Customer Engagement

How customers and consumer behaviour have been changing due to technology and other forces is of prime interest. This book addresses the central questions regarding emerging consumer behaviour. These are: How does social media affect this behaviour? How and at what points do emotions affect consumer decisions and what triggers this? How should engagement be conceptualized, defined and measured? How do social media and other marketing activities create engagement?

The book draws on the rich, extensive knowledge of the authors, who are pioneers in the field. The book's editors have identified the weakness in the current knowledge and aim to address this gap by touching on significant conceptual and empirical contributions to this emerging literature stream, providing readers with a comprehensive, contemporary perspective of customer engagement. The book also endeavours to develop a richer narrative around the notion of social media and customer engagement, and the non-monetary notion of social media within new media-based social networks.

Roderick J. Brodie is a Professor at the Department of Marketing, University of Auckland, New Zealand.

Linda D. Hollebeek is a Senior Lecturer at the Graduate School of Management, University of Auckland, New Zealand. She is also Associate Professor (Adjunct) at the NHH Norwegian School of Economics, Bergen, Norway.

Jodie Conduit is a Senior Lecturer at the Adelaide Business School, University of Adelaide, Australia.

Customer Engagement
Contemporary issues and challenges

Edited by Roderick J. Brodie,
Linda D. Hollebeek and
Jodie Conduit

Routledge
Taylor & Francis Group

LONDON AND NEW YORK

First published 2016 by Routledge

2 Park Square, Milton Park, Abingdon, Oxfordshire OX14 4RN
711 Third Avenue, New York, NY 10017

Routledge is an imprint of the Taylor & Francis Group, an informa business

First issued in paperback 2017

British Library Cataloguing in Publication Data
A catalogue record for this book is available from the British Library

Library of Congress Cataloging-in-Publication Data
Customer engagement : contemporary issues and challenges /
   edited by Roderick J. Brodie, Linda D. Hollebeek and Jodie Conduit.
      pages cm
   Includes bibliographical references and index.
   1. Consumer behavior.   2. Customer relations.   3. Marketing
research.   I. Brodie, R. J., editor.   II. Hollebeek, Linda D., editor.
III.   Conduit, Jodie., editor.
   HF5415.32.C875 2015
   658.8′342—dc23
   2015027509

ISBN: 978-1-138-84738-5 (hbk)
ISBN: 978-0-8153-5073-6 (pbk)

Typeset in Galliard
by Apex CoVantage, LLC

Contents

Figures

Tables

Contributors

Matthew Alexander is a Senior Lecturer at the Strathclyde Business School, University of Strathclyde, UK.

Frank Alpert is an Associate Professor of Marketing at the UQ Business School, University of Queensland, Australia.

David Ballantyne is an Associate Professor at the Department of Marketing, University of Otago, New Zealand.

Sharon E. Beatty is a Professor of Marketing at the Culverhouse College of Commerce, University of Alabama, USA.

Sander F. M. Beckers is a PhD candidate at the Department of Marketing, Faculty of Economics and Business, University of Groningen, the Netherlands.

Sergio Biggemann is a Senior Lecturer at the Department of Marketing, University of Otago, New Zealand.

Enrique Bigné is a Professor of Marketing at the School of Economics, University of Valencia, Spain.

Jana Lay-Hwa Bowden is a Senior Lecturer at the Department of Marketing and Management, Faculty of Business and Economics, Macquarie University, Australia.

Christoph F. Breidbach is a Lecturer at the Department of Computing and Information Systems, The University of Melbourne, Australia.

Roderick J. Brodie is a Professor at the Department of Marketing University of Auckland, New Zealand.

Bobby J. Calder is a Professor of Marketing at the Kellogg School of Management, Northwestern University, USA.

Jodie Conduit is a Senior Lecturer at the Adelaide Business School, University of Adelaide, Australia.

Vivek Dalela is an Associate Professor at the Department of Marketing, Seidman College of Business, Grand Valley State University, USA.

Arne De Keyser is an Assistant Professor of Marketing at the EDHEC Business School, France.

Rebecca Dolan is a PhD candidate at the Adelaide Business School, The University of Adelaide, Australia.

John Fahy is a Professor at the Department of Management and Marketing, University of Limerick, Limerick, Ireland.

Linda D. Hollebeek is a Senior Lecturer at the Graduate School of Management, University of Auckland, New Zealand. She is also Associate Professor (Adjunct) at the NHH Norwegian School of Economics, Bergen, Norway.

Antonio Hyder is Director of Research at Hackers & Founders, Mountain View, CA, USA.

Elina Jaakkola is a Senior Research Fellow in Marketing at the Turku School of Economics, University of Turku, Finland.

Biljana Juric is a Senior Lecturer at the Department of Marketing University of Auckland, New Zealand.

Ceridywn King is an Associate Professor in the School of Tourism and Hospitality Management, Temple University, USA.

Vilma Luoma-Aho is a Professor at the Department of Communication, University of Jyväskylä, Finland.

Edward C. Malthouse is a Professor of Integrated Marketing Communications, Medill School, Northwestern University, USA.

Kay Naumann is a PhD candidate at the Department of Marketing and Management, Faculty of Business and Economics, Macquarie University, Australia.

Sylvia Ng is a PhD candidate at the Adelaide Business School, University of Adelaide, Australia.

Carolin Plewa is a Senior Lecturer at the Adelaide Business School, University of Adelaide, Australia.

Carissa Roberts is the Insights and Analysis Manager of Engaged Marketing, Brisbane, Australia.

Christopher Roberts is the Managing Director of Engaged Marketing, Brisbane, Australia.

Sandra D. Smith is a Lecturer at the Department of Marketing, University of Auckland, New Zealand.

Kevin Kam Fung So is an Assistant Professor at the School of Hotel Restaurant and Tourism Management, University of South Carolina, USA.

Beverley Sparks is a Professor at the Griffith Business School, Griffith University, Australia.

Jillian C. Sweeney is a Professor at the University of Western Australia Business School, University of Western Australia, Australia.

Jenny van Doorn is an Associate Professor at the Department of Marketing, Faculty of Economics and Business, University of Groningen, the Netherlands.

Mark Vandenbosch is a Professor of Marketing at the Ivey School of Business, Western University, Canada.

Peter C. Verhoef is a Professor at the Department of Marketing, Faculty of Economics and Business, University of Groningen, the Netherlands.

Katrien Verleye is a Postdoctoral Researcher at the Centre for Service Intelligence, Ghent University, Belgium.

Shiri D. Vivek is an Associate Professor at the Department of Marketing and Supply Chain Management, College of Business, Eastern Michigan University, USA.

George Wilks is a research student at the Department of Marketing, University of Auckland, New Zealand.

Kamer Yuksel is a PhD candidate at the Department of Marketing, University of Otago, New Zealand.

Preface

*Roderick J. Brodie, Linda D. Hollebeek
and Jodie Conduit*

The enduring importance of understanding customers and the customer experience is well recognised by both marketing practitioners and academics. Thus,
the issue of how consumers' attitudes and behaviours are changing as a result
of rapid technological advancements, coupled with and among other factors, is
of prime scholarly interest. In recent years, marketing has experienced a paradigm
shift, which recognises that consumers are no longer passive recipients of organisational strategies, but rather, increasingly demand interactivity and the ability
to generate value-in-use. In order to capture the nature of customers' interactive
experiences the concept of engagement is replacing more traditional relational
concepts, including involvement and participation (Brodie et al., 2011). The
notion of 'customer engagement' originated from industry leaders seeking to
manage and motivate their customers beyond the realms of individual service
delivery touch-points, and motivate them to interact and connect with focal
brands. However, with terminology exhibiting a lack of consistency, a fragmented
state of the field has resulted, as illustrated by the development of numerous
tools and frameworks for building consumer engagement in the popular business
press.

The importance of understanding key customer-based trends, including the
increasing importance of the customer experience and the customer journey,
has been recognised as a top tier research priority for the period of 2014–2016
by the Marketing Science Institute (MSI, 2014; msi.org). Specifically, the
MSI recognises that understanding today's customers requires the adoption
of multi-faceted, multi-layered perspectives, which includes the suggestion of
the need for theorising, developing, and validating new concepts and ideas.
The MSI pose a number of questions: What new customer behaviours have
emerged in a multi-media, multi-screen, and multi-channel environment?
How do social media and digital technology change customer experiences
and the consumer path to purchase? What are the best ways to model the
consumer decision journey? Are other models more appropriate than the
decision funnel? What is the role of habit and inertia in consumer decision
making? How and at what points do emotions affect consumer decisions?
How are they triggered? How should qualitative and quantitative methods

be combined to understand the total customer experience? However, central to answering these questions is:

> How should engagement be conceptualised, defined, and measured? How do social media and other marketing activities create engagement?

Recent marketing literature has provided insight regarding customer engagement as a psychological mind-set comprising focal cognitive, emotional, and behavioural dimensions (Brodie et al., 2011). While several authors have explored customer engagement in different contexts and proposed influences on, and outcomes of, customer engagement (e.g. Bowden 2009; Van Doorn et al., 2010; Brodie et al., 2011; Hollebeek, 2011; Vivek et al., 2012; Hollebeek et al., 2014;), a number of significant conceptual and empirical contributions remain to be made to this emerging literature stream. Our book consists of four broad sections reflecting different, yet interrelated strands of engagement research, and comprises 15 chapters written by 39 authors from North America, Europe, and Australasia, who are thought leaders on the emerging research topic of customer engagement.

Part I: Engagement conceptualisations

Chapter 1, which is titled 'Customer engagement behaviours and value co-creation', is authored by Matthew Alexander and Elina Jaakkola. This chapter examines how different customer engagement behaviours contribute to value creation by the focal customer, the focal firm, and other stakeholders within broader service systems. Drawing on a broad range of literature, the chapter outlines direct and indirect value outcomes emerging through co-developing, influencing, augmenting, and mobilising behaviours. It proposes a general framework for the value co-creation which is triggered and affected by these four types of customer engagement behaviours.

Chapter 2, which is titled 'Economic outcomes of customer engagement: emerging findings, contemporary theoretical perspectives, and future challenges', is authored by Sander F.M. Beckers, Jenny van Doorn and Peter C. Verhoef. The chapter responds to the need for further research examining focal firm-level outcomes of customer engagement. In constructing their argument, the authors draw on theories from economic, behavioural, and hybrid economic/behavioural theoretical domains to develop a conceptual framework from which priorities for further research are also identified.

Chapter 3, which is authored by Shiri D. Vivek, Vivek Dalela and Sharon E. Beatty, is titled 'Partner engagement: a perspective on B2B engagement'. To date, scholarly research has largely focused on customer engagement with little attention given to how firms engage business clients. This chapter offers a preliminary effort towards understanding the concept of customer engagement in the B2B context. It considers partner engagement as episodes of intense exchange in the relationship between two independent, but interdependent, entities and explores environmental and relational factors that trigger this engagement.

Chapter 4, which is authored by Linda D. Hollebeek, is titled 'Exploring customer engagement: a multi-stakeholder perspective'. This chapter adopts a multi-stakeholder perspective and addresses customer engagement from a hybrid service-dominant logic/social exchange theory-informed perspective. It culminates in the development of an integrative multi-stakeholder conceptualisation of customer engagement, which outlines investments and returns across CE cognitions, emotions and behaviours.

Part II: Engagement, social media and technology

Chapter 5, which is titled 'Creating brand engagement on digital, social and mobile media', is authored by Edward C. Malthouse, Bobby J. Calder and Mark Vandenbosch. This chapter addresses the process of creating engagement. It is hypothesised that engagement results from experiential contact points that prompt cognitive elaboration about how a brand helps consumers achieve their goals. The research supports the view that experiences that cause consumers to reflect and elaborate on the connection between a brand and life goals will increase engagement and therefore purchase behaviour. The findings suggest that engagement created by virtue of this process is not produced by simply being 'on' any particular type of media, including digital, social, or mobile. Hence marketers need to design specific experiences to establish brand–life goal(s) connections in consumers' minds.

Chapter 6 is authored by Rebecca Dolan, Jodie Conduit and John Fahy, and is titled 'Social media engagement: a construct of positively and negatively valenced engagement behaviours'. This chapter explores the different types of engagement behaviours exhibited by users on social media platforms. It demonstrates that social media engagement behaviour comprises six distinct types, including creating, contributing, consuming, dormancy, detaching, and destructing. Several forms of engagement behaviours, including knowledge seeking, sharing experiences, co-developing, socialising, advocating, and affirming are used to identify specific creative engagement behaviours. Further, the proposed construct recognises the valence and various intensities at which social media engagement behaviour manifests.

Chapter 7, which is titled 'Nature and purpose of engagement platforms', is authored by Christoph F. Breidbach and Roderick J. Brodie. This chapter examines the nature and purpose of engagement platforms and their role in the changing service landscape of the twenty-first century. It explores the intersection of Information and Communication Technology (ICT), service, and engagement platforms, and suggests the need to move beyond singular engagement platforms, towards holistic engagement ecosystems. In particular, this contention is illustrated by examining the engagement ecosystem of leading company Amazon.com.

Chapter 8 is authored by Katrien Verleye and Arne De Keyser, and is titled 'Customer engagement in technology-based and high-contact interfaces'. In both high-contact and technology-based interfaces, contemporary firms introduce tools that foster customer engagement in new product and service development and innovation. This chapter elaborates on key characteristics and motivational drivers underlying customer engagement, and draws on self-determination theory to discuss how engaged customers expect unique combinations of extrinsic, internalised extrinsic and intrinsic benefits. The authors stipulate that firm investments in experimentation, community-building, and gamification can help generate these benefits. Further, the integration of these tools in technology-based and high-contact service interfaces may help firms to encourage and support customers in demonstrating shared inventiveness, co-design, and other discretionary behaviours.

Chapter 9, which is authored by Antonio Hyder and Enrique Bigné, is titled 'Website engagement'. The authors reflect on the increasing importance of engagement in online settings and in the broader digital consumer industry. Despite the growing use of the term 'website engagement', it is yet to be conceptualised from an academic perspective. This chapter responds to this need by developing a measurement tool to measure website engagement consisting of five dimensions: positive affect, focused attention, challenge, curiosity and involvement. Implications of this application are also examined.

Part III: Managerial applications of engagement

Chapter 10, which is authored by Christopher Roberts, Frank Alpert and Carissa Roberts, is titled 'Strategic drivers of customer and employee engagement: practical applications'. The chapter first describes a published consulting model (the Total Engagement Model), which is used to drive and model customer engagement. Second, the authors reflect on a series of general observations extracted from their five-year consumer benchmarking study, which outlines the key distinguishing factors characterising loyalty leaders in relation to customer engagement. Further, the importance of employee engagement in driving customer engagement is highlighted by drawing on survey evidence. Finally, five case studies are used to illustrate the application of the Total Engagement Model.

Chapter 11 is titled 'Customer engagement with a service offering: a framework for complex services' and is authored by Sylvia Ng, Carolin Plewa and Jillian C. Sweeney. This chapter explores the multi-faceted nature of customer engagement in the context of complex services. It investigates how customers engage with a service offering and provides further insight into the activities associated with cognitive, affective and behavioural engagement as observed in the finance industry. Further, the authors identify several influences and consequences of customer engagement that could be extended to other complex services.

Chapter 12, which is authored by Kamer Yuksel, David Ballantyne, and Sergio Biggemann, is titled 'Brand co-creation through social actor engagement'. This chapter adopts an illustrative case to examine a particular company's brand development experience and associated engagement. The concept of social actor engagement is developed as a means to understand how brand management is changing within a broader network configuration of brand experience.

Chapter 13, which is titled 'Extending the tourism experience: the role of customer engagement', is authored by Kevin Kam Fung So, Ceridywn King and Beverley Sparks. Examining engagement within the context of tourism services, this chapter identifies a set of key tourism-based customer engagement behaviours. The chapter examines the role of online reviews, travel blogs and social networks to facilitate customer engagement pre, during and post tourism experience.

Part IV: Emerging customer engagement contexts

Chapter 14, which is authored by Jana Lay-Hwa Bowden, Vilma Luoma-Aho and Kay Naumann, is titled 'Developing a spectrum of positive to negative citizen engagement'. This chapter examines customer engagement theory within a public sector context. It illustrates a spectrum of types of citizen engagement, which includes strongly positively valenced engagement, passive and weakly negative disengagement, and highly activated, dedicated and destructive negative engagement. The role of vertical brand engagement networks and horizontal citizen-to-citizen actor networks on the propensity for each of these types of engagement to transpire is discussed. Policy and managerial implications are also explored.

Chapter 15, which is titled 'Negative customer brand engagement: an overview of conceptual and blog-based findings', is authored by Biljana Juric, Sandra D. Smith and George Wilks. Specifically, these authors argue that a piecemeal approach to solely examining the positive aspects of customer brand engagement is no longer sufficient. In response to this gap, this chapter focuses on the negative aspects of customer brand engagement. The authors develop a conceptual model, which is applied using blog analysis, to examine negative aspects of customer brand engagement.

The 15 chapters in this book provide a rich theoretical understanding and new conceptual and empirical insights into customer engagement and its role in contemporary service systems. Customer engagement is a multi-dimensional and complex phenomenon, with all of the chapters elaborating on specific aspects of its conceptualisation and implementation in various settings. As a whole, these chapters bring forth a greater level of understanding of the general nature and role of customer engagement and how it manifests in many complex environments. The chapters also highlight important areas for future research and therefore should lead the research agenda in this topic area. We hope that this book proves to be useful for academic researchers interested in the research field and also increases managerial awareness of the phenomenon of customer engagement and how it can be effectively utilised for business success. The editorial team would sincerely like to thank the contributors to this book for their efforts and support in producing a high-quality publication.

References

Bowden, J. H. (2009). The process of customer engagement: A conceptual framework. *Journal of Marketing Theory and Practice, 17* (1), 63–74.

Brodie, R. J., Hollebeek, L. D., Juric, B. and Ilic, A. (2011). Customer engagement: Conceptual domain, fundamental propositions and implications for research. *Journal of Service Research, 14* (3), 1–20.

Hollebeek, L. D. (2011). Demystifying customer brand engagement: Exploring the loyalty nexus. *Journal of Marketing Management, 27* (7–8), 785–807.

Hollebeek, L. D., Glynn, M. and Brodie, R. J. (2014), Consumer brand engagement in social media: Conceptualization, scale development and validation. *Journal of Interactive Marketing, 28* (2), 149–165.

Van Doorn, J., Lemon, K. E., Mittal, V., Naβ, S., Pick, D., Pirner, P. and Verhoef, P. C. (2010). Customer engagement behaviour: Theoretical foundations and research directions. *Journal of Service Research, 13* (3), 253–266.

Vivek, S. D., Beatty, S. and Morgan, R. M. (2012). Customer engagement: Exploring customer relationships beyond purchase. *Journal of Marketing Theory & Practice, 20* (2), 122–146.

Part I

Engagement conceptualisations

1 Customer engagement behaviours and value co-creation

Matthew Alexander and Elina Jaakkola

Introduction

Contemporary markets are increasingly interconnected, with actors no longer seen as part of linear value chains, but existing in networks of service systems where interaction, collaboration and experience sharing take place (Jaakkola, Helkkula and Aarikka-Stenroos, 2015; Lusch and Vargo, 2014; Chen, Drennan and Andrews, 2012). In such markets, traditional boundaries between the roles of 'customer' and 'provider' are losing clarity, highlighted by the emergence of concepts such as *prosumers* and *post-consumers* (Carù and Cova, 2015; Cova and Dalli, 2009). Customers are not satisfied with the limited role of a buyer, receiver and user of a firm's offering at the end of the value chain, but proactively engage in crafting the offering according to their personal needs and wants, and seek to also engage other stakeholders (such as other consumers, communities, firms or government organisations) in the service system to contribute their resources towards common aims (Jaakkola and Alexander, 2014). Examples include customers rating products and services in various online marketplaces, co-creating experiences in brand communities, co-designing and innovating products and services, and arranging boycotts against firms and products perceived as doing harm (e.g. Carù and Cova, 2015; Fournier and Avery, 2011; Füller, 2010; Libai et al., 2010). To capture the various customer activities and behaviours beyond the traditional role of a buyer and user that affect the firm, an overarching concept *customer engagement* (CE) has been introduced (Brodie, Hollebeek, Jurić, and Ilić, 2011; Van Doorn et al., 2010).

Emergent CE research has reported that various customer engagement behaviours (CEBs) have implications for value creation by the active customers themselves, the focal firm and also other stakeholders in the service system (Brodie, Ilic, Juric, and Hollebeek, 2013; Jaakkola and Alexander, 2014). Value creation occurs through the integration of resources in interaction between actors (Grönroos and Voima, 2012; Lusch and Vargo, 2014), and due to its dynamic and interdependent, networked nature, value creation is best understood at the level of service systems, rather than individual (e.g. the firm) or dyadic actors (e.g. firm–customer) (Lusch and Vargo, 2014). Nevertheless, extant studies have predominantly focused on the value outcomes of a particular type of

CEB, such as customers influencing others through word-of-mouth, or outcomes for particular actors, such as the firm or the customer (e.g. Adjei, Noble, and Noble, 2010; Schau, Muñiz Jr, and Arnould, 2009) Furthermore, the value implications of CE have mainly been viewed in certain isolated settings such as brand communities (Brodie et al., 2013) or with the perspective of how firms could manage it (Verleye, Gemmel, and Rangarajan, 2013). Therefore, a holistic understanding of the broad spectrum of CEBs and their implications for different stakeholders has been missing, and the 'big picture' of how CE relates to value co-creation on a service system level is only just emerging (Jaakkola and Alexander, 2014).

This chapter examines how different CEBs contribute to value creation by the focal customer, the focal firm and other stakeholders within service systems. Drawing on a broad range of literature, the chapter outlines the various direct and indirect value outcomes emerging through four types of CEB identified by Jaakkola and Alexander (2014), and proposes a general framework for the value co-creation, which is triggered and affected by CEB. Thereby this chapter integrates currently fragmented research findings on CEB-affected value co-creation and facilitates future research on this topic.

This chapter is organised as follows. The next section provides definitions for CE and CEB and discusses the conceptual scope of CEB. Then we elaborate on four different types of CEBs. The subsequent section elaborates on the role that CEB plays in value co-creation on the service system level, followed by conclusions and implications for practitioners and researchers.

Customer engagement behaviour as a concept

Brodie et al. (2011) view CE as a psychological state, which results from interactive experiences between a customer and a focal agent or object (an organisation or brand, e.g. see Hollebeek, 2011). This chapter focuses on the behavioural manifestations of CE through which 'customers make voluntary resource contributions that have a brand or firm focus but go beyond what is fundamental to transactions, occur in interactions between the focal object and/or other actors, and result from motivational drivers' (Jaakkola and Alexander, 2014, p. 248). Given the various roles customers may play in the marketplace, it is essential to differentiate CEB from other similar, yet for our purposes distinctly different, concepts (e.g. co-creation) to highlight that CEBs are conceptually distinct from these.

Service marketing and management research has long acknowledged that in the service context, customers may engage in *customer participation* or *co-production*, which refers to the extent to which a customer is directly participating in the delivery or production of a product or service (Bendapudi and Leone, 2003). Critically we see co-production as in-built in many service encounters, such as airlines offering online check-in only. As a result, co-production is rarely voluntary or of an extra-role nature, but a core element in the service transaction. Even in circumstances where customers can choose whether to co-produce or not, the interaction is firm-driven and associated with the output of the firm (Vargo, 2008). We also differentiate CEB from *scripted forms of behaviour* within a service encounter (such as compliance with airport security or following instructions when purchasing furniture in an IKEA store). These behaviours are closely aligned with research into the service encounter (e.g. Bitner, 1992) where it is recognised that customers adopt specific roles (Solomon, Surprenant, Czepiel, and Gutman, 1985). While customers do have control over their behaviour in these situations, their activities are often associated with specified roles and scripts which are, again, firm-driven. CEB can also be differentiated from other voluntary or extra-role behaviours, such as *customer voluntary performance* or *customer citizenship behaviours* (Ahearne, Bhattacharya, and Gruen, 2005; Bettencourt, 1997; Rosenbaum and Massiah, 2007). The various concepts discussed above centre on customer provision of enhanced contributions occurring largely within the service encounter and being more or less driven or controlled by the firm. CEB, although centred on a focal object, such as a firm or a brand, are exogenous customer actions, driven by customers' own motivations, rather than those of the firm, and typically extend beyond transactions/ purchase (Brodie et al., 2011; Van Doorn et al., 2010).

Brodie et al. (2011) view CE to exist within a nomological network, that is, with specific antecedents (such as involvement or rapport) and consequences (such as commitment or loyalty), and several studies have explored customer motivations for engaging in behaviours beyond transactions. Some authors see traditional marketing concepts, such as satisfaction, commitment and trust playing a role alongside customer goals and resources (Brodie et al., 2011; Van Doorn et al., 2010). Other research suggests that customers engage with an expectation of benefits from the engagement (Füller, 2010; Nambisan and Baron, 2009). Finally, there is also a sense that the firm can play some kind of facilitative role with the provision of appropriate platforms (e.g. firm-hosted social networking sites) for engagement behaviour to occur with appropriate rewards for customers (see Jaakkola and Alexander, 2014; Kumar et al., 2010).

Given CEBs take place beyond transactions (Van Doorn et al., 2010), as well as the customer–firm dyad, a discussion of value creation at a systemic level is appropriate, yet explored only recently (Jaakkola and Alexander, 2014). Recent developments in Service-Dominant logic and beyond see resource integration as a key feature of marketing interactions (Grönroos and Voima, 2012; Lusch and Vargo, 2014). Resources exchanged are affected by their compatibility with personal value processes and customer context (Vargo and Lusch, 2008). Of particular relevance to CE is a reduction in the importance of the transaction around the array of resources that can be transferred between actors within service systems (Chandler and Vargo, 2011; Edvardsson, Tronvoll, and Gruber, 2011). These service systems are configurations of value creation comprising a range of parties and their own networks that can collectively influence and enable value co-creation (Edvardsson et al., 2011). Extant literature offers many examples where customer actions influence value creation beyond the customer– firm dyad and where benefits can be shared with customers' own networks and beyond to other relevant stakeholders (Nambisan and Baron, 2009; Schau et al., 2009). The following section introduces four distinct types of CEB identified by Jaakkola and Alexander (2014), and examines the value outcomes of such CEBs.

Types of customer engagement behaviours

Initial research on CEB discussed two types of CEB: first, customer participation in innovation and new product development, and second, the role of customers in inducing other potential users to interact with a brand via referral programs, word-of-mouth and other types of customer-to-customer interaction (Kumar et al., 2010; Brodie et al., 2013). Jaakkola and Alexander (2014) classify these first two types, respectively, as *co-developing behaviour* and *influencing behaviour*. In their empirical study of community adoption of railway stations a further two behaviours – *augmenting* and *mobilising behaviours* – were identified. Research has demonstrated that the different forms of CEBs can take place in online settings, such as brand communities, social media and blogs (Brodie et al., 2011), and also in offline environments (Jaakkola and Alexander, 2014). The role of these four types of CEB in value co-creation will be explored in more detail in the following sections.

Co-developing behaviour

Co-developer behaviour can be defined as 'customer contributions of resources such as knowledge, skills, and time, to facilitate the focal firm's development of its offering' (Jaakkola and Alexander, 2014; p. 255). Involving customers as co-developers of the firm's offering is well-established as an important factor contributing to successful product and service development (e.g. Carbonell, Rodríguez, and Pujari, 2009). Co-developing behaviours may include providing ideas for new products, participating in design contests and development competitions, and serving in customer panels or as members in the innovation team (e.g. Edvardsson, Kristensson, Magnusson, and Sundström, 2012; Nambisan and Baron, 2009). For example, the online forum 'My Starbucks Idea' (cf. http://mystarbucksidea.force.com/) invites customers to suggest ideas for the development and improvement of Starbucks' drink and food assortment, service experience and ways of community involvement. The firm can make use of its customers' resources to benefit product development, but retain ultimate control of the extent to which customer resources will be utilised when developing the offering.

Many studies indicate that customers engage in co-development because of their dissatisfaction with existing offerings and their desire to enhance the development of products or services that better fulfil their needs (e.g. Füller, 2010; Jaakkola and Alexander, 2014). Financial rewards sometimes motivate co-development, for example in the form of monetary prizes for winning development contests (Hoyer et al., 2010). For example, when BMW launched a contest to improve the luggage compartment of BMW, they advertised prizes worth 10.000 € to motivate people to invest sufficient resources in the design (cf. https://www.bmwgroup-cocreationlab.com/cocreation/project/trunk-contest). Other studies also highlight the role of psychological benefits: customers seek appreciation and reputational gains by displaying their ideas and product-related expertise (Nambisan and Baron, 2009; Füller, 2010). By participating in innovation forums or projects, customers may also benefit from gaining product or technology-related knowledge which facilitates their learning (Nambisan and Baron, 2009). Providers can facilitate co-development behaviours by offering resources to aid customer contributions, for example in the form of well-functioning feedback and innovation platforms and tools (Hoyer et al., 2010; Von Hippel, 2005), and by being open and appreciative towards customers' suggestions (Jaakkola and Alexander, 2014).

Research demonstrates that customers' co-developing behaviour is very beneficial for the provider. Besides offering the firm invaluable insights regarding the functionality of the product/service in the user's context, customers may possess knowledge, skills and expertise that significantly add to the firms' resources (Hoyer et al., 2010). For example, when developing its programmable Mindstorms robot, Lego gained leverage on the original design through making the source code available, organising competitions and even including a 'right to hack' into the software license, and thereby the firm benefited from the unique skills of its lead user community (cf. http://www.innovation-portal.info/wp-content/uploads/Lego1.pdf). Customer engagement in new service development has been demonstrated to have a positive effect on the speed of technical innovation, and indirectly facilitates sales performance and competitive superiority of the firm (Carbonell et al., 2009).

Influencing behaviour

Influencing behaviour refers to 'customer contributions of resources such as knowledge, experience and time, to affect other actors' perceptions, preferences or knowledge regarding the focal firm' (Jaakkola and Alexander, 2014, p. 256). In the midst of a complex myriad of providers and offerings, customers are increasingly reliant on each other for gaining trustworthy information for finding and evaluating brands, products, and services (Libai et al., 2010). Insights from more experienced users help customers to mitigate the risks perceived in selecting providers and reduce their dependency on communications from the firm. Influencing behaviour can take the form of word-of-mouth, eWOM, recommendations and referrals, testimonials and customer references, and may include the sharing of positive or negative experiences, as well as product- or firm-related information (Jaakkola, Aarikka-Stenroos, and Kimmel, 2014).

The development of online channels has contributed significantly to the increasing connectivity of customers who find and share information though social networking sites, blogs, and online communities, and can post reviews on virtually any type of engagement platform they have consumed to be available to a global audience (Hennig-Thurau, Gwinner, Walsh, and Gremler, 2004; Libai et al., 2010). Consumers are also reported to craft actual advertisements and broadcast them online, thus taking over the marketing function traditionally executed by the firm (Berthon, Pitt, and Campbell, 2008). Influencing behaviour, therefore, has very broad applicability, and particularly customers who are perceived as experts in the field may change the preferences and purchase intentions of a multitude of people with one single blog post or product review (Adjei et al., 2010).

For the focal customer, the value of engaging in influencing behaviour relates to their power to reward or punish the firm for good or bad service, respectively. Customers who are satisfied or dissatisfied with a provider want to reciprocate the experience by recommending the provider or warning others not to transact with the provider (Blazevic et al., 2013). Customers also engage in influencing behaviour in order to telegraph their expertise and generate publicity (self-promotion) (Berthon et al., 2008; Hennig-Thurau et al., 2004).

Research has shown that customers' influencing behaviour can affect its audience in several ways. The information and experiences shared by customers serve as resources for other customers' purchase process, and affect their purchase decision-making especially when it is associated with greater perceived risk (Bansal and Voyer, 2000). Particularly influential is information provided by opinion leaders who are known experts in particular product fields and are trusted by opinion seekers to provide knowledgeable advice (Litvin et al., 2008). Influencing behaviour also affects other stakeholders' expectations about the content and value of the service: learning about other customers' experiences helps prospective customers to adjust their expectations to a realistic level (Jaakkola et al., 2014). From the firm perspective, positive influencing behaviour, such as favourable WOM, impacts the perceived value of the firm's offering and customer loyalty (Gruen, Osmonbekov, and Czaplewski, 2006), and may lead to customer acquisition, increased sales and faster diffusion of new offerings (Adjei et al., 2010; Libai et al., 2010). At the same time, influencing behaviour can also have negative outcomes, such as consumers' deteriorated brand perceptions when the message speaks against the firm or its offering (Hollebeek and Chen, 2014).

Augmenting behaviour

Augmenting behaviour is defined as 'customer contributions of resources such as knowledge, skills, labour and time, to directly augment and add to the focal firm's offering beyond that which is fundamental to the transaction' (Jaakkola and Alexander, 2014, p. 254). This behaviour is exemplified by customers acting on their own initiative to adapt, modify and create new uses or content surrounding a focal firm or band. Unlike co-development where the firm is in charge of realising the development and might or might not take customers' contributions into account, augmenting behaviour refers to customers' realising the modification of an offering, regardless of whether it is intended or preferred by the focal firm (Jaakkola and Alexander, 2014).

Many existing studies reveal augmentation of an intangible nature. This can be as simple as a customer's contribution to an online community (Seraj, 2012; Sussan, 2012) where the addition of user-generated content or customer-to-customer interaction allows customers to confer their own meaning onto the brand, thereby adding additional value to the firm's offering (Ferrell and Ferrell, 2012). Provision of an engagement platform (Breidbach, Brodie, and Hollebeek, 2014; Sawhney, Verona, and Prandelli, 2005) by the firm can achieve additional augmentation benefits within a service system. For example, the use of Nike+ by customers has created a form of collectivised achievement platform, where customers engage each other in challenges (such as the 2009 men vs women campaign; cf. http://marketing.blogs.ie.edu/archives/2009/03/the-nike-challenge-men-vs-women.php). Other intangible augmentation might be found within P3 (peer-to-peer problem solving) communities, such as those discussed by Dholakia et al. (2009). In these communities, customers solve problems such as those relating to appliance repair of IT equipment, thereby augmenting the existing knowledge offerings of the firm.

Not all augmenting behaviour is intangible. Von Hippel (2005, p. 64) discusses how product and services users frequently innovate for themselves, rather than 'relying on manufacturers to act as their (often very imperfect agents)'. Von Hippel (2005, p. 66) presents evidence that '10%–40% of users engage in developing or modifying products', which leads to greater functional capability and other improvements. These modifications are further evidenced in studies of brand communities (Schau et al., 2009), where the 'Brand Use' practices identified include the customisation and commodification of various products, and geographical communities where local residents can take ownership of public buildings and customise them in ways meaningful to the community (Hamilton and Alexander, 2013).

For customers, the value outcomes of augmenting behaviour appear to be clear. Customer benefits include adapted products or services through customisation with offerings better suited to fit their goals and needs (Epp and Price, 2011); they benefit through the social welfare associated with collaborative effort as well as the social, cultural and intellectual value of interacting with brand communities. For firms, additional insight is gained through adaptations made by customers that complement existing innovation and increase intellectual capital (Dholakia et al., 2009; Sussan, 2012). There is also a view that deeper relationships between customers could be built through augmenting behaviour (Ramaswamy, 2008). Sussan (2012) observes how consumer-to-consumer (C2C) interactions are likely to increase over time with more traditional business-to-business (B2C) relationships diminishing. This trend would suggest that in the future firms would act more as facilitators (rather than controllers) of engaged behaviours occurring between a range of actors.

For other stakeholders augmented products and services are akin to open source benefits, meaning that the benefits from augmenting behaviour should ripple out into the wider service system. Augmenting behaviour can therefore make products or services more appealing to other customers generating value for themselves, the firm and other stakeholders.

Mobilising behaviour

The final form of CEB is *mobilising behaviour*, which occurs when engaged customers go beyond influencing other stakeholders' perceptions to stimulate real actions towards a focal firm. Mobilising behaviour is defined as 'customer contributions of resources, such as relationships and time, to mobilise other stakeholders' actions towards the focal firm' (Jaakkola and Alexander, 2014, p. 256).

Mobilising behaviour is perhaps best understood with reference to socially responsible customer action where other actors are marshalled to behave in a certain way towards a focal organisation. This might be through either 'boycotts' or 'buycotts' of certain products (Paek and Nelson, 2009). Recent examples would include the mass student boycott of clothing manufacturer Fruit of the Loom, who was forced to reverse its decision to close a factory in Honduras it had earlier shut down after workers had become unionised. The boycott campaign started in 2009 with 96 US colleges cancelling their contracts with the company, and 10 UK universities followed in action that cost the organisation around $50 million (example from Ethical Consumer: www.ethicalconsumer.org/boycott). In political marketing, parties seed supporters using social media to share ideas and, more importantly, to become self-organising groups that mobilise support around campaigns (Harris and Harrigan, 2011). 'Buycotts' (also known as anti-boycotts) see customers attempting to galvanise support for a firm, such as in 2009 when conservative Americans arranged a buycott of Whole Foods Market as a counter to a boycott by liberals who objective to its CEOs opposition to President Obama's healthcare reforms (cf. http://www.dailyfinance.com/2009/09/02/whole-foods-buycott-turns-grocery-store-into-cultural-battlegr/). In the recent independence referendum in Scotland the Scottish National party mobilised widespread support through social media and other initiatives, which galvanised supporters to design and circulate their own ideas around the campaign through community leafleting (Adamson and Lynch, 2013); the results of which contributed to a growth in support which nearly beat the combined strength of all the other political parties in the UK. Social media has, in fact, become the go-to mechanism to turn the tables on organisations to force them to change decisions (such as Gap's failed rebrand in 2010, which was met with a furious response on social media and the old logo restored in six days), or make better ones (such as Domino's Pizza using its biggest social media critics to contribute to a recipe change exercise; Fournier and Avery, 2011). These examples suggest that mobilising behaviour can force firms to listen more carefully to the needs of its customers.

There are also examples of mobilising behaviour used, not to force the focal firm to change or renege on a decision, but to enable a firm to make a positive change. The website Carrotmob (cf. www.carrotmob.org) provides a platform that facilitates groups of people to contribute resources (in this case money) to enable or support business, which in return makes investments or improvements desired by the customers. Recent examples include money raised by investors to support a health food shop in investing in low-energy lighting, or raising funds to enable a café in Budapest, Hungary to reduce its water footprint. These recent mobilising behaviour initiatives are further examples of the influence customers have when moving from supporter to critic to investor.

Customers benefit from mobilising behaviour by forcing (or encouraging) firms to change behaviours or decisions, or by making investments in things customers care about, which stimulate engagement behaviours. They also benefit from the improvements that other stakeholders' contributions towards the offering bring about, and enjoy a sense of accomplishment and empowerment (Jaakkola and Alexander, 2014). Value outcomes for the firm may involve positive or negative change in sales and customer acquisition, depending on whether mobilisation aims at 'boycott' or 'buycott'. The actions of mobilised customers, once again, provide benefits for other stakeholders and may stimulate a change in attitude or behaviour towards the focal firm.

How CEB contributes to value creation

As revealed by the literature review on the four types of CEBs addressed, CEBs accrue a range of value outcomes for the focal customer, the focal firm, as well as other stakeholders, (such as other or prospective customers). Table 1.1 summarises these value outcomes. It is evident that research thus far has mainly focused on the positive outcomes of CEB; its negative consequences having predominantly been discussed with relation to influencing behaviour.

By assimilating the literature on value creation and the outcomes of CEB, we present a theoretical framework for the role of customer engagement in value co-creation in a multi-stakeholder service system (Figure 1.1). The framework builds on the view that value co-creation occurs through integration of resources between actors (Lusch and Vargo, 2014). Through CEB (mobilising, influencing, co-developing and augmenting behaviour), engaged customers contribute diverse resources, such as knowledge, skills, experience and labour towards the focal firm and/or other stakeholders. These resources contributed by engaged customers may modify and/or augment the offering itself, or the resources may affect other stakeholders' perceptions, knowledge, preferences, expectations or actions towards the firm or its offering that affect their willingness to contribute resources towards the firm (Jaakkola and Alexander, 2014). In these interactions, focal customers also receive resources, such as improved

Table 1.1 Summary of value outcomes of customer engagement behaviours

Type of CEB	Value outcomes for the focal customer	Value outcomes for the firm	Value outcomes for other stakeholders
Co-developing behaviour	• Gaining products/ services that better serve their needs • Monetary rewards • Social rewards such as admiration	• Insights into users' needs and wants • Innovative ideas • Development resources such as expertise and skills	• Benefits from improved offerings
Influencing behaviour	• Power to reward/punish the provider for good/bad experience • Signalling expertise • Social prestige and attention	• New customer acquisition • Decreased/ increased sales • More knowledgeable customers	• Reduction of perceived risk in purchase decisions • Reliable source of information about the provider/ offering • Adjusting expectations
Augmenting behaviour	• Customised offerings better suited to goals and needs • Social benefits associated with collaborative effort • Social, cultural and intellectual value through C2C interaction	• Additional insight gained through customer augmentation • Improved offerings more relevant to clients • Fostering of deeper relationships	• Benefits from improved offerings
Mobilising behaviour	• Forcing (or encouraging) firms to change behaviours or decisions • Ensuring firms invest in things customers care about • Gathering support and recognition around a common cause	• Ability to make strategic investments that are valued by customers • Decreased/ increased sales	• Benefits from improved offerings • Benefits from participation in common causes

offerings (Füller, 2010), financial resources (Hoyer et al., 2010) or social prestige (Berthon et al., 2008) that further motivate their engagement behaviours. Figure 1.1 posits that CEB affects value co-creation processes 1) between the engaged customers and the focal firm, 2) between the engaged customers and other stakeholders, and 3) between other stakeholders and the focal firm. Next, we elaborate on these three relationships.

First, CEB affects *value co-creation between engaged customers and the focal firm:* through CEB, the exchange between the customer and the firm extends from what is fundamental to the transaction to customers contributing a broad range of resources such as time, knowledge and effort towards the firm (Jaakkola and Alexander, 2014). Engaged customers may contribute resources such as knowledge, skills, expertise and time to extend and add to the focal firms' offering (augmenting), or they can facilitate firm-led product/service development with their resources (co-developing).

For the focal firm, CEB provides a source of a range of resources that contribute to its offering development and marketing in ways that may be beyond what it could do alone. If the firm is able and willing to integrate the customer's resource contributions with its own resources, in other words, use customer's input such as product ideas and user expertise in product/service development, the firm is able to develop improved offerings that have a better value potential for the customer. Customer resources could also make the firm's offering unique, and provide the firm with considerable benefits and cost savings (Carbonell et al., 2009; Von Hippel, 2005).

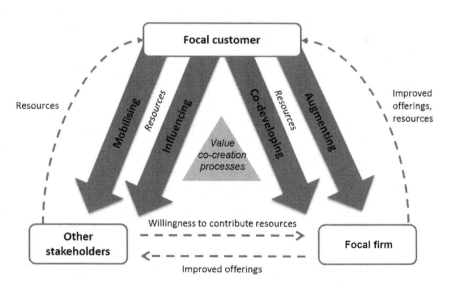

Figure 1.1 How customer engagement behaviours contribute to value co-creation between different stakeholders

Sometimes the firm cannot control the way customer contributions modify the offering, as customers augment the offering independently, for example, by generating new meanings for a brand by engaging in C2C interaction in a brand community, which may, in turn, create an additional source of value for the customer (McAlexander, Schouten, and Koening, 2002; Schau et al., 2009). Firms can provide a platform for such behaviour (Breidbach et al., 2014), or it may take place entirely outside the firm domain. In order to encourage their co-developing and augmenting behaviour, firms may also offer new resources for focal customers, such as monetary rewards (Hoyer et al., 2010) or user toolkits (von Hippel, 2005), or rely on the social benefits (such as building new relationships) and functional benefits (such as problem solving) gained by engaged customers (Dholakia et al., 2009).

Second, CEB may initiate and influence *value co-creation processes between the focal customer and other stakeholders.* Customers may invest their resources such as time, effort, relationships, experience and information to affect other stakeholders' perceptions, preferences or knowledge of the focal firm (influencing behaviour) or to affect other stakeholders' actions towards the focal firm (mobilising behaviour; Jaakkola and Alexander, 2014).

Other stakeholders, such as prospective customers, benefit from the information and experience shared by the focal customer as it helps them to find, evaluate and select providers and offerings that best fit their needs and situation (Jaakkola et al., 2014). Other customers are considered as trustworthy sources of information and they can decrease the risk perceived by other stakeholders. As indicated in Figure 1.1, other stakeholders in the service system may reciprocate through their own resources, such as time and knowledge manifested, for example, in recognition and appreciation towards the focal customer legitimising their actions, which further encourages CEB (Brodie et al., 2013; Jaakkola and Alexander, 2014). Engaged customers may also experience social benefits (such as building new relationships) and functional benefits (such as problem solving; Dholakia et al., 2009).

Finally, CEB affects the *value process between the other stakeholders and the focal firm* (Figure 1.1). The co-developing and augmenting behaviours by focal customer resources also impact the value potential of the firm's offering for other stakeholders (Jaakkola and Alexander, 2014). For example, when Starbucks develops a new coffee beverage based on a customer's idea, the improved offering can be enjoyed by a vast number of other stakeholders as well. Furthermore, information and experiences shared through influencing behaviour make the focal firm either more or less appealing for other stakeholders as well, who are therefore willing to contribute either more or fewer resources towards the firm. Through mobilising behaviour, engaged customers directly affect other stakeholders' resource contributions (e.g. increased or decreased buying) towards the focal firm.

Our framework indicates that CEB can activate an iterative, cyclical process where a growing number of stakeholders contribute their resources to value co-creation (cf. Arnould, Price, and Malshe, 2006), resulting in various value outcomes that emerge for each party in their respective value processes (cf.

Grönroos and Voima 2012). The positive outcomes (Table 1.1) for each party further motivate them to engage in, or support CEB (cf. Brodie et al. 2013; Jaakkola and Alexander, 2014).

Conclusions

This chapter has discussed how customer engagement behaviours contribute to value co-creation within service systems. The framework developed (Figure 1.1) suggests that CEB accrue value outcomes for the focal customer, focal firm and also other stakeholders via the application of resources offered (and subsequently) gained by each party through exchange and interaction. Focal customers benefit from the modified offering of the focal firm, as they co-create it with their resources, and also through the contributions made by other stakeholders. The focal firm benefits from CEB through the provision of resources that contribute to its offering in ways that may be beyond what it might otherwise achieve alone. Customer resources could make the firm value proposition unique, and the various CEBs could result in considerable benefits and cost savings for the firm through improved products and services (augmenting/co-developing), or the attraction of new customers and resources (influencing/mobilising). We see our framework as a critical juncture in research on CE and value co-creation as it draws research attention beyond firm-focused interpretations of CE towards a more contemporary systemic perspective.

To link the systemic value co-creation cycle induced by CEB with the broader literature on customer engagement, Figure 1.2 outlines the nomological network that brings together customer engagement and value co-creation (Brodie et al., 2011; Van Doorn et al., 2010). The framework indicates that customer engagement is facilitated by certain characteristics of the focal customer, focal firm and context (e.g. characteristics of other customers within the setting). These

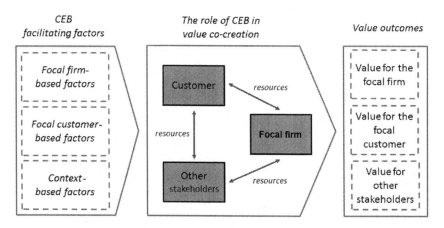

Figure 1.2 Customer engagement and value co-creation nomological network

'facilitating factors' stimulate the provision of resources that are exchanged between customer, firm and other stakeholders (as represented in Figure 1.1), subsequently affecting the firm's offering and/or other stakeholders' knowledge, preferences or expectations regarding the offering. Thereby customers affect the value processes of other customers either directly, or by transforming the offering of the focal firm with their contributions.

Customer satisfaction, trust and commitment may both represent CEB facilitating factors and CEB outcomes, and customers' motivation to engage relates to their expectation of value outcomes. Also, the firm's actions and attitudes towards CEB are closely linked to outcomes for both the customer and the firm itself, as indicated by Jaakkola and Alexander (2014).

In this chapter we have shown how customers make diverse resource contributions towards the focal firm and/other stakeholders centring on four CEBs that modify and/or augment the offering of the firm, and/or affect other stakeholders' perceptions, preferences, expectations or actions towards the firm or its offering. We argue that through customer activities, value co-creation has become a systemic process where the drivers for and outcomes of customer resource contributions are iterative and cyclical, and where positive outcomes for each party further motivate them to engage more and make additional resource contributions. In this way we further underline the importance of the customer for contemporary organisations by highlighting their contributions to value co-creation beyond more commonly understood roles of buyers and users in dyadic exchanges.

Managerial implications

This chapter has demonstrated how engaged customers, through behaviours exhibited and executed outside of regular service encounters, can build additional value for firms beyond that which they might gain with a more traditional approach to firm-customer relationships. Indeed, such is the advance of customer activity enacted beyond transactions that firms may not be able to rely on traditional value chains to develop, market or create new products and services as effectively as they have in the past. Undoubtedly there are tantalising opportunities for firms to enhance and differentiate their offerings through endeavours associated with customer augmentation and co-development of products and services. Firms are also increasingly reliant on customers to influence other customers' and stakeholders' attitudes and behaviours towards the firm. These interactive behaviours by engaged customers represent many indirect revenue-generating opportunities through co-developing, influencing and augmenting behaviours. Additionally, in the case of mobilising behaviours, engagement behaviours might also result in direct revenue generation if firms (or their customers) can be mobilised around a common cause or 'buycott'.

However, the flip side of CEB faced by firms relates to the extent to which the firm is able to retain control of their offerings and their wider marketing narrative. Augmenting behaviour, in particular, sees the customer taking control of modifications of offerings and, on that basis, may make changes or adaptations which the firm does not wish or did not intend. Moreover, influencing and mobilising behaviours are already well-established ways customers are using to criticise firms and dissuade them from making changes to their offerings, which Fournier and Avery (2011) suggest makes firms use marketing more as a public relations exercise than any influencing behaviour of their own. With many multi-national organisations viewed now as targets, ripe for criticism, the actions of engaged customers are likely to continue to impact firms in ways they do not expect or appreciate.

Avenues for future research

By using our framework future researchers can continue to make sense of the dramatic changes affecting the relationships that customers have with focal firms and their wider service systems. With stronger conceptual foundations, future research on customer engagement is able to explore more confidently the impacts that CEBs have on service systems in general. A fruitful approach for future research would be to study the evolution and life cycle of CE over time: What are the typical development cycles for CE and CEB? Are there any key conditions under which CE and CEB either grows or reduces? When may CEBs cease to exist, for example during dormancy (Brodie et al., 2013) or decline? We also encourage more research on the different contexts and platforms for CEB. Potential areas to explore are, for example, the key differences between online versus offline CEBs, and if there are any particular types of online CEBs not captured by extant research.

Our review on the range of behavioural manifestations of CE indicates that we know more about the positive, compared to negative outcomes of CEB. Furthermore, we do not yet understand the implications on firms if customers become weary of making additional contributions or when engaged customers work in direct opposition to the firm. More research is therefore needed to investigate negatively valenced CEB (Hollebeek and Chen, 2014), and the negative implications that different types of CEBs may have on the focal customer, the firm or other stakeholders in the service system. Additionally, work on CE to-date assumes customers are highly motivated to work with specific firms and makes no provision for engagement across firms and sectors. Future research, therefore, may wish to consider how self-selection bias may impact on specific CEB outcomes.

With regard to the four CEBs discussed in this chapter, future researchers should explore how firms can adapt to a loss of control associated with augmenting behaviour and/or the effects on the focal firm when augmentations change the firm offering beyond that with which it is comfortable. Mobilising behaviours represent unique situational and contextual problems (or opportunities) for firms, and future research would need to understand how firms can either stimulate the positive, or mitigate the effects of negative, mobilising situations. Although co-developing and influencing behaviours are well-understood, research on their systemic effects is still nascent and firms will, increasingly, need greater understanding of the implications of working with (or perhaps working for) engaged customers.

References

Adamson, K., and Lynch, P. (2013). *Yes Scotland and Better Together: Mobilizing and Neutralising National Identity for the 2014 Independence Referendum.* Paper presented at the Political Studies Association annual conference, Cardiff.

Adjei, M. T., Noble, S. M., and Noble, C. H. (2010). The influence of C2C communications in online brand communities on customer purchase behavior. *Journal of the Academy of Marketing Science, 38*(5), 634–653.

Ahearne, M., Bhattacharya, C. B., and Gruen, T. (2005). Antecedents and consequences of customer-company identification: expanding the role of relationship marketing. *Journal of Applied Psychology, 90*(3), 574.

Arnould, E. J., Price, L. L., and Malshe, A. (2006). Toward a cultural resource-based theory of the customer. In R. F. Lusch and S. L. Vargo (Eds.), *The Service-Dominant Logic of Marketing: Dialog, Debate and Directions* (320–333).

Bendapudi, N., and Leone, R. P. (2003). Psychological implications of consumer involvement in co-production. *Journal of Marketing, 67*(1), 14–28.

Berthon, P., Pitt, L., and Campbell, C. (2008). Ad lib: when customers create the ad. *California Management Review [T], 50*(4), 6–30

Bettencourt, L. A. (1997). Customer voluntary performance: customers as partners in service delivery. *Journal of Retailing, 73*(3), 383–406.

Bitner, M. J. (1992). Servicescapes: the impact of physical surroundings on customers and employees. *The Journal of Marketing, 56*(2), 57–71.

Blazevic, V., Hammedi, W., Garnefeld, I., Rust, R. T., Keiningham, T., Andreassen, T. W., and Donthu, N. (2013). Beyond traditional word-of-mouth: an expanded model of customer-driven influence. *Journal of Service Management, 24*(3), 294–313.

Breidbach, C., Brodie, R., and Hollebeek, L. (2014). Beyond virtuality: from engagement platforms to engagement ecosystems. *Managing Service Quality,* 24(6), 592–611.

Brodie, R. J., Hollebeek, L. D., Jurić, B., and Ilić, A. (2011). Customer engagement: conceptual domain, fundamental propositions, and implications for research. *Journal of Service Research, 14*(3), 252–271.

Brodie, R. J., Ilic, A., Juric, B., and Hollebeek, L. (2013). Consumer engagement in a virtual brand community: An exploratory analysis. *Journal of Business Research, 66*(1), 105–114.

Carbonell, P., Rodríguez, E., Ana L, and Pujari, D. (2009). Customer involvement in new service development: an examination of antecedents and outcomes. *Journal of Product Innovation Management, 26*(5), 536–550.

Carù, A., and Cova, B. (2015). Co-creating the collective service experience. *Journal of Service Management, 26*(2), 276–294.

Chandler, J. D., and Vargo, S. L. (2011). Contextualization and value-in-context: how context frames exchange. *Marketing Theory, 11*(1), 35–49.

Chen, T., Drennan, J., and Andrews, L. (2012). Experience sharing. *Journal of Marketing Management,* 28(13–14), 1535–1552.

Cova, B., and Dalli, D. (2009). Working consumers: the next step in marketing theory? *Marketing Theory, 9*(3), 315–339.

Dholakia, U. M., Blazevic, V., Wiertz, C., and Algesheimer, R. (2009). Communal service delivery: how customers benefit from participation in firm-hosted virtual P3 communities. *Journal of Service Research, 12*(2), 208.

Edvardsson, B., Kristensson, P., Magnusson, P., and Sundström, E. (2012). Customer integration within service development – A review of methods and an analysis of insitu and exsitu contributions. *Technovation, 32*(7), 419–429.

Edvardsson, B., Tronvoll, B., and Gruber, T. (2011). Expanding understanding of service exchange and value co-creation: a social construction approach. *Journal of the Academy of Marketing Science, 39*(2), 327–339.

Epp, A. M., and Price, L. L. (2011). Designing Solutions Around Customer Network Identity Goals. *Journal of Marketing, 75*(2), 36–54.

Ferrell, L., and Ferrell, O. (2012). Redirecting direct selling: High-touch embraces high-tech. *Business Horizons, 55*(3), 273–281.

Fournier, S., and Avery, J. (2011). The uninvited brand. *Business Horizons, 54*, 193–207.

Füller, J. (2010). Refining virtual co-creation from a consumer perspective. *California Management Review, 52*(2), 98–122.

Grönroos, C., and Voima, P. (2012). Critical service logic: making sense of value creation and co-creation. *Journal of the Academy of Marketing Science, 41*(2), 1–18.

Gruen, T. W., Osmonbekov, T., and Czaplewski, A. J. (2006). eWOM: The impact of customer-to-customer online know-how exchange on customer value and loyalty. *Journal of Business Research, 59*(4), 449–456.

Hamilton, K., and Alexander, M. (2013). Organic Community Tourism: A Cocreated Approach. *Annals of Tourism Research, 42*(July), 169–190.

Harris, L., and Harrigan, P. (2011). Social media in politics: the ultimate voter engagement tool or simply an echo chamber. *Journal of Political Marketing, 14*(3), 251–283.

Hennig-Thurau, T., Gwinner, K. P., Walsh, G., and Gremler, D. D. (2004). Electronic word-of-mouth via consumer-opinion platforms: What motivates consumers to articulate themselves on the Internet? *Journal of Interactive Marketing, 18*(1), 38–52.

Hollebeek, L. D. (2011). Demystifying customer brand engagement: Exploring the loyalty nexus. *Journal of Marketing Management, 27*(7–8), 785–807.

Hollebeek, L., and Chen, T. (2014). Exploring positively-versus negatively-valenced brand engagement: a conceptual model. *Journal of Product & Brand Management, 23*(1), 62–74.

Hoyer, W. D., Chandy, R., Dorotic, M., Krafft, M., and Singh, S. S. (2010). Consumer cocreation in new product development. *Journal of Service Research, 13*(3), 283–296.

Jaakkola, E., Aarikka-Stenroos, L., and Kimmel, A. J. (2014). Leveraging customer experience communication. In J. Kandampully (Ed.), *Customer Experience Management: Enhancing Experience and Value through Service Management.* USA: Kendall Hunt.

Jaakkola, E., and Alexander, M. (2014). The role of customer engagement behavior in value co-creation: a service system perspective. *Journal of Service Research, 17*(3), 247–261.

Jaakkola, E., Helkkula, A., and Aarikka-Stenroos, L. (2015). Service experience cocreation: conceptualization, implications, and future research directions. *Journal of Service Management, 26*(2), 182–205.

Kumar, V., Aksoy, L., Donkers, B., Venkatesan, R., Wiesel, T., and Tillmanns, S. (2010). Undervalued or overvalued customers: capturing total customer engagement value. *Journal of Service Research, 13*(3), 297–310.

Libai, B., Bolton, R., Bügel, M.S., de Ruyter, K., Götz, O., Risselada, H., and Stephen, A.T. (2010). Customer-to-customer interactions: broadening the scope of word of mouth research. *Journal of Service Research, 13*(3), 267–282.

Litvin, S., Goldsmith, R., Pan, B. (2008) Electronic word-of-mouth in hospitality and tourism management. *Tourism Management, 29*(3), 458–468.

Lusch, R.F., and Vargo, S.L. (2014). *Service-Dominant Logic: Premises, Perspectives, Possibilities*. Cambridge University Press.

McAlexander, J.H., Schouten, J.W., and Koening, H.F. (2002). Building brand communities. *Journal of Marketing, 61*(January), 38–54.

Nambisan, S., and Baron, R.A. (2009). Virtual customer environments: testing a model of voluntary participation in value co creation activities. *Journal of Product Innovation Management, 26*(4), 388–406.

Paek, H.-J., and Nelson, M.R. (2009). To buy or not to buy: Determinants of socially responsible consumer behavior and consumer reactions to cause-related and boycotting ads. *Journal of Current Issues & Research in Advertising, 31*(2), 75–90.

Ramaswamy, V. (2008). Co-creating value through customers' experiences: the Nike case. *Strategy & Leadership, 36*(5), 9–14.

Rosenbaum, M.S., and Massiah, C.A. (2007). When customers receive support from other customers: exploring the influence of intercustomer social support on customer voluntary performance. *Journal of Service Research, 9*(3), 257–270.

Sawhney, M., Verona, G., and Prandelli, E. (2005). Collaborating to create: the Internet as a platform for customer engagement in product innovation. *Journal of Interactive Marketing, 19*(4), 4–17.

Schau, H.J., Muñiz Jr, A.M., and Arnould, E.J. (2009). How brand community practices create value. *Journal of Marketing, 73*(5), 30–51.

Seraj, M. (2012). We create, we connect, we respect, therefore we are: intellectual, social, and cultural value in online communities. *Journal of Interactive Marketing, 26*(4), 209–222.

Solomon, M.R., Surprenant, C., Czepiel, J.A., and Gutman, E.G. (1985). A role theory perspective on dyadic interactions: the service encounter. *Journal of Marketing, 49*(1), 99–111.

Sussan, F. (2012). Consumer interaction as intellectual capital. *Journal of Intellectual Capital, 13*(1), 81–105.

Van Doorn, J., Lemon, K.N., Mittal, V., Nass, S., Pick, D., Pirner, P., and Verhoef, P.C. (2010). Customer engagement behavior: theoretical foundations and research directions. *Journal of Service Research, 13*(3), 253–266.

Vargo, S.L. (2008). Customer integration and value creation: paradigmatic traps and perspectives. *Journal of Service Research, 11*(2), 211–215.

Vargo, S.L., and Lusch, R.F. (2008). Service-dominant logic: continuing the evolution. *Journal of the Academy of Marketing Science, 36*(1), 1–10.

Verleye, K., Gemmel, P., and Rangarajan, D. (2013). Managing engagement behaviors in a network of customers and stakeholders evidence from the nursing home sector. *Journal of Service Research, 17*(1), 68–84.

Von Hippel, E. (2005). Democratizing innovation: the evolving phenomenon of user innovation. *Journal für Betriebswirtschaft, 55*(1), 63–78.

2 Economic outcomes of customer engagement

Emerging findings, contemporary theoretical perspectives, and future challenges

Sander F. M. Beckers, Jenny van Doorn and Peter C. Verhoef

Introduction

Customers nowadays are very active on social media and social networks, in which they, for instance, discuss companies and their brands (Hennig-Thurau et al., 2010). Key facilitating factors in this area include social media (e.g. Facebook and Twitter), which have increased the connectivity of customers and firms (e.g. Liu-Thompkins and Rogerson, 2012). As a result, customer value becomes more important for companies. For instance, the share of customer value in enterprise valuation is rising (from less than 10 per cent in 2003 to almost 20 per cent in 2013; Binder and Hanssens, 2015), research company Forrester speaks about a new era of 'the age of the customer' (Band, 2012), many companies have increased investment in CRM technologies (Band, 2010), and over 80 per cent of chief marketing officers report to expect a rising use of online customer behaviour data within their companies (cf. www.cmosurvey.org).

As such, companies have shifted their strategic focus from building brands to building customer relationships (Binder and Hanssens, 2015), especially due to the growing influence of customer relationships on economic (firm-level) outcomes. Within the building of customer relationships an evolution is taking place; before the emergence of customer relationship management (CRM) the relationship between firms and customers was largely unidirectional (i.e. from firm to customer). Later, with the start of customer relationship management (roughly around 1990), this relationship became bidirectional, and presently (roughly from 2005 onwards) the relationship between firms and customers goes beyond bidirectionality into one of co-operation (Beckers, Risselada and Verhoef, 2013). In this next frontier, often labelled as 'customer engagement' – rather than being passive recipients of companies' actions – customers provide value to, and cocreate value with, companies (Beckers, Risselada and Verhoef, 2013). This cocreation is often in conclave with other customers and/or firms within interactive social networks (e.g. Risselada, Verhoef and Bijmolt, 2014).

Customer engagement has thus become a very important topic for companies (Brodie et al., 2011; Verhoef, Reinartz and Krafft, 2010). In this chapter we will investigate emerging findings, contemporary theoretical perspectives, and future challenges with respect to the economic outcomes of customer engagement. To do so we first need to define 'customer engagement'. Despite the term having different meanings for different people (Bolton, 2011), academic literature views customer engagement as a multi-faceted construct with cognitive, emotional, and behavioural dimensions (Brodie et al., 2011). Nevertheless, debate exists regarding the exact definition and boundaries of the customer engagement construct (e.g. Bolton, 2011; Brodie and Hollebeek, 2011; Van Doorn, 2011). Despite this debate, consensus exists in the literature that customer engagement goes beyond traditional customer management constructs, such as loyalty and satisfaction (especially prominent and fruitful is the work by Hollebeek and colleagues on this terrain; for instance Hollebeek (2011), especially Table 3 on p. 793; and Hollebeek, Glynn and Brodie (2014)). Moreover, there is consensus that the cognitive and emotional dimensions; typically, result in non-transactional behavioural manifestations of engagement.

These manifestations can take different forms, such as customer word-of-mouth, customer cocreation in new product development, and customer feedback (cf. Bijmolt et al., 2010; Verhoef, Reinartz and Krafft, 2010). Writing a review on TripAdvisor, participating in Lay's Chips flavour creation competition, filling out a satisfaction survey, commenting on a company's Facebook page, and so on are all examples of behaviours that fall within the behavioural dimension of the customer engagement construct. Such behaviours can sometimes make or break a company and its brand and thus, have clear economic implications. For instance, a Twitter campaign by McDonalds was 'hijacked' by customers who started to make fun of the company (Verhoef Beckers and Van Doorn, 2013). Customers nowadays add value for companies through transactions, but also through non-transactional behaviours. This value addition can be in the form of providing customer knowledge, providing product referrals to other customers and/or influencing other customers (Kumar et al., 2010). Benefits of these value-added activities for companies are numerous, and range from more efficient and effective value creation to enhancing customer relationships, although these behaviours can also be a double-edged sword since they might not always be positive (Beckers, Van Doorn and Verhoef, 2015).

Not surprisingly, given how customer engagement has a clear and growing impact on companies, recently both academics and practitioners have begun to empirically investigate the economic outcomes of customer engagement and interactivity. Numerous studies have emerged on this topic; however, to our knowledge there is currently not an overview available of the empirical findings regarding the consequences of customer engagement. We feel, given the current state of research, that the time is ripe for such an overview. Therefore, the first aim of our chapter is to provide an overview of emerging and converging findings of the consequences (in terms of customer-level, firm-level, and other-level outcomes) of customer engagement. From our overview we conclude that research on the firm-level outcomes of customer engagement as an overarching construct is largely lacking to date. We feel that research on firm-level outcomes of the overall customer engagement construct can benefit from applying a unified theoretical perspective in order to analyse the underlying rationale that through customer engagement customers become co-producers of value. Yet, we observe that unified theoretical perspectives on economic outcomes of customer engagement, and its key drivers, remain underdeveloped to date. In response to this observed research gap, our second objective is to introduce relevant contemporary theoretical perspectives (i.e. transaction cost economics, the resource-based view, and social exchange theory) on firm-level effectiveness of (the company's strategies with respect to) customer engagement. We thereby aim to examine the theoretical foundations for customer engagement and firm performance. Specifically, we investigate theories originating in all various theoretical domains (i.e. economic, behavioural, and economic/behavioural domains) that are deemed relevant for relationship marketing (Odekerken-Schröder, 1999), thereby providing a comprehensive view. In doing so, we focus on the behavioural dimension of the customer engagement construct, since this represents the managerial focal point for most organisations in terms of driving the economic outcomes of customer engagement (Bolton, 2011).

Our chapter proceeds as follows. In the next session we summarise recent empirical findings on the economic outcomes of customer engagement. Based on our summary we argue that current literature could focus more on firm-level performance consequences of the overall customer engagement construct and potential contingencies associated with these outcomes. In doing so, we believe it is particularly worthwhile to apply an overarching theoretical framework. We, therefore, in the following section, present the foundations of various traditional organisational theories and discuss their applicability in order to analyse the economic outcomes of customer engagement. In the final section we explore future research directions.

Emerging findings on customer engagement outcomes

As specified in the Introduction, recently a lot of (academic) research on customer engagement has emerged. Customer engagement was one of the Marketing Science Institute's top research priorities (MSI, 2010), and the underlying changes in customers and customer experiences continue to be so today (MSI, 2014). In Table 2.1 we provide an overview of the findings on the outcomes of customer engagement (behaviours). We do not claim that our overview is exhaustive (given the contemporary interest in customer engagement as a research topic such an overview would be virtually impossible to provide), yet we included the most cited exemplary papers within the domain, and we complemented these key papers with some of the most recent work (primarily from the major marketing journals, such as the *Journal of Marketing* and the *Journal of Marketing Research*). We focused on empirical findings from quantitative research, since they, amongst others, test the propositions developed in some of the earlier conceptual and qualitative research, which have had true merit in laying the foundations of the customer engagement construct. Following Van Doorn et al.

Table 2.1 Overview of exemplary and key research on the outcomes of customer engagement

Author(s)	Year	Outcome construct	Type of CE studied	Main finding(s)
		Customer level		
Fuchs, Prandelli, and Schreier	2010	Cognitive	Cocreation	Customers feel a sense of psychological ownership when they are involved in product selection, which increases their product demand
Scott and Craig-Lees	2010	Cognitive	Customer engagement	Product recognition is enhanced by audience engagement
Brodie et al.	2013	Cognitive, attitudinal, and emotional	Customer engagement	Customer engagement leads to connection and emotional bonding, customer empowerment, customer loyalty and satisfaction, and trust and commitment
Bagozzi and Dholakia	2006b	Attitudinal	Community participation	Participation in online support community leads to intentions of additional positive behaviours (e.g., spending money, cocreation) towards the company
Bendapudi and Leone	2003	Attitudinal	Cocreation	Customers have a self-service bias when they participate in co-production, which reduces their satisfaction towards the firm
Calder, Malthouse, and Schaedel	2009	Attitudinal	Customer engagement	Online engagement positively impacts attitude towards advertisement
Gruen, Osmonbekev, and Czaplewski	2006	Attitudinal	Word-of-mouth	Customer know-how exchange positively impacts product value perception and recommendation intentions
Heidenreich et al.	2015	Attitudinal	Cocreation	Failure in high cocreation services lead to larger reduction in satisfaction than failure in low cocreation services
McAlexander, Schouten, and Koenig	2002	Attitudinal	Community participation	Brandfest participation positively impacts attitude towards the brand, the company, and fellow customers

Ofir and Simonson	2001	Attitudinal	Voice	When customers (anticipate they) are asked for their opinion a negativity bias can occur which reduced their satisfaction
So, King, and Sparks	2014	Attitudinal	Customer engagement	Customer engagement positively impacts loyalty intentions
Algesheimer, Dholakia, and Herrmann	2005	Attitudinal, emotional	Community participation	Community engagement, on the positive side, leads to participation, continuation, and recommendation intentions. But on the negative side community engagement leads to normative pressure and ultimately reactance
Hollebeek, Glynn, and Brodie	2014	Attitudinal, emotional	Customer engagement	Consumer brand engagement, especially the affection component, has a positive influence on self-brand connection and brand usage intent
Beckers et al.	2015	Attitudinal, cross-customer	Community participation	Online customer community support increases customer satisfaction, static online support decreases customer satisfaction. Effects differ between users and upper managers.
Algesheimer et al.	2010	Behavioural	Community participation	Community usage makes customers more efficient and conservative; they for instance spend less money.
Bayus	2013	Behavioural	Cocreation	Customers whose previous cocreation ideas were implemented propose less diverse ideas
Bone et al.	2015	Behavioural	Community participation	Usage of online community support decreases usage of the more costly traditional offline customer support
Borle et al.	2007	Behavioural	Voice	Customer satisfaction survey participation increases customer purchase behaviour
Ludwig et al.	2013	Behavioural	Word-of-mouth	When reviews have greater increases in positive content the impact on conversion behaviour becomes smaller, the same pattern does not hold for negative content

(*Continued*)

Table 2.1 (Continued)

Author(s)	Year	Outcome construct	Type of CE studied	Main finding(s)
Manchanda, Packard, and Pattabhiramaiah	2015	Behavioural	Community participation	Customers that are active within communities spend more, especially those customers that contribute content by posting and those with more social ties in the community
Zhu et al.	2012	Behavioural	Community participation	Online community participants make riskier financial decisions than non-participants
Sprott, Czellar, and Spangenberg	2009	Time, cognitive, and attitudinal	Customer engagement	High brand engaged consumers are less time-sensitive and price-sensitive regarding the brand. They also pay more attention to the brand, have a better recall of the brand, and a higher preference for the brand
Firm level				
Beckers, Van Doorn, and Verhoef	2015	Shareholder value	Customer engagement (Word-of-mouth, voice, cocreation)	Stimulating customer engagement reduces shareholder value
Chen, Liu, and Zhang	2012	Shareholder value	Word-of-mouth	Relative valence of a review influences stock return in the direction of their valence
Luo	2009	Shareholder value	Word-of-mouth	Negative word-of-mouth reduces a firm's cash flow and stock price
Tirunillai and Tellis	2012	Shareholder value	Word-of-mouth	Word-of-mouth is correlated with stock performance and negative word-of-mouth can negatively impact stock performance
Schmitt, Skiera, and Van den Bulte	2011	Financial	Word-of-mouth	Customers that are acquired through referral programs are more valuable, have a higher contribution margin, and a higher retention rate

Trusov, Bucklin, and Pauwels	2009	Financial	Word-of-mouth	Word-of-mouth referrals are more effective in driving customer acquisition than traditional advertising activity
Villanueva, Yoo, and Hanssens	2008	Financial	Word-of-mouth	Customers that are acquired through marketing actions are more valuable in the short-run, yet customers that are acquired through word-of-mouth are more valuable in the long run
Berger, Sorenson, and Rasmussen	2010	Sales	Word-of-mouth	Negative word-of-mouth can increase sales for products with low prior awareness and reduce sales for well-known products
Chevalier and Mayzlin	2006	Sales	Word-of-mouth	When reviews get more positive sales increase. Negative reviews are more influential than positive reviews.
Chintagunta et al.	2010	Sales	Word-of-mouth	Positive word-of-mouth drives sales. It is the valence of word-of-mouth that matters and not the volume.
Floyd et al.	2014	Sales	Word-of-mouth	Meta-analysis documents that retail sales elasticity of review valence is .69 and retail sales elasticity of review volume is .35
Godes and Mayzlin	2009	Sales	Word-of-mouth	Word-of-mouth is most effective in driving sales for products with low initial awareness
Gopinath et al.	2014	Sales	Word-of-mouth	Only the valence of word-of-mouth has an impact on sales
Ho-Dac, Carson, and Moore	2013	Sales	Word-of-mouth	Online reviews impact sales of weak brands and do not impact sales of strong brands
Kumar et al.	2013	Sales	Word-of-mouth	Social media conversations can drive customer influence effect and customer influence value
Lilien et al.	2002	Sales	Cocreation	Cocreation projects involving lead users result in larger sales value

(*Continued*)

Table 2.1 (Continued)

Author(s)	Year	Outcome construct	Type of CE studied	Main finding(s)
Tang, Fang, and Wang	2014	Sales	Word-of-mouth	Mixed-neutral (balanced positive and negative) user generated content enhances the effectiveness of user generated content, whereas indifferent-neutral (neither positive nor negative claims) user generated content decreases the effectiveness of user generated content
You, Vadakkepatt, and Joshi	2015	Sales	Word-of-mouth	Meta-analysis shows that the sales elasticity of electronic word-of-mouth volume and valence are .236 and .417, respectively
Chan, Yim, and Lam	2010	Employee	Cocreation	Customer cocreation can cause job stress among a company's employees
Fang	2008	Product	Cocreation	The effect of customer participation on product innovation and speed to market can be positive or negative depending on customer network connectivity and new product development process interdependence
Noordhoff et al.	2011	Product	Cocreation	In a B2B setting embedded ties with customers hurt supplier innovation due to fear of opportunism
Other				
Thompson and Sinha	2008	Cross-brand	Community participation	Brand community participation decreases adoption of new products from competing brands
Chen, Wang, and Xie	2011	Cross-customer, sales	Word-of-mouth	Negative word-of-mouth has more influence on sales than positive word-of-mouth. Only positive (not negative) observational learning has an (positive) impact on sales.

Moreau, Bonney, and Herd	2011	Cross-customer	Cocreation	Customers that customize products for other customers have a higher willingness-to-pay than customers that customize for themselves
Thompson and Malaviya	2013	Cross-customer	Cocreation	Disclosing that an advertisement is cocreated by another customer can cause two opposite effects: scepticism about the ad creator competence and identification with the ad creator

Notes: We ordered the table based on outcome level studied, followed by respectively the studied construct and name of the author(s). We classified the outcomes studied into customer-level, firm-level, and other-level outcomes (based, for instance, on Van Doorn et al. 2010) and distinguished various types of customer engagement investigated (customer engagement as an overarching construct or distinct behavioural manifestations of customer engagement; word-of-mouth, voice, cocreation, or community participation).

(2010), we classified the outcomes studied into customer-level, firm-level, and other-level, and distinguished various types of customer engagement investigated (customer engagement as an overarching construct or distinct behavioural manifestations of customer engagement, word-of-mouth, voice, cocreation, or community participation).

In reviewing Table 2.1 we observe two main insights:

- The outcomes of customer engagement are mostly positive. Specifically, 21 papers examined report positive outcomes as key findings, such as increased satisfaction and sales. However, negative outcomes are also shown: 11 papers in Table 2.1 report negative outcomes as core findings, such as employee job stress and decreased shareholder value. The remaining 15 papers report both positive as well as negative main outcomes (e.g. negative and positive word-of-mouth effects).
- Most research studies the effectiveness of a single customer engagement (behavioural) manifestation in isolation (i.e. 40 out of 47 papers), instead of the overarching multi-faceted customer engagement construct (i.e. a mere 7 out of 47 papers examined study the overarching engagement construct).

Other observations from Table 2.1 include:

- Among the studies that study a single customer engagement behaviour in isolation, (e) word-of-mouth (e.g. online reviews) has received the most attention (i.e. out of 40 papers focusing on a single customer engagement behaviour, 19 papers solely address word-of-mouth), especially with firm sales as a key outcome variable (i.e. 10 included papers limit their focus to the effect of word-of-mouth on firm sales). We also identify two recent meta-analyses; one in the *Journal of Marketing* (You, Vadakkepatt and Joshi, 2015) documenting a sales elasticity of electronic word-of-mouth volume of .236 and a sales elasticity of electronic word-of-mouth valence of .417. A second meta-analysis, which appeared in the *Journal of Retailing* (Floyd et al., 2014), indicated that the retail sales elasticity of review volume and review valence are .34 and .69, respectively.

- Customer engagement behaviours are separately linked to firm-level consequences, but overarching construct outcomes of customer engagement are almost always studied at the customer level (i.e. 6 out of the 7 papers that study the consequences of the overall customer engagement construct have a customer-level dependent variable, herein survey methodology is the most popular research method).
- The effect of customer engagement on other stakeholders, that is, besides firms and customers, are largely overlooked: only 6 out of 47 studies in Table 2.1 investigate the effect of customer engagement on employees, shareholders, or competitors, and we did not identify any empirical studies addressing the effects of customer engagement on society at large (e.g. consumer welfare, economic and social surplus, the government, public policy makers).

Thus, although the outcomes of focal behavioural manifestations of customer engagement in isolation have been studied in relative depth, studies investigating the outcomes of (customer) engagement as an overarching construct are few to date. Most 'studies have been predominantly exploratory in nature, thus generating a lack of empirical research in this area to date' (Hollebeek, Glynn and Brodie, 2014, p. 149). The few empirical studies that study the outcomes of the overarching customer engagement construct typically focus on customer-level outcomes. We propose that future research should focus on the firm-level outcomes of customer engagement as an overarching construct. Research can benefit from adopting an integrative perspective on customer engagement, instead of focusing on a single manifestation of customer engagement. Distinct customer engagement behaviours arise out of the cognitive and emotional dimension of customer engagement, and have in common that they change the way value is created between firms and customers (Beckers, Risselada and Verhoef, 2013). Next, we argue that contemporary theoretical perspectives are especially fruitful to study the firm-level consequences of customer engagement as an overarching construct, which we apply by presenting a number of relevant theoretical perspectives.

Contemporary theoretical perspectives on the firm-level outcomes of customer engagement

Our review about studies of customer engagement outcomes highlights the need to develop a unified view on the firm-level outcomes of the overall customer engagement construct. In doing so, we believe it is particularly worthwhile to apply a cohesive theoretical perspective. Such perspective can exploit the communality underlying the overarching customer engagement construct that customers become co-producers of value (e.g. Prahalad and Ramaswamy, 2004a, Beckers, Risselada and Verhoef, 2013). Different traditional (organisational) theories have their own viewpoint on the benefits and drawbacks of this communality, and thus how this translates into firm-level performance. A unified theoretical perspective could also be used to determine systematic contingencies of the outcomes of (firm's strategies with respect to) customer engagement. Nevertheless, we feel such theoretical perspectives are underdeveloped to date. Therefore, in this section, we will introduce three relevant contemporary theoretical perspectives: transaction cost economics, the resource-based view, and social exchange theory. We selected these theories based on their applicability in a customer engagement setting and their complementarity arising from each belonging to a separate relevant theoretical domain (and collectively covering all relevant domains) for relationship marketing (Odekerken-Schröder, 1999). Since our focus is on firm-level outcomes, we explicitly incorporate analysis of firm strategies to drive these outcomes.

We summarise the anticipated firm-level outcomes of customer engagement based on the various theoretical perspectives in Table 2.2. Table 2.2 also contains an overview of the key process, i.e. the underlying rationale, and key moderators by which each theory anticipates customer engagement to translate into firm performance.

Table 2.2 Summary of anticipated firm-level outcome effects of customer engagement

Theory	Type of effect	Prediction	Rationale
TCE	Main effect	On average, the (firm-level) outcomes of customer engagement are negative	Managing customer engagement leads to behavioural uncertainty (that is, risk of potential negative engagement behaviours), since companies have no safeguarding mechanism to enforce positive outcomes
TCE	Moderator: Customer relationship investments	Companies with more customer relationship investments obtain lower firm-level outcomes	Relationship specific investments are being put on the line when managing customer engagement, especially since no safeguards against opportunistic behaviours are available
TCE	Moderator: Demand uncertainty	Firm-level outcomes are reduced under demand uncertainty	Under demand uncertainty customer input is more likely to be obsolete and misdirected, since customers' future wants and needs are unstable and unknown

(*Continued*)

Table 2.2 (Continued)

Theory	Type of effect	Prediction	Rationale
TCE	Moderator: Frequency	Frequency reduces firm-level outcomes	With more frequent activity it becomes more efficient to produce in-house instead of relying on customers' contributions and risks of negative outcomes are higher because customers become more empowered
RBV	Main effect	On average, the firm-level outcomes of customer engagement are positive	Customer engagement can aid companies in building resources that are valuable, rare, and inimitable or non-substitutable (i.e. strategic resources)
RBV	Moderator: Corporate reputation	Firm-level outcomes are reduced when a company has a good reputation	Corporate reputation is a strategic resource that can be built through managing customer engagement; if a company already possess this resource, customer engagement efforts might be redundant
RBV	Moderator: Customer loyalty	Firm-level outcomes are reduced when a company has a loyal customer base	Customer engagement enhances the strategic resource of having a loyal customer base; customer engagement efforts are redundant if a company already possess such customer base
RBV	Moderator: Internal (R&D) resources	Companies with more internal (R&D) resources obtain lower firm-level outcomes	Internal (R&D) resources and benefitting from the wisdom of the crowd through their customer engagement might be substitutes
SET	Main effect	On average, the firm-level outcomes of customer engagement are positive/negative	Customers make a cost/benefit trade-off when exchanging with companies; this implies for the (management of) customer engagement two opposing effects: potential benefits are enhanced, but potential costs are also enhanced

Note: TCE stands for transaction cost economics, RBV stands for resource-based view, and SET stands for social exchange theory.

Transaction cost economics

The first theoretical perspective that we investigate to identify the firm-level performance of customer engagement (and contingencies thereof) is transaction cost economics. When stimulating customer engagement and the resulting customer engagement behaviours, companies seek joint value creation with customers and involve customers in activities that were traditionally performed in-house (e.g. Prahalad and Ramaswamy, 2004a). For instance, by stimulating word-of-mouth companies partially outsource advertising and acquisition to customers (e.g. Libai, 2011; Villanueva, Yoo and Hanssens, 2008). This means that a company decides to what extent it involves its customers in value creation. This decision is similar to a traditional make, buy, or ally decision, as is common in transaction cost economics. We, therefore, argue that classical elements of transaction cost theory can help explain the economic outcomes of customer engagement.

The basic premise of transaction cost theory is that the benefits of competition establish outsourcing (i.e. market governance) as a default option for organising production. However, in some circumstances leading to market failure, the costs of outsourcing exceed its benefits, and in-house production (i.e. hierarchical governance) is more efficient. Elements that can lead to potential market failure are relationship-specific investments, uncertainty, and frequency (Geyskens, Steenkamp and Kumar, 2006). These elements are also relevant with respect to the firm's management of customer engagement.

However, rather than a classical market versus hierarchical governance dichotomy, (most) firm-initiated customer engagement behaviours entail hybrid governance mechanisms, and involving customers in value creation differs from traditional inter-organisational arrangements in important ways. In traditional outsourcing agreements, co-operating firms create value *for* customers, rather than *with* them, and are contractually bound by formal governance mechanisms (e.g. Kim, 1999; Mooi and Gilliland, 2013). By contrast, involving customers in the production process makes formal governance more difficult, because the size and heterogeneity of the customer base prevents contractual binding. Furthermore, the types of value creation behaviours customers undertake generally are 'noncontractible' (Dyer, 1997). Creative activities in particular (e.g. innovation inputs, novel solutions to business problems, designing appealing advertising content) cannot be captured effectively in contracts (neither in an employer-employee relationship, nor in a buyer-supplier relationship), because human creative efforts and abilities are too heterogeneous to standardise or specify (Benkler, 2006; Weber, 2004).

Therefore, instead of market governance, when firms initiate and/or manage customer engagement behaviours some form of hybrid governance mechanism is required. Customer value cocreation seeks joint outcomes (Prahalad and Ramaswamy, 2004a), which represents a social form of production; therefore, the particular hybrid governance form companies use to stimulate customer engagement behaviours likely reflects a social transactional framework (Benkler, 2006). Rather than relying on economic incentives and formal and explicit controls, which is typical for market governance, a social transactional framework uses social norms and informal and implicit control mechanisms to encourage participants to self-identify their tasks (e.g. deciding to participate by contributing to a company's online community; Rindfleisch et al., 2010). This approach thus avoids the transaction costs associated with specifying customers' creative efforts for pricing or managerial command; therefore, the transaction costs for customer input in value creation are lowest in a social production governance mode (Benkler, 2006; Cook, 2008). Just as customer engagement behaviours change value creation, this novel, hybrid governance mode can be viewed as a new economic institution reflecting social forms of production, with joint effort and outcomes (Cook, 2008; Rindfleisch et al., 2010).

Main effect: behavioural uncertainty

Still, the central governance issue that companies face when involving customers in value creation, by stimulating customer engagement behaviours, is behavioural uncertainty. Especially since no strong market or traditional inter-organisational governance mechanisms (e.g. contractual binding, regular progress meetings, long-term relationship incentives) are applicable in order to induce customers to comply with company objectives, value creation based on customer engagement behaviours is risky for companies (Hoyer et al., 2010). That is, these behaviours may be value enhancing (e.g. low-cost new product development; Hoyer et al., 2010), but they also can be value destroying (e.g. negative word-of-mouth; Luo, 2009). The problem of performance ambiguity arises when stimulating customer engagement behaviours, because companies give away control over value creation activities to customers (Cook, 2008), without any means to enforce positive outcomes. Furthermore, the social transactional governance mode seeks joint value, instead of benefits accruing to an individual firm (Sawhney and Prandelli, 2000), yet the need for companies to capture the created value hinders the efficiency, thereby increasing transaction costs (Benkler, 2006; Ghosh and John, 1999).

Next, we argue that this central governance issue of performance ambiguity may be attenuated or enhanced, depending on its interplay with three other circumstances identified in the transaction cost literature to generate market failure. These other circumstances are relationship-specific investments, external uncertainty, and frequency.

Moderator: relationship-specific investment

Relationship-specific investments are tailored to a specific external party. According to transaction cost economics, such investments increase the risk of market failure because they cannot be deployed outside the relationship. By making investments specific to an independent partner, the focal firm becomes more dependent on (Geyskens, Steenkamp and Kumar, 2006) and thus more vulnerable to opportunistic behaviour (i.e. 'self-interest seeking with guile') by the other party (Williamson, 1985). When companies stimulate customer engagement behaviours, they grow to depend on customers, putting, for instance, their brand name capital and its associated benefits at stake in this customer-firm interaction (Ghosh and John, 1999). Therefore, when stimulating customer engagement behaviours, companies need a safeguarding mechanism to protect their relationship-specific investments and prevent opportunistic behaviour. However, in a customer engagement setting, there are no strong market mechanisms available to achieve these outcomes. Relationship-specific investments in a customer engagement setting are all investments made by a company in order to strengthen the bond with its customers, for instance investments in corporate image, brand name capital, and post-sale service. Hence the risk of stimulating customer engagement behaviours is particularly acute for companies that have invested in customer relationships.

Moderator: external uncertainty

With respect to external uncertainty, transaction cost economics distinguishes demand from technological uncertainty (Geyskens, Steenkamp and Kumar, 2006). We consider demand uncertainty more relevant for the management of customer engagement, because it arises directly from the partner's transactional behaviour (i.e. the customer). Managing customer engagement behaviours is not so much to uncover future technological requirements; instead, it should better reveal customers' needs and wants (Hoyer et al., 2010; Kumar et al., 2010). Therefore, we focus our attention on demand uncertainty.

When demand is uncertain it is hard to predict the requested volume for a company's offering, due to market fluctuations (Walker and Weber, 1984). In inter-organisational relationships, it can lead to co-ordination difficulties, in terms of specification or modification, which, in turn, raise transaction costs (Geyskens, Steenkamp and Kumar, 2006). With regard to customers involved in value creation, demand uncertainty arises because their needs and wants change rapidly (Anderson, Day and Rangan, 1997), and therefore companies need to closely monitor them (Gatignon and Xuereb, 1997; Kohli and Jaworski, 1990). However, customer engagement management goes beyond listening to customers and traditional market research by letting customers participate in value creation. Yet, when customers are in the driver's seat and take a level of control of value creation activities (Hoyer et al., 2010), the firm's flexibility diminishes. Such flexibility, however, is necessary in unstable environments, to ensure adaptivity and avoid obsolescence (Anderson, Day and Rangan, 1997). In a rapidly changing environment the feedback customers provide to the company, the recommendations they make to their peers, and their cocreation input may be valuable currently, but not for the future per se. In this case, stimulating customer engagement behaviours increases (rather than decreases) demand uncertainty for companies, and creates an exchange hazard associated with acting on obsolete customer input in the value chain. Customers may not be able to foresee what their future needs are. As automotive pioneer Henry Ford is said to have put it: 'If I had asked people what they wanted, they would have said faster horses' (e.g. Vlaskovits, 2011). Under demand uncertainty customers, therefore, may either make mistakes in their value-adding engagement activities, or overestimate their contribution ability (Benkler, 2006). Therefore, social transactional governance incurs transaction costs associated with correcting and eliminating poor outcomes, in 'parallel [with] quality control problems faced by firms and markets' (Benkler, 2006, p. 112). The central governance concern of performance ambiguity is amplified with demand uncertainty, because customers may engage not just in negative efforts, but also misdirected effort (e.g. constructive customer engagement behaviours that turn out to be obsolete).

Moderator: frequency

The transaction cost economics element frequency refers to the amount or recurrence of transactions (Geyskens, Steenkamp and Kumar, 2006). When transactions are more frequent, the firm enjoys the advantages of a repeating game with a strategic partner, which reduces opportunism threats (Dyer, 1997), and facilitates the recovery of the overhead costs associated with organising such transactions (Williamson, 1985). However, when firms manage customer engagement (behaviours), these advantages may disappear, considering the vastness and heterogeneity among the group of potential customers. The same customers do not respond to all customer engagement initiatives per se, and their responses vary substantially across such initiatives. Even if a company frequently involves customers in value creation, ex-ante ambiguity about their responses is unlikely to decline, as it would if they developed a solid relationship through a recurring game with a single partner. By contrast, the overhead cost benefits may still apply; that is, the fixed costs of performing the value-added function, such as customer acquisition, can be recovered more easily when the frequency of performing the function increases (Anderson and Schmittlein, 1984; Williamson, 1985).

In addition, a company that involves customers more frequently in value creation loses more substantial control over value-adding functions and empowers customers (Hoyer et al., 2010). These customers may learn to recognise their greater power and knowledge about products and quality, which they may exploit to achieve premium returns (Anderson and Jap, 2005). Hence initiative frequency may lead to more safeguards, although the number and heterogeneity of customers complicates this process. On the other hand, overhead costs can be better recovered with higher initiative frequency. Further, customers become more empowered, which would lead to higher transaction costs/higher opportunity costs, due to a higher propensity of misdirected effort.

Conclusion

To conclude, with respect to the economic outcomes of customer engagement, transaction cost theory identifies behavioural uncertainty as a main exchange hazard, since companies have no means to enforce positive outcomes. This indicates that according to transaction cost theory, on average, firm-level outcomes of (company's strategies with respect to) customer engagement are negative. This behavioural uncertainty may be enhanced by making relationship-specific investments (these investments become vulnerable), demand uncertainty (which may cause obsoleteness and misdirected behaviour), and frequency (in-house production becomes more efficient and customer empowerment increases). Hence, firm-level outcomes are, according to transaction cost theory, even more negative for companies that have invested in customer relationships, operate in turbulent environments, and/or solicit customer engagement multiple times.

Resource-based view

Besides transaction cost economics, it is insightful to investigate the merits of additional perspectives on customer engagement. One such perspective lies in adopting a resource-based view on customer engagement. This perspective seems insightful since it departs from a different theoretical standpoint (Odekerken-Schröder, 1999). At the heart of the distinction between both theoretical perspectives is whether the mechanism to be explained that underlies a company's customer engagement initiative is 'a fear of opportunism (as posited by transaction cost economists), or a quest for sustainable advantage (as posed by resource-based view theorists)' (Schilling and Steensma, 2002, p. 387). Since power is shifting from companies to customers (as explained earlier and due to the rise of new digital media, which resulted in a more open economy, and consequently changed customer behaviour; see for instance seminal work by Lynch Jr. and Ariely, 2000, and Prahalad and Ramaswamy, 2004b) customers are becoming less dependent upon companies. 'In fact, the balance of power in value creation is tipping in favour of consumers' (Prahalad and Ramaswamy, 2004b, p. 1). Additionally, for most products there is not a monopolistic market, but rather, markets typically become more competitive and customers have the choice where to take their business (World Economic Forum, 2015). In light of these factors, companies do face a strong need to safeguard against potential opportunistic behaviour of customers. Yet, at the same time companies also face a strong need for differentiation in order to survive in the competitive landscapes they operate in. Therefore, both a transaction cost perspective and a resource-based view on customer engagement have merit.

The resource-based view of the firm claims that firms represent collections of strategic resources and are inherently heterogeneous in terms of their resource possession (Wernerfelt, 1984). Firms leverage their strategic resources 'to create competitive advantages, which in turn confer performance advantages' (Crook et al., 2008, p. 1142). Resources must meet certain criteria in order to be a source of sustainable competitive advantage. Crucial characteristics that render resources strategic (i.e. a source of sustained competitive advantage) are value, rareness, and inimitability (e.g. Hoopes, Madsen and Walker, 2003; Peteraf, 1993).

Main effect: building of strategic resources

Through managing customer engagement companies can build such strategic resources in two ways. First, previous literature classifies corporate reputation (e.g. Crook et al., 2008) and customer loyalty (e.g. Wernerfelt, 1984) as resources that adhere to the aforementioned characteristics – thus, both corporate reputation and customer loyalty are by themselves strategic resources. Managing customer engagement (behaviours) is a way for companies to enhance both corporate reputation (e.g. Van Doorn et al., 2010) and customer loyalty (e.g. Hollebeek, Glynn and Brodie, 2014). For instance, by being active within brand communities, customer attachment to the focal brand tends to increase, as well as attract other brand users, subsequently driving customer loyalty (e.g. Algesheimer, Dholakia and Herrmann, 2005; Bagozzi and Dholakia, 2006a). Further, the way a company manages a brand community influences customers' level of trust in the company (Porter and Donthu, 2008), and will ultimately affect the company's reputation (Walsh and Beatty, 2007).

Second, by stimulating customer engagement behaviours, companies attempt to gain access to a strategic resource, which resides within their customer base, that is, the wisdom of the crowd. A prime source of value for companies seeking to stimulate customer engagement behaviour is customer knowledge value (Kumar et al., 2010). Through customer engagement, customers are able to contribute relevant emotional, cognitive, and/or physical resources (Hollebeek, 2011), which provide companies with unique knowledge. Unique knowledge, in turn, is identified under the resource-based view as a strategic resource (Crook et al., 2008); customer knowledge and creative efforts adhere to the characteristics that render resources strategic: (1) value, (2) inimitability, and (3) rarity. Such knowledge is invaluable (1) to firms for a number of reasons, for example customer participation in cocreation (for instance, by providing creative solutions and revealing information regarding customer needs) has the potential to enhance the success of new products (e.g. Fang, Palmatier and Evans, 2008). Customers' knowledge and skill contribution (e.g. their creative effort) is also difficult to imitate or substitute (2), since they are protected by knowledge barriers. 'They cannot be imitated by competitors because they are subtle and hard to understand because they involve talents that are elusive' (Miller and Schamsie, 1996, p. 522).

They also tend to be rare (3), 'given the zero cost of existing information and the declining cost of communication and processing, human capacity becomes the primary scarce resource in the networked information economy' (Benkler, 2006, p. 52). Thus, by tapping into the wisdom of the crowd through engagement initiatives, such as the establishment of brand communities, companies complement their internal resources with the strategic resources posed within their (external) customer base and a whole new resource spectrum emerges (O'Hern and Rindfleisch, 2009). This suggests that 'market scholars should view a firm's resources and capabilities from a broader network-based (embodied) perspective, rather than focusing narrowly on its internal (embedded) assets' (O'Hern and Rindfleisch, 2009, p. 100).

Access to these external resources is controlled by the customers themselves, since they hold the intellectual property rights of their own ideas (Hoyer et al., 2010). Yet, given the earlier discussion regarding the importance of these resources, companies should be willing to go to great lengths to obtain these resources, for instance, by paying substantial amounts of money. Not surprisingly, we observe such occurrences in practice. An example is Lay's, a potato chip manufacturer, which rewards the winner of a flavour suggestion contest with one million U.S. dollars, or 1 per cent of the one-year net sales of the flavour (cf. www.dousaflavor.com).

Moderators: current and internal resources

Nevertheless, these resources may not have the same value for all companies. Specific contingencies thus exist to the economic outcomes of customer engagement from a resource-based perspective. Namely, the usefulness of customers' resource contribution for a company is a surrogate for the company's valuation of these resources. Whether the wisdom of the crowd is valuable for a company depends, amongst others, on the company's own resource possession. If a company already possesses strong customer relationships, a good corporate reputation, and/or many internal R&D resources and capabilities, tapping into the wisdom of the crowd may be redundant (e.g. Beckers, Van Doorn and Verhoef, 2015).

Beyond resource redundancy, there are additional caveats in creating strategic resources through customer engagement management. First, a disadvantage of relying on customer knowledge value is a potential loss of critical internal know-how, and an increase in the dependence on customers (Gassmann, Kausch and Enkel, 2010). Second, when customers contribute their intellectual property (e.g. creativity), the question emerges as to the ownership of these resources, and to the ownership of value-creating activities provided by customers that arise out of these resources (Gassmann, Kausch, and Enkel, 2010; Hoyer et al., 2010). For instance, to avoid this potential drawback, Lay's potato chips employs a strict policy in their previously mentioned flavour suggestion contest (www.dousaflavor.com). How to best govern customer engagement and how to optimally motivate customers to provide their resources (i.e. how to best access resources controlled by the customers themselves), represent intriguing questions for future research. A lot of academic research is emerging on how customers could be motivated towards enhanced levels of engagement. Broadly speaking customers could be motivated by financial incentives, but also through social, psychological, and/or technical incentives (e.g. Hoyer et al., 2010; Nambisan and Baron, 2009). For instance, recent research suggests that by giving financial incentives people provide fewer, but better ideas (Torres, 2015).

Conclusion

To conclude, the resource-based view implies for the economic outcomes of customer engagement that customer engagement (behaviours) can be used to build and create resources, which are valuable, rare, and inimitable or non-substitutable. Although questions may arise as to the ownership of these resources, our analysis suggests, in general, that firm-level outcomes of (company's strategies with respect to) customer engagement tend to be positive from a resource-based view perspective. However, this positive effect may be attenuated for companies that already have a good reputation, a loyal customer base, and/or much internal R&D knowledge and capabilities (they already possess these strategic resources and therefore customer engagement efforts to build these resources may be redundant).

Social exchange theory

Besides a transaction cost view and a resource-based view, it is insightful to investigate the applicability of social exchange theory in a customer engagement setting. Social exchange theory complements the former theoretical perspectives because it is built on a different theoretical foundation, namely behavioural theory (Odekerken-Schröder, 1999).

The basic tenet of social exchange theory, developed by Blau (1964), is that (social) exchange results from a process in which the actors undertake cost-benefit analyses. Specifically, actors engage in relationships as long as they expect optimised and positive equity arising from these relationships (e.g. Cropanzano and Mitchell, 2005; Emerson, 1976). In technical terms, 'a resource will continue to flow only if there is a valued return contingent upon it' (Emerson, 1976, p. 359). The building of social exchange through frequent interaction creates interdependence and reciprocity in the relationship, which under the right conditions have the possibility to create highly valuable relationships between the parties involved (Cropanzano and Mitchell, 2005).

Main effect: increasing benefits within cost/benefit trade-off

The theory has important implications for customer engagement as the next step within relationship marketing (cf. also Hollebeek, 2011). Exchange is a construct that lies at the heart of marketing in general (already noted by Bagozzi back in 1975) and relationship marketing in particular (Morgan and Hunt, 1994). Within relationship marketing, and in line with social exchange theory, the focus is on building long-term relationships with customers, rather than short-term, single transactional exchanges (Luo, 2002). By focusing on customer engagement, companies have the potential to further enhance customer relationships (Beckers, Van Doorn and Verhoef, 2015). Stimulating customer engagement behaviours creates additional customer-firm interaction points (Hoyer et al., 2010). This connectivity has the potential to build and enhance customer-firm relationships through mere additional interactions, since (according to social exchange theory) as long as the parties involved adhere to certain 'rules', 'relationships evolve over time into trusting, loyal, and mutual commitments' (Cropanzano and Mitchell, 2005, p. 875). An activity as small as filling out a customer satisfaction survey can serve to deepen customer relationships (Borle et al., 2007). Beyond mere additional interactions, the customer-firm social exchange through customer engagement adds value for both customers and firms beyond the transactional side of their relationship. From the customer's perspective they can benefit financially (e.g. receive rewards), psychological (e.g. having fun), social (e.g. feeling a sense of community), and technological (e.g. learning about a product) from customer engagement behaviours (e.g. Hoyer et al., 2010; Nambisan and Baron, 2009). Additional customer-firm interactions beyond purchase can, thus, increase the benefits accruing from exchange relationships for a customer with a focal company, such that customers will remain loyal. The reciprocity element of social exchange theory also implies that if customers receive a more favourable service experience, they are likely to return the favour by engaging in positive behaviours towards the firm (Hollebeek, 2011).

Hence on the positive side, social exchange theory implies for customer engagement that it aids companies in providing additional benefits, beyond the transaction, to customers and therefore customers would be more likely to continue the relationship. Companies that were effective in creating mutually beneficial, trustworthy relationships with customers through customer engagement include Starbucks with its customer idea platform (www.mystarbucksidea.com), Ford with its Fiesta movement (McCracken, 2010), and Harley-Davidson with its brand community (e.g. Algesheimer, Dholakia and Herrmann, 2005; McAlexander, Schouten and Koenig, 2002).

Main effect: increasing costs within cost/benefit trade-off

On the negative side, social exchange theory posits that customers undertake explicit cost-benefit analyses such that they may end the relationship if the relationship-related costs are perceived to outweigh its benefits. Therefore, if a company develops a customer engagement strategy it should make sure to develop a suitable level of perceived benefits to their customers. In other words, to explain the economic outcomes of customer engagement, companies should always keep in mind whether customers receive sufficient benefits from their exchange relationship with a focal company, rather than looking only at the company's individual benefits. While this seems a trivial remark, in practice companies are not always sufficiently responsive and trustworthy towards their customers. There are numerous well-known examples of companies' lacking responsiveness, for instance: Tiger Airlines marked an online complaint on its Facebook page as irrelevant and tried to hide the complaint, thereby causing an outrage amongst customers (sproutsocial.com); Boeing responded to an 8-year-old they were not interested in unsolicited ideas, which did not run well among their customer base (Clifford, 2010); and, perhaps the most famous of all even with its own Wikipedia page, United Airlines did not respond appropriately after having broken a musician's guitar (www.youtube.com).

Key lessons from social exchange theory for these companies in particular, and companies in general, are that 'exchange requires a bidirectional transaction – something has to be given and something returned. For this reason, interdependence, which involves mutual and complementary arrangements, is considered a defining characteristic of social exchange (Molm, 1994)' (Cropanzano and Mitchell, 2005, p. 876). Further, 'although companies are not inclined to interact with consumers at all points in the value chain, opportunities for exchanges between the company and the consumer neither begin nor end when a consumer purchases something from a company. Indeed, the point of exchange need not be restricted to where the company and the consumer trade money for finished goods or services' (Prahalad and Ramaswamy, 2004b, p. 5). Thus, as transactions and relationships can be seen as occurring through social exchange they bring responsibilities, obligations, and reciprocity for both parties involved (Emerson, 1976). With the development of novel communication channels, such as social media, customers become empowered and have increasing ability to follow-up on companies in events where they did not hold up their end of the bargain (e.g. Prahalad and Ramaswamy, 2004b). After all, the relationship between firms and customers is no longer unidirectional (Beckers, Risselada and Verhoef, 2013). When managing customer engagement companies should prevent potential losses (such as losing face) to customers (Fombelle, Bone and Lemon, 2014). They should be responsive, yet have a fine line to walk, since overreacting does not create additional value (Knox and Van Oest, 2014) and providing the wrong incentives and benefits to the wrong customers could backfire (Füller, 2010) Social exchange theory implies that especially private rewards, such as gaining reputation or knowledge within online communities, are effective in motivating customers to engage in positive exchange behaviours (Nambisan and Baron, 2010).

Conclusion

To conclude, social exchange theory posits that customers undertake an explicit cost/benefit-analysis when prolonging their relationship with a company. For the management of customer engagement, on the positive side, this implies that firms could create highly beneficial interactions and exchanges, thereby increasing the relationship benefits, which can, in turn, grow both traditional customer lifetime value and contemporary customer engagement value (Kumar et al., 2010). On the other hand, social exchange theory also states that when building relationships there are responsibilities and obligations for both parties involved. When managing customer engagement to build customer relationships there is a risk for companies not upholding these obligations, thereby increasing costs for customers, and facing ultimate customer churn and/or retaliation. Hence, according to social exchange theory the firm-level consequences of customer engagement can be either positive or negative, mediated by whether customer perceived value is positive or negative.

Conclusion and future research directions

Customer engagement and its key outcomes is an area of prime importance for companies, as reflected in the emergence of both academic and business research on this topic. Outcomes investigated range from customers' cognitions and emotions, to company sales and shareholder value. However, our overview shows that customer engagement (behavioural) manifestations have often been studied in isolation to date, and that the few studies investigating customer engagement as an overarching construct primarily investigate particular customer-level (rather than firm-level) outcomes. Further, contingencies of the economic outcomes arising from unified theoretical perspectives on customer engagement are lacking in the literature to date. Therefore, we presented three contemporary theoretical perspectives (i.e. transaction cost economics, the resource-based view, and social exchange theory) to assess the economic outcomes of customer engagement. We summarised our conclusions drawn from these theories regarding the firm-level consequences of customer engagement in Figure 2.1. Specifically, we did so by displaying the mechanism (and potential contingencies of this mechanism) by which each theory foresees customer engagement to translate into firm-level performance. Due to behavioural uncertainty transaction cost economics expects a negative impact of customer engagement on firm performance (which may be enhanced by relationship-specific investments, demand uncertainty, and frequency), while the resource-based view would suggest a positive impact of customer engagement on firm performance due to the building of strategic resources (which may be attenuated for companies with strong customer relationships, a good corporate reputation, and/or many internal R&D resources and capabilities). By contrast, social exchange theory is unsure about the impact of customer engagement on firm performance, since according to social exchange

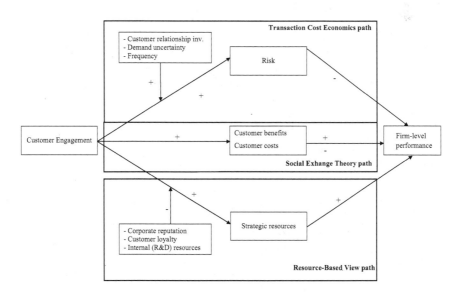

Figure 2.1 Theoretical paths to firm-level customer engagement consequences

theory engagement can enhance costs as well as benefits for customers in exchanging with a focal company.

These theoretical perspectives and our overall discussion regarding the economic outcomes of customer engagement bring forth important future research avenues. Some of the most fundamental and inspiring arising research questions are as follows:

- What is the 'best' unified theoretical perspective on customer engagement outcomes?
  - Which perspective has superior explanatory power in terms of performance variance?
  - Which perspective is the most informative for managers?
  - Which perspective is the most informative for policy makers?
  - Are there any other (unified) theoretical perspectives that can be utilised besides transaction cost economics, the resource-based view, and social exchange theory, to better explain or predict the economic outcomes of customer engagement? For instance, given that customers are taking over roles traditionally performed by company employees, rather than viewing customer engagement from the perspective of a customer/firm relationship, it could also be viewed as an employer/employee relationship. From the latter viewpoint especially, a principal-agent perspective is expected to be fruitful (e.g. Eisenhardt, 1989).
  - Should the perspective employed be dependent on the particular customer engagement dimension under investigation? For instance, our resource-based view reasoning seems most appropriate with respect to customer cocreation in new product development.
- What is the average firm-level consequence of customer engagement?
  - Transaction cost economics would suggest a negative main effect, the resource-based view would suggest a positive main effect, whereas social exchange theory is uncertain about whether the main effect is positive or negative (cf. Figure 2.1). Future research, therefore, could empirically determine an overall effect of customer engagement on firm-level performance (perhaps by utilising a meta-analytical approach).
- What are the mediators of the economic outcomes of customer engagement?
  - With respect to firm-level outcomes, from a transaction cost viewpoint behavioural uncertainty, and consequently, firm risk is expected to operate as a primary mediator, while the resource-based view indicates that the building of strategic resources is the main mediating process. By contrast, social exchange theory dictates customer perceived value (cost-benefit trade-off) to be the key mediator (Figure 2.1).
- What are potential other mediators? For instance, what are the most important mediators for focal customer-level outcomes?

- To illustrate, transaction cost economics predicts moderating effects of demand uncertainty, customer relationship investments, and frequency. On the other hand, the resource-based view predicts moderating effects of corporate reputation, customer loyalty, and internal (R&D) resources (Figure 2.1).

- What are the contingencies of the consequences of customer engagement?

  - What are potential other moderators? An important question is, for instance, how effects differ between various manifestations of customer engagement (e.g. word-of-mouth, voice, cocreation, community participation)?

- What are the effects of customer engagement on other stakeholders apart from firms and customers?

  - What are the effects on shareholders? Beckers, Van Doorn and Verhoef (2015), for instance, show that stimulating customer engagement can reduce shareholder value.
  - What are the effects on employees? To illustrate, the main finding of Chan, Yim and Lam (2010) is that customer cocreation can cause job stress among a company's employees. Another interesting topic relates to the interrelationship between customer engagement and employee engagement.
  - What are the effects on competitors? Thompson and Sinha (2008) explicitly focus on this question. Their findings indicated that community participation decreases adoption of new products from competing brands. What are other potential outcomes on competitors?
  - What are the effects on society at large? Amongst others in terms of consumer welfare, economic and social surplus, the government, and/ or policy makers?

- How do we quantify the economic outcomes of customer engagement?

  - Which methods are best suited? To illustrate, studies that investigate customer-level outcomes of customer engagement primarily utilise survey methodology. How does this methodology relate to experimental research in order to capture the outcomes of customer engagement (for instance, are these methods complementary, or substitutes)? Can triangulation be applied?
  - Which metric is best suited? Sales effects are popular at the firm-level (e.g. 11 of the 21 firm-level studies included in Table 2.1 have firm sales as the key outcome metric), and satisfaction is the most popular metric at the customer-level (although at the customer-level outcome metrics are more diverse; that is, only 5 out of the 22 customer-level studies included in Table 2.1 use customer satisfaction as the key outcome metric). What is the value of these metrics relative to other metrics, such as return-on-investment?

- Which type of data is needed? In recent business practice and literature much attention is given to 'big data' (e.g. McAfee and Brynjolfsson, 2012) and as specified in the Introduction, companies are predicted to make increasing use of online customer behaviour data (www.cmo-survey.org). Is big data the most useful type of data to study the consequences of customer engagement?

All in all, we believe customer engagement represents a highly relevant topic for both academics and practitioners. We are pleased to see that research has begun to investigate the (economic) outcomes of customer engagement, and hope that future research continues to emerge on the effectiveness of the nascent, inspiring topic of customer engagement. We also hope that future research will take up the remaining challenges, such as by investigating the research questions posed in this section.

References

Algesheimer, R., Dholakia, U. M. and Herrmann, A., 2005. The social influence of brand community: Evidence from European car clubs. *Journal of Marketing*, 69(3), 19–34.

Algesheimer, R., Borle, S., Dholakia, U. M. and Singh, S. S., 2010. The impact of customer community participation on customer behaviors: An empirical investigation. *Marketing Science*, 29(4), 756–769.

Anderson, E., Day, G. S. and Rangan, V. K., 1997. Strategic channel design. *Sloan Management Review*, 38(4), 59–69.

Anderson, E. and Jap, S. D., 2005. The dark-side of close relationships. *Sloan Management Review*, 46(3), 75–82.

Anderson, E. and Schmittlein, D. C., 1984. Integration of the sales force: An empirical examination. *Rand Journal of Economics*, 15(3), 385–395.

Bagozzi, R. P., 1975. Marketing as exchange. *Journal of Marketing*, 39(4), 32–39.

Bagozzi, R. P. and Dholakia, U. M., 2006a. Antecedents and purchase consequences of customer partition in small group brand communities. *International Journal of Research in Marketing*, 23, 45–61.

Bagozzi, R. P. and Dholakia, U. M., 2006b. Open source software user communities. *Management Science*, 52(7), 1099–1115.

Band, W., 2010. The Forrester wave™: CRM suites for large organizations, Q2 2010. Available at: <http://crmdynamics.blob.core.windows.net/xps-docs/06–16–10SuitesLarge.pdf> [Accessed 16 April 2015].

Band, W., 2012. The Forrester wave™: CRM suites for midsize organizations, Q3 2012. Available at: <http://www.sugarcrm.com/sites/default/files/whitepapers/The_Forrester_Wave__CRM_Mid_0.pdf> [Accessed 16 April 2015].

Bayus, B. L., 2013. Crowdsourcing new product ideas over time: An analysis of the Dell IdeaStorm community. *Management Science*, 59(1), 226–244.

Beckers, S. F. M., Bone, S. A., Fombelle, P. W., Van Doorn, J., Verhoef, P. C. and Ray, K. R., 2015. Happy users, grumpy bosses: How B2B customer support channels impact user and upper management satisfaction. Working paper, University of Groningen.

Beckers, S. F. M., Risselada, H. and Verhoef, P. C., 2013. Customer engagement: A new frontier in customer value management. In: Rust, R. T. and Huang, M.-H., eds. *Handbook of service marketing research*. Cheltham, UK: Edward Elgar Publishing Ltd., 97–120.

Beckers, S. F. M., Van Doorn, J. and Verhoef, P. C., 2015. When should companies stimulate customer engagement behaviors? A shareholder evaluation. Working paper, University of Groningen.

Bendapudi, N. and Leone, R. P., 2003. Psychological implications of customer participation in co-production. *Journal of Marketing*, 67(1), 14–28.

Benkler, Y., 2006. *The wealth of networks: How social production transforms markets and freedom*. New Haven, CT: Yale University Press.

Berger, J., Sorensen, A. T. and Rasmussen, S. J., 2010. Positive effects of negative publicity: When negative reviews increase sales. *Marketing Science*, 29(5), 815–827.

Bijmolt, T. H. A., Leeflang, P. S. H., Block, F., Eisenbeiss, M., Hardie, B. G. S., Lemmens, A. and Staffert, P., 2010. Analytics for customer engagement. *Journal of Service Research*, 13(3), 341–356.

Binder, C. and Hanssens, D. M., 2015. Why strong customer relationships trump powerful brands. Harvard business review weblog, [blog] 14 April. Available at: <https://hbr.org/2015/04/why-strong-customer-relationships-trump-powerful-brands> [Accessed 16 April 2015].

Blau, P. M., 1964. *Exchange and power in social life*. New York, NY: John Wiley.

Bolton, R. N., 2011. Customer engagement: opportunities and challenges for organizations. *Journal of Service Research*, 14(3), 272–274.

Bone, S. A., Fombelle, P. W., Ray, K. R. and Lemon, K. N., 2015. How customer participation in B2B peer-to-peer problem-solving communities influences the need for traditional customer service. *Journal of Service Research*, 18(1), 23–38.

Borle, S., Dholakia, U. M., Singh, S. S. and Westbrook, R. A., 2007. The impact of survey participation on subsequent customer behavior: An empirical investigation. *Marketing Science*, 26(5), 711–726.

Brodie, R. J. and Hollebeek, L. D., 2011. Advancing and consolidating knowledge about customer engagement. *Journal of Service Research*, 14(3), 283–284.

Brodie, R. J., Hollebeek, L. D., Jurić, B. and Ilić, A., 2011. Customer engagement: Conceptual domain, fundamental propositions, and implications for research. *Journal of Service Research*, 14(3), 252–271.

Brodie, R. J., Ilic, A., Juric, B. and Hollebeek, L. D., 2013. Consumer engagement in a virtual brand community: An exploratory analysis. *Journal of Business Research*, 66(1), 105–114.

Calder, B. J., Malthouse, E. C. and Schaedel, U., 2009. An experimental study of the relationship between online engagement and advertising effectiveness. *Journal of Interactive Marketing*, 23(4), 321–331.

Chan, K. W., Yim, C. K. and Lam, S. S. K., 2010. Is customer participation in value creation a double-edged sword? Evidence from professional financial services across cultures. *Journal of Marketing*, 74(3), 48–64.

Chen, Y., Liu Y. and Zhang, J., 2012. When do third-party product reviews affect firm value and what can firms do? The case of media critics and professional movie reviews. *Journal of Marketing*, 76(2), 116–134.

Chen, Y., Wang, Q. and Xie, J., 2011. Online social interactions: A natural experiment on word of mouth versus observational learning. *Journal of Marketing Research*, 48(2) 238–254.

Chevalier, J. A. and Mayzlin, D., 2006. The effect of word of mouth on sales: Online book reviews. *Journal of Marketing Research*, 43(3), 345–354.

Chintagunta, P. K., Gopinath, S. and Venkataraman, S., 2010. The effects of online user review on movie box office performance: Accounting for sequential rollout and aggregation across local markets. *Marketing Science*, 29(5), 944–957.

Clifford, S., 2010. Boeing's social-media lesson. The New York Times media decoder blog, [blog] 3 May. Available at: <http://mediadecoder.blogs.nytimes.com/2010/05/03/boeings-social-media-lesson/> [Accessed 19 April 2015].

Cook, S., 2008. The contribution revolution. *Harvard Business Review*, 86(10), 60–69.

Crook, T. R., Ketchen Jr., D. J., Combs, J. G. and Todd, S. Y., 2008. Strategic resources and performance: A meta-analysis. *Strategic Management Journal*, 29, 1141–1154.

Cropanzano, R. and Mitchell, M. S., 2005. Social exchange theory: An interdisciplinary review. *Journal of Management*, 31, 874–900.

Dyer, J. H., 1997. Effective interfirm collaboration: How firms minimize transaction costs and maximize transaction value. *Strategic Management Journal*, 18, 535–556.

Eisenhardt, K. M., 1989. Agency theory: An assessment and review. *The Academy of Management Review*, 14(1), 57–74.

Emerson, R. M., 1976. Social exchange theory. *Annual Review of Sociology*, 2, 335–362.

Fang, Er., 2008. Customer participation and the trade-off between new product innovativeness and speed to market. *Journal of Marketing*, 72(4), 90–104.

Fang, Er., Palmatier, R. W. and Evans, K .R., 2008. Influence of customer participation on creating and sharing of new product value. *Journal of the Academy of Marketing Science*, 36, 322–336.

Floyd, K., Freling, R., Alhoqail, S., Cho, H. Y. and Freling, T., 2014. How online product reviews affect retail sales: A meta-analysis. *Journal of Retailing*, 90(2), 217–232.

Fombelle, P. W., Bone, S. A. and Lemon, K. N., 2014. Open to your ideas: The effect of firm acknowledgement of consumer ideas on consumer face and future idea sharing. Working paper, Northeastern University.

Fuchs, Ch., Prandelli, E. and Schreier, M., 2010. The psychological effects of empowerment strategies on consumers' product demand. *Journal of Marketing*, 74(1), 65–79.

Füller, J., 2010. Refining virtual co-creation from a consumer perspective. *California Management Review*, 52(2), 98–122.

Gassmann, O., Kausch, Ch. and Enkel, E., 2010. Negative side effects of customer integration. *International Journal of Technology Management*, 50(1), 43–62.

Gatignon, H. and Xuereb, J. -M., 1997. Strategic orientation of the firm and new product performance. *Journal of Marketing Research*, 34(1), 77–90.

Geyskens, I., Steenkamp, J. -B. E. M. and Kumar, N., 2006. Make, buy, or ally: A transaction cost theory meta-analysis. *Academy of Management Journal*, 49(3), 519–543.

Ghosh, M. and John, G., 1999. Governance value analysis and marketing strategy. *Journal of Marketing*, 63(4), pp. 131–145.

Godes, D. and Mayzlin, D., 2009. Firm-created word-of-mouth communication: Evidence from a field test. *Marketing Science*, 28(4), 721–739.

Gopinath, S., Thomas, J. S. and Krishnamurthi, L., 2014. Investigating the relationship between the content of online word of mouth, advertising, and brand performance. *Marketing Science*, 33(2), 241–258.

Gruen, T. W., Osmonbekov, T. & Czaplewski, A. J., 2006. eWOM: The impact of customer-to-customer online know-how exchange on customer value and loyalty. *Journal of Business Research*, 59, 449–456

Heidenreich, S., Wittkowski, K., Handrich, M. and Falk, T., 2015. The dark side of customer co-creation: Exploring the consequences of failed co-created services. *Journal of the Academy of Marketing Science*, 43(3), 279–296.

Hennig-Thurau, Th., Malthouse, E. C., Friege, Ch., Gensler, S., Lobschat, L., Rangaswamy, A. and Skiera, B., 2010. The impact of new media on customer relationships. *Journal of Service Research*, 13(3), 311–330.

Hollebeek, L. D., 2011. Exploring customer brand engagement: Definition and themes. *Journal of Strategic Marketing*, 19(7), 555–573.

Hollebeek, L. D., Glynn, M. and Brodie, R. J., 2014. Consumer brand engagement in social media: Conceptualization, scale development and validation. *Journal of Interactive Marketing*, 28(2), 149–165.

Hoopes, D. G., Madsen, T. L. and Walker, G., 2003. Guest editors' introduction to the special issue: Why is there a resource-based view: Toward a theory of competitive heterogeneity. *Strategic Management Journal*, 24, 889–902.

Ho-Dac, N. N., Carson, S. J. and Moore, W. L., 2013. The effects of positive and negative online customer reviews: Do brand strength and category maturity matter? *Journal of Marketing*, 77(6), 37–53.

Hoyer, W. D., Chandy, R., Dorotic, M., Krafft, M. and Singh, S. S., 2010. Consumer co-creation in new product development. *Journal of Service Research*, 13(3), 283–296.

Kim, K., 1999. On determinants of joint action in industrial distributor-supplier relationships: Beyond economic efficiency. *International Journal of Research in Marketing*, 16, 217–236.

Knox, G. and Van Oest, R., 2014. Customer complaints and recovery effectiveness: A customer base approach. *Journal of Marketing*, 78(5), 42–57.

Kohli, A. K. and Jaworski, B. J., 1990. Market orientation: The construct, research propositions, and managerial implications. *Journal of Marketing*, 54(2), 1–18.

Kumar, V., Aksoy, L., Donkers, B., Venkatesan, R., Wiesel, Th. and Tillmanns, S., 2010. Undervalued or overvalued customers: Capturing total customer engagement value. *Journal of Service Research*, 13(3), 297–310.

Kumar, V., Bhaskaran, V., Mirchandani, R. and Shah, M., 2013. Creating a measurable social media marketing strategy: increasing the value and ROI of intangibles and tangibles for Hokey Pokey. *Marketing Science*, 32(2), 194–212.

Libai, B., 2011. Comment: The perils of focusing on highly engaged customers. *Journal of Service Research*, 14(3), 275–276.

Lilien, G. L., Morrison, P. D., Searls, K., Sonnack, M. and Von Hippel, E., 2002. Performance assessment of the lead user idea-generation process for new product development. *Management Science*, 48(8), 1042–1059.

Liu-Thompkins, Y. M. and Rogerson, M., 2012. Rising to stardom: An empirical investigation of the diffusion of user-generated content. *Journal of Interactive Marketing*, 26, 71–82.

Ludwig, S., De Ruyter, L., Friedman, M., Brüggen, E. C., Wetzels, M. and Pfann, G., 2013. More than words: The influence of affective content and linguistic style matches in online reviews on conversion rates. *Journal of Marketing*, 77(1), 87–103.

Luo, X., 2002. Trust production and privacy concerns on the Internet: A framework based on relationship marketing and social exchange theory. *Industrial Marketing Management*, 31, 111–118.

Luo, X., 2009. Quantifying the long-term impact of negative word of mouth on cash flows and stock prices. *Marketing Science*, 28(1), 148–165.

Lynch Jr., J. G. and Ariely, D., 2000. Wine online: Search costs affect competition on price, quality, and distribution. *Marketing Science*, 19(1), 83–103.

Manchanda, P., Packard, G. and Pattabhiramaiah, A., 2015. Social dollars: The economic impact of customer participation in a firm-sponsored online customer community. *Marketing Science*, forthcoming.

Marketing Science Institute, 2010. 2010–2012 Research Priorities. Boston, MA: Marketing Science Institute.

Marketing Science Institute, 2014. 2014–2016 Research Priorities. Boston, MA: Marketing Science Institute.

McAfee, A. and Brynjolfsson, E., 2012. Big data: The management revolution. *Harvard Business Review*, 90(10), 60–68.

McAlexander, J. H., Schouten, J. W. and Koenig, H. F., 2002. Building brand community. *Journal of Marketing*, 66(1), 38–54.

McCracken, G. 2010. How Ford got social marketing right. Harvard business review weblog, [blog] 7 January. Available at: <https://hbr.org/2010/01/ford-recently-wrapped-the-firs/> [Accessed 17 April 2015].

Miller, D. and Schamsie, J., 1996. The resource-based view of the firm in two environments: The Hollywood film studios from 1936 to 1965. *Academy of Management Journal*, 39(3), 519–543.

Mooi, E. A. and Gilliland, D. I., 2013. How contracts and enforcement explain transaction outcomes. *International Journal of Research in Marketing*, 30(4), 395–405.

Moreau, C. P., Bonney, L. and Herd, K. B., 2011. It's the thought (and the effort) that counts: How customizing for others differs from customizing for oneself. *Journal of Marketing*, 75(5), 120–133.

Morgan, R. M. and Hunt, S. D., 1994. The commitment-trust theory of relationship marketing. *Journal of Marketing*, 58(3), 20–38.

Nambisan, S. and Baron, R. A., 2009. Virtual customer environments: Testing a model of voluntary participation in value co-creation activities. *Journal of Product Innovation Management*, 26, 388–406.

Nambisan, S. and Baron, R. A., 2010. Different roles, different strokes: Organizing virtual customer environments to promote two types of customer contributions. *Organization Studies*, 21(2), 554–572.

Noordhoff, C. B., Kyriakopoulos, K., Moorman, Ch., Pauwels, P. and Dellaert, B. G. C., 2011. The bright side and dark side of embedded ties in business-to-business innovation. *Journal of Marketing*, 75(5), 4–52.

Odekerken-Schröder, G., 1999. The role of the buyer in affecting buyer-seller relationships: Empirical studies in a retail context. Ph.D. thesis, Maastricht University.

Ofir, C. and Simonson, I., 2001. In search of negative customer feedback: The effect of expecting to evaluate on satisfaction evaluations. *Journal of Marketing Research*, 38(2), 170–182.

O'Hern, M. S. and Rindfleisch, A., 2009. Customer co-creation: A typology and research agenda. In: Malholtra, N. K., ed. *Review of marketing research*. New York, NY: M.E. Sharpe, 84–106.

Peteraf, M. A., 1993. The cornerstones of competitive advantage: A resource-based view. *Strategic Management Journal*, 14(3), 179–191.

Porter, C. E. and Donthu, N., 2008. Cultivating trust and harvesting value in virtual communities. *Management Science*, 54(1), 113–128.

Prahalad, C. K. and Ramaswamy, V., 2004a. Co-creation experiences: The next practice in value creation. *Journal of Interactive Marketing*, 18(3), 5–14.

Prahalad, C. K. and Ramaswamy, V., 2004b. The co-creation connection. Strategy and Business, 27, pp. 1–12.

Rindfleisch, A., Antia, K., Bercovitz, J., Brown, J. R., Cannon, J., Carson, S. J. and Wathne, K. H., 2010. Transaction cost, opportunism and governance: Contextual considerations and future research opportunities. *Marketing Letters*, 21(3), 211–222.

Risselada, H., Verhoef, P. C. and Bijmolt, T. H. A., 2014. Dynamic effects of social influence and direct marketing on the adoption of high-technology products. *Journal of Marketing*, 78(2), 52–68.

Sawhney, M. and Prandelli, E., 2000. Communities of creation: Managing distributed innovation in turbulent markets. *California Management Review*, 42(4), 24–54.

Schilling, M. A. and Steensma, H. K., 2002. Disentangling the theories of firm boundaries: A path model and empirical test. *Organization Science*, 13(4), 387–401.

Schmitt, P., Skiera B., & Van den Bulte, Ch., 2011. Referral programs and customer value. *Journal of Marketing*, 75(1), 46–59.

Scott, J. and Craig-Lees, M., 2010. Audience engagement and its effects on product placement recognition. *Journal of Promotion Management*, 16, 39–58.

So, K. K. F., King, C. & Sparks, B., 2014. Customer engagement with tourism brands: Scale development and validation. *Journal of Hospitality and Tourism Research*, 38(3), 304–329.

Sprott, D., Czellar, S. and Spangenberg, E., 2009. The importance of a general measure of brand engagement on market behavior: Development and validation of a scale. *Journal of Marketing Research*, 46(1), 92–104.

Tang, T., Fang, Er. and Wang, F., 2014. Is neutral really neutral? The effects of neutral user-generated content on product sales. *Journal of Marketing*, 78(4), 41–58.

Thompson, D. and Malaviya, P., 2013. Consumer-generated ads: Does awareness of advertising co-creation help or hurt persuasion? *Journal of Marketing*, 77(3), 33–47.

Thompson, S. A. and Sinha, R. K. 2008. Brand communities and new product adoption: The influence and limits of oppositional loyalty. *Journal of Marketing*, 72(6), 65–80.

Tirunillai, S. and Tellis, G. J., 2012. Does chatter really matter? Dynamics of user-generated content and stock performance. *Marketing Science*, 31(2), 198–215.

Torres, N., 2015. Financial rewards make people suggest fewer but better ideas. Harvard Business review weblog, [blog] May. Available at: <https://hbr.org/2015/02/financial-rewards-make-people-suggest-fewer-but-better-ideas> [Accessed 20 April 2015].

Trusov, M., Bucklin, R. E. & Pauwels, K., 2009, Effects of word-of-mouth versus traditional marketing: Findings from an internet social networking site. *Journal of Marketing*, 73(5), 90–102.

Van Doorn, J., 2011. Comment: Customer engagement: Essence, dimensionality, and boundaries. *Journal of Service Research*, 14(3), 280–282.

Van Doorn, J., Lemon, K. N., Mittal, V., Nass, S., Pick, D., Pirner, P. and Verhoef, P. C., 2010. Customer engagement behavior: Theoretical foundations and research directions. *Journal of Service Research*, 13(3), 253–266.

Verhoef, P. C., Beckers, S.F.M. and Van Doorn, J., 2013. Understand the perils of co-creation. *Harvard Business Review*, 91(9), 28.

Verhoef, P. C., Reinartz, W. J., and Krafft, M., 2010. Customer engagement as a new perspective in customer management. *Journal of Service Research*, 13(3), 247–252.

Villanueva, J., Yoo, S. and Hanssens, D. M., 2008. The impact of marketing-induced versus word-of-mouth customer acquisition on customer equity growth. *Journal of Marketing Research*, 45(1), 48–59.

Vlaskovits, P., 2011. Henry Ford, innovation, and that "faster horse" quote. Harvard Business review weblog, [blog] 29 August. Available at: <https://hbr.org/2011/08/henry-ford-never-said-the-fast/> [Accessed 22 April 2015].

Walker, G. and Weber, D., 1984. A transaction cost approach to make-or-buy decisions. *Administrative Science Quarterly*, 29, 373–391.

Walsh, G. and Beatty, S. E., 2007. Customer-based corporate reputation of a service firm: Scale development and validation. *Journal of the Academy of Marketing Science*, 35, 127–143.

Weber, S., 2004. *The success of open source*. Cambridge, MA: Harvard University Press.

Wernerfelt, B., 1984. A resource-based view of the firm. *Strategic Management Journal*, 5(2), 171–180.

Williamson, O. F., 1985. *The economic institutions of capitalism*. New York, NY: The Free Press.

World Economic Forum, 2015. The global competitiveness report 2014–2015. Available at: <http://www3.weforum.org/docs/WEF_GlobalCompetitivenessReport_2014–15.pdf> [Accessed 22 April 2015].

You, Y., Vadakkepatt, G. G. and Joshi, A. M., 2015. A meta-analysis of electronic word-of-mouth elasticity. *Journal of Marketing*, 79(2), 19–39.

Zhu, R., Dholakia, U. M., Chen, X. and Algesheimer, R., 2012. Does online community participation foster risky financial behavior? *Journal of Marketing Research*, 49(3), 394–407.

3 Partner engagement

A perspective on B2B engagement

Shiri D. Vivek, Vivek Dalela and Sharon E. Beatty

Introduction

Researchers and practitioners have shown a deep interest in the notion of 'engagement' in the last decade, with significant attention going towards building an understanding of customer engagement (CE). With more concrete conceptualisations and measures being developed, significant scholarly progress has been made in our understanding of engagement in customer-to-customer (C2C) and business-to-customer (B2C) interactions (Sashi, 2012, Vivek et al., 2014). However, researchers either assume that business partners are highly similar to end customers, or neglect the importance of engagement in business-to-business (B2B) relationships. This notion intriguing businesses is evident from its continued presence as a priority area, as stated by the Marketing Science Institute (MSI) since 2006, as well as practitioners' increasing use of the term.

Several chapters in this book elaborate on the concept of engagement from the perspective of the customer. Although many firms consider CE important, the term often has different meanings for different people (Bolton 2011). While some scholars view it as a psychological state, others tend to focus on CE behaviours. Generally, CE is now widely considered as a context-specific, multi-dimensional concept, which is expressed in the form of relevant cognitive, emotional and behavioural dimensions. It is also considered dependent on situational conditions (Brodie et al., 2011). Thus, the challenge for researchers is to examine CE manifestations in specific contexts.

In the past decade, since the discussion of engagement started in business circles, market research and consulting companies – such as Nielsen Media Research, the Gallup Group, Pricewaterhouse Coopers LLP and Allegiance – have been offering modules and advice focused on customer engagement. Some of this advice focused on big data, and others addressed the relationship side of engagement. Businesses have been simultaneously developing customer engagement strategies focusing on C2C relationships as well as B2C relationships. In any case, the focus, either clear or implied, has been on the end customer. In this way, research has made significant progress in understanding B2C engagement, but scholarly research has not taken even initial steps to enhance our understanding of how businesses engage their business clients, that is, business-to-business partner engagement (B2B-PE).

B2B perspective on customer engagement

Here, we will discuss how an average business likely interprets the concept of customer engagement with respect to its clients and how the final consumer, probably unwittingly, has come to garner the lion's share of a firm's engagement efforts. While involving the customers is often considered a top priority, many other equally important stakeholders tend to get overlooked by organisations. For example, entities such as channel partners, third-party service providers, IT services vendors and many other supply chain partners often play a critical role in ensuring a firm's market success. However, companies tend to pay more attention to engaging the end customer as compared to its B2B partners. What could be the possible reasons behind such an approach? Are end customer relationships inherently different compared to the relationships the firm has with its B2B partners? Are business partners' expectations drastically different from the expectations of the end customer? If that is not the case, then are companies making a mistake in ignoring their business partners relative to engagement? Moreover, it is important to remember that these stakeholders share several characteristics with the customers whom the businesses are trying to engage.

Researchers have established that engaging customers in co-creation has positive consequences for product design and development (Hoyer et al., 2010). Similarly, operations and supply chain research have established the importance of other stakeholders in co-creating products and services. The widespread availability of social media gives business partners the same opportunities as end customers, to interact with others in the community. In fact, partners in the channels of distribution are subject to drivers and emotions similar to those of the end customer. Organisations should actively nurture a culture of engagement with their business partners so that, like customers, even the business partners engage with each other and are more likely to take an active interest in the network's success. While a channel partner may meet their monthly goal on a regular basis, an engaged partner is more likely to get involved effectively in dynamic business situations requiring initiative.

As discussed earlier, there are a number of similarities between the two contexts of engagement under discussion, consumer markets and business markets. In their exploration, Brodie et al. (2011) also found that since 2007, about a third of articles mentioning the terms 'engage' or 'engagement' were doing so in a B2B context. However, following that, considerable research progress has been made relative to CE in consumer markets. On the other hand, minimal attention has been paid to understanding engagement in business-to-business (B2B) markets. Besides stating the similarities, scholars also recognise that B2B markets have unique needs since they often deal with complex decision making groups and team-based interactions within and between firms (Bolton, 2011).

Although the B2B partner engages in many similar ways as a B2C customer, there are a host of differences that make this context unique. First, B2B markets are inhabited by more rational buyers with less emphasis on the emotional dimension, which is considered essential in end-customer context (Hollebeek, 2011). Therefore, the role and importance of emotions in B2B engagement is likely to differ from that in the consumer context. Further, co-creation and innovation result from engaging both business as well as end customers. However, co-creation and innovation within B2B relationships is more industry- and process-specific, while the same is more service or design oriented in a B2C context. For instance, a manufacturer may work with a supplier to make large-scale process changes to alter features across a product line using the feedback from end users, creating value in an all-encompassing process. On the other hand, in a service industry involving only the consumer (such as Subway) co-creation is performed *during* the design or delivery stage (of a meal, for example) on a much smaller individual scale, inherently creating value-in-use (Gronroos, 2011).

The Marketing Science Institute 2014–2016 priorities for research have focused on both contexts by using the term customer more generically; however, academic research on engagement tends to focus on co-creation with end customers. A B2B partner includes a supplier, channel partner or any other entity supporting the servicing of end customer, while the B2C context refers specifically to the end customer. The understanding of business processes, as well as mutuality of business and financial goals, are more relevant in the B2B context where the benefits of a partnership are shared by both parties and thus a collaborative partner is also likely to have less self-interest than in the B2C context. These differences are likely to influence the nature of engagement in the two contexts, specifically in terms of the relational strategies used by the involved parties. Given that the need to study engagement among B2B partners has been identified but the literature is still in its initial stages, in this chapter, we draw from the existing literature to develop a preliminary understanding of partner engagement in a B2B context. Further, although research on collaboration has made significant progress, researchers have not focused on the effective engagement of collaborating teams that work in highly dynamic business environments. Thus, we set out to explore the nature of B2B partner engagement (B2B-PE) and its association with related concepts. In the following sections, we discuss how engagement fits into the larger picture of collaborations with B2B partners and make certain assumptions about its relationship with existing relationship marketing concepts.

Engagement: threads of the collaboration tapestry

Research on collaboration has shown that competitive advantage from inter-organisational business relationships can be generated by moving away from market relationships to mutual partnerships (Paulraj et al., 2008). Jap (1999) considered coordination between exchange partners, and idiosyncratic investments as the primary differentiators of collaborative exchange relationships from arm's length exchanges. Dyer and Singh (1998) argued that a business's critical resources may be embedded in inter-firm resources and routines. They identified relationship-specific assets, knowledge sharing routines, complementary resources/capabilities and effective governance as the sources of competitive advantage in cooperative relationships. Nyaga, Whipple and Lynch (2010) argue that value-adding relational norms of information sharing, joint relationship efforts and dedicated investments form the basis for a collaborative relationship. Some researchers have also indicated the importance of personal relations and social exchanges in successful collaborations (for instance, Ploetner and Ehret, 2006). Empirical evidence corroborates the potentially important role of collaborations in creating economic value and competitive advantage (Gulati and Singh, 1998, Sarkar, Echambadi, and Harrison, 2001, Lambe, Spekman and Hunt, 2002).

Collaboration assumes the presence of experience between alliance partners and a long-term horizon as a necessary condition for successful collaboration (Jap 1999; Nyaga, Whipple and Lynch 2010). Research has also addressed the extent to which the length of relationship serves as a proxy for trust and mutuality of objectives in collaborative relationships. For several decades, close collaborative relationships have been considered synonymous with good relationships. However, citing the increasing number of failed B2B relationships, more recent research has challenged this assumption (Anderson and Jap, 2005).

In the early stages of relationship research, Dwyer, Schurr and Oh (1987) suggested that awareness, exploration, expansion, commitment and dissolution represented the five stages of a collaborative relationship. A plethora of research followed, taking snapshots of these stages to determine their nature. Even this in-depth look at the collaboration stages seems to lack the details necessary to understand the transitions in collaborative relationships adequately (Palmatier, 2013).

Most scholars agree that the exact nature of these relational dynamics remains elusive because extant research has often failed to account for the information contained in the discrete events in a relationship's trajectory (Palmatier et al., 2006). Challenged by the shortening response times in this dynamic environment and the complexity of developing new collaborations quickly, recent practitioner literature has begun to focus on short-term discrete events in inter-organisational relationships. So while collaboration may reflect consistent, positive results in the long run, a closer look at any short-term period in a business relationship might expose inconsistencies in the exchange dynamics of the relationship. The discrete events featuring higher-than-baseline levels of exchange in a collaborative relationship's trajectory may be thought of as instances of B2B partner engagement, while the periods showing no change in trajectory may be considered as quotidiary or baseline. In any long-term relationship, the long-run evaluation flattens out the wrinkles and inconsistencies experienced on a day-to-day basis, resulting in a net effect of positive collaboration.

Thus, we define B2B partner engagement (B2B-PE) as the *episodes of intense inter-organisational resource and social exchanges between two independent or interdependent business entities, directed towards common outcomes.* The outcomes are specific to a business situation created either due to market environment or other factors, such as several auto makers' recent attempts to join hands with some suppliers in order to innovate products, or Boeing's attempts to co-ordinate with suppliers to eliminate causes of fire in the Dreamliner, its most recent commercial jet. These entities involve one or more groups of people on both sides, rather than just individuals. Such episodes may be triggered by various internal and external factors at any stage in an exchange relationship between these entities. Engagement may be initiated by any of the partners and could be positively or negatively valenced. B2B-PE has a different set of resource requirements than B2C-CE and needs to be studied in isolation to better understand the quality of outcomes in inter-organisational relationships, as this engagement may play a crucial role in influencing collaboration in the future and the subsequent success of a relationship.

Influence of customer engagement in B2B relationships

In this section we present our preliminary understanding of how partner engagement will influence or be influenced by other relationship factors in a B2B context. We draw our ideas from the existing managerial and academic literature. Our analysis of the managerial press and academic research suggests that B2B partner engagement, an episodic social and resource exchange process, is focused on a specific outcome, which influences future collaboration between two independent but interdependent parties and the achievement of the specific outcomes. The conceptual framework of relationships in B2B partner engagement is depicted in Figure 3.1.

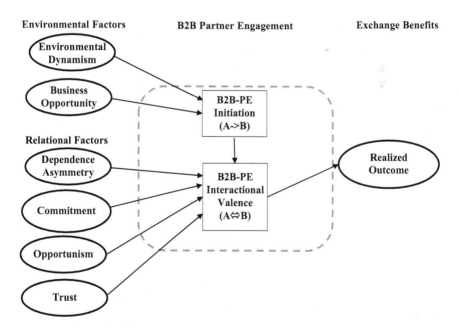

Figure 3.1 Conceptual framework of B2B partner engagement episode

Note: The Model above conceptualises the process of a single B2B CE episode between two parties, A and B. An aggregation of many such episodes over a period in a relationship determines the nature of collaboration between parties A and B.

58 *Shiri D. Vivek et al.*

The episodes of engagement of the business customer may be triggered by a combination of environmental and relational factors. Environmental dynamism and/or identification of a new business opportunity might trigger one partner (Firm A) to engage another partner (Firm B). Further, imbalance in the mutual dependence of A and B, oscillation or deterioration of commitment between the parties, a perception that one party is behaving opportunistically, as well as the level of trust between the parties determines the valence of this episode between the parties. The valence of any engagement episode then influences the realisation of immediate outcomes. These engagement episodes between two parties serve as building blocks in all phases of a collaborative relationship, thus influencing the nature of collaboration in the long run. In the following sections, we discuss these relationships in detail.

B2B-PE valence and collaboration

A positive long-term exchange relationship, such as collaboration with an alliance, or a partnership to service the end customer, is a series of discrete exchange episodes, or *interactions*, that result in an economic or social outcome. B2B-PE captures the inter-organisational processes and exchanges within an episode that determines the level of mutuality in the relationship in future. Unlike collaboration, which is a positive association between two business entities, B2B-PE could be positive or negative. Under conditions of agency conflict, engagement efforts from Firm A might not result in an immediate positive response from B, spiralling the interactions into negative engagement between the two parties. Negative responses and subsequent negative interaction in an episode with a business customer will have an antagonistic influence on the future relationship between the parties. On the other hand, a positive response from B to the engagement initiatives of A could lead to positive engagement. In the future then, positively valenced engagement may lead to collaboration between the two parties. Overall, the valence of the engagement efforts will influence future collaboration between A and B, such that negatively valenced engagement will have a negative influence on future collaboration and positively valenced engagement is likely to have a positive influence on future collaboration. We now discuss the antecedent factors that influence engagement initiatives between partners.

Environmental factors in B2B-PE

Environmental factors are those outside the control of either member in a business-to-business collaborative relationship. They include environmental dynamism and business opportunities. While environmental factors may be outside control, appropriate reactions may include engagement efforts – or not. Successful management of engagement efforts relies on an understanding of these factors.

Environmental dynamism and B2B-PE

As mentioned, prior research suggests that the number of years spent in a relationship influence the development of trust (Doney and Cannon, 1997), which also drives successful collaborations. Additionally, when firms are in vulnerable strategic positions resulting from difficult or dynamic environments (Jap, 1999), as well as risky business strategies, they are more likely to depend on cooperative inter-organisational relationships (Eisenhardt and Schoonhoven, 1996). Today's fast-paced, dynamic business environment calls for faster reactions and responses by the firms. Such time pressures challenge a business's ability to form new collaborations in response to dynamic environmental demands. Moreover, although collaborations can provide the critical resources, legitimacy and market power needed in such situations, many business collaborations might be facing a relationship low, such as Lewicki et al.'s (1998) low-trust, low-distrust relationships. However, since new collaborations can take time to form, time-pressured businesses facing vulnerable strategic positions are more likely to attempt to engage existing partners to improve the state of collaboration with them. Thus, a dynamic external environment may boost the motivation of a business partner to engage in an action plan with a low-relationship business partner.

While sometimes dynamic business environments call for action to survive the rough weather, a positive business environment offers opportunities for growth. An environmental factor that is likely to influence engagement in a B2B setting is the perception of opportunity in the business environment. We discuss this relationship next.

Business opportunity and partner engagement

In a dynamic business environment, market opportunities arise frequently and require a quick response from businesses. The success of a business network depends on providing consumers with time and place utility by ensuring that the right products are in the right place at the right time (Agarwal, Shankar, and Tiwari, 2007). To remain competitive in the marketplace, many firms now rely on the capabilities of external partners to meet the evolving needs of customers (Christopher, 2000). In recent decades, a large variety of collaborative networks have emerged in response to the market- and response-time-related challenges faced by the businesses. These range from highly integrated supply chains to virtual organisational networks. Through these networks, firms seek complementarities and joint activities to allow them to participate in competitive market opportunities. Firms faced with time-pressured market opportunities are more likely to engage with either existing or new partners with a clear objective of responding to the business opportunity. For instance, a business responding to a market opportunity might partner with an existing supplier to develop a new product or participate in a 'dynamic virtual organisation' that is 'established in a short time to respond to a competitive market opportunity, and has a short life cycle, dissolving when the short-term purpose of the organization is accomplished' (Camarinha-Matos and Afsarmanesh, 2005, p. 440). We argue that businesses wishing to respond to time sensitive market opportunities will engage partners more.

Relational factors in B2B-PE

Within any business-to-business collaboration, a perceived change in the elements within the relationship may trigger engagement efforts from one firm to another. These relational factors include dependence asymmetry, commitment, opportunism and trust. Understanding relational factors within the framework of B2B-PE is critical to managing such engagement efforts successfully.

Dependence asymmetry and B2B-PE

Dependence research has established the influence of dependence asymmetry on inter-organisational relationships (Scheer, Miao and Palmatier, 2014). Based on Scheer, Miao and Palmatier 2014 we argue that the balance in dependency has a unique and substantial influence on how one partner engages the other. Prior research has established that the mutual dependence of collaborating partners is not always symmetrical. As Emerson (1962) emphasised, firm A's dependence on Firm B will be increased if B can help A accomplish a desired goal that is otherwise more difficult or impossible to achieve. Firm A could be motivated to invest either because the goal is important to them, or because B has more discretion over the resources, or because of the magnitude of the exchange itself. For instance, firm A would be more dependent if the outcome determines their competitive position, or if firm B is the sole or the largest supplier of a technology of importance to A's business. In such situations of dependency, firms engage in *bonding behaviours* in order to create close connections. To bond further, the members on both sides might develop personal friendships creating opportunities for interaction beyond work. The two businesses wanting to bond might create specialised procedures and dedicate more resources to the interaction between the two partners (Heide and John, 1988).

Unilateral dependence in an engagement might decrease relational efforts from the parties involved. Furthermore, partners faced with dependence asymmetries might engage each other more in order to determine the direction the partnership will take in the future. However, if the dependence is equal and high on both sides, efforts for a relationship are also likely to be high, such as the existence of normative contracts (Lusch and Brown, 1996). Therefore, the higher the dependence on both sides, the more the influence will flow both ways, thus leading to higher positive engagement.

Commitment and B2B-PE

Researchers in the past have established that relationships between firms are fundamentally dynamic and operate differently over time (Dwyer, Schurr and

Oh, 1987; Jap and Anderson, 2007). However, researchers have mostly studied static snap shots of business-to-business relationships at different ages or stages. This has led to a loss of information contained in the discrete events in a relationship's trajectory leading to a neglect of relationship processes at the transition of relationship dynamics (Palmatier et al., 2006). More recently, Palmatier et al. (2013) found that the rate and direction of commitment between partners change over time and have a significant effect on performance. While some relationships may experience oscillation of commitment, others may experience continuous deterioration of commitment. Partnerships linger in states of deterioration, where the partners are surprisingly loyal but passive (Anderson and Jap, 2012). These findings partially explain why a large number of partnerships fail. Research on successful collaborations recommends several factors that could save such relationships; however, not much attention has been paid to the intermittent efforts of relational partners to shock the relationship out of a passive state. We argue that when commitment is low and one party needs the partner's cooperation to achieve a specific outcome, they make attempts to engage the partner. However, the response of the partner might be influenced by the level of commitment, thus affecting the overall valence of engagement interactions between the two parties.

Opportunism and B2B-PE

More recently, B2B research has recognised that close relationships are not always synonymous with good relationships (Anderson and Jap, 2012, Palmatier et al., 2013). While marketing research focuses on the growing expectations in long-term relationships, strategic management research centres on the growing instability and vulnerability of long-term partnerships. There are even temporary failures in long-term relationships, resulting from occasional differences (Rindfleisch and Heide, 1997). Referring to the dark side of close relationships, Anderson and Jap, (2012, p. 75) identify a phenomena where 'relationships that appear to be doing well are often the most vulnerable to the forces of destruction that are quietly building beneath the surface of the relationship'. Opportunism, self-interest seeking with guile, has been the most commonly studied factor influencing this downward spiral. Recently, research attention has also been focused on the differences in active and passive opportunism and their implications (Seggie, Griffith and Jap, 2013). Active opportunism includes opportunism by commission, while passive opportunism is conceptualised as opportunism by omission (Wathne and Heide, 2000). Whatever the form, while opportunism may be clearly evident in some relationships, dealing with a suspected breach of trust is reported to be a difficult relational task (Anderson and Jap 2005). Seggie, Griffith and Jap (2013) report constructive discussion and venting as two active responses to acts of opportunism where the buyer gives the supplier a chance for retrieval and recovery of the situation. Party B's response to these and other active attempts at engagement is further influenced by the opportunism operating at Party B's end. In this manner, by influencing the action-reaction sequence, the level of opportunism ends up determining the overall valence of engagement between the two parties. Therefore, by initiating engagement in an environment of opportunism, one party in the relationship may be trying to engage the other party, while giving them an opportunity to recover from the situation. The response to this initiation and the subsequent interaction determines the overall valence of engagement between the two parties.

B2B-PE in such a situation helps companies to evaluate the present state of their relationship to understand future prospects. First, engaging a partner might help the business determine whether the opportunism is active or passive. Continued engagement, and its subsequent valence, resulting from the interaction, might further determine future relationship prospects.

Trust and B2B-PE

Trust, belief in the reliability and integrity of the exchange partner, has been a key variable for investigation in inter-organisational relationships. Researchers argue that positive outcomes over time increase trust and commitment between the interacting parties. Trust has been used as a key factor in explaining partnership performance, as well as the structure and governance in exchange relationships. Although past research used length of relationship as a proxy for trust, or assumed that interactions over time affect trust in a relationship, a meta-analytic conclusion drawn by Vanneste, Puranam, and Kretschmer (2014) argued that the correlation between trust and relationship duration is positive but small. This indicates that there are certain factors that actively moderate the association between length of relationship and trust. Trust seems to have a unique cyclical relationship with engagement in a B2B context. We believe that more trust between the partners will lead to an overall positive interaction, that is, positively valenced engagement. However, an imbalance in the level of trust might negatively influence the interaction, the partners thereby experiencing negative engagement. If a partner responds positively to an engagement initiative, this will likely enhance trust. However, if this response is negative, or even neutral, it could subsequently lower the trust, which will be evident in the next episode of engagement.

Discussion

Overview

Our literature review offers a preliminary effort towards understanding the concept of customer engagement as it applies to the B2B context. We explored the existing literature to answer the question 'What is meant by customer engagement in a business-to-business context?' Further, we feel that the concept of customer engagement in B2B is best characterised as partner engagement. First and foremost, our research indicates that relationships, howsoever good they might seem overall, are more dynamic in nature than previously indicated by researchers. Collaborative relationships not only face different stages of evolution, there are highs and lows even in a given stage of an evolving collaborative relationship. Engagement is an episode of intense exchange in the minor and major transitions in relationships between two independent, but interdependent, entities. Another important aspect of engagement is its valence. While collaboration involves positive and mutual exchange between two parties, the valence of an engagement episode could be positive or negative. The direction of the valence is likely to have a significant influence on the future of the relationship between these parties.

When we dug deeper to explore the association of collaboration with various relational constructs, we found indications of counter-intuitive associations. The literature reports a negative relationship of dependence asymmetry and opportunism with collaboration. If partners experience asymmetrical dependence, the more dependent partner may engage the less dependent partner. The outcome of this engagement will then contribute to shaping the collaboration in future. Further, opportunism is likely to have a positive relationship with engagement. Additionally, while more trust leads to higher collaboration, it may not have the same influence over partner engagement. However, distrust could lead to negatively valenced engagement, which is not likely to have a strong positive association with future collaboration.

Managerial implications

Managerial literature has been exploring the meaning and implications of 'engagement' for a number of years now; however, to our knowledge, no systematic attempt has been made to explore its nature in a business-to-business context. Our research answers some preliminary questions about 'what is engagement?'. Our exploration helps managers understand the counter-intuitive predictors and effects of engaging a partner for a specific outcome. In the short term, businesses might engage partners in an episodic manner. However, the implications of engaging and its valence have a long-term influence on the nature of relationship with the entity a business engages with. Therefore, our work lends deeper insights to managers into the strategic use of engagement episodes as a way of achieving business outcomes and influencing the direction of ties in the long term. Further, the proposed relationships provide a framework for managers considering the dynamic nature of relationships. Businesses often forge partnerships to gain support in dynamic environments. However, when put to test, some businesses are surprised to discover passive and active opportunism and indifference caused by unequal dependence on each other. A better understanding of partner engagement may give managers insight into how to respond when they find that the partner has 'moved on'. With our continued research, we hope to further develop a systematic understanding of engagement and its role in developing stronger business relationships.

Future research directions

This work is meant to move the conversation on customer engagement forward by addressing partner engagement in a business-to-business context. Our work was aimed at developing an initial conceptualisation of B2B-PE. However, further field work is needed to understand the degree to which these relationships are reasonable and generalisable. Although this work only scratches the tip of the B2B-PE iceberg, it provides an initial conceptualisation of the factors that might influence the initiation and valence of B2B-PE events and suggests the importance of studying these ideas more thoroughly. Researchers need to explore engagement in a large number of industries and at different levels in supply chains to comprehensively understand its nature, elements, dimensionality and strategic utility.

In addition, marketers need to consider how to assess the value of 'engaging' new versus existing partners. For example, is engaging a partner in a temporary network of organisations – one that will disintegrate after developing a new product – different from engaging a partner with which a business has had a long experience? Which organisational outcomes, other than financial and collaborative are influenced by partner engagement? How should return on investment of these programs be measured? In order to enable practitioners to make full use of the construct and academics to continue exploring the construct, future research needs to focus in the direction of developing a measure of B2B-PE and testing its applicability across contexts.

References

Agarwal, A., Shankar, R., and Tiwari, M.K. (2007) "Modeling Agility of Supply Chain." *Industrial Marketing Management*, 36(4): 443–57.

Anderson, E., and Jap, S.D. (2005) "The Dark Side of Close Relationships." *MIT Sloan Management Review*, 46(3): 75–82.

Anderson, E., and Jap, S. (2012) "The Dark Side of Close Relationships." *Sloan Management Review*, 46(3): 75–82.

Bolton, R. (2011). "Customer Engagement: Opportunities and Challenges for Organizations." *Journal of Service Research*, 14(3): 272–274.

Brodie, R. J., Hollebeek, L. D., Jurić, B., and Ilić, A. (2011). "Customer Engagement: Conceptual Domain, Fundamental Propositions, and Implications for Research." *Journal of Service Research*, 14(3): 252–271.

Camarinha-Matos, L. M., and Afsarmanesh, H. (2005) "Collaborative Networks: A New Scientific Discipline." *Journal of Intelligent Manufacturing*, 16(4–5): 439–52.

Christopher, M. (2000) "The Agile Supply Chain: Competing in Volatile Markets." *Industrial Marketing Management*, (29): 37–44.

Doney, P. M., and Cannon, J. P. (1997) "An Examination of the Nature of Trust in Buyer-Seller Relationships." *Journal of Marketing*, 61(2):35–51.

Dwyer, F. F., Schurr, P. H., and Oh, S. (1987) "Developing Buyer-Seller Partnerships." *Journal of Marketing*, 51(2): 11–27.

Dyer, J.H., and Singh, H. (1998) "The Relational View: Cooperative Strategy and Sources of Interorganizational Competitive Advantage." *Academy of Management Review*, 23(4): 660–79.

Eisenhardt, K. M., and Schoonhoven, C. B. (1996) "Resource-Based View of Strategic Alliance Formation: Strategic and Social Effects in Entrepreneurial Firms." *Organization Science*, 7(2): 136–50.

Emerson, R. M. (1962) "Power-Dependence Relations." *American Psychological Review*, 27 (1):31–41.

Gulati, R., and Singh, H. (1998). "The Architecture of Cooperation: Managing Coordination Costs and Appropriation Concerns in Strategic Alliances." *Administrative Science Quarterly*, 43(4): 781–814.

Gronroos, C. (2011) "Value Co-creation in Service Logic: A Critical Analysis." *Marketing Theory*, 11(3): 279–301

Heide, J. B., and John, G. (1988) "The Role of Dependence Balancing In Safeguarding Transaction-Specific Assets in Conventional Channels." *Journal of Marketing*, 52(1):20–35.

Hollebeek, L. D. (2011) "Demystifying Customer Brand Engagement Exploring the Loyalty Nexus." *Journal of Marketing Management*, 27(7–8): 785–807.

Hoyer, W. D., Chandy, R., Dorotic, M., Krafft, M. and Singh, S. (2010), "Consumer Co-Creation in New Product Development." *Journal of Service Research*, 3(3): 283–296.

Jap, S. D. (1999) "Pie-Expansion Efforts: Collaboration Processes in Buyer-Supplier Relationships." *Journal of Marketing Research*, 36(4):461–75.

Jap, S. D., and Anderson, E. (2007) "Testing a Life-Cycle Theory of Cooperative Interorganizational Relationships: Movement across Stages and Performance." *Management Science*, 53(2): 260–75.

Lambe, C. J., Spekman, R. E., and Hunt, S. D. (2002) "Alliance Competence, Resources, and Alliance Success: Conceptualization, Measurement, and Initial Test." *Journal of the Academy of Marketing Science*, 30(2): 141–58.

Lewicki, R. J., Mcallister, D. J., and Bies, R. J. (1998) "Trust and Distrust: New Relationships and Realities." *Academy of Management Review*, 23(3): 438–458.

Lusch, R. F., and Brown, J. R. (1996) "Interdependency, Contracting, and Relational Behavior in Marketing Channels." *Journal of Marketing*, 60(4): 19–38.

Nyaga, G. N., Whipple, J. M., and Lynch, D. F. (2010) "Examining Supply Chain Relationships: Do Buyer and Supplier Perspectives on Collaborative Relationships Differ?" *Journal of Operations Management*, 28(2): 101–14.

Palmatier, R. W., Dant, R. P., Grewal, D. and Evans, K. R. (2006) "Factors Influencing the Effectiveness of Relationship Marketing: A Meta-Analysis." *Journal of Marketing*, 70(4): 136–53.

Palmatier, R. W., Houston, M. B., Dant, R. P., and Grewal, D. (2013) "Relationship Velocity: Toward a Theory of Relationship Dynamics." *Journal of Marketing*, 77 (1): 13–30.

Paulraj, A., Lado, A. A., and Chen, I. A. (2008) "Inter-Organizational Communication as a Relational Competency: Antecedents and Performance Outcomes in Collaborative Buyer–Supplier Relationships." *Journal of Operations Management*, 26(1): 45–64.

Ploetner, O., and Ehret, M. (2006) "From Relationships to Partnerships – New Forms of Cooperation between Buyer and Seller." *Industrial Marketing Management*, 35(1): 4–9.

Rindfleisch, A., and Heide, J. B. (1997) "Transaction Cost Analysis: Past, Present, and Future Applications." *Journal of Marketing*, 61(4): 30–54.

Sarkar, M., Echambadi, R., and Harrison, J. (2001) "Alliance Entrepreneurship and Firm Market Performance." *Strategic Management Journal*, 22(6–7): 701–11.

Sashi, C. M. (2012) "Customer Engagement, Buyer-Seller Relationships, and Social Media," *Management Decision*, 50(2): 253–272.

Scheer, L. K., Miao, C. F., and Palmatier, R. W. (2014) Dependence and Interdependence in Marketing Relationships: Meta-analytic Insights." *Journal of the Academy of Marketing Science,* available at: http://download.springer.com/static/pdf/165/art%253A10.1007%252Fs11747–014–0418–1.pdf?auth66=1420580885_c826db70332fcb6ef77bbcb9cb28289c&ext=.pdf

Seggie, S. H., Griffith, D. A., and Jap, S. D. (2013) "Passive and Active Opportunism in Interorganizational Exchange." *Journal of Marketing*, 77(6): 73–90.

Vanneste, B. S., Puranam, P., and Kretschmer, T. (2014). "Trust over Time in Exchange Relationships: Meta-Analysis and Theory." *Strategic Management Journal*, 35(12): 1891–1902.

Wathne, K. H., and Heide, J. B. (2000) "Opportunism in Interfirm Relationships: Forms, Outcomes, and Solutions." *Journal of Marketing*, 64(4): 36–51.

Vivek, S. D., Beatty, S. E., Dalela, V. and Morgan, R. M. (2014) "A Generalized Multidimensional Scale for Measuring Customer Engagement." *Journal of Marketing Theory and Practice*, 22(4): 401–20.

4 Exploring customer engagement

A multi-stakeholder perspective

Linda D. Hollebeek

Introduction

After generating significant initial interest in the business practice literature (Appelbaum, 2001), the 'customer engagement' (CE) concept is rapidly gaining traction in the academic marketing literature (Verleye et al., 2013; Jaakkola and Alexander, 2014; Leeflang, 2011). Specifically, a number of authors has heralded the potentially superior contributions of this nascent concept to predicting or explaining focal consumer behaviours and specific behavioural outcomes, including consumer commitment and loyalty, relative to conventional concepts (e.g. customer satisfaction or involvement; Mollen and Wilson, 2010; Bowden, 2009; Brodie et al., 2011, 2013; Sprott et al., 2009; MSI, 2014).

The CE concept has been found to have particular relevance in focal marketing contexts typified by highly interactive, co-creative or experiential consumer dynamics (Abdul-Ghani, Hyde and Marshall, 2010; Verhoef, Reinartz and Krafft, 2010; Gebauer, Füller and Pezzei, 2012; Van Doorn et al., 2010). As such, the literature suggests CE may be adopted to optimise or facilitate specific customer/provider interactions, the development of value-laden business relationships, as well as the subsequent achievement of superior performance outcomes, including sales growth and cost reductions (Martin, 1998; Ashley, Noble, Donthu and Lemon, 2011; Leeflang, 2011; Hollebeek, 2011a/b, 2012).

A number of authors posit the theoretical foundations underlying CE to be reflective of the grand theoretical service-dominant (S-D) logic framework (Vargo and Lusch, 2004, 2008). Consistent with, and building upon this perspective, the findings reported in this chapter indicate that customers' specific expression of their engagement with a focal object (e.g. a brand) may be explained by referring to the conceptual underpinnings of social exchange theory (SET), which posits that individuals are motivated to reciprocate specific favourably perceived actions and behaviours (e.g. by firms) by displaying favourable behaviours in return (e.g. exhibiting elevated levels of cognitive, emotional and/or behavioural activity (i.e., CE) in specific brand interactions; Blau, 1964; Pervan et al., 2009).

The following example illustrates the nature of key dynamics observed at the interface of S-D logic, SET and CE. Specifically, the role of many contemporary consumers is not only to perceive, experience or extract relevant value from specific contexts (Cronin et al., 1997), but also to contribute to, or participate in, their production, including as part-time employees or co-producers (Prahalad and Ramaswamy, 2004). Further, the reciprocal (i.e. SET-based), two-way nature of CE exhibits close conceptual alignment with the co-creation concept, which represents a key theoretical foundation of S-D logic (Brodie et al., 2011; Spencer and Cova, 2012; Purvis and Purvis, 2012). Based on this rationale, the key contributions of this chapter reside in the following two areas: (i) the adoption of a multi-stakeholder perspective (i.e. consumer, manager, and academic conceptions) on CE, which is not known to exist in the literature to date and which is expected to provide an enhanced understanding of the multi-faceted CE concept observed within broader service ecosystems; and (ii) the conceptual linking of CE to an integrative S-D logic/SET-informed perspective, which culminates in the development of a multi-stakeholder conceptual model of CE.

This chapter is structured as follows. First, recent engagement research published within the marketing discipline is reviewed in the next section. Despite providing pioneering insights, the reviewed research, however, is limited to addressing a single-, rather than a multi-stakeholder perspective on CE. Based on this observed research gap a multi-stakeholder perspective of CE is developed in the next section, followed by an overview of exploratory insights obtained into CE, as informed by multiple stakeholder groups. Next, the research question and methodology guiding the enquiry are introduced, followed by an overview of the key findings. The chapter concludes with an overview of key limitations and implications arising from this research.

Engagement research in marketing

An overview of selected engagement research published in the marketing literature is provided in Table 4.1. Despite the debate regarding the interpretation of CE, Brodie et al. (2011) identify the notion of 'interactive experience' between a specific engagement subject (e.g. a customer) and object (e.g. a brand) as a core hallmark typifying CE, thus highlighting the two-way, interactive nature underlying the engagement concept (Bolton, 2011; Jaakkola and Alexander, 2014; Robinson et al., 2004; Gambetti and Graffigna, 2010; Brodie and Hollebeek, 2011; Ramani and Kumar, 2008).

Van Doorn et al. (2010) identify CE as a multidimensional concept comprising relevant cognitive, emotional and behavioural dimensions, although their specific expression may vary across contexts. To illustrate, while Mollen and Wilson (2010) identify 'active sustained processing' and 'experiential/instrumental value' as online engagement dimensions, other authors conceptualise offline CE applications by employing the distinct facets of absorption, vigour and dedication (Patterson, Yu and De Ruyter, 2006; So et al., 2014). Despite the debate surrounding the specific dimensionality of engagement, our literature review revealed three generic dimensions characterising CE, including cognitive, emotional and behavioural facets (e.g. Calder et al., 2009; Patterson et al., 2006; Hollebeek, 2011b, 2012; Phillips and MacQuarrie, 2010; Vivek et al., 2012).

Table 4.1 Overview – Selected engagement research in marketing

Author(s)	Concept	Definition
Gambetti and Graffigna (2010)	Engagement	The authors differentiate between: (i) Soft, relational; and (ii) Pragmatic, managerial aspects of engagement.
Van Doorn et al. (2010)	Customer engagement behaviour	Customers' behavioural manifestation towards a brand or firm, beyond purchase, resulting from motivational drivers, including word-of-mouth activity, helping other customers, blogging and writing reviews (cf. also Jaakkola and Alexander, 2014; Verleye et al., 2013).
Hollebeek (2011a); Hollebeek et al. (2014)	Customer brand engagement	(2011a) – The level of expression of an individual customer's motivational, brand-related and context-dependent state of mind characterised by a degree of activation, identification and absorption in brand interactions. (2014) – A consumer's positively valenced brand-related cognitive, emotional and behavioural activity during or related to focal consumer/brand interactions.
Mollen and Wilson (2010)	Engagement	A cognitive and affective commitment to an active relationship with the brand as personified by the website or other computer-mediated entities designed to communicate brand value (cf. also Calder et al., 2009).
Abdul-Ghani et al. (2010)	Engagement	Requires consumer connection (e.g. with media), and implies utilitarian, hedonic and social benefits that are the bases of [consumer] engagement with a specific consumer-to-consumer auction site.
Vivek et al. (2012)	Customer engagement	The intensity of an individual's participation and connection with the organisation's offerings and activities initiated by either the customer or the organisation.
Higgins and Scholer (2009)	Engagement	A state of being involved, occupied, fully absorbed or engrossed in something (i.e. sustained attention), generating the consequences of a particular attraction or repulsion force. The more engaged individuals are to approach or repel a target, the more value is added to or subtracted from it.

(*Continued*)

Table 4.1 (Continued)

Author(s)	Concept	Definition
Bowden (2009)	Customer engagement	A psychological process that models the underlying mechanisms by which customer loyalty forms for new customers of a service brand, as well as the mechanisms by which loyalty may be maintained for repeat purchase customers of a service brand.
Patterson et al. (2006)	Customer engagement	The level of a customer's physical, cognitive and emotional presence in their relationship with a service organisation.
Brodie et al. (2011)	Customer engagement	A motivational state that occurs by virtue of interactive, co-creative customer experiences with a focal agent/object (e.g. a brand) in focal service relationships.

As stated in the Introduction, a multi-stakeholder S-D logic/SET-informed perspective is adopted in this study. Specifically, SET posits, broadly, that customers will reciprocate positive thoughts, feelings and behaviours towards a specific individual (e.g. service employee) or object (e.g. a brand) upon receiving specific benefits from interacting with these (Blau, 1964; Pervan et al., 2009; Abdul-Ghani et al., 2010). Referring to the literature, which cites brands to have specific personalities, analogous to human beings (Aaker, 1997; Hosany et al., 2006), the SET perspective engenders particular relevance with respect to consumers' willingness to reciprocate (e.g. by interacting with, or providing positive word-of-mouth regarding, focal brands), thus contributing to these individuals' engagement with particular objects (Libai, 2011; Hollebeek, 2011a; Van Doorn et al., 2010; Sawhney et al., 2005; Saks, 2006).

SET addresses customers' underlying motivation for making specific, proactive contributions to focal brand interactions, and any perceived returns extracted from such interactions (Pervan and Bove, 2009). Hence a customer in an exchange may perceive what (s)he gives as a cost, while viewing what (s)he receives as a reward (Homans, 1958; Pervan et al., 2009). Consequently, the individual modifies his/her behaviour as the difference between the two (i.e. profit) changes (Homans, 1974). This cost/reward perspective corresponds to the interactive nature of engagement (Abdul-Ghani et al., 2010; Robinson et al., 2004; Lusch and Vargo, 2010). Based on this observation, this chapter seeks to conceptualise the interactive, reciprocal nature characterising the CE concept from a hybrid S-D logic/SET-informed perspective.

Research question and approach

Based on the observed gap in the literature, the following research question was developed to guide the enquiry: '*What are consumer, manager, and academic experts' conceptions of the term 'customer engagement'?*' To investigate this research question, an open-ended e-mail survey was adopted by drawing on a sample of 35 consumers (14 male), 33 managers (19 male) and 11 academic experts who are active in the field of CE research (6 male).

Consumers were recruited through advertisements posted on community notice boards in a large Pacific Coast city. Specifically, prospective participants were able to contact the researcher by phone, e-mail or postal mail regarding their participation in the research. While the majority of consumers ($n = 35$) and managers ($n = 33$) were sourced locally, the majority of the academic experts were sourced from relevant countries worldwide ($n = 9$). In contrast to the consumer respondents, the main researcher knew the managers and academic experts comprising the sample. The respondents were solicited via e-mail (Yun and Trumbo, 2000). The informants' ages ranged from 20 to 66.

The respondents were instructed to e-mail the survey, which took approximately 15 minutes to complete, back to the main researcher in completed form for subsequent data processing and analysis. The data were then classified by respondent category (i.e. consumer, manager, or academic expert) and tabled for analysis. The majority of completed e-mail surveys (93%) were received within three days following the initial e-mail contact with the respondent. Further, in this chapter the respondents' names are omitted to protect their privacy (De Vaus, 2002). Instead, a respondent coding schedule was used in the analysis to facilitate the identification of the informants.

The data were analysed using content and thematic analysis. In contrast to content analysis, thematic analysis incorporates the entire conversation as the potential unit of analysis (Thomsen, Straubhaar, and Bolyard, 1998), and as such extracts super/sub-ordinate themes from the data. The analysis was conducted at two levels, including open and axial coding (e.g. Spiggle, 1994). Open coding refers to the process of identifying themes in the data with the objective of creating descriptive categories as a preliminary framework for analysis (Strauss and Corbin, 1998). Specifically, the themes were generated inductively from the raw data, and deductively from theory and prior research (Taylor and Bogdan, 1984; Hyde, 2000).

Key themes emergent from the data were identified at the manifest level (i.e. directly observable in the data), and at the latent level (i.e. underlying the phenomenon of interest; Boyatzis, 1998). Open codes were developed from text, which varied in length from several words to paragraphs. Some passages exemplified more than a single category, resulting in multiple codes designated to particular passages of text. Further, a portion of the data did not contain any meaningful information and thus remained uncoded.

In axial coding the analyst develops a category or construct, by specifying 'the conditions giving rise to it; the context in which it is embedded; the action/interactional strategies by which it is handled, managed, and carried out; and the outcome of those strategies' (Strauss and Corbin, 1990: p. 97; Spiggle, 1994: p. 495). More specifically, axial coding entails the re-examination of the identified themes in order to determine focal linkages to core, higher-order categories comprising sets of relevant concepts, and/or offering explanations of the phenomenon of interest (Glaser and Strauss, 1967; Strauss and Corbin, 1998).

Hence the identified themes were analysed and compared by drawing on open coding in novel ways, as focal hierarchical (i.e. super- and sub-ordinate) theme structures began to emerge from the data. Overall, open/axial coding represents an iterative process whereby themes initially identified using open coding merit further scrutiny and/or linking to the core CE concept during the axial coding stage. The key findings emergent from the analysis are reported in the next section.

Key findings

Overview: CE stakeholder data

An overview of the findings classified by consumer (C), manager (M) and academic expert (AE) data is presented in Table 4.2. Scrutiny of Table 4.2 reveals the existence of two-way, interactive experiences as a key hallmark of CE, as examined from a multi-stakeholder perspective, thus concurring with the findings from previous CE research (e.g. Patterson et al., 2006; Brodie et al., 2011; Leeflang, 2011; Hollebeek, 2011b; Robinson et al., 2004) and extending these to the multi-stakeholder perspective on CE. The findings also reflected an enhanced importance of direct incorporation of a more explicit interactive perspective on CE, relative to those reported, typically, in previous CE research (e.g. Sprott et al., 2009).

Each of the respondents used one or more terms describing their interactive experiences with a focal brand or organisation, including 'interaction' ($n = 51$, i.e. 93%), 'connection' ($n = 42$, i.e. 76%), 'communication' ($n = 41$, i.e. 75%), 'relationship' ($n = 39$, i.e. 71%), 'participation' ($n = 35$, i.e. 63%), or 'dialogue' ($n = 30$, i.e. 54%), which represent stakeholders' cognitive, emotional and/or behavioural CE. Further, specific interactive experience types identified included (i) Product/service-related consultations with service personnel, (ii) Purchase, (iii) Visiting the brand's website and (iv) Conversing with others about the brand (online and/or offline), thus reflecting a number of different engagement objects and activities (Hollebeek et al., 2014).

The findings also differed across the focal CE stakeholder groups in a number of ways. First, while consumers, typically, highlighted the nature of CE as interaction expressed through connection (e.g. to a brand), processing depth, passion and affinity towards the engagement object (e.g. brand, product, organisation), the managers tended to focus more on specific firm-based tactics or strategies that may be used to engage customers (e.g. marketing communications, customer

Table 4.2 Consumer, manager and academic experts' conceptions of CE

Consumers (C)	1. A firm's genuine, sustained interest in customer needs/feelings, reciprocated by the customer by purchasing/partaking in brand interactions. 2. Firm-initiated, as well as proactive, customer-initiated interactions with a brand. 3. The way in which a company interacts with a customer. 4. The depth of processing in interactions and link between a customer and a brand. 5. A relationship with a product/brand, how well the customer knows the brand. 6. Feeling connected to a brand/service provider and what it stands for. 7. Customer passion for the brand. 8. Feeling affinity and being energised and inspired by the brand. 9. The extent to which a customer cares about a brand beyond its consumption utility.
Managers (M)	1. A close, two-way relationship between a customer and the business. 2. The way in which the customer relates and interacts with the brand. 3. The interaction and a call for action for customers (e.g. go to website, order product). 4. Customer/firm communication/relationship and having educated customers. 5. Customer passion for your brand, them 'believing' in it. 6. Customers' genuine interest in a brand beyond the purchase transaction. 7. Being connected [to your customer], creating energy/buzz, being active. 8. Customer/firm communication and proactive customer collaboration. 9. Having customers excited about, and interacting positively with, the firm.
Academic Experts (AE)	1. A mutual, two-way relationship [centred on] proactive communication. 2. Interaction-based concept, where value may be co-created with other actors. 3. A multi-faceted, interpersonal concept based on customer/firm interaction. 4. Relational interaction/exchange and co-creation of value augmenting the brand. 5. An individual's collective brand experience (thoughts, feelings and actions). 6. Energising customers to contribute to joint co-creation processes. 7. Communication using brand touch points to promote customer brand familiarity.

education, calls to action for customers). Finally, although the findings attained from academic experts also emphasised the importance of interaction underlying CE, these respondents also focused on the multi-dimensional nature underlying CE (e.g. Brodie et al., 2011), which may include specific expressions of customers' cognitive, emotional and behavioural engagement (Gambetti and Graffigna, 2010).

Consistent with the principles underlying SET, the respondents indicated being motivated to reciprocate specific favourably perceived firm actions and behaviours through exhibiting elevated levels of cognitive, emotional and/ or behavioural activity in specific brand interactions, as exemplified by the following respondent statement (C1):

> CE reflects a firm's genuine, sustained interest in customer needs/feelings, [which is] reciprocated by the customer by purchasing or partaking in brand interactions.

Specifically, by referring to focal interactively generated, potentially co-creative value the respondent taps into the conceptual domain of S-D logic (Vargo and Lusch, 2004). Further, the reported notion of customer based reciprocity reflects SET (Pervan et al., 2009); the customer's level of brand-related cognitive, emotional and behavioural activity displayed during focal brand interactions reflects CE (Brodie et al., 2011; Hollebeek et al., 2014; Hollebeek, 2011b). Based on these findings, an integrative, multi-stakeholder conceptualisation of CE is developed in the next section, which details the specific cognitively, emotionally and behaviourally based CE themes extracted from the analysis.

Customer engagement conceptualisation

The present findings, which are based on a multi-stakeholder perspective on CE, as reported in the preceding sections, suggest a more explicit reciprocal nature underlying CE, relative to perspectives reported in the current literature. Specifically, the findings indicated an interplay of specific customer-perceived cognitive, emotional and behavioural sacrifices/costs, versus particular perceived benefits extracted from specific brand interactions (Abdul-Ghani et al., 2010; Hollebeek, 2011b), compared to previous research conceptualising engagement in marketing. Adopting this bilateral S-D logic/SET-informed 'cost/benefit' perspective, CE is defined here as:

> The level of perceived cognitive, emotional and behavioural investment in, and ensuing perceived returns extracted from, a customer's interactive brand experience.

The proposed CE definition differs, conceptually, from the concept of 'customer value' in the following manner. Customer value is defined as 'a customer's overall assessment of the utility of a product/service based on perceptions of

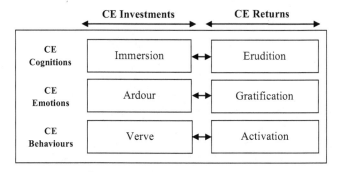

Figure 4.1 Multi-stakeholder model of customer engagement (CE)
Notes – cf. also Hollebeek (2011c)

what is received and what is given' (Zeithaml, 1988). While both CE and customer value are viewed to reflect the notion of 'perceived investment/returns (or: cost/benefit), the conceptual scope of CE is limited to consumers' *intra-interaction* cognitive, emotional and behavioural activity (Hollebeek, 2011a). Customer value, by contrast, represents a customer's *overall assessment* regarding the performance of a product or service offering, thus reflecting a significantly broader theoretical domain.

The newly developed conceptual model, which incorporates the key CE themes emergent from the data, is shown in Figure 4.1. Based on the literature review and findings reported in this chapter, CE is represented from a tripartite perspective typified by specific cognitions, emotions and behaviours (Patterson et al., 2006; Brodie et al., 2011; Higgins, 2006), each of which are shown on individual rows of the model. Moreover, the column headed 'CE investments' reflects the levels of particular types of cognitive, emotional and behavioural customer-perceived inputs or contributions to focal brand interactions.

The column headed 'CE returns' shows specific types of customer-perceived benefits from engaging in focal brand interactions. Specific cognitive, emotional and behavioural CE returns were found to emerge from particular CE investments within the respective cognitive, emotional and behavioural CE dimensions. For example, respondent C2 refers to CE as 'proactive, customer-initiated interactions with a brand', thus reflecting specific benefits accruing from CE. By contrast, M6 refers to CE as 'customers' genuine interest in a brand beyond the purchase transaction', thus referring to the potential existence of focal investments made by customers into their relationship with a focal engagement object (e.g. a brand).

The cognitive dimension of CE, *'immersion'* (shown on the top row of Figure 4.1) is defined as a customer's level of concentration on a specific inter-active experience (e.g. Table 4.2: C4, M6, AE5). Immersion, or an theoretically analogous engagement dimension, is also observed in previous research, including

Schaufeli et al.'s (2002) 'absorption' and Hollebeek et al.'s (2014) 'cognitive processing'. Immersion, in turn, generates a particular degree of '*erudition*', that is, a customer's level of knowledge about the engagement object (e.g. Table 4.2: C5, M4, AE7), thus reflecting the dynamic, interactive nature of CE across a series of customer/brand interactions. Erudition reflects a customer's level of interactively generated knowledge about a focal engagement object (e.g. a brand); thereby differentiating the concept from '(brand) awareness', which does not require the undertaking of focal brand interactions per se. The two-way arrow linking these specific CE themes, as shown in Figure 4.1, highlights their interactive, reciprocal nature, thus concurring with the theoretical foundations underlying a hybrid S-D logic/SET-informed perspective of CE, as addressed earlier in this chapter. Analogously, two-way arrows linking the specific emotional and behavioural CE themes (i.e. ardour/gratification, verve/activation), respectively, are included in Figure 4.1, representing the bilateral association between these concepts.

Second, the newly developed concept of '*ardour*' addresses a customer's level of positive emotion for the brand during a particular interactive experience, and thus displays conceptual congruence to Appelbaum's (2001) 'passion', which the authors include as a component of CE (Table 4.2, e.g. C9, M5, M9, AE2). Ardour, in turn, generates a particular level of '*gratification*', that is, a customer's level of enjoyment or pleasure extracted from a particular interactive experience (Scott and Craig-Lees, 2010; e.g. Table 4.2: C7, M2, AE4). Similar to the present observation, authors including Hollebeek et al. (2014) propose the notion of positive emotion as a dimension of consumer brand engagement (cf. also Patterson et al., 2006; Schaufeli et al., 2002). Emerging perspectives in the literature, however, posit that not all forms of CE will result, necessarily, in favourable firm-related outcomes (for a more in-depth discussion regarding positively and negatively valenced expressions of CE refer to Hollebeek and Chen, 2014).

Third, '*verve*' reflects a customer's level of energy, time and/or effort expended on a particular interactive experience (e.g. Table 4.2: C1, C2, M3, M7, AE1), and as such reflects the behavioural dimension of CE. Verve, in turn, generates '*activation*', which refers to the extent to which a customer feels energised and/or invigorated by a particular interactive experience (e.g. Table 4.2: C8, M8, AE6). While verve represents a newly developed CE-based concept in the literature, the notion of 'activation' has been reported in previous CE research (e.g. Hollebeek et al., 2014). Further, the behavioural dimension of CE also reflects customer engagement behaviours (CEBs; Van Doorn et al., 2010; Jaakkola and Alexander, 2014; Verleye et al., 2013).

Based on the adopted hybrid S-D logic/SET-informed 'cost/benefit' perspective, '*net CE*' reflects a customer's perceived total cognitive, emotional and behavioural investment in a specific interactive experience *less* the individual's perceived total cognitive, emotional and behavioural returns extracted from the interactive experience. As such, net CE is positive when the level of total perceived CE returns *exceeds* the level of perceived CE investments in a particular interactive experience, and vice versa. Further, CE equals zero when the level of perceived CE investments is identical to the level of perceived returns extracted from a particular interactive experience.

Moreover, for specific interactive experiences, customers may adopt particular 'zones of tolerance' for the requisite levels of focal CE themes and/or dimensions (Kettinger and Lee, 2005; Yap and Sweeney, 2007), although little in this area is known to date. Interestingly, despite S-D logic-based claims arguing against the importance of specific transactional (or goods-based) exchange, the present findings suggest the existence of a hybrid S-D logic (i.e. value-in-use based)/SET (i.e. more transactional) perspective. Based on the key findings emergent from this research, an overview of relevant research limitations and implications is provided in the next section.

Conclusions, limitations and implications

This chapter has developed an integrative, multi-stakeholder CE conceptualisation based on the findings attained from an open-ended e-mail survey on a sample of 79 informants representing the specific CE stakeholder groups of consumers (n = 35), managers (n = 33) and academic experts (n = 11). The contributions of this chapter are in two key areas: (i) The adoption of a multi-stakeholder perspective (i.e. consumer, manager and academic conceptions) on CE, which is not known to exist in the literature to date, and which is expected to provide an enhanced understanding of the multi-faceted CE concept observed within broader service ecosystems; and (ii) The conceptual linking of CE to an integrative S-D logic/SET-informed perspective, which culminates in the development of a multi-stakeholder conceptual model of CE.

Despite the insights gleaned, this research is also subject to a number of key limitations, which are summarised in Table 4.3. To illustrate, while S-D logic and SET perspectives on CE have been proposed independently (but not explicitly collectively) in the literature, the currently nascent state of CE research may engender relevance of exploring alternative and/or complementary perspectives onto this emerging concept, including Consumer Culture Theory (Arnould and Thompson, 2005). Further, the proposed CE conceptualisation requires empirical testing and validation adopting large-scale, quantitative methods of enquiry (e.g. SEM; Calder et al., 2009).

In addition to its scholarly contributions, this research also provides a number of managerial implications. First, it enhances practitioners' understanding of the emerging CE concept, which despite being heralded in the business practice literature for its promising contributions, including providing superior explicability or predictability of specific consumer behaviour outcomes (including loyalty; Bowden, 2009), has received relatively little systematic enquiry, including conceptual and empirical development to date (Hollebeek and Chen, 2014). As such, managers may wish to use the findings presented in this chapter to clarify the nature and dynamics underlying the CE concept from an integrative, multi-stakeholder perspective, which draws on focal consumer, practitioner and academic expert conceptions of CE.

Table 4.3 Overview – Limitations and key marketing research implications

Limitation	Key marketing research implication(s)
Conceptual foundations: SET/S-D logic perspective of CE	• Which theoretical perspective(s), other than or complementary to the hybrid SET/S-D logic view, may researchers use to explain or predict focal CE levels? • Further empirical testing and validation of the SET/S-D logic CE interface is required to substantiate claims made in this area across specific sets of contextual contingencies. • Does the level of customer reciprocity of favourably perceived firm actions/ behaviours, as advocated under SET and/or the S-D logic, differ across distinctly perceived or positioned service brands (e.g. utilitarian vs. hedonic brands)? ◦ For example, which types of brands are most likely to engender optimal levels of CE with the brand?

Methodology:
Exploratory research
	• Empirical testing/verification of the proposed CE conceptualisation and quantification of CE levels using large-scale, quantitative methodology (e.g. SEM) are required.
	• Establishment of a generalisable CE conceptualisation across (a) contexts and/or (b) over time, that is, by using longitudinal methods (e.g. time series analysis).
	  ◦ For example, does the proposed conceptual model hold in iteratively modelled CE processes over time?
	• Establishment of CE discriminant validity vs. interrelated constructs, including focal CE antecedents/ consequences
	  ◦ For example, implications of CE on brand loyalty.

Second, the CE research agenda outlined in Table 4.3 provides insight into the current state of CE research, which highlights the need for further scholarly enquiry in this area before managers are able to fully leverage the anticipated benefits of CE, including contributions to enhanced customer loyalty and improved organisational performance (Bijmolt et al., 2010; Roberts and Alpert,

2010). Specifically, such research includes the development of a CE measurement or quantification instrument, which practitioners may adopt upon its development and validation (Leeflang, 2011; Hollebeek, 2011a, 2014).

References

Aaker, J. A. (1997). Dimensions of brand personality. *Journal of Marketing Research, 34* (3), 347–356.

Abdul-Ghani, E., Hyde, K. and Marshall, R. (2010). Emic and etic interpretations of engagement with a consumer-to-consumer online auction site. *Journal of Business Research, 64* (10), 1060–1066.

Appelbaum A. (2001). The constant consumer. *Gallup Management Journal,* Available at: http://gmj.gallup.com/content/745/Constant-Customer.aspx [Accessed 29 October 2014].

Arnould, E. and Thompson, C. J. (2005). Consumer culture theory: Twenty years of research *Journal of Consumer Research, 31* (4), 868–882.

Ashley, C., Noble, S. M., Donthu, N. and Lemon, K. N. (2011). Why customers won't relate: Obstacles to relationship marketing engagement. *Journal of Business Research, 64* (7), 749–756.

Bijmolt, T.H.A., Leeflang, P.S.H., Block, F., Eisenbeiss, M., Hardie, B.G.S., Lemmens, A. and Saffert, P. (2010). Analytics for customer engagement. *Journal of Service Research, 3* (3), 341–356.

Blau, P. (1964). *Exchange and Power in Social Life.* Wiley, New York.

Bolton, R. N. (2011). Customer engagement: Opportunities and challenges for organizations. *Journal of Service Research, 14*(3), 272–274.

Bowden, J. H. (2009). The process of customer engagement: A conceptual framework. *Journal of Marketing Theory and Practice, 17* (1), 63–74.

Boyatzis, R. E. (1998). *Transforming Qualitative Information: Thematic Analysis and Code Development.* Thousand Oaks: Sage Publications.

Brodie, R. J. and Hollebeek, L. D. (2011). Advancing and consolidating knowledge about customer engagement. *Journal of Service Research, 14* (3), 283–284.

Brodie, R. J., Hollebeek, L. D., Juric, B. and Ilic, A. (2011). Customer engagement: Conceptual domain, fundamental propositions and implications for research. *Journal of Service Research, 14* (3), 1–20.

Brodie, R. J., Ilic, A., Juric, B. and Hollebeek, L. D. (2013). Consumer engagement in a virtual brand community: An exploratory analysis. *Journal of Business Research, 66* (1), 105–114.

Calder, B. J., Malthouse, E. C. and Schaedel, U. (2009). An experimental study of the relationship between online engagement and advertising effectiveness. *Journal of Interactive Marketing, 23* (4), 321–331.

Cronin, J. J., Brady, M. K., Jr., Brand, R. R., Hightower, R., Jr. and Shemwell, D. J. (1997). A cross-sectional test of the effect and conceptualization of service value. *Journal of Services Marketing, 11* (6), 375–391.

De Vaus, D. A. (2002). *Surveys in Social Research.* 5th edition, Crow's Nest, NSW: Allen & Unwin.

Gambetti, R. C. and Graffigna, G. (2010). The concept of engagement: A systematic analysis of the ongoing marketing debate. *International Journal of Market Research, 52* (6), 801–826.

Gebauer, J., Füller, J. and Pezzei, R. (2012). The dark and bright side of co-creation: Triggers of member online behavior in online innovation communities. *Journal of Business Research*, http://dx.doi.org/10.1016/j.jbusres.2012.09.013.

Glaser, B. G. and Strauss, A. L. (1967). *The Discovery of Grounded Theory: Strategies for Qualitative Research.* New York: Aldine Transaction.

Higgins, E. T. (2006). Value from hedonic experience *and* engagement. *Psychological Review, 113* (3), 439–460.

Higgins, E. T. and Scholer, A. A. (2009). Engaging the consumer: The science and art of the value creation process. *Journal of Consumer Psychology, 19* (2), 100–114.

Hollebeek, L. D. (2011a). Demystifying customer brand engagement: Exploring the loyalty nexus. *Journal of Marketing Management, 27* (7–8), 785–807.

Hollebeek, L. D. (2011b). Exploring customer brand engagement: Definition and themes. *Journal of Strategic Marketing, 19* (7), 555–573.

Hollebeek, L. D. (2011c). Customer engagement: Consumer, managerial and academic conceptions. EMAC 2011 Proceedings.

Hollebeek, L. D. (2012). The customer engagement/value interface: An exploratory investigation. *Australasian Marketing Journal, 21* (1), 17–24.

Hollebeek, L. D. and Chen, T. (2014). Exploring Positively- vs. Negatively-Valenced Brand Engagement: A Conceptual Model, Journal of Product & Brand Management, *23* (1), 62–74.

Hollebeek, L. D., Glynn, M. and Brodie, R. J. (2014), Consumer brand engagement in social media: conceptualization, scale development and validation. *Journal of Interactive Marketing, 28* (2), 149–165.

Homans, G. C. (1958). Social behavior as exchange. *American Journal of Sociology, 63* (6), 597–606.

Homans, G. C. (1974). *Social Behavior: Its Elementary Forms.* New York: Harcourt Brace Jovanovich.

Hosany, S., Ekinci, Y. and Uysal, M. (2006). Destination image and destination personality: An application of branding theories to tourism places. *Journal of Business Research, 59* (5), 638–642.

Hyde, K. F. (2000). Recognising deductive processes in qualitative research. *Qualitative Market Research: An International Journal, 3* (2), 82–90.

Jaakkola, E. and Alexander, M. (2014). The role of customer engagement behavior in value co-creation: A service system perspective, *Journal of Service Research,* DOI: 10.1177/1094670514529187.

Kettinger, W. J. and Lee, C. C. (2005). Zones of tolerance: Alternative scales for measuring information systems service quality. *MIS Quarterly, 29* (4), 607–623.

Leeflang, P. (2011). Paving the way for 'distinguished marketing.' *International Journal of Research in Marketing, 28* (2), 76–88.

Libai, B. R. (2011). The perils of focusing on highly engaged customers. *Journal of Service Research, 14* (3), 275–276.

Lusch, R. F. and Vargo, S. L. (2010). S-D logic: Accommodating, integrating, transdisciplinary. *Grand Service Challenge*, University of Cambridge, 23 September.

Lusch, R. F., Vargo, S. L. and Tanniru, M. (2010). Service, value networks and learning. *Journal of the Academy of Marketing Science, 38* (1), 19–31.

Martin, C. L. (1998). Relationship marketing: A high-involvement product attribute approach. *Journal of Product & Brand Management, 7* (1), 6–26.

Mollen, A. and Wilson, H. (2010). Engagement, telepresence and interactivity in online consumer experience: Reconciling scholastic and managerial perspectives. *Journal of Business Research*, 63 (9/10), 919–925.

MSI (Marketing Science Institute) (2014). *Research Priorities 2010–2012*. Cambridge, MA, Available at: www.msi.org [Accessed 13 August 2014].

Patterson, P., Yu, T. and De Ruyter, K. (2006). Understanding customer engagement in services. *Proceedings of ANZMAC 2006 Conference*, Brisbane, 4–6 December.

Pervan, S. J., Bove, L. L. and Johnson, L. (2009). Reciprocity as a key stabilizing norm of interpersonal marketing relationships: Scale development and validation. *Industrial Marketing Management*, 38 (1), 60–70.

Phillips, B. J. and McQuarrie, E. F. (2010). Narrative and persuasion in fashion advertising. *Journal of Consumer Research*, 37 (3), 368–392.

Prahalad, C. K. and Ramaswamy, V. (2004). Co-creation experiences: The next practice in value creation. *Journal of Interactive Marketing*, 18 (3), 5–14.

Purvis, M. K. and Purvis, M. A. (2012). Institutional expertise in the service-dominant logic: Knowing how and knowing what. *Journal of Marketing Management*, 28 (13–14), 1626–1641.

Ramani, G. and Kumar, V. (2008). Interaction orientation and firm performance. *Journal of Marketing*, 72 (1), 27–45.

Roberts, C. and Alpert, F. (2010). Total customer engagement: Designing and aligning key strategic elements to achieve growth. *Journal of Product & Brand Management*, 19 (3), 198–209.

Robinson, D., Perryman, S. P. and Hayday, S. (2004). *The Drivers of Employee Engagement*. IES Report 408, Institute for Employment Studies, Available at: http://www.employment-studies.co.uk/summary/summary.php?id=408 [Accessed 3 September 2014].

Saks, A. M. (2006). Antecedents and consequences of employee engagement. *Journal of Managerial Psychology*, 21 (7), 600–619.

Sawhney, M., Verona, G. and Prandelli, E. (2005). Collaborating to create: The internet as a platform for customer engagement in product innovation. *Journal of Interactive Marketing*, 19 (4), 4–17.

Schau, H. J. and Muñiz, A. M., Jr. (2004). If you can't find it create it: An analysis of consumer engagement with Xena: Warrior Princess. In: Kahn, B. E. and Luce, M. F. (Eds.), *Advances in Consumer Research*, 31, Toronto: Association for Consumer Research, 545–547.

Scott, J. and Craig-Lees, M. (2010). Audience engagement and its effects on product placement recognition, *Journal of Promotion Management*, 16 (1/2), 39–58.

So, K., King, C., Sparks, B. and Wang, Y. (2014). The role of customer engagement in building consumer loyalty to tourism brands, *Journal of Travel Research*, DOI: 10.1177/0047287514541008.

Spencer, R. and Cova, B. (2012), Market solutions: Breaking free from dyad-centric logic and broadening the scope of the S-D logic. *Journal of Marketing Management*, 28 (13–14), 1571–1587.

Spiggle, S. (1994). Analysis and interpretation of qualitative data in consumer research. *Journal of Consumer Research*, 21 (3), 491–503.

Sprott, D., Czellar, S. and Spangenberg, E. (2009). The importance of a general measure of brand engagement on market behavior: Development and validation of a scale. *Journal of Marketing Research*, 46 (1), 92–104.

Strauss, A. and Corbin, J. (1990). *Basics of Qualitative Research: Grounded Theory Procedures and Techniques*. Beverly Hills, CA: Sage.

Strauss, A. and Corbin, J. (1998), *Basics of Qualitative Research*. Thousand Oaks, CA: Sage Publications.

Taylor, S. J. and Bogdan, R. (1984). *Introduction to Qualitative Research Methods: The Search for Meanings*. New York: John Wiley & Sons.

Thomsen, S. R., Straubhaar, J. D. and Bolyard, D. M. (1998). Ethnomethodology and the study of online communities: Exploring the cyber streets. *Information Research*, *4* (1), Available at: http://informationr.net/ir/4–1/paper50.html [Accessed 18 September 2012].

Van Doorn, J., Lemon, K. E., Mittal, V., Na , S., Pick, D., Pirner, P. and Verhoef, P. C. (2010). Customer engagement behavior: Theoretical foundations and research directions. *Journal of Service Research*, *13* (3), 253–266.

Vargo, S. and Lusch, R. (2004). Evolving to a new dominant logic for marketing. *Journal of Marketing*, *68* (1), 1–17.

Vargo, S. L. and Lusch, R. F. (2008). Service-dominant logic: Continuing the evolution. *Journal of the Academy of Marketing Science*, *36* (1), 1–10.

Verhoef, P. C., Reinartz, W. J. and Krafft, M. (2010). Customer engagement as a new perspective in customer management. *Journal of Service Research*, *13* (3), 247–252.

Verleye, K., Gemmel, P. and Rangarajan, D. (2013). Managing engagement behaviors in a network of customers and stakeholders: Evidence from the nursing home sector, *Journal of Service Research*, DOI: 10.1177/1094670513494015.

Vivek, S. D., Beatty, S. and Morgan, R. M. (2012). Customer engagement: Exploring customer relationships beyond purchase. *Journal of Marketing Theory & Practice*, *20* (2), 122–146.

Yap, K. and Sweeney, J. C. (2007). Zone-of-tolerance moderates the service quality-outcome relationship. *Journal of Services Marketing*, *21* (2), 137–148.

Yi, Y. and Gong, T. (2012), Customer value co-creation behaviour: Scale development and validation. *Journal of Business Research*, In Press, DOI: 10.1016/j.jbusres.2012.02.026.

Yun, G. W. and Trumbo, C. W. (2000). Comparative response to a survey executed by post, e-mail & web form. *Journal of Computer-Mediated Communication*, *6* (1), DOI: 10.1111/j.1083–6101.2000.tb00112.x; Available at: http://onlinelibrary.wiley.com.ezproxy.auckland.ac.nz/doi/10.1111/j.1083–6101.2000.tb00112.x/full [Accessed 2 November 2013].

Zeithaml, Valarie A. (1988). Consumer perceptions of price, quality, and value: A means-end model and synthesis of evidence, *Journal of Marketing*, 52 (3), 2–21.

Part II

Engagement, interactivity, social media and technology

5 Creating brand engagement on digital, social and mobile media

Edward C. Malthouse, Bobby J. Calder and Mark Vandenbosch

Introduction

As digital, social and mobile media platforms become more common, customer engagement is becoming increasingly important. Consumers are no longer limited to a passive role in their relationships with firms. They can easily create their own brand-relevant, user-generated content (UGC) and distribute it to large audiences. The possibility of this type of engagement is changing the way that firms interact with their customers (e.g. Malthouse et al., 2013). While most firms now react to UGC, especially when it is negative (e.g. Van Noort and Willemsen, 2012), companies increasingly have the opportunity to engage proactively with consumers.

It is sometimes assumed that digital, social, and mobile platforms foster engagement in and of themselves. That is, by their very nature these platforms are more interactive, so they must by this very fact increase engagement. However, such a view rests on an overly simplistic view of engagement.

There has been extensive work on defining engagement as an important new marketing construct that is not synonymous with the properties of any particular media platform (Brodie et al., 2011, 2013; Hollebeek, 2011a; Hollebeek, 2011b; Hollebeek et al., 2014). There is agreement that 'customer engagement (CE) is a *psychological state* that occurs by virtue of *interactive, cocreative experiences* with a *focal agent/object* (e.g. a brand) in focal service relationships . . . [and is a] dynamic, iterative process' (Brodie et al., 2011, p. 260). In other words, engagement should be thought of as the result of certain types of experiences with a brand, where some of these experiences may be designed for the express purpose of creating stronger engagement. But how does this process of creating engagement work if it is not simply a matter of exposing brands 'on' certain kinds of platforms?

This chapter deals with the process of creating engagement. Specifically, we hypothesise that engagement results from experiential contact points that prompt *cognitive elaboration* about how a brand helps consumers achieve *goals* in their lives. We provide the results of one natural experiment testing this hypothesis in detail and cite other work that tests it in different ways. We discuss how to harness this insight in digital, social and mobile environments and cite relevant examples from marketing practice.

Creating engagement through experiences connecting to goals or values

Our analysis of engagement expands on the framework proposed by Calder and Malthouse (2008, Figure 5.2) and Calder et al. (2009, Figure 5.1). Consistent with the Brodie et al.'s (2011) aforementioned definition, Calder and Malthouse think of engagement as being rooted in one or more experiences that reflect consumers' goals or values, and that engagement causes various consequences, such as product purchase and usage. It should thus be an understanding of experiences that shows the way to creating engagement. As Calder and Malthouse (2008) discuss, these experiences reflect the individual's interaction with the product over time as a way of accomplishing personal life goals or manifesting larger values. Isaac et al. (2015) extend this notion further by explicitly defining engagement as 'a multilevel, multidimensional construct that is reflected by the thoughts and feelings consumers have about one or more rich experiences involved in reaching a personal life goal or value'. Experiences are at the intersection of personal goals and values in consumers' lives and their connection to the brand in a way that adds value to the brand. A brand that connects with consumers' lives in this way will foster engagement and thus attract the customer's loyalty, prompting repurchase and use. As distinct from just the notion of an experiential brand, the architect of an engaging brand must understand and articulate how the brand contributes to specific goals or values.

The evaluation versus the design perspective

It is important to note that engagement can be approached from two useful perspectives. From one perspective, a marketer can measure how engaging a brand is at a point in time. A marketer could employ generic questions about experiences with a brand. For example, Brakus et al. (2009) suggested four dimensions of brand experience – sensory, affective, intellectual and behavioural. Hollebeek et al. (2014) measure cognitive (i.e. cognitive processing), emotional (i.e. affection) and behavioural (i.e. activation) dimensions of consumer brand engagement. The Calder-Malthouse approach employs direct measures of experiences based on potential consumer beliefs and feelings about the extent to which a brand links to a goal or value in a qualitatively meaningful way. Two examples of goal/values and associated measurement items are given next.

Utilitarian experience

It (brand) shows me how to do things the right way.
You learn to improve yourself from this (brand).
It (brand) helps me to make up my mind.
I learn a lot about things to do or places to go from this (brand).

Social experience

I often bring up things I have seen about this (brand) in conversations with other people.

I especially like to follow what other people post about this (brand).

I frequently send things or links to things regarding this (brand) on the web to friends and family.

These items are generally crafted to reflect the way some consumers might talk about their actual experiences with the specific brand in question.

Based on agree-disagree responses to assess scale items like these by Calder and Malthouse a second-order factor measurement model may be used. Overall, engagement is derived from a set of goal/value-relevant experiences as measured by the items associated with each particular experience. A number of studies provide evidence for the validity of this approach to evaluating engagement.

The design perspective

Apart from evaluating consumers' present level of engagement with a brand, a marketer may be more action-oriented. The concern is with designing some marketing activity that produces greater engagement with the brand. From this perspective, a marketer wants to design experiences that create engagement. Here engagement can be thought of more as an independent variable to be manipulated, rather than as an outcome variable to be measured.

The marketer wants to design activities in which consumers will experience the connection of the brand with a life goal or value. The objective is to have consumers actually or virtually *engage* with the brand in the pursuit of the goal or value. The experience is one of active goal pursuit. It is the engagement created by this pursuit that produces a stronger relationship with the brand.

To anticipate the sort of marketing activity used in the research reported later in this chapter, the marketer could, for example, design a contest using digital, social or mobile media. This contest could be one in which consumers describe how a brand is linked to some goal or value that is important in the their life. The contest is thus designed to create an activity in which the consumer incrementally *experiences* engagement with the brand.

Both the evaluation and the design perspective are consistent with the view that engagement flows from experiences that connect the consumer with a goal or value. With the design perspective, however, we are applying this theory as a guide to constructing the marketing activity. The intention is to have the consumer experience the brand in this special way.

The process of employing a marketing activity (i.e. activation) in this way can be diagrammed as in Figure 5.1 (Calder and Malthouse, 2003). From this

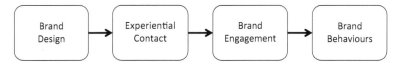

Figure 5.1 A process for creating engagement

perspective it is apparent how and why digital, social and mobile useful can be very powerful tools for producing engagement. The capability to have consumers involved in goal-relevant, user-generated content fits perfectly with this perspective.

As a footnote to this discussion, we point out that the design perspective clarifies a common point of confusion about engagement. Engagement is often confused with the act of consuming the brand. Engagement is often defined to include terms such as paying more attention to the brand, or 'leaning forward', or undertaking search behaviours. However, these should be regarded as potential *consequences* of engagement. Engagement itself stems from experiences in which the brand is actually or virtually connected with a goal/value. Marketers should focus on designing these experiences, experiences that, in turn, produce positive changes in brand behaviours, where these behaviours may *reflect* an increase in engagement.

Two example activities from marketing practice

The marketing task becomes one of designing experiences in which the consumer makes the connection between a particular life goal and a focal brand. As noted, digital, social and mobile media are especially well-suited to design interactive, co-creative experiences. They enable customers to actively make, and cognitively elaborate on, the connection of the brand to a particular life goal. In effect, customers actively elaborate on, or think through, their relationship with the brand. Such elaboration is known to have powerful effects on the formation of attitudes (e.g. Petty and Cacioppo, 1986). Again, the act of elaborating reinforces the role of the brand experience in connecting to goals/values and thereby produces a greater sense of engagement.

We again emphasise the importance of the intersection of brand and life goals/values in an actual experience. A contact point could simply ask consumers to elaborate on the positives of a brand, but this would not produce engagement as defined here. There must be an experience that leads to an active connection of the brand to a life goal/value.

Kit Kat example of engagement activation

We begin with a practical example to make these ideas more concrete. To illustrate the process of creating engagement by designing brand-life goal connection experiences, we consider some examples from the Kit Kat candy bar's use of Facebook. We contrast two actual Kit Kat promotions. The first promotion was called the Fan of the Month. Customer were invited to post a picture of themselves taking a break with Kit Kat, or comment on, like or share other pictures. For example, a fan named Robin posted a picture (Figure 5.2) of her eating a Kit Kat on top of a mountain she had just climbed. This is a perfect example of the intersection. The Kit Kat brand has long associated itself with the event of taking a break. Inviting customers to post pictures causes elaboration in that the customers must think about the benefit of having a Kit Kat when they need it most. Robin has customised the Kit Kat benefit – for her it provides much-needed energy after an arduous climb. The picture reminds her and others of the value of taking a break with Kit Kat.

The second promotion, called the Game Time Give Away, invited Kit Kat customers to give their email address on Facebook in order to win an NFL beverage pail, t-shirt, pen or other NFL merchandise. It is easy to find other examples of such promotions, where customers get something in return for giving their contact information. Such promotions may be an effective way of gathering names to build a database of customers and may produce benefits by associating Kit Kat with the NFL brand, but we argue that it is ineffective at creating engagement. The act of providing an email address itself does not cause the consumer to make and elaborate on a connection between the brand and a life goal.

Figure 5.2 Kit Kat example using social media contests

Mein burger example of engagement activation

As a second example, consider a marketing program from McDonald's designed to engage German customers. The McDonald's 'Burger Battle' invited customers to design their own sandwich. An interactive website provides consumers with a set of possible ingredients that can be dragged onto a canvas to create a new sandwich. The consumer names the creation, shares it on social media and encourages friends to vote for it. Those with the most votes are made in test kitchens and evaluated by juries, and the finalists are made and sold in McDonald's stores in Germany for a period of time. This is a clear example of co-creation, where consumers contribute to the design of the product and participate in the creation of value, but consider the contest from the perspective of personal goals. One can imagine a German consumer being attracted to certain aspects of the McDonald's brand such as the convenience, speed and image, but not like the food itself. This contest asks consumers to elaborate on how the food offerings could be made more palatable to them. For example, one finalist was the *McBrezel* ('McPretzel'), featuring *leberkäse* ('liver cheese'), a kind of Bavarian meatloaf that is close to the heart of Germans. Participation also facilitates social interaction, since consumers must get their friends to vote for their sandwich.

Testing the goal-elaboration hypothesis

Our central hypothesis is that cognitive elaboration about how a brand helps consumers achieve goal(s) in their lives will create engagement and thus affect purchase behaviour. We test this hypothesis with data from the Air Miles Reward Program (AMRP), which has been operating in Canada since 1992, and is not affiliated with Air Canada or any other airline. As a coalition loyalty program, members collect miles from over 100 sponsors spanning nearly all purchase categories, including groceries, gasoline, apparel and credit card purchases. Members collect 'miles' by swiping their AMRP card at the time of purchase. Sponsors compensate AMRP on the basis of the number of miles issued to members, so mile accumulation by members is proportional to AMRP's revenue. Collected miles can be exchanged for rewards such as travel (e.g., airline tickets, hotels), merchandise (e.g. toasters, blenders) and gift cards (e.g. gas, movies, groceries, home improvement). AMRP pays for the reward.

Activity on AMRP's social media page

AMRP maintained a social media website for members to discuss the program and its benefits, which they discontinued in 2013. Posts made by members can be linked to their mile accumulation, which is proportional to spending. Thus, this data set provides a unique opportunity to measure the effect of participation in social media forums on actual purchase behaviours with the brand. Figure 5.3

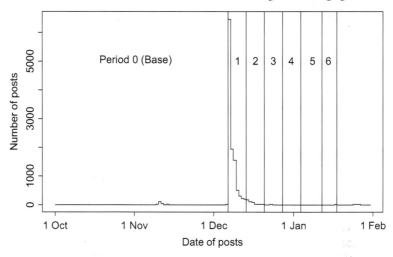

Figure 5.3 Number of posts to the AMRP social media

shows a histogram of the number of posts to the AMRP social media site from 1 October 2010 through 17 January 2011. Posting to the site is sporadic, with few posts on most days – the median number of posts per day for the date range (1 Oct –17 Jan) is only 6. There are, however, large spikes in activity. The maximum number of posts on a single day was 6,455, which occurred on 7 December 2010 and was caused by an email sent on that day announcing what we call the *winter contest*.

The winter contest invited members to 'simply share with us what rewards you are redeeming for this winter season and we'll give you 10 bonus reward miles'. The contest specifically asks respondents to specify and elaborate on a personal goal. There was a limit of one reward per customer ID, and the offer was valid until 20 December 2010. Out of 11,740 total posts between 7–20 December, 9,911 were in response to the winter contest. These posts were made by 7,089 unique customer ID values that could be matched with the transaction history, with 82 per cent posting only one time.

We study the effects of the winter contest on mile accumulation during the six-week period from 7 December 2010–17 January 2011. AMRP did not have any other UGC contests during this period, nor in the two-month period before the contest, which reduces the risks of confounds. Figure 5.3 shows that there was little activity on the site except for the winter contest. We study the effects separately on each of the six week-long periods, indexed by t, after the email. This will enable us to assess the immediate effect (e.g. week $t = 1$) as well as longer-term effects during subsequent weeks. The period 1 Jan–6 December 2010 is the *pre-period* ($t = 0$), used to establish a baseline measure of mile accumulation per week and account for customer heterogeneity.

Responses to the winter contest varied in length. Some wrote one or two words, e.g., 'blender' or 'digital camera'. One poster even wrote that he wanted 'a new wife'. Others wrote several sentences explaining why they wanted a particular reward, for example, 'haven't seen my mother in several years and I want to get a ticket to visit her on her 80th birthday'. Summing words across posts, the average number of words written by each participant was 17.2 and the quartiles were 8, 13 and 21 words.

Variable operationalisation and study design

AMRP provided the mile accumulation history for 141,308 members, which included all promotion participants, a random sample of non-participants who had received the email advertising the promotion, and a random sample of non-participants who had received no information on the promotion. The vertical lines in Figure 5.3 demarcate seven *study periods*. For each member i, we obtained the average number of miles per week accumulated during the pre-period ($t = 0$) and each of the six post-email periods ($t = 1, . . ., 6$). The number of miles accumulated is labelled y_{it}. Note that Christmas occurs during week 3 and New Year Eve during week 4. A total of 279,016 people who received the email opened it. Elaboration is measured by the number of words written by a member.

Matching with propensity scoring models to control for selection bias

To evaluate the effects of entering the social media contest, we have before-after-with-control-group quasi-experimental designs. Pre-measures (miles per week) account for heterogeneity across customers, and the control group accounts for confounds in the future periods such as history. While this design is robust to most threats to internal validity, a potential problem with it is that members self-select into participating in the contest. It turns out that those who elect to enter (treatment group) have systematically higher levels of log mile accumulation during the pre-period than those who do not (control group). It is not surprising that customers with higher purchase activity are more likely to engage on AMRP's social media site. Having a design with pre-measures of mile accumulation addresses this selection bias to some extent, but the design can be strengthened further through matching with propensity scoring models.

The goal is to identify a comparable control group that is as similar as possible to the treatment group as of the time of the contest. Propensity scoring models achieve this by predicting whether or not a member is in the treatment group from relevant member measures known at the time of the contest using logistic regression. The predicted probabilities of those in the treatment group are then matched with those not treated to identify a 'twin'. Details of our propensity scoring model can be found in Malthouse et al. (2015). We used a wide variety of variables from the pre-period including the level of spending at different types of sponsors and the number of rewards earned.

Results

For each of the six future time periods, we regress y_t ($t = 1, \ldots, 6$) on a dummy variable indicating whether or not the member entered the contest, elaboration measured by the total number of words written (0 for those who did not enter), and the total pre-period miles to control for customer heterogeneity. We estimate the following multiplicative model with least squares using the 7,089 who entered into the contest and their matched controls, selected from the 37,350 who opened the email but did not participate, for a total sample size of 14,178. Our model is:

$$\log (y_t + 1) = \beta_0 + \beta_1 \log (y_0 + 1) + \beta_2 \text{ enter} + \beta_3 \log (\text{wc} + 1)$$

The first term controls for pre-period miles, enter is a dummy indicating whether the member entered into the contest, and wc is the word count, which measures the level of cognitive elaboration. All mile variables are highly right skewed with outliers and the log transformation stabilises the variance to address homoscedasticity (for $t = 1, \ldots, 6$), symmetrises the distributions and reduces the influence of extreme observations.

Table 5.1 provides the regression estimates for the six time periods. First consider the 'Full model', with three predictors in it. Miles in the pre-period is a strong predictor of miles in the subsequent periods. The elaboration effects are statistically significant ($P < .05$) in weeks 1, 2, 3 and 5, and nearly significant in period 6 ($t = 1.86$, $P = .063$). The slope estimates for elaboration are plotted with 95 per cent confidence intervals in Figure 5.4. The plot shows that elaboration has a consistent, long-term, positive effect on future behaviour after controlling for pre-period miles, although there is a drop in week 4. The elaboration effect seems to reduce in week 6. Our explanation for the non-significant effect and small drop in the effect for week 4 is that it was after Christmas and includes New Year's Eve. This holiday period is systematically different from the rest of the year, where Canadians are not following their usual routine. Thus, the goal-elaboration hypothesis is supported, except possibly during the New Year Eve period.

The second column gives the variance inflation factors, VIFs. For pre-period miles VIF is approximately 1, indicating that it is nearly unrelated to the treatment variable 'enter' and elaboration. This is a consequence of the matching and suggests that pre-period miles will not confound the treatment variables. Entering into the promotion and elaboration have VIF ≈ 7.2, indicating the variables are highly confounded, which is due to those not entering all having a word count of zero. Without accounting for elaboration, the effect of entering will be overstated (omitted-variable bias). We, therefore, present the results both with elaboration ('full model') and without elaboration ('reduced model'). The effects for

Table 5.1 Regression estimates for entry model

	Variance Inflation Factor	1 7–13 Dec	2 14–20 Dec	3 21–27 Dec	4 28 Dec–3 Jan	5 4–11 Jan	6 12–19 Jan
Full model (3 predictors, n = 14,178)							
Intercept		0.24***	−0.28***	−0.27***	−0.21***	0.37***	0.41***
Log (pre miles + 1)	1.01	0.78***	0.85***	0.76***	0.62***	0.758***	0.79***
Enter	7.25	0.04	−0.18*	−0.14	−0.01	−0.13+	−0.10+
Log (wc + 1)	7.25	0.08**	0.09***	0.071*	0.04	0.07*	0.05*
Reduced model (2 predictors, without word count)							
Intercept		0.25***	−0.29***	−0.27***	−0.22***	0.37***	0.41***
Log (pre miles + 1)	1.00	0.78***	0.85***	0.76***	0.62***	0.75***	0.79***
Enter	1.00	0.24***	0.06*	0.05+	0.08**	0.04	−0.03

Note

*** means $P < .001$, ** $P < .01$, * $P < .05$ and + $P < .1$

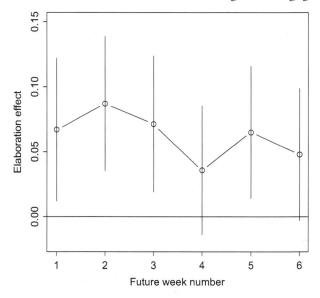

Figure 5.4 Elaboration effect over time with 95 per cent confidence bands

the models are different. If we do not account for elaboration (Reduced model), there is a large initial 28 per cent increase during the first week ($e^{0.243} = 1.28$, $P < .001$), a substantially smaller, yet significant, effect in weeks 2–4, and insignificant effects during weeks 5–6. If we control for elaboration (full), the effects of entering into the promotion vanish: elaboration is what drives the future increase in purchase behaviour, not mere entry. Our hypothesis is confirmed.

Implications

Engagement through mobile devices

Having confirmed the goal-elaboration hypothesis, we now discuss applications in other digital environments. Mobile devices provide unique opportunities and challenges for organisations to engage with their customers because customers tend to have their devices with them all the time, providing ubiquitous access to the Internet from anywhere and at any time. Consumers compulsively check their devices for a variety of reasons such as reading emails, keeping up with posts on Facebook or Twitter, reading the news and shopping. They also use their devices for entertainment such as listening to music, watching videos or playing games. Brands would like for customers to have the same compulsive desire to interact with it as they do to interact with their friends and media. We consider the question of how mobile devices can be used to engage customers to increase loyalty, and cite empirical evidence in support of our claims.

Mobile devices are commonly used to deliver ads, but forcing ads on consumers who do not want to see them will not create engagement (although it probably has the similar effects as traditional, out-bound TV or print advertising). Our contention is that engagement contact points create experiences that prompt cognitive elaboration at the intersection of personal goals and the brand. If a brand is to create such experiences with mobile media, it should first consider how the mobile contact points will create value for customers and which goals it will help achieve.

Much research has been done over the past 50 years to understand experiences with media in general. Uses and gratification (U&G) theory suggests that consumers achieve four general types of goals (gratifications) from media consumption: *utilitarian, identity expression, social* and *hedonic* (e.g. McQuail, 1987, pp. 82–83). The Calder-Malthouse media experience studies break these general areas out into more specific types of experiences (e.g., hedonic) and provide measurement scales (e.g. Malthouse et al., 2007; Calder et al., 2009; Calder and Malthouse, 2008).

It is easy to find examples of mobile applications that successfully create engagement by helping consumers achieve these goals. For example, consider check-in apps such as Foursquare, which allow consumers to check in at locations and post short comments. To see how such apps create engagement we must understand how they contribute to personal goals. By declaring to the world that someone is at a certain restaurant or store, the customer may be expressing his/her *identity* (e.g. see Peck and Malthouse, 2011, ch. 7). Consumers are consciously associating themselves with some brand. A consumer who checks in at an independent microbrew pub wants the world to know that he shares the values of the pub. The consumer may also satisfy *social* goals (Peck and Malthouse, 2011, ch. 14), either by attracting friends in the vicinity to stop by, or by having an online discussion about what unusual toppings to get on the pizzas served at the pub or which beers go best with which dishes.

Many apps focus on satisfying utilitarian goals (e.g. see Peck and Malthouse, 2011, ch. 5) such as providing information. A canonical example of a utilitarian app is a transit tracker that gives the arrival times of buses and trains, and offers advice on the route that minimises travel times between a starting point and destination. Airline apps give departure and arrival information, allow customers to manage bookings and seat assignments, and provide information about frequent flyer status. The USAA insurance company for military personnel offers an app that facilitates banking interactions for servicemen stationed abroad, such as the ability to scan a check for deposit. The outdoor recreation retailer REI offers a snow report app for skiers. Kraft Foods offers the iFood Assistant app giving access to a recipe database with meal solutions. Other utilitarian goals that can be satisfied in mobile media include learning the hours of a restaurant or store, making a reservation at a restaurant, or determining whether some item is in stock at some store location.

Although consumers spend a large fraction of their time on mobile devices with hedonic apps such as games, video, music and news, it is more difficult to find examples where companies create hedonic experiences for consumers. One widely cited example is the Audi A4 Driving Challenge, which allows iPhone users to steer an A4 sedan through progressively more challenging driving courses. The app uses the iPhone's accelerometer for steering. This videogame app creates a hedonic experience for consumers, while also giving them a virtual experience with the product.

It is important to note that creating mobile engagement often involves a third party. Sometimes a company will create its own branded app and customers will download and use it (e.g. an airline app, Kraft's iFood, REI's snow finder), but customers will frequently engage with the focal brand on a third-party website, such as FourSquare, websites that feature reviews (e.g. Amazon or other retailers), other review sites (e.g. Yelp), search engines (e.g. Google collects information such as store hours) or mapping sites (e.g. Google maps, Bing, MapQuest). We now summarise two studies that relate mobile engagement to subsequent purchase behaviours.

Airmiles app

AMRP, previously discussed with the elaboration study, launched a mobile app. Members can check in at sponsor locations, track their mile balance and browse rewards. The app can satisfy the utilitarian, identity expressing and social goals previously discussed. Additionally, it is intended to gamify the point-collection process. Just as Fitbit users frequently monitor their steps toward a daily fitness goal, members are able to monitor their progress toward a reward goal.

The effects of this app have been examined by the conference paper Kim et al. (2015) and the full-length paper Viswanathan et al. (2015). The analyses shows that after members adopt the mobile app their purchases increase over matched controls who elected not adopt the app. Moreover, future spending has a positive association with the frequency of check-ins and logins, which can be considered indicators of elaboration.

Grocery delivery service shopping app

Wang et al. (2015) examine the effects of a mobile app launched by an Internet grocery service. In the past, the company sold groceries exclusively on their website, and delivered orders with their private fleet of trucks. Several years ago it launched a shopping app that customers could use to compose, modify and place orders. Previous discussions of engagement have not included shopping environments, and one may question whether shopping can be part of engagement. As an aside, there are many examples of contact points that exist in a grey area between the customer engagement behaviours (CEBs; Van Doorn et al., 2010 and purchase, such as an auto manufacturer's website that allows a consumer to design and customise a car, and then share it with friends on Facebook. This would clearly be a CEB if the customer has no intention of purchasing the car, creating hedonic, identity expressing and social experiences.

The customer is participating in co-creation by configuring the options of the car and promoting it on Facebook. But if the customer actually orders the car then it is also shopping. We argue that the process of shopping can be an example of engagement if it is creating experiences.

This app is designed to create a hassle-free shopping experience. When a customer notices that she needs (more of) some product, she can immediately add it to an order using the mobile device from anywhere. This is meant to be an improvement over the traditional shopping list written on paper, which may not be with the shopper when she notices the need, and is more likely to be misplaced than a smartphone. The app contributes to a personal goal and builds on the brand's intended use.

Using similar matching methods as the elaboration study, Wang et al. (2015) reach several conclusions. First, the order rate (number of orders per year) increases after customers adopt the app, especially for low-spending customers. The average order amount also increases for low-spending customers. Thus, such an app is an effective way to increase the profitability of weaker customers, a universal objective of firms.

Their second finding is that customers do not use the mobile device equally for all products: the app is used more for habitual purchases that they already have a history of purchasing. They explain this finding with screen size. It is more difficult to navigate and study items on a mobile screen than on a PC, lending itself to adding products with which the consumer is already familiar to the order rather than those requiring more consideration. Typing is more difficult without a keyboard (speech recognition programs, such as iPhone's Siri address this issue, but are not perfectly accurate at the present time). A shopper using a PC can have multiple windows open, comparing the features of products, reading reviews and comparing prices. These tasks are more cumbersome on a mobile phone.

A third finding from this study is that the number of shopping channels used by the customer is positively associated with customer value. While the direction of causality is questionable (do better customers use multiple channels, or does using multiple channels cause a customer to be better?), this suggests that increasing the number of engagement channels will improve customer value.

Wearable devices and the future

There is currently excitement around wearable devices such as the Apple watch and Microsoft's Band. Much of the discussion centres on potential fitness applications: such devices track the level of physical activity and monitor physiological variables (e.g. heart rate). These data track progress toward personal fitness goals and can motivate their users to complete their daily regime. They can also be shared on social media with a network of friends who may join in celebration when goals are achieved, or cajole them into action when they lag behind. Similar monitoring and peer networks are used in helping diabetes patients (e.g. Greene et al. 2011). The challenge for marketers is to create contact points that exploit the same goal-oriented engagement dynamics as those around health and fitness.

Engagement through content

An emerging way for brands to communicate with their customers is through *owned media* that contains *content*. This is in direct contrast to traditional advertising approaches that use *paid media* to deliver overt *ad messages,* where the brand would pay some media vehicle for access to its audience, such as the viewers of a TV program or readers of a magazine. With content marketing, the brand creates its own media property and attracts an audience by providing content that is of value to its consumers. One of the reasons for this trend of moving to content is that it's thought to be a highly effective way of creating engagement. As such, it involves the same issues in connecting brands to life goals.

For example, consider the website of a computer company such as Microsoft. The web designers should not think of the website as a media vehicle to carry ad messages, because a large fraction of visitors are not visiting the website to be exposed to ad messages. Although some visitors will come for information about products and purchase them, others will visit for more utilitarian reasons such as advice on getting the most out of products they have already purchased, tutorials for learning new applications and technical support. Such utilitarian content has been a staple component of computer magazines for decades, but in this case it is being created by a computer company rather than a by a journalism organisation. Clearly such a contact point is well-suited to produce the 'interactive, cocreative customer experiences', especially when consumers contribute to discussions about the products, write solutions to problems raised in discussion forums, and distribute scripts and macros for others to use.

Our focus is on creating engagement in digital environments, but the goal-oriented engagement content is often delivered across multiple media channels including non-digital ones such as print. In particular, the definition of a magazine has evolved from being a paper product with staples and ink to that of an idea that is manifested across different media channels (e.g. see Peck and Malthouse, 2011, ch. 16). Relevant examples are *Asda Magazine* and *Tesco Magazine* from the UK supermarket chains Asda and Tesco.

The print manifestations of the magazines have the second and third largest circulations among all magazines in the UK, and offer digital, social and mobile touch points such as how-to videos and blogs. The @TescoLiving Twitter account has more than 41,000 followers, and both are active on Facebook, Pinterest, Instagram and other social media platforms. Likewise, *Costco Connection,* from the discount warehouse store Costco, has the third largest circulation in the US. As mentioned earlier, consumer package good manufacturers such as Kraft are also creating content to engage with their customers; Kraft's *What's Cooking* is the most circulated magazine in Canada, and complements their 'iFood

Assistant' app, how-to videos on their website and 'Tips & Ideas' page with consumer comments.

These examples illustrate how a brand can create engagement through content showing how the brand can help consumers achieve personal goals. Goals could be getting some software program to do a particular task in the case of Microsoft, or finding recipe suggestions in the case of Kraft, Asda and Tesco. The brands clearly have something to offer towards such personal goals.

Conclusion

The studies we have presented all support the view that experiences that cause consumers to reflect and elaborate on the connection between a brand and life goals will increase engagement and therefore purchase behaviour. Engagement is created through this process. Engagement is not produced by simply being 'on' a certain kind of media, digital, social, mobile or otherwise. Marketers must design specific experiences using these media to make the brand-life goal(s) connection and elaborate on it.

References

Brodie, R. J., Hollebeek, L. D., Juric, B., and Ilic, A. (2011). Customer engagement: conceptual domain, fundamental propositions, and implications for research. *Journal of Service Research*, *14*(3), 252–271.

Brodie, R. J., Ilic, A., Juric, B., and Hollebeek, L. (2013). Consumer engagement in a virtual brand community: An exploratory analysis. *Journal of Business Research*, *66*(1), 105–114.

Brakus, J. J., Schmitt, B. H. and Zarantonello, L. (2009). Brand experience: What is it? How is it measured? Does it affect loyalty? *Journal of Marketing*, *73*(3), 52–68.

Calder, B. J. and Malthouse, E. (2003). What is integrated marketing? In Iacobucci, D. and Calder, B. (Ed.), *Kellogg on integrated marketing*. Wiley.

Calder, B. J., and Malthouse, E. C. (2008). Media engagement and advertising effectiveness. In Calder, B. (Ed.), *Kellogg on advertising and media*, 1–36. Wiley.

Calder, B. J., Malthouse, E. C., and Schaedel, U. (2009). An experimental study of the relationship between online engagement and advertising effectiveness. *Journal of Interactive Marketing*, *23*(4), 321–331.

Greene, J. A., Choudhry, N. K., Kilabuk, E., Shrank, W. H. (2011). Online social networking by patients with diabetes: a qualitative evaluation of communication with Facebook. *Journal of General Internal Medicine*, 26, 287–292.

Hollebeek, L. D. (2011a). Demystifying customer brand engagement: Exploring the loyalty nexus. *Journal of Marketing Management*, *27*(7–8), 785–807.

Hollebeek, L. (2011b). Exploring customer brand engagement: definition and themes. *Journal of Strategic Marketing*, *19*(7), 555–573.

Hollebeek, L. D., Glynn, M. S., and Brodie, R. J. (2014). Consumer brand engagement in social media: Conceptualization, scale development and validation. *Journal of Interactive Marketing*, *28*(2), 149–165.

Isaac, M., Calder, B. J. and Malthouse, E. C. (2015). Capturing consumer experiences: A context-specific approach to measuring engagement. *Journal of Advertising Research*, Forthcoming. Available at SSRN: http://dx.doi.org/10.2139/ssrn.2608149

Kim, S. J., Wang, R. J. H., and Malthouse, E. C. (2015). The effects of adopting and using a brand's mobile application on consumers subsequent purchase behaviors. *Journal of Interactive Marketing*, 31, 28–41.

Malthouse, E. C., Haenlein, M., Skiera, B., Wege, E., and Zhang, M. (2013). Managing customer relationships in the social media era: introducing the social CRM house. *Journal of Interactive Marketing*, *27*(4), 270–280.

Malthouse, E. C., Calder, B. J., and Tamhane, A. (2007). The effects of media context experiences on advertising effectiveness. *Journal of Advertising*, *36*(3), 7–18.

Malthouse, E. C., Vandenbosch, M., Calder, B. and Kim, S. J. (2015). The New Strategic Role of Promotions Using Digital Media. Working paper, Spiegel Research Center, Northwestern University.

McQuail, D. (1987). *Mass communication theory: An introduction*. Sage Publications, Inc.

Peck, A., and Malthouse, E. C. (Eds.). (2011). *Medill on media engagement*. Hampton Press.

Petty, R. E., and Cacioppo, J. T. (1986). The elaboration likelihood model of persuasion. *Advances in experimental social psychology*, 19, 123–205.

Van Doorn, J., Lemon, K. N., Mittal, V., Nass, S., Pick, D., Pirner, P., and Verhoef, P. C. (2010). Customer engagement behavior: Theoretical foundations and research directions. *Journal of Service Research*, *13*(3), 253–266.

Van Noort, G., and Willemsen, L. M. (2012). Online damage control: The effects of proactive versus reactive webcare interventions in consumer-generated and brand-generated platforms. *Journal of Interactive Marketing*, *26*(3), 131–140.

Visvanathan, V., Hollebeek, L., Maslowska, E., Malthouse, E., Kim, S. J., and Xie, W. (2015). The Dynamic Inter-Relationship between Customer Engagement with Mobile Apps and Ensuing Marketplace Behaviors. Working paper.

Wang, R.J.H., Malthouse, E. C., and Krishnamurthi, L. (2015). On the Go: How Mobile Shopping Affects Customer Purchase Behavior. *Journal of Retailing* *91*(2), 271–234.

6 Social media engagement

A construct of positively and negatively valenced engagement behaviours

Rebecca Dolan, Jodie Conduit and John Fahy

Introduction

The advent of social media has changed the way customers and organisations interact. Customers have transformed from passive recipients of marketing content, to active participants in the brand message. While the traditional marketing communications paradigm is characterised by a high degree of managerial control and one-way brand messages, customer interactions with the brand and with each other through social media results in brand-related dialogues regarding which managers have little direct control in terms of the content, timing and frequency (Mangold and Faulds, 2009). Social media sites provide an ideal platform for brand-related advocacy (Chu and Kim, 2011; Riegner, 2007), customer-led content generation (Vivek, Beatty, and Morgan, 2012), and customer-to-customer interaction (Heller Baird and Parasnis, 2011). Organisations are increasingly recognising and utilising this opportunity, with more than 15 million brands registered with the social media site Facebook (Koetsier, 2013) As businesses seek to communicate with customers through the social medium more effectively, it offers a significant research area for scholars to better anticipate and understand consumer engagement in online social groups and subsequent brand-related behaviours (Pagani, Hofacker, and Goldsmith, 2011; Pelling and White, 2009). This chapter seeks to provide a deeper understanding of the engagement behaviours customers exhibit on social media, through the identification and explanation of different types of engagement behaviour in this forum.

Whilst there is no consensus on a definition of customer engagement, general agreement exists that it emerges from specific interactive experiences (Brodie, Hollebeek, Jurić, and Ilić, 2011). Extant literature focuses on understanding the dimensions and characteristics of engagement (van Doorn, Lemon, Mittal, Nass, Pick, Pirner and Verhoef, 2010), and there is an increasing interest in context-specific manifestations of customer engagement, specifically in the social media environment (Gummerus, Liljander, Weman, and Pihlström, 2012; Hollebeek and Chen, 2014; Hollebeek, Glynn, and Brodie, 2014). To date, conceptual explanations of customer engagement have focused heavily on delineating the dimensions of engagement (Brodie et al., 2011) and investigating its antecedents and consequences (Gambetti, Graffigna, and Biraghi, 2012; Nambisan and Baron, 2007; Van Doorn et al., 2010). Whilst authors have discussed valence, form/modality, scope, nature of impact, customer goals and intensity (Hollebeek, and Chen, 2014; Van Doorn et al., 2010), a cohesive construct that specifically examines the valence, different forms and intensity of engagement behaviour within social media remains undeveloped.

To further understand the dynamic nature of customer engagement in online and offline environments (Brodie, Ilic, and Hollebeek, 2013; Hollebeek, 2011; Jaakkola and Alexander, 2014; Vivek et al., 2012), this chapter extends our understanding of engagement behaviour, and provides an appreciation of the nature, valence and intensity of specific social media engagement behaviours (Brodie et al., 2011). Our examination takes a 'user,' rather than 'customer' perspective and captures the engagement behaviours of all active and passive followers of a brand on social media, including customers, non-paying customers and non-brand users that interact with the brand's social media presence. The development of the social media engagement behaviour construct provides clarity to managers and engagement researchers who wish to further understand how social media users behaviourally engage with brands. .

This chapter puts forth a social media engagement behaviour construct that identifies and explicates the different types of engagement behaviours that users exhibit in social media platforms. It demonstrates that social media engagement behaviour consists of six distinct types: *creating, contributing, consuming, dormancy, detaching and destructing*. Further, we draw from existing literature and discuss several forms of creating engagement behaviours, including *knowledge seeking, sharing experiences, co-developing, socialising and advocating* (Brodie et al., 2013) and *affirming* to identify specific creative engagement behaviours. The construct recognises the various intensities at which social media engagement behaviour may manifest. While *creating, contributing* and *destructing* represent active engagement behaviours that potentially impact on other social media users, *consuming, dormancy* and *detaching* are more passive and/or individualised forms of engagement. The construct also highlights the critical role of negatively valenced engagement behaviour within social media platforms. The majority of research conducted on the engagement concept in marketing has focused on positively valenced expressions of customer engagement, failing to recognise and incorporate negatively valenced expressions. The identification and understanding of negatively valenced engagement behaviour adds to a more cohesive understanding of engagement behaviour, as called for by Hollebeek and Chen (2014). We show that negatively valenced engagement behaviours exist within social media at two levels: *detachment* and *destruction*. Awareness of both positively valenced and negatively valenced engagement behaviours amongst social media users is critical for managers, who must develop procedures by which to facilitate positively valenced, and mitigate negatively valenced behaviours within social media forums.

Jointly, these insights demonstrate the importance of exploring the levels and valence of engagement behaviour in social media, such as Facebook, Twitter,

Instagram and YouTube. This chapter is structured as follows. The next section provides an introduction to the area of engagement behaviour from the marketing literature, of which social media engagement behaviour is a subset. This is followed by the presentation of a new perspective on social media engagement behaviour. We provide a detailed exploration of six social media engagement behaviour types: creating, contributing, consuming, dormancy, detaching and destructing. Finally, we discuss the ensuing managerial and scholarly implications of the typology.

Social media engagement behaviour

Overview

Customer engagement is interactive and context-dependent in nature (Brodie et al., 2011; Calder, Malthouse, and Schaedel, 2009; Gummerus et al., 2012). To comprehensively understand customer engagement, examination of specific focal objects of engagement is required. For example, focal objects of customer engagement include product or service offerings (Brodie et al., 2011), media (Calder et al., 2009) and activities and events (Vivek et al., 2012). While customers engage with a firm or brand through the multiple touch-points and service encounters, constituting the entire brand experience, there is little research that examines engagement with a specific focal object. In this chapter we focus on one particular type of touch-point: social media. Our examination of engagement behaviour focuses on a singular focal object of engagement (i.e. social media), and therefore does not reflect customer brand engagement in its entirety. Our examination within this context-specific environment will provide greater insight into the behavioural manifestations of engagement within social media platforms, as we seek to understand the nature of engagement at different intensities and with different valence (Brodie et al., 2011; Vivek et al., 2012).

A range of customer engagement definitions have emerged in recent years (see Brodie et al, 2011, Vivek et al., 2014), commonly including a three-dimensional perspective of engagement, including cognitive, affective and behavioural components (Brodie et al., 2013). In this chapter, we focus on the examination of the behavioural manifestation of engagement, consistent with previous studies of engagement and social media (e.g. Gummerus et al., 2012; Van Doorn et al., 2010). Customer engagement behaviour, defined as 'a customer's behavioural manifestations that have a brand or firm focus, beyond purchase' (Van Doorn et al., 2010, p. 254) has been described as the ultimate tool in measuring engagement within social media platforms (Park, Kee, and Valenzuela, 2009; Raacke and Bonds-Raacke, 2008; Van Doorn et al., 2010). Firms develop brand-related social media sites with the express purpose of engaging their consumers (Gensler, Völckner, Liu-Thompkins, and Wiertz, 2013) and with behavioural engagement measures, the nature of this engagement can be monitored and evaluated. However, as yet, no meaningful frameworks have been developed to assist managers in understanding the various types of behavioural engagement that occur.

The proliferation of social media platforms and corresponding consumer adoption in recent years has precipitated a paradigm shift, significantly altering the ways customers behave and engage with brands. The social media paradigm allows for interactive and dynamic communications between customers and brands, and among users of a brand's social media forum. The social media environment offers users a touch-point through which they can actively and behaviourally engage with brands through reading, commenting, reviewing and sharing information online (Calder et al., 2009). Further, social media engagement behaviours can be positive or negative in nature and can be targeted at a wide audience, including the brand, other customers, users and the general public (Van Doorn et al., 2010).

Intensity and valence of engagement

Customers engage with focal brands and brand related content within social media platforms (Chu, 2011; Chung and Austria, 2010; Hollebeek et al., 2014). Traditional user categorisations distinguish between users who create content such as 'posters', compared to those who are members of a community but do not post, referred to as 'lurkers' (Nonnecke and Preece, 1999; Preece, Nonnecke, and Andrews, 2004). This basic categorisation of online users is limited in its general nature and fails to take into account the diverse number of possible roles available to users in dynamic platforms. Previous research categorised social media users who 'like' brands on Facebook into groups based on their brand loyalty, brand love, use of self-expressive brands and word of mouth (Wallace, Buil, De Chernatony, and Hogan, 2014). In an attempt to define customer engagement levels within social media, scholars have also characterised engagement behaviours on a continuum of low to high activity (Muntinga, Moorman, and Smit, 2011). Muntinga and colleagues (2011) argued users with low intensity levels of engagement were epitomised as *consuming* content, medium levels of engagement behaviour were characterised by *contributing* to content and the most active and intense levels of engagement behaviour were represented by *creating* content. Additionally, practice-oriented research focuses on the practices related to brand communities (Schau, Muñiz, and Arnould, 2009) and finds that value is created through participation in online communities as a result of activities, such as welcoming, empathizing and governing. However, these approaches to conceptualising engagement behaviour lack a detailed exploration of the different intensity and valence of activities that customers engage in.

The social media engagement behaviour construct outlined in this chapter proposes six distinct types of behaviour that epitomise a hierarchy of social media engagement and reflect the positively or negatively valenced nature of the behaviour. The construct incorporates lower intensity and more passive engagement behaviours, such as dormancy and consumption. Additionally, it recognises more active engagement behaviours with a moderate intensity: detachment and contribution. Finally, the construct demonstrates the occurrence of highly active engagement behaviour, such as creation and destruction. Whilst recognising the different forms of social media engagement behaviour, the construct also reflects the valence of behaviours. Table 6.1 outlines each of types of social media engagement behaviour, with their respective definitions and examples.

Table 6.1 Positively and negatively valenced social media engagement behaviours

	Definition	*Examples*
Creating	Users engage with brands and other users by creating positively valenced content on social media platforms. Creating epitomises a highly active level of social media engagement behaviour. Creating users exhibit specific creating behaviours of knowledge seeking, sharing experiences, advocating, socialising, co-developing and affirming.	*Knowledge Seeking:* Content is created by users with the objective of learning, through the acquisition of competencies that consumers apply to purchase consumption decisions. *Sharing Experiences:* Users provide content that is designed to disseminate personal relevant information, knowledge and experiences. *Advocating:* Users recommend specific brands, products/services and organisations, or ways of using products and brands. *Socialising:* Users' content reflects two-way, non-functional interactions. *Co-developing:* Users' content assists in the development of new products and services. *Affirming:* Users create content with the aim of disseminating support, encouragement and acknowledgement of the focal firm, brand or organisation's success.
Contributing	Users contribute to existing content in social media platforms. Contributing users exhibit a moderate level of positively valenced social media engagement behaviour.	Facebook: 'like' content and 'share' content to personal profile or friend's profile. Twitter: 'favourite' brand-related tweets, 're-tweet' brand-related content to personal profile. Instagram: 'like' brand-related images, 're-gram' brand-related images to personal profile. YouTube: 'like' content, share video to personal social networks.

Consuming	Users passively consume content without any form of active reciprocation or contribution. Consuming users demonstrate a minimum level of positive, passive social media engagement behaviour.	Viewing brand-related video. Listening to brand-related audio. Viewing pictures and photos posted by the brand. Reading brand posts. Reading post comment threads and conversations. Reading product/brand reviews within the social media page.
Dormancy	A temporary state of inactive, passive engagement by users who may have previously interacted with the focal brand.	Brand-related content is delivered to the user via the social media news feed or home page but the user takes no action.
Detachment	Users take action to remove content of the brand appearing in their news feed or equivalent home page. Detaching users exhibit a moderate level of negatively valenced social media engagement behaviour.	'Unliking' or 'unsubscribing' to a social media brand page. 'Unfollowing' a brand on social media. Terminating a subscription for further updates and content from the brand. Selecting to hide future posts.
Destruction	Negative, active contributions to existing content on social media platforms are created by destructive users. Destructive users represent a highest level of negatively active social media engagement behaviour.	Conversing negatively on brand-related content. Making negative contributions to brand forums. Publicly rating products and brands negatively. Commenting negatively on posts, blogs, videos and pictures posted by the brand. Writing a public complaint on the brand page. Writing negative product reviews and testimonials on social media content. Reporting brand or brand-related social media content for misconduct of use on social media.

The extent to which users engage with brand-related social media platforms in both a positively and negatively valenced manner is an important consideration. Positively valenced engagement behaviour is reflected in favourable or affirmative behaviours, whereas negatively valenced engagement behaviour is exhibited through unfavourable behaviours (Hollebeek and Chen, 2014). Positively valenced behaviours often reflect heightened levels of customer engagement and include activities such as 'sharing' a brand post to a friend with a recommendation to experience the offer (Van Doorn et al., 2010). Extant literature pays little attention to negatively valenced behaviours that involve such activities as customers frequenting anti-brand communities, or visiting social media platforms to vent negative feelings and views about brands.

Social media engagement behaviour construct

Studies addressing the processes and levels of social behaviour in the online context provide foundational insights, however, theoretical coherence of the concept and corresponding measurement techniques remain sparse. We present a construct of engagement behaviour specific to the social media context. This construct offers value to engagement researchers through the context-specific detailed investigation of engagement behaviour. Further, the description of various engagement behaviours offers managerial clarity regarding exactly how users engage, both positively and negatively, within social media platforms. The construct captures the varying intensity of specific engagement behaviours that users exhibit in social media platforms. We propose six types of social media engagement behaviour in Table 6.1. The construct includes a neutral inactive level termed dormancy, three positively valenced behaviours (consuming, contributing and creating) and two negatively valenced behaviours (detachment and destruction).

Creating

Users who create original content within social media platforms exhibit the highest level of positively valenced social media engagement behaviour. Users make unique, positive, active contributions to social media content by disseminating their knowledge, resources and experiences (Brodie et al., 2013). This behaviour goes beyond relaying (e.g. sharing, liking) content created by the brand and reflects a user contribution to the brand's social media site. Although not all user comments and content creation is favourable towards a brand, our categorisation recognises the creation of negative content as *destructing* engagement behaviours and these will be discussed in detail in a later section. Therefore, within our typology of social media engagement behaviour, we posit that positively valenced, active and highly engaged users fall under the *creating* type of engagement behaviour. They exhibit interactive creation behaviours specific to social media platforms including knowledge seeking, sharing experiences, advocating, socialising and co-developing (Brodie et al., 2013). In addition to the five creation behaviours identified from previous literature, we propose an additional creation behaviour termed 'affirming' that was identified as a separate behaviour from our analysis of social media data.

The nature of the creation engagement behaviours is explored and illustrated throughout the following sections using examples of content posted by users (brand fans) of a sample of 12 Australian wine brands. The brands selected for the analysis ranged from small, family owned wineries with small social media following of less than 1,000 Facebook fans, to larger corporate brands with over 20,000 Facebook fans. In order to derive and code comments according to the themes arising through the literature, a content analysis was conducted. In total, 5,569 comments were captured over a 12-month period in 2013. The comments were analysed through the use of qualitative analysis software NVivo 10 and the social media analysis add-on NCapture. NCapture is a web browser extension that captures content from web pages, online PDFs and social media pages for analysis in NVivo 10.

The analysis of this data identified six unique 'creating' engagement behaviours specific to social media platforms. These different categories reflect the objective and intent of the content that is created and posted to the social media site by users. These categories may occur independently or in conjunction (e.g. sharing experiences and advocating). These categories were identified as knowledge seeking, sharing experiences, advocating, socialising, co-developing and affirming. Each of the creation behaviours are discussed in the following sections.

Knowledge seeking

Users create content within social platforms with the objective of learning, through the acquisition of knowledge from other users that can be applied to purchase and consumption decision-making (Brodie et al., 2013). Social media platforms can enable and increase the collaboration and learning from customers in various ways, such as providing and receiving feedback regarding new products and services (Kärkkäinen, Jussila, and Leino, 2012). Customer-related learning can benefit both the supplier and receivers of information (i.e. the brand and the customer), as both parties learn by receiving and adopting novel information and knowledge (Kärkkäinen et al., 2012). This exchange has been referred to as 'interactive learning', described as the informal exchange and sharing of knowledge resources with suppliers and/or customers that is conducive to the firm (Meeus, Oerlemans, and Hage, 2001). Social media platforms have been credited with facilitating processes of interactive learning, including facilitating the mobilisation of tacit knowledge (Ribiere and Tuggle, 2010), enhancing information and knowledge sharing (Levy, 2009) and facilitating knowledge acquisition (Schneckenberg, 2009).

To illustrate the concept of knowledge seeking, the following comments were extracted from the public Facebook page of an Australian wine brand. For example:

> User: Does noble rot also change the taste or flavour in accordance with aging in the barrel?

Brand: If you choose to age it in a barrel, it will definitely change the flavour of the wine. Last year we fermented a portion of the wine in a new French oak barrique, and the remainder in a stainless steel tank. The two wines were completely different, but combined well together in the final blend.

User: How do you find the MV6? It is popular in Victoria but doesn't seem as favoured here when you talk to winemakers. Also 777 is meant to be fantastic. Wines I have tasted made from it have a lovely perfume, reasonable colour but lacking a bit in body. What has been your experience?

Brand: 777 ripens a lot earlier than other clones in our experience, but we co-ferment our clones as we pick across the slope in a top pick, middle pick & bottom pick fashion. We find we get better complexity that way rather than harvesting and fermenting the clones separately. MV6 is often more advanced baume wise, and generally adds more of the red berry characteristics. D4V2 and the 114 & 115 clones are my personal favourites.

These statements illustrate the potential role of social media platforms in facilitating the creation of content through which users of the focal page can acquire and develop brand-related knowledge.

Sharing experiences

Users create knowledge through content which disseminates personally relevant information, knowledge and experiences (Brodie et al., 2013; Jaakkola and Alexander, 2014). Users share their personal experiences and knowledge in this way through storytelling. Traditionally it has been difficult for managers to acquire knowledge of customer conversations, opinions and desires (Gorry and Westbrook, 2011). Few managers could hear customers speak in their own words and ways about their experiences (Gorry and Westbrook, 2011). However, within social media platforms, the barrier is reduced as customers freely comment and create stories regarding their brand experiences and perceptions. In a social media platform, user sharing of their personal knowledge and information allows them to pass along their experiences about services or products purchased (Black and Kelley, 2009). For example:

User: . . . supposedly a cellar hand hooked up a water-fitting ahead of their centrifugal pump to push through the lines to their tank and catch out, however the head pressure in this case was far greater than the site's water pressure (perhaps it was rain water), resulting in wine travelling back up the water pipe. The result of this, so the story goes, was that one of the ladies in the office turned on the tap and out came wine. Definitely one for Mythbusters I reckon.

User: Oh my goodness. I'd have pretty much done just about anything to be involved with that wine tasting! Gave a very special bottle of your wine to a stupid ex once to help get rid of him!!! MAJOR regret. Hope those involved are extremely grateful and savour every moment. Cheers in major style.

These statements illustrate the user content creation on a social media brand page with the objective of sharing personal knowledge, experiences and information. Through such forms of content creation, users co-create knowledge and experiences within social media platforms. This concept goes beyond the practice of forwarding brand posts, as users are actively creating the content to share with the social media community.

Advocating

Advocating is an expression of engagement, which occurs when users recommend their preference for specific brands, products/services and organisations or ways of using products and brands (Sashi, 2012). This form of content creation is aimed at influencing other user's perceptions, preferences or knowledge regarding the brand (Jaakkola and Alexander, 2014). Advocating may occur through positive electronic word-of-mouth (e-WOM; Van Doorn et al., 2010), the significance of which is well recognised in the marketing and advertising literature (Engel, Kegerreis, and Blackwell, 1969; Gilly, Graham, Wolfinbarger, and Yale, 1998). Social media platforms represent an ideal tool for e-WOM, as consumers freely create and disseminate brand-related information in their established social networks composed of friends, classmates and other acquaintances (Vollmer and Precourt, 2008). Further, advocating focal brands and brand-related experiences through e-WOM behaviours on social media will likely impact purchase behaviour and increase customer value (Van Doorn et al., 2010).

Advocating users create content within social media platforms to specifically endorse and promote brand-related products and services. To illustrate, the user comments below illustrate advocating behaviour in relation to a wine brand's product related post:

User: This stuff is liquid gold!
User: The '98 Merlot was a surprising stand out. All the wines are winners though and extremely good value. I'm coming back for more!

Socialising

Socialising creation behaviour denotes two way, non-functional interactions (Brodie et al., 2013). The social value derived from membership in social media platforms has been argued to drive the adoption and usage levels of the platforms (Hennig-Thurau et al., 2010). Social media platforms, incorporating brand pages, provide greater opportunities for interactions where consumers can derive social value from computer-mediated interactions with one another (De Vries and Carlson, 2014). Within social media platforms members perceive other members as similar to themselves and have the opportunity to interact, meet and communicate with each other (Jahn and Kunz, 2012). It has been suggested that a higher perception of social-interaction value of social media brand pages may lead to the customer using the page more frequently, subsequently becoming more engaged with the brand (De Vries and Carlson, 2014). Social-interactive engagement occurs in online communities, whereby users experience intrinsic enjoyment and value the input from the larger community of users (Calder et al., 2009). Social engagement has been identified as a fundamental dimension of engagement online (Calder et al., 2009) and offline (Altschwager, Conduit, and Goodman, 2013).

Users who exhibit a high level of socialising behaviour interact on a brand's social media page and may develop a sense of belonging and feeling of knowing each other (Park et al., 2009). This form of content is created with the sole purpose of interacting and communicating with the brand and other members in a social manner. This is distinct to the behaviour of sharing experiences, in which users share personal relevant information, knowledge and experiences within the social media platform (Brodie et al., 2013). Social interactions can be in response to a comment made by another user, or in response to the brand itself. In the context of Facebook, users often utilise the page and relevant posts to create content, tagging a friend or other user. To illustrate, the following comments were created in response to a wine brand posting a new product release date through their Facebook Page:

> User: [Tagged friend of user] I'll be able to drink by then!
> Friend of user: [Tagged user] Yay!!!! It feels like years since we have shared a bottle, lol!

Similarly, the following comments were created by users of a brand Facebook page following a post regarding an upcoming brand event:

> User: [Tagged friend of user]
> Friend of user: Already onto it [User] Cathy and I have it in the diary!
> User: [tagged friends of user], we need to go here for a long lazy lunch!!
> Friend of User: Hey [User] sounds awesome not too sure if can do it by 31st may have to be in Sept/ Oct but definitely in on this one xxx.

The comments above illustrate engagement through the brand's social media page as a platform for social interaction with existing users and friends within the social network.

Co-developing

Users contribute by assisting in the development of new products, services, brands or brand meanings (Brodie et al., 2013). Users engaged in co-developing behaviours assist in the collaborative innovation of new products and services, allowing firms to draw upon customer knowledge, experience and capabilities (Greer and Lei, 2012). When customers are involved in design and innovation processes, there is a positive impact on new product performance (Menguc, Auh, and Yannopoulos, 2014). Within the social media context, collaborative innovation occurs when users contribute their knowledge, resources and skills to facilitate the focal firm's developing of its offering, through sharing ideas for improved products and services (Jaakkola and Alexander, 2014). Users also answer questions or quizzes related to the brand within social media platforms, which provides the organisation with customer insight for future development of its offerings. The use of questions and quizzes as a form of gamification in order to engage users in solving problems has been found to increase user contributions and engagement (Huotari and Hamari, 2012).

To illustrate, one brand posted an update to their social media page seeking ideas for activities at an upcoming wine tasting event. The following comment was made in response demonstrates a community member who was contributing their knowledge and ideas in order to contribute to the brand's offering:

> User: What about wine Monopoly? Buying wineries and vineyards, getting awards and getting $200 every time you finish vintage. The punishment for over imbibing or not appreciating a good red could be prison. There could be chance cards for overwatering vines, downy mildew etc., the possibilities are endless.

Affirming

Affirming denotes the specific creation of content by users with the aim of disseminating their support, encouragement and acknowledgement of the brand's success. Drawing from self-concept theory (Mehta, 1999; Sirgy, 1982), affirming behaviour refers to the words and deeds of others that act to reinforce an individual's perceptions of competencies, traits and values (Schmidt and Scholl, 2004). Types of affirming behaviour include positive feedback directed towards the brand, recognition of skills and worth and recognition of significant achievements (Schmidt and Scholl, 2004). In social media platforms, affirming behaviour occurs in a customer-to-brand manner whereby users and customers recognise and communicate the brand's skills, worth and significant achievements. Affirming behaviour differs from advocating or word-of-mouth behaviour in that the content is directed toward the brand. Comparatively, advocating behaviour occurs when users engage in user-to-user interactions with the aim of recommending brands, products and services (Jaakkola and Alexander, 2014). Affirming allows users who are highly engaged a way of demonstrating their appreciation and support for the focal brand. To illustrate, the following comments were made by users in response to a social media post, which highlighted recent awards received by the brand:

> User: Big congrats to you guys, well done!
> User: Congratulations to [Brand]. I heartily agree with the judges' choice. Well deserved.

We posit that the 'creating' form of social media engagement behaviour consists of the six creation behaviours as described thus far. The occurrence of creating engagement behaviours can be triggered when a consumer recognises a need to solve a problem or satisfy a want, performs a search, identifies relevant social media platforms and posts a comment. The nature of the posted comment and resultant conversations characterise the creation of knowledge seeking, sharing experiences, advocating, socialising, co-developing and affirming behaviours. Our construct of social media engagement behaviour recognises that whilst customers can be actively and positively engaged with the brand through the six creating behaviours, additional behaviours may occur within a social media environment. These are less active in nature; however still represent a positively valenced expression of engagement through contributing to and consuming brand related content.

Contributing

The second overarching social media engagement behaviour proposed, Contributing, sees users forward or contribute to existing content; however, they do not create any additional or new content in the form of writing a comment or post. Contributing users represent a moderate level of positively valenced social media engagement behaviour. Through functions such as 'sharing' content on Facebook, and 're-tweeting' messages on Twitter, users contribute by forwarding brand content. Users are, therefore, distributors of pre-existing content, passing along information to members of their own social networks. Additionally, users contribute to content by indicating their preferences for specific social media content through the 'Like' function on Facebook and Instagram, tagging friends and other users in comments, and functions such as the 'favourite' option on Twitter. Through these actions, users contribute to the popularity of social media content and become message senders for the focal brand, passing on content to actors within their own networks. When users undertake these actions, they not only increase the original reach and exposure of the social media content, they also become advocates of the focal brand. This increases the likelihood of friends and other social media users engaging with the brand (Chu, 2011).

Consuming

Consuming is defined as the passive consumption of brand-related content through reading reviews, discussion and comments, viewing photos, watching videos and clicking on content and links. Consuming reflects the minimum level of positively valenced social media engagement behaviour. Consumption behaviour is passive, whereby consumers exhibit a level of participation, however, do not actively contribute to or create content. Through the consumption of content within social media platforms, individuals may extract individual value. Users' behaviour is individualistic and independent of other users, and thus will not impact on other users of the social media platform. Reading discussions (e.g. to find information) is a form of passive participation, whereas posting comments is active participation (Gummerus et al., 2012; Shang, Chen, and Liao, 2006). Only a small number of customers actively interact with content and other members, with most customers using brand communities to consume content as a source of information, reading messages rather than contributing through likes, shares and comments (Gummerus et al., 2012). A significant number of users within social media fall into the category of consuming. Consuming customers may consciously choose not to contribute to the social media site for several reasons including a desire for privacy, time pressures and an overload of messages (Nonnecke and Preece, 1999). Hence, we make a distinction in non-contributing behaviour between consuming behaviours and dormancy.

Dormancy

A dormant user is one who has made zero active or passive contributions to the community. Users do not behaviourally engage with the brand passively or actively, through consuming, contributing to or creating content. Rather, dormant users exhibit a temporary state of inactive behavioural engagement (Brodie et al., 2013). This state does not necessarily reflect inactive cognitive or emotional engagement, but there is no visible interaction between the user and the brand from the perspective of an independent observer (e.g. another user). Users exhibiting dormant behaviour are often referred to as lurkers (Muller, Shami, Millen, and Feinberg, 2010; Takahashi, Fujimoto, and Yamasaki, 2003). Dormant users are considered as neutral in their engagement behaviour valence, and do not exhibit negatively valenced engagement behaviours, such as detachment or destruction. Studies of Facebook user behaviour have indicated a significant rate of dormancy, with less than 5 per cent of Facebook users engaging with the brand they are a fan of, regardless of product category (Nelson-Field and Taylor, 2012). Such a high rate of inactive users presents a challenge for marketers, particularly those wishing to increase expressions of social media engagement behaviour. To date, little research has been established in the social media forum to determine effective communication efforts and strategies that may act to facilitate superior levels of engagement amongst existing users that remain dormant.

Detaching

Detaching users exhibit private, yet active social media engagement behaviour. This negatively valenced option involves users actively and yet privately removing themselves from social media brand pages through selecting to hide brand-related content, or 'unlike' and 'unsubscribe' from the page. Detachment represents a moderate level of negatively valenced social media engagement behaviour. Detaching users have made a decision to terminate their interaction with the brand, meaning there is a temporary or permanent conclusion to the consumers' behavioural engagement with the brand community. As users privately and quietly remove themselves from the platform, it is unlikely to impact on other users of the page.

Customer detachment from a brand relationship is observed in interpersonal relationship scholarly research through the concept of relationship ending (Duck and Perlman, 1985). Similarly, relationship termination, withdrawal, dissolution, discontinuation, uncoupling and break-up reflect similar processes of detachment (Stewart, 1998). Referring to detachment as a process of disengagement, Bowden, Gabbott, and Naumann (2015) define disengagement as a process, stimulated by a trauma or disturbance leading to relationship termination, dependent on prior levels of engagement (p. 6):

> A process by which a customer-brand relationship experiences a trauma or disturbance which may lead to relationship termination; which involves a range of trigger based events; which varies in intensity and trajectory; which occurs within a specific set of category conditions and which is dependent on prior level of customer engagement.

This view of customer disengagement suggests a permanent state of detachment. However, disengagement with or detachment from a focal brand or brand community may be more temporary in nature. Consumers may choose to re-join the community, following the trauma or disturbance. For example, Facebook offers users a number of ways to adjust and detach from their relationships with brand pages. First, users may choose to hide content, whereby they click to hide a specific post from appearing in their news feed. This represents a low level of detachment where users disengage from a specific piece of brand content or information, rather than the brand itself. Secondly, users select to hide all content. This option allows the user to block all future posts from appearing in their news feed. This represented a moderate level of detachment where users disengage from all brand content or information in the future. These users may remain as brand 'fans', maintaining their membership; however, they choose to opt out of receiving any communication from the brand, this differs from dormant users, who still receive the communication but do not visibly interact with it. Finally, detaching users can permanently detach from the social media page by unliking the page. This form of detaching behaviour reflects a more lasting stage of disengagement, where users choose to terminate their relationship with the virtual brand community.

Destructing

Destructive social media users make negatively valenced active contributions to social media brand pages. Negatively valenced, destructive content is created by users within social media platforms with the aim to disseminate negative word-of-mouth, or e-WOM, and vent negative brand-related feelings, causing a destruction of brand value (Bowden et al., 2015; Hollebeek and Chen, 2014; Plé and Cáceres, 2010). While co-creation refers to the process in which providers and customers collaboratively create value, co-destruction refers to the collaborative destruction, or diminishment of value by providers and customers (Plé and Cáceres, 2010). Destructive behaviour can be driven by users' perceived reputation of the brand, product involvement, self-confidence, perceived worthiness of complaining and proximity of others and attitudes to the business in general (Lau and Ng, 2001).

Social media platforms provide dissatisfied users with the opportunity to reach a larger audience, and hence in recent years individuals have turned to online pages to share negative experiences and make complaints to brands. To illustrate, in June 2014, a mother turned to a wine brand's Facebook page to share her anger towards the brand, claiming she was forced to express breast milk in public after the winery denied her access to a private area during a wine festival. The customer's negatively valenced destructive brand engagement behaviour included a lengthy recount of her unsatisfactory treatment by employees. The post was shared more than 11,000 times, causing significant negative publicity and national news coverage for the brand. The brand was forced to shut down their Facebook page and stated 'we are not social media experts and were unsure of how to cope with the negativity' (Jones, 2014). In response to this negatively valenced social media engagement behaviour, the McLaren Vale Grape and Wine Tourism Association developed a new program, aimed to reinforce the message that breastfeeding mothers are welcome to the region. The association's 135 cellar doors and tourism venues were required to display 'breastfeeding friendly' stickers in addition to compulsory staff training (Jones, 2014). This demonstrates the impact on the business of destructive contributions to social media content.

In addition to independently creating destructive brand-related content within social platforms, some platforms such as Facebook offer users the ability to assist in the determination of inappropriate content. For example, the 'report post' function allows users to make an official report regarding a specific post. If the reported post is found to violate community standards, Facebook will permanently delete the content. Hence, users have the ability to remove content created by the brand or other users.

Summary and implications

We investigate specific engagement behaviours within social media, focusing on two key areas: the valence of the behaviour, and the intensity at which it is exhibited. We present a new, cohesive construct of social media customer engagement behaviour. In particular, we note that users express three levels of positively valenced engagement behaviour: consumption, contribution and creation, in addition to two levels of negatively valenced engagement behaviour: detachment and destruction.

Implications for marketing theory

The social media engagement behaviour construct contributes to the literature on social media and interactive marketing in general and the extant literature on customer engagement behaviour in particular. The construct responds to the call for the development of a broader conceptualisation of engagement behaviour, which incorporates the notions of focal positively, as well as potentially negatively valenced customer expressions when considering the engagement concept, as suggested by Hollebeek and Chen (2014). We extend the concept of negatively valenced engagement as discussed by Hollebeek and Chen (2014) and Brodie et al. (2013) through the description of various forms of negatively valenced social media engagement behaviour. In addition to the critical consideration of social media engagement behaviour valence, we provide a more comprehensive understanding of social media engagement behaviour intensities through our comparison of low (passive) engagement behaviour and high (active) engagement behaviour. We demonstrate that social media engagement behaviours vary in their active and passive nature. This is reflected in the multi-level nature of the developed construct.

We suggest six types of behaviour – creating, contributing, consuming, dormancy, detachment and destruction – in order to explain the passive and active nature of social media engagement behaviour. Further, we have unpacked 'creating' to demonstrate several specific creation behaviours, including knowledge seeking, sharing experiences, socialising, advocating, co-developing and affirming. These forms of engagement are reflected in the work of Brodie et al. (2013) and Jaakkola and Alexander (2014). The affirming category was deduced from a content analysis of over 5,000 comments made within Australian wine brand social media pages. This introduces a new form of engagement behaviour into the literature, reflecting a user-initiated interaction between the user and the brand.

Implications for marketing practice

Marketing managers in charge of social media activities face difficult decisions when designing digital content and campaigns for their products. Whilst previous scholars have suggested that marketing practitioners can measure online social media engagement behaviour through measures such as 'likes', 'shares' and 'comments' (Cvijikj and Michahelles, 2013; De Vries, Gensler, and Leeflang, 2012; Lee, Hosanagar, and Nair, 2013), we suggest that a far more comprehensive understanding of how users engage, both positively and negatively is key to social media marketing success. Through adoption of a more comprehensive perspective incorporating intensity and valence of engagement behaviours, marketing practitioners should structure and deliver communications content, such as social media posts, in such a way that promotes and encourages positively valenced, active social media engagement behaviours. The development of the social media engagement behaviour construct provides clarity to managers who wish to understand exactly how consumers engage with a focal brand.

Further research

Given the paucity of research on social media engagement behaviours, further research is required in order to explore different types of engagement behaviours in online communities. The dynamic nature of the levels of customer engagement behaviours proposed in this chapter merit further attention. Specifically, customer propensity for each type of engagement behaviour and customer progression through or within the six types of social media engagement behaviour offers an interesting avenue for future research. An examination of how likely consumers are to migrate from one level of engagement to another and the nature of consumers at each level would also be of particular interest. Understanding this process will offer strategic direction for marketing practitioners who want to develop active and positively valenced engagement behaviours among customers.

An understanding of the profiles of users within each of the social media engagement behaviour types and the context in which each of the segments engages in more active engagement behaviours would be an interesting avenue for further exploration. In addition, understanding the nature of the social media content that drives customers to engage at different levels of intensity and with difference valence would be useful for strategic managers and social media content designers. In particular, further exploring the nature of dormant users and what triggers consumption, contributing and creating behaviours would be of interest.

Social media engagement behaviours may occur in interactive, cyclical or unpredictable patterns, warranting further research. As suggested by Gummerus et al. (2012), further research is required in order to determine the measurement of customer engagement and its proximal constructs. However, in an ongoing relationship it is difficult to separate the antecedents of customer engagement from its moderators and consequences, as it is likely that a circular logic exists (Gummerus et al., 2012). Moreover, whilst this construct focuses on the specific interactive experiences between consumers and brands, interactions between consumers and other agencies, including business and governments, warrants further attention as called for by Brodie et al. (2011).

Additionally, as brand communities through various social media platforms continue to emerge, important questions develop concerning engagement behaviours across multiple platforms. Academic research is necessary in order to determine the differences in customer engagement behaviours across various forms of online brand communities. Moreover, whilst the development of our construct focuses on social media engagement behaviours, there is a need to study engagement behaviours across the multiple touch-points in which customers engage with a firm. A consideration of engagement behaviours across all channels and touch-points by which customers engage with the firm will enable future scholars to understand the synergistic effects of multiple forms of customer engagement with the brand. This could also include examination and comparison of online versus offline customer engagement.

Customer engagement has commonly been characterised through the three dimensional perspective, incorporating cognitive, affective and behavioural components (e.g. Brodie et al., 2011). Within our chapter, we focus exclusively on the specific behavioural manifestation of engagement in one context: social media. An incorporating of cognitive and affective engagement in the social media forum would provide a more comprehensive understanding of customer engagement in this context.

Finally, for social media sites that provide an opportunity to purchase or link to the sales platform, there is an opportunity to understand the relationship between social media engagement behaviours and purchase behaviours. This would provide marketing managers with a clearer, although still incomplete, understanding of the return on investment of the social media strategy. An evaluation of the dollar investment of increasing a customer's engagement from dormant to actively engaged could be translated into sales propensity.

References

Altschwager, T., Conduit, J., and Goodman, S. (2013). *Branded Marketing Events: Facilitating Customer Brand Engagement.* Paper presented at the International Conference of the Academy of Wine Business Research, Ontario, Canada.

Black, H.G. and Kelley, S.W. (2009). A storytelling perspective on online customer reviews reporting service failure and recovery. *Journal of Travel & Tourism Marketing,* 26, 169–179.

Bowden, J. Gabbott, M. and Naumann, K. (2014). Service relationships and the customer disengagement – engagement conundrum. *Journal of Marketing Management,* 1–33.

Bowden, J. L., Gabbott, M., & Naumann, K. (2015). Service relationships and the customer disengagement–engagement conundrum. *Journal of Marketing Management,* 31(7–8), 774–806.

Brodie, R.J., Hollebeek, L., Jurić, B. and Ilić, A. (2011). Customer engagement conceptual domain, fundamental propositions, and implications for research. *Journal of Service Research,* 14, 252–271.

Brodie, R.J., Ilic, A., Jurić, B. and Hollebeek, L. (2013). Consumer engagement in a virtual brand community: An exploratory analysis. *Journal of Business Research,* 66, 105–114.

Calder, B.J., Malthouse, E.C. and Schaedel, U. (2009). An experimental study of the relationship between online engagement and advertising effectiveness. *Journal of Interactive Marketing (Mergent, Inc.),* 23, 321–331.

Chu, S.-C. (2011). Viral advertising in social media: Participation in Facebook groups and responses among college-aged users. *Journal of Interactive Advertising,* 12, 30–43.

Chu, S.-C. and Kim, Y. (2011). Determinants of consumer engagement in electronic word-of-mouth (eWOM) in social networking sites. *International Journal of Advertising,* 30, 47–75.

Chung, C. and Austria, K. (2010). Social media gratification and attitude toward social media marketing messages: a study of the effect of social media marketing messages on online shopping value. *Proceedings of the Northeast Business & Economics Association*.

Cvijikj, I. P. and Michahelles, F. (2013). Online engagement factors on Facebook brand pages. *Social Network Analysis and Mining*, 3, 843–861.

De Vries, N. J. and Carlson, J. (2014). Examining the drivers and brand performance implications of customer engagement with brands in the social media environment. *Journal of Brand Management*, 21, 495–515.

De Vries, L., Gensler, S. and Leeflang, P. S. (2012). Popularity of brand posts on brand fan pages: an investigation of the effects of social media marketing. *Journal of Interactive Marketing*, 26, 83–91.

Duck, S. E. and Perlman, D. E. (1985). *Understanding personal relationships: An interdisciplinary approach*. Sage Publications, Inc.

Engel, J. F., Kegerreis, R. J. and Blackwell, R. D. (1969). Word-of-mouth communication by the innovator. *The Journal of Marketing*, 33, 15–19.

Gambetti, R. C., Graffigna, G. and Biraghi, S. (2012). The Grounded Theory approach to consumer-brand engagement. *International Journal of Market Research*, 54, 659–687.

Gensler, S., Völckner, F., Liu-Thompkins, Y., and Wiertz, C. (2013). Managing brands in the social media environment. *Journal of Interactive Marketing*, 27, 242–256.

Gilly, M. C., Graham, J. L., Wolfinbarger, M. F. and Yale, L. J. (1998). A dyadic study of interpersonal information search. *Journal of the Academy of Marketing Science*, 26, 83–100.

Gorry, G. A. and Westbrook, R. A. (2011). Can you hear me now? Learning from customer stories. *Business Horizons*, 54, 575–584.

Greer, C. R. and Lei, D. (2012). Collaborative innovation with customers: a review of the literature and suggestions for future research. *International Journal of Management Reviews*, 14, 63–84.

Gummerus, J., Liljander, V., Weman, E. and Pihlström, M. (2012). Customer engagement in a Facebook brand community. *Management Research Review*, 35, 857–877.

Heller Baird, C. and Parasnis, G. (2011). From social media to social customer relationship management. *Strategy & Leadership*, 39(5), 30–37.

Hennig-Thurau, T., Malthouse, E. C., Friege, C., Gensler, S., Lobschat, L., Rangaswamy, A. and Skiera, B. (2010). The impact of new media on customer relationships. *Journal of Service Research*, 13, 311–330.

Hollebeek, L. D. (2011). Demystifying customer brand engagement: Exploring the loyalty nexus. *Journal of Marketing Management*, 27, 785–807.

Hollebeek, L. D. and Chen, T. (2014). Exploring positively-versus negatively-valenced brand engagement: a conceptual model. *Journal of Product and Brand Management*, 23, 62–74.

Hollebeek, L. D., Glynn, M. S. and Brodie, R. J. (2014). Consumer brand engagement in social media: Conceptualization, scale development and validation. *Journal of Interactive Marketing*, 28, 149–165.

Huotari, K. and Hamari, J. (2012). *Defining gamification: a service marketing perspective*. Paper presented at the Proceeding of the 16th International Academic MindTrek Conference.

Jaakkola, E. and Alexander, M. (2014). The role of customer engagement behavior in value co-creation: A service system perspective. *Journal of Service Research*, 17(3), 247–261.

Jahn, B. and Kunz, W. (2012). How to transform consumers into fans of your brand. *Journal of Service Management*, 23, 344–361.

Jones, E. (2014). McLaren Vale wineries urged to offer breastfeeding mums private areas after Rikki Forrest forced to express milk in public. *The Advertiser.*

Kärkkäinen, H., Jussila, J. J. and Leino, M. (2012). Learning from and with customers with social media: A model for social customer learning. *International Journal of Management, Knowledge and Learning*, 1, 5–25.

Koetsier, J. (2013). *Facebook: 15 million businesses, companies, and organizations now have a Facebook page* [Online]. Available: http://venturebeat.com/2013/03/05/facebook-15-million-businesses-companies-and-organizations-now-have-a-facebook-page/ [Accessed 12 December 2013].

Lau, G. T. and Ng, S. (2001). Individual and situational factors influencing negative word-of-mouth behaviour. *Canadian Journal of Administrative Sciences/Revue Canadienne des Sciences de l'Administration*, 18, 163–178.

Lee, D., Hosanagar, K. and Nair, H. S. (2013). The effect of advertising content on consumer engagement: Evidence from Facebook. *Available at SSRN.*

Levy, M. (2009). WEB 2.0 implications on knowledge management. *Journal of Knowledge Management*, 13, 120–134.

Mangold, W. G., and Faulds, D. J. (2009). Social media: The new hybrid element of the promotion mix. *Business Horizons*, 52, 357–365.

Meeus, M. T., Oerlemans, L. A. and Hage, J. (2001). Patterns of interactive learning in a high-tech region. *Organization Studies*, 22, 145–172.

Mehta, A. (1999). Using self-concept to assess advertising effectiveness. *Journal of Advertising Research*, 39, 81–89.

Menguc, B., Auh, S. and Yannopoulos, P. (2014). Customer and supplier involvement in design: The moderating role of incremental and radical innovation capability. *Journal of Product Innovation Management*, 31, 313–328.

Muller, M., Shami, N. S., Millen, D. R. and Feinberg, J. (2010). We are all lurkers: Consuming behaviors among authors and readers in an enterprise file-sharing service. Proceedings of the 16th ACM international conference on Supporting group work, 2010. ACM, 201–210.

Muntinga, D. G., Moorman, M. and Smit, E. G. (2011). Introducing COBRAs. *International Journal of Advertising*, 30, 13–46.

Nambisan, S. and Baron, R. A. (2007). Interactions in virtual customer environments: Implications for product support and customer relationship management. *Journal of Interactive Marketing*, 21, 42–62.

Nelson-Field, K. and Taylor, J. (2012). Facebook fans: A fan for life? Admap: Warc.

Nonnecke, B. and Preece, J. (1999). Shedding light on lurkers in online communities. *Ethnographic Studies in Real and Virtual Environments: Inhabited Information Spaces and Connected Communities, Edinburgh*, 123–128.

Pagani, M., Hofacker, C. F. and Goldsmith, R. E. (2011). The influence of personality on active and passive use of social networking sites. *Psychology and Marketing*, 28, 441–456.

Park, N., Kee, K. F. and Valenzuela, S. (2009). Being immersed in social networking environment: Facebook groups, uses and gratifications, and social outcomes. *CyberPsychology and Behavior*, 12, 729–733.

Pelling, E. L. and White, K. M. (2009). The theory of planned behavior applied to young people's use of social networking web sites. *CyberPsychology and Behavior*, 12, 755–759.

Plé, L. and Cáceres, R. C. (2010). Not always co-creation: Introducing interactional co-destruction of value in service-dominant logic. *Journal of Services Marketing*, 24, 430–437.

Preece, J., Nonnecke, B. and Andrews, D. (2004). The top five reasons for lurking: Improving community experiences for everyone. *Computers in Human Behavior*, 20, 201–223.

Raacke, J. and Bonds-Raacke, J. (2008). MySpace and Facebook: Applying the uses and gratifications theory to exploring friend-networking sites. *CyberPsychology and Behavior*, 11, 169–174.

Ribiere, V. M. and Tuggle, F. D. (2010). Fostering innovation with KM 2.0. *Vine*, 40, 90–101.

Riegner, C. (2007). Word of mouth on the web: The impact of web 2.0 on consumer purchase decisions. *Journal of Advertising Research*, 47, 436–447.

Sashi, C. (2012). Customer engagement, buyer-seller relationships, and social media. *Management Decision*, 50, 253–272.

Schau, H. J., Muñiz Jr, A. M. and Arnould, E. J. (2009). How brand community practices create value. *Journal of Marketing*, 73, 30–51.

Schmidt, C. T. and Scholl, R. W. (2004). *Motivation: Affirming behavior* [Online]. Available: http://www.uri.edu/research/lrc/scholl/webnotes/Motivation_Affirming.htm [Accessed 1 February 2015].

Schneckenberg, D. (2009). Web 2.0 and the empowerment of the knowledge worker. *Journal of Knowledge Management*, 13, 509–520.

Shang, R. A., Chen, Y. C. and Liao, H. J. (2006). The value of participation in virtual consumer communities on brand loyalty. *Internet Research*, 16, 398–418.

Sirgy, M. J. (1982). Self-Concept in Consumer Behavior: A Critical Review. *Journal of Consumer Research*, 9, 287–300.

Stewart, K. (1998). The customer exit process-a review and research agenda. *Journal of Marketing Management*, 14, 235–250.

Takahashi, M., Fujimoto, M. and Yamasaki, N. (2003) The active lurker: Influence of an in-house online community on its outside environment. Proceedings of the 2003 international ACM SIGGROUP conference on Supporting group work, 2003. ACM, 1–10.

Van Doorn, J., Lemon, K. N., Mittal, V., Nass, S., Pick, D., Pirner, P. and Verhoef, P. C. (2010). Customer engagement behavior: theoretical foundations and research directions. *Journal of Service Research*, 13, 253–266.

Vivek, S. D., Beatty, S. E., Dalela, V. and Morgan, R. M. (2014). A generalized multidimensional scale for measuring customer engagement. *Journal of Marketing Theory and Practice*, 22(4), 401–420.

Vivek, S. D., Beatty, S. E. and Morgan, R. M. (2012). Customer engagement: Exploring customer relationships beyond purchase. *The Journal of Marketing Theory and Practice*, 20, 122–146.

Vollmer, C. and Precourt, G. (2008). *Always on: Advertising, marketing, and media in an era of consumer control*. McGraw Hill Professional.

Wallace, E., Buil, I., De Chernatony, L. and Hogan, M. (2014). Who likes you and why? A typology of Facebook fans. *Journal Of Advertising Research*, 54(1), 92–109.

7 Nature and purpose of engagement platforms

Christoph F. Breidbach and
Roderick J. Brodie

Introduction

The ever-increasing sophistication of Information and Communication Technology (ICT) has transformed service interactions since the late 1990s (Davis, Spohrer, and Maglio, 2011). Today, ICTs, such as video or teleconferencing, can replace face-to-face (F2F) service exchanges in contexts ranging from consulting to telemedicine, which has led to *technology-enabled value co-creation processes* (Breidbach, Kolb, and Srinivasan, 2013). Other service contexts, such as retail banks, equally expanded their customer-facing interactions from physical, into virtual realms. For example, a decade and a half ago, Wells Fargo's traditional bricks-and-mortar retail banks were supplemented with an online banking platform, thus generating *self-service environments* (Bitner, Ostrom, and Meuter, 2002). Online platforms based on self-service are now pervasive in retailing and other contexts, including business-to-customer, business-to-business, and customer-to-customer interfaces.

Attempts to understand the implications resulting from shifting physical to technology-enabled and self-service processes dominated much of the nascent service research literature to date (e.g. Froehle and Roth, 2004; Makarem, et al., 2009). However, such a unidirectional perspective is now obsolete as yet another, and seemingly paradoxical, reverse trend can been observed: service firms are beginning to expand what used to be entirely *virtual* customer-firm interactions into the realm of additional, *physical* environments. For example, Microsoft now operates dedicated bricks-and-mortar retail stores, thereby complementing its otherwise exclusive online presence. Similarly, tech giants such as Google or Amazon maintain dedicated ad-hoc retail outlets (e.g. at airports), and offer a plethora of branded technical devices (e.g. Amazon's 'Firefly' phone), which allow customers to interact with, and experience, the digital service ecosystem that these firms maintain. Ultimately, what used to be a clear-cut distinction between exclusively virtual and physical interfaces no longer applies to the service landscape of the twenty-first century.

Today, collections of boundary spanning, integrative, physical/virtual platforms represent the focal point of many service ecosystems (Breidbach, Brodie, and Hollebeek, 2014). In order to study the transforming service landscape, new theoretical lenses and concepts are needed (Maglio and Breidbach, 2014; Maglio, Kwan, and Spohrer, 2015). One particularly promising concept to generate new insights in this context is the *engagement platform*, which transforms the structure of economies and societies, therefore representing both the means and ends of value creation (Charkabarti and Ramaswamy, 2014; Smedlund and Faghankhani, 2015). Furthermore, engagement platforms are conceptually closely aligned with practitioners' terminology (Frow, et al., 2015), and can bridge the theoretical and empirical domains associated with service-dominant (SD) logic (Vargo and Lusch, 2004) through middle-range theory (Brodie, Pels, and Saren, 2011). The managerial importance for understanding the nature of engagement is also highlighted by the Marketing Science Institute's 2014–2016 research priorities, which lists customer engagement as a Tier 1 entry. The Global Perspectives on Service Research, which are coordinated by researchers at the Center for Service Leadership at Arizona State University, also include engagement in the topic 'enhancing the service experience'. However, despite the potential benefits, the conceptual foundations underlying engagement platforms remain ambiguous, and more research in this important area of inquiry is needed (Brodie, et al., 2011; Charkabarti and Ramaswamy, 2014; Frow, et al., 2015; Smedlund and Faghankhani, 2015; Breidbach, Chandler and Maglio, 2015).

In this chapter, we examine the nature and purpose of engagement platforms and their role in the changing service landscape of the twenty-first century. First, we explore the intersection of ICT, service, and engagement platforms. Second, we review the body of literature related to service ecosystems, to subsequently draw on emerging research that moves its focus beyond singular engagement platforms to holistic engagement ecosystems (e.g. Breidbach, et al., 2014). We support this argument by illustrating how platform leader Amazon.com designed an engagement ecosystem, consisting of multiple complementary engagement platforms. Finally, we explore the issue of engagement ecosystem design, which we link to further managerial implications.

Engagement platforms

The engagement platform concept emerged in the marketing literature to describe 'purpose-built, ICT-enabled environments containing artifacts, interfaces, processes and people permitting organisations to co-create value with their customers' (Ramaswamy, 2009). The link between engagement platforms and ICTs is unsurprising, given that the engagement concept itself has been considered to be the 'definitive umbrella term' (Mollen and Wilson, 2010, p. 1) when attempting to understand interactions between human economic actors within ICT-mediated environments (Sawhney et al., 2005). While early work focused on engagement platforms as ICT-enabled artifacts *only*, the wider marketing literature subsequently provided additional, although often ambiguous, definitions to conceptualise engagement platforms.

Charkabarti and Ramaswamy (2014) differentiate between co-production platforms (e.g. an ICT-enabled environment that allows individuals to contribute to the design of a physical good) and co-consumption platforms (which provide consumption experiences, such as social media). In addition, Ramaswamy and Gouillart (2010) describe, rather than define, engagement platforms using the criteria of transparency, access, dialogue, and reflexivity. First, 'transparency' implies that an actor's interactions with the engagement platform is visible to a wider audience (e.g. on social networking sites). Second, 'accessibility' enables actors to integrate resources into the platform, for example, by adding or sharing content. Actors thereby modify the nature and characteristics of the platform itself, and engagement platforms facilitate 'dialogue' amongst multiple actors, since the exchange of resources is considered a prerequisite for value co-creation (Prahalad and Ramaswamy, 2004; Ramaswamy and Guillard, 2010). Finally, 'reflexivity' implies an engagement platform is capable of adapting to changes from within.

Engagement platforms are increasingly conceptualised beyond ICT-driven realms. For example, Nenonen et al. (2012) provide a classification system that differentiates between digital engagement platforms, processes, tools, and physical spaces. Frow et al. (2015, p. 10) provide a similar typology which consists of

(1) digital applications, such as websites that extend the reach and speed of interactions with multiple and diverse actors . . . ; (2) tools or products . . . to connect actors (e.g. software companies providing software developer toolkits); (3) physical resources, where collaborators come together occasionally for mutual benefit . . . (e.g. retail formats such as Apple stores); (4) joint processes involving multiple actors . . . and (5) dedicated personnel groups, such as call centre teams.

Finally, Storbacka, et al. (2015) define engagement platforms through the perspective of actor-network theory as 'multi-sided intermediaries that actors leverage to engage with other actors to co-create value' (p. 21). As such, the authors argue that engagement platforms always assume the role of an intermediary, and do not enable the cognitive state of engagement that an actor may experience beyond an individual transaction (Van Doorn et al., 2010).

Here, we draw on our earlier work and define engagement platforms as 'physical or virtual touch points designed to provide structural support for the exchange and integration of resources, and thereby co-creation of value between actors in a service system' (Breidbach et al., 2014, p. 596). Since all points of interaction represent opportunities for the emergence of value (Vargo and Lusch, 2004), engagement platforms can be considered as the basis for facilitating such value-generating interactions and experiences through resource exchanges (Breidbach et al., 2014). Brodie et al. (2011) highlight that the process of engagement occurs within a dynamic, iterative process of service relationships between actors (e.g. customers), and engagement objects (e.g. the firm or brand). From an SD-logic perspective, such interactive, co-creative experiences may be interpreted as particular forms of engaging (Lusch and Vargo, 2010). Consequently, engagement platforms are centered on a focal engagement object and attempt to enhance an actor's ability to experience engagement with the object. These interactions, however, occur within larger service ecosystems, thus making it necessary to explore them in this context (Breidbach et al., 2014).

Service ecosystems

The service ecosystems concept draws on the established literature on business ecosystems (e.g. Moore, 1994), and moves from a narrow firm-centric, or even dyadic, customer–supplier perspective, to a much broader view, including multiple stakeholders or 'actors'. During the last decade, ecosystems emerged as a central concept within the wider business and management disciplines, with Google Scholar identifying just 48 entries using the term 'business ecosystem' in the year 2000, but over 700 entries in the year 2014. Similarly, 48 entries for the term 'service ecosystem' existed in Google Scholar in the year 2000, but over 300 entries in 2014. Finally, in the context of SD-logic, the term ecosystem emerged for the first time in 2005, and has grown to over 350 entries since.

The growing popularity of the ecosystem concept raises the question of what additional insights may emerge that are not reflected in the more general discourse about business networks. Iansiti and Levien (2004) identify properties of biological ecosystems that can provide additional insights into how the structure and dynamics of business networks can be conceptualised. First, ecosystems consist of large numbers of loosely interconnected participants that depend on each other for their performance and survival. Second, participants are mutually dependent, meaning that outcomes can only be influenced and not controlled. Third, the system is subject to continuous change and, finally, hubs of participants regulate the ecosystem.

While Iansiti and Levien (2004) recognise the limitations of the biological ecosystem metaphor, they do acknowledge the benefits when focusing managerial attention on features of modern business networks that are ignored by conventional singular-level theories. Specifically, an ecosystem perspective can assist in understanding how networks of individuals and groups of individuals are connected, and how value based on competitive and collaborative advantage emerges. For example, by managing the supply chain through an ecosystem perspective, Wal-Mart generates over 65 per cent of its cost advantage through collaboration in global procurement, centralised buying, and other operating activities.

Mars, Bronstein and Lusch (2012) extend the biological ecosystem metaphor into service research. They argue that, unlike most organisations, biological systems are not designed, but based on natural selection. As individual organisms interact with one another in the context of their natural environment, a set of intertwined networks of relationships emerge. In contrast, service ecosystems emerge in a more deterministic fashion, because its actors develop and pursue strategies that lead to structures (institutions), which help to manage risk and uncertainty. Furthermore, both biological and service ecosystems depend on key actors, and interactions that are linked to resources and information, as well as the resilience in the system (Mars et al., 2012).

Ultimately, an ecosystem perspective is beneficial to understanding the dynamics in many service and other business contexts, including this work on the nature and purpose of engagement platforms. However, such a shift in thinking requires altering one's perspective from a singular engagement platform as the unit of analysis, towards a holistic lens that is centered on the entire engagement ecosystem.

From engagement platforms to engagement ecosystems

Institutional and individual actors interact and engage with one another through engagement platforms, which are embedded within service ecosystems (Vargo and Lusch, 2010), innovation ecosystems (Adner and Kapoor, 2010), or ecologies of innovation (Dougherty and Dunne, 2011). Engagement platforms are therefore not constrained to ICT-mediated environments only, nor do they exist or act in isolation from other actors or platforms within the system. It is evident that a more holistic understanding of the role and nature of engagement platforms is necessary when attempting to explain the emergence, evolution, and interaction of individual platforms, especially when exploring the actions of platform leaders (Gawer and Cusumano, 2008) or keystone firms (Iansiti and Levien, 2004) like Apple, Google, or Amazon. Each of those organisations uses their individual technical (e.g. iOS) *and* physical platforms (e.g. Apple Store), to orchestrate a service ecosystem, consisting of networks of firms and customers. Conceptualising engagement platforms as singular entities cannot identify, describe, or understand the complex interdependencies that arise from multiple complementary engagement platforms within service ecosystems today.

A holistic understanding of the configuration of *all* platforms maintained by an organisation may generate more substantial insights (Breidbach et al., 2014). We define *engagement ecosystems* as: 'dynamic constellation of interdependent physical and virtual engagement platforms that a focal actor uses to interact with other actors in its service ecosystem' (Breidbach et al., 2014, p. 600). For example, the focal actor could be Amazon and other actors in its service ecosystem could be customers and other organisations. Exploring the interaction between a keystone firm like Amazon and other actors through an engagement ecosystem lens will allow us to gain holistic insights into the specific co-creative interactions between *all* actors across *all* interfaces. This conceptual shift in thinking thereby extends our understanding of how each individual engagement platform contributes to value co-creation processes. In order to accomplish this, we suggested exploring the *nature* of each engagement platform within the system (i.e. physical or virtual interface), as well as their *purpose* (Breidbach et al., 2014).

In what follows, we will analyse Amazon's engagement ecosystem and highlight the nature and purpose of each engagement platform archetypes therein.

We then provide a discussion of managerially relevant behavioural patterns that can help practitioners to design, and manage, the most effective engagement ecosystem in the context of their own organisations.

Amazon's engagement ecosystem

Amazon is a keystone firm that emerged at the turn of the twenty-first century in an entirely virtual manner. Amazon was unprecedented at the time of its inception since it never experienced the technology-induced shift from a physical, bricks-and-mortar, towards a virtual context that many established service firms like, for example, retail banks undertook to remain competitive. Today, however, Amazon has expanded its previously entirely virtual presence (e.g. Amazon.com) into an integrative virtual/physical engagement ecosystem that spans multiple engagement platforms ranging from branded technical devices (e.g. Firefly phone), to physical retail outlets (e.g. Amazon Locker).

Amazon's engagement ecosystem can best be understood by initially considering the *nature* of each engagement platform (i.e. physical or virtual interface), as well as their individual *purpose*. This approach allows us to identify four engagement platform archetypes – namely (i) *Operating*, (ii) *Instrumental*, (iii) *Enabling*, and (iv) *Supplying* platforms – and to explain their role, characteristics, and implications for Amazon's engagement ecosystem performance (drawing on Breidbach et al., 2014). Figure 7.1 presents a conceptual model of Amazon's engagement ecosystem.

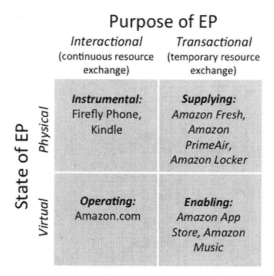

Figure 7.1 Conceptual framework of Amazon's engagement ecosystem (based on Breidbach, et al., 2014)

Operating engagement platforms enable organisations to generate revenues whilst co-creating benefits during customer-to-firm or customer-to-customer interactions. Amazon.com is such an operating platform, and consists of a highly interactive marketplace where individual actors continuously exchange and integrate resources for their own and other's benefit. Specifically, Amazon not only generates revenues by selling physical items such as books or smartphones through its operating platform, but the platform itself represents a value proposition since it enables other sellers to reach a wide audience of potential customers. Furthermore, all actors on the platform can engage with one another beyond transactions, for example, by rating products or other actors. While an operating platform could also exist in the physical world, it must remain highly interactive beyond transactions, in order to maintain its hallmark of engagement (Brodie et al., 2011).

Instrumental engagement platforms enable a group of economic actors to access a firm's operating platform. They represent physical artifacts that facilitate the continuous exchange of resources, either within specific actor-to-actor or actor-to-firm networks. Instrumental platforms, such as Amazon's 'Kindle' reader are, by themselves, typically without any immediate benefit, since they need to be integrated with further applications that enable a user to experience the service embedded into this operand resource. A 'Kindle' may just be an expensive paperweight, but once loaded with eBooks, this instrumental platform enables the user to experience Amazon's ecosystem through use. Another example is Amazon's 'Firefly' phone. The device is pre-loaded with software that recognises physical items (e.g. a jar of Nutella) that are 'photographed' by the user. Once a picture has been taken, this instrumental platform automatically directs the user back to Amazon's operating platform (e.g. the online store), where the user of the 'Firefly' phone can purchase whatever item he or she photographed previously. As such, the instrumental platform is a complementary artifact, and specifically designed to support the operating platform. However, it uniquely differs from comparable technical artifacts such as Apple's iPhone, which could be used to access Amazon.com, but that do not provide the same seamless purchasing experience as the Firefly phone.

Enabling engagement platforms are necessary for the functioning of the instrumental platforms. They provide the software applications or content to users, which are required to fully benefit from the intended capabilities of the instrumental platform. Amazon's App Store or Apple's 'iTunes' are examples for what we define as enabling engagement platforms. These artifacts are designed for transactional, and somewhat transient, actor-firm exchanges.

Finally, *supplying* platforms, such as Amazon's physical delivery stations 'Amazon Locker', as well as Amazon's 'PrimeAir' delivery drones presented in 2014, or the grocery delivery 'Fresh', facilitate the transition of Amazon from a purely virtual, to a more integrative virtual/physical ecosystem. They enable the firm to interact with customers through novel means in the physical world. Table 7.1 summarises the characteristics of each of the four engagement platform archetypes presented here.

Table 7.1 Key definitions and characteristics of engagement platform archetypes (based on Breidbach et al., 2014)

Engagement Platform Archetype	Definition	Key Characteristics	Example
Operating Platform (OP)	OPs enable firms to generate revenues by virtue of co-creating a perceived benefit during customer-to-firm, and/or customer-to-customer interactions.	– Facilitates interactivity and value co-creation with customers. – Designed to generate revenue for the firm through continuous exchange of resources. – May comprise specific online (virtual) and/or offline (physical) environments.	– Amazon.com
Instrumental Platform (IP)	IPs enable customer to access a service provider's OP. As such, possession of or access to an IP is a prerequisite for customers intending to co-create value with the firm.	– Physical artifact that needs to be integrated with applications/software to experience its full potential. – Designed to facilitate the continuous exchange of resources within customer-to-customer or customer-to-firm.	– Firefly phone – Kindle reader
Enabling Platform (EP)	EPs are designed to facilitate transactional customer-firm exchanges, and are typically accessed by customers through IPs.	– Virtual artifact that supports OP performance (e.g. allows customer to access specific applications/software).	– Amazon App Store – Amazon Music
Supplying Platform (SEP)	SEPs provide a touch-point for customer-firm and customer-to-customer interactions, in order to shape prospective customers' experiences with IPs.	– Facilitate the firm's transition from a purely virtual, to more integrative virtual/physical realms. – Experiential and interactive (resource exchange possible but not necessary).	– Amazon Fresh – Amazon PrimeAir – Amazon Locker

The service landscape of the future will likely continue to be characterised by service interactions that span digital and physical value propositions and platforms. The boundaries between the physical and virtual worlds will likely dissolve entirely, especially as we move into the age of wearable computing and the 'Internet-of-Things'. However, engagement and engagement ecosystems represent valuable concepts that can provide practitioners with the necessary terminology and understanding when attempting to overcome challenges associated with the increased prevalence of technology in all aspects of human economic exchange. As such, a final issue to consider when exploring the nature and purpose of engagement platforms is the question of how these artifacts can ideally be designed. In the next section, we draw on the management literature for this purpose, where the concept of architecture has been used to guide design processes.

Designing engagement ecosystems

The architecture and design of any complex system requires creating 'an abstract description of the entities of a system and how they are related' (Whitney, 2002, p. 2). Thus, the architecture of an engagement ecosystem requires describing not only the system's overall components (e.g. the types of engagement platforms), but also the constraints that govern the relationships among these components, in order to allow them to interact effectively and efficiently.

Every effective engagement ecosystems consists of individual physical and virtual platforms, and is capable of enhancing an organisation's ability to successfully exchange resources, and therefore to co-create value. Such an outcome would generate higher revenues and superior organisational performance. As such, the optimal configuration of an engagement ecosystem may be perceived as a dynamic capability, and therefore as a type of competitive advantage (Teece, et al., 1997). Increasing the quantity and quality/nature (e.g. physical and virtual) of engagement platforms may be one first step to alter the configuration of an existing engagement ecosystem. This would also increase its accessibility and reflexivity that, according to Ramaswamy and Gouillart (2010), represent key success criteria. The most important step forward for any practitioner is to recognise that moving beyond individual engagement platforms and towards holistic engagement ecosystems will be key to facilitate novel interactive experiences between keystone firms (e.g. the engagement object) and customers (e.g. the engagement subject).

Practitioners should furthermore consider the ideal configuration of their engagement ecosystem with respect to facilitating customer engagement and co-creation processes when designing new, or altering existing engagement ecosystems. Storbacka et al. (2015) recently introduced a generic actor perspective within service ecosystems that may be beneficial here. By viewing all ecosystem actors as able to interact, the engagement concept can be applied to a much richer set of actor combinations, including dyads such as human-to-human (H2H), human-to-technology (H2T), technology-to-technology (T2T), triads of human-to-human-and-technology (H2H&T); human-and-technology-to-human-and-technology (H&T2H&T) and finally, networks of many-humans-to-human (MH2H) and many-humans-to-technology (MH2T). Of these combinations, many can be seen as organisations. Hence, a human may engage with a firm's technology (e.g. customer using internet banking), and a firm, using humans and technology, may engage with another firm's humans and technologies (a supplier engages with a buyer, involving both personal engagement between sales person and purchaser). A focal actor wishing to facilitate engagement through an engagement ecosystem needs to consider how various combinations support its design objectives. Practitioners need to pay attention to set of actor combinations and different 'engagement' antecedents and consequences when implementing engagement ecosystems.

Implications

While truly radical technological changes may be in the far future, our present work generates immediate managerial implications that go beyond the design of an engagement ecosystem. First, guaranteeing the accessibility of each individual engagement platform is an important prerequisite to the performance of service firms in the twenty-first century. For technology firms like Amazon, the accessibility of their operating platform (e.g. Amazon.com) is of the utmost importance, since their revenues are generated there. The prerequisite to ensure the accessibility and usability of its operating platform lies in Amazon's ability to control both the instrumental engagement platforms such as its 'Firefly Phone', as well as the enabling platforms. The managerial discourse around engagement platforms, therefore, needs to increasingly focus on the interaction of all platforms, and on understanding performance implications for the entire engagement ecosystem.

Organisations that can ensure their customers' positive experience within their operating platforms will likely be able to secure their customers continued use of their value propositions. Such positive use-experience will likely result in enhanced levels of customer engagement and, subsequently improve firm performance through cost reductions, sales growth, or company referrals (Kumar, Petersen, and Leone, 2010).

Managers could also consider enhancing their ability to control both the instrumental and the enabling platforms by introducing physical supplying platforms (e.g. retail stores), if their organisational boundaries permit this. Concepts such as 'multi-channel' and 'omni-channel' have been introduced in the context of the retail research literature already (e.g. Verhoef, Neslin and Vroomen, 2007), and attempts to incorporate the advantages of physical stores with the information-rich experience of online shopping are another avenue. Understanding and perceiving this context through the lens of engagement and engagement ecosystems provides the necessary foundation to develop a 'touch point architecture' for customer engagement (Dhebar, 2013), by managing the quality of a customer's service experiences throughout physical stores, websites, social media, and other channels.

Finally, almost all digital organisations, including Amazon, collect data about their customers' behaviour and preferences. Controlling the instrumental and enabling platforms, once again, represents a necessary prerequisite for managers, as it enables the collection of large customer datasets, which can be analysed using big data analytics (Huang and Rust, 2013). Ultimately, by generating an enhanced understanding of their customers, practitioners may alter their relevant engagement ecosystems, most importantly the operating platform. Specifically, such practice would ensure the reflexivity of the engagement ecosystem, a key prerequisite for its success (Ramaswamy and Gouillart, 2010).

References

Adner, R. and Kapoor, R. (2010), "Value creation in innovation ecosystems: how the structure of technological interdependence affects firm performance in new technology generations," *Strategic Management Journal,* 31(3), 303–333.

Bitner, M. J., Ostrom, A. and Meuter, M. L. (2002), "Implementing successful self-service technologies," *Academy of Management Perspectives,* 16(4), 96–108.

Breidbach, C. F., Brodie, R. and Hollebeek, L. (2014), "Beyond virtuality: from engagement platforms to engagement ecosystems," *Managing Service Quality,* 24(6), 592–611.

Breidbach, C. F., Chandler, J. D. and Maglio, P. P. (2015), "The duality of second screens: A phenomenological study of multi-platform engagement and service experiences," *Proceedings of the 48th Hawaii International Conference on System Sciences (HICSS),* Kauai, HI, 1432–1441.

Breidbach, C. F., Kolb, D. G. and Srinivasan, A. (2013), "Connectivity in service systems: Does technology-enablement impact the ability of a service system to co-create value?," *Journal of Service Research,* 16(3), 428–441.

Brodie, R. J. Hollebeek, L. D. Juric, B. and Ilic, A. (2011), "Customer engagement: Conceptual domain, fundamental propositions and implications for research," *Journal of Service Research,* 14(3), 252–271.

Brodie, R. J., Saren, M. and Pels, J. (2011). "Theorizing about the service dominant logic: The bridging role of middle range theory," *Marketing Theory,* 11(1), 75–91.

Charkabarti, A. and Ramaswamy, V. (2014), "Re-thinking the concept of surplus: Embracing co-creation experiences in economics," *B E Journal of Economic Analysis & Policy,* 14(4), 1283–1297.

Davis, M. M., Spohrer, J. C. and Maglio, P. P. (2011), "Guest editorial: How technology is changing the design and delivery of services," *Operations Management Research,* 4(1–2), 1–5.

Dhebar, A. (2013), "Toward compelling customer touchpoint architecture," *Business Horizons,* 56(2), 199–205.

Dougherty, D. and Dunne, D. (2011), "Organizing ecologies of complex innovation," *Organization Science,* 22(5), 1214–1223.

Froehle, C. M. and Roth, A. V. (2004), "New measurement scales for evaluating perceptions of the technology-mediated customer service experience," *Journal of Operations Management,* 22(1), 1–21.

Frow, P., Nenonen, S., Payne, A. and Storbacka, K. (2015), "Managing co-creation design: A strategic approach to innovation," *British Journal of Management,* Online first.

Gawer, A. and Cusumano, M.A. (2008), "How companies become platform leaders," *MIT Sloan Management Review*, 29(2), 28–38.

Huang, M. and Rust, R. (2013), "IT-related service: A multidisciplinary perspective," *Journal of Service Research*, 16(3), 38–52.

Iansiti, M. and Levien, R. (2004), "Strategy as ecology," *Harvard Business Review*, 82(3), 68–81.

Kumar, V., Petersen, J. A. and Leone, R. P. (2010), "Driving profitability by encouraging customer referrals: Who, when, and how," *Journal of Marketing*, 74(5), 1–17.

Lusch, R. F. and Vargo, S. L. (2010), "S-D logic: Accommodating, integrating, transdisciplinary," *Grand Service Challenge*, University of Cambridge, 23 September.

Makarem, S.C., Mudambi, S.M. and Podoshen, J.S. (2009), "Satisfaction in Technology-Enabled Service Encounters," *Journal of Services Marketing*, 23(3), 134–144.

Maglio, P.P. and Breidbach, C.F. (2014), "Service Science: Toward Systematic Service System Innovation." Bridging Data and Decisions, *INFORMS Tutorials Series*. Ed. by A. Newman, J. Leung, and J.C. Smith. Catonsville, MD, 161–170.

Maglio, P.P., Kwan, S.K. and Spohrer, J. (2015), "Commentary-toward a research agenda for human-centered service system innovation," *Service Science*, 7(1), 1–10.

Mars, M.M., Bronstein, J.L. and Lusch, R.F. (2012). "The value of a metaphor: Organizations and ecosystems." *Organizational Dynamics*, 41(4), 271–280.

Mollen, A. and Wilson, H. (2010), "Engagement, telepresence, and interactivity in online consumer experience: Reconciling scholastic and managerial perspectives," *Journal of Business Research*, 63(9–10), 919–925.

Moore, J.F. (1994). "Predators and prey: a new ecology of competition." *Harvard Business Review*, 71(3), 75–86.

Nenonen, S., Frow, P., Payne, A. and Storbacka, K. (2012), "Co-creating in actor networks: Identifying attractive morphotypes," Paper presented at the Global Marketing Conference, Seoul, 19–22 July.

Prahalad, C. K. and Ramaswamy, V. (2004), "Co-creation experiences: The next practice in value creation," *Journal of Interactive Marketing*, 18(3), 5–14.

Ramaswamy, V. (2009), "Leading the transformation to co-creation of value," *Strategy & Leadership*, 37(2), 32–37.

Ramaswamy, V. and Gouillart, F. (2010), "Building the co-creative enterprise," *Harvard Business Review*, Available at: http://techarbour.com/demosite/wp-content/uploads/2011/02/r1010j-pdf-eng.pdf [Accessed April 29, 2013].

Sawhney, M., Verona, G. and Prandelli, E. (2005), "Collaborating to create: The internet as a platform for customer engagement in product innovation," *Journal of Interactive Marketing*, 19(4), 4–17.

Smedlund, A. and Faghankhani, H. (2015), "Platform orchestration for efficiency, development and innovation," *Proceedings of the 48th Hawaii International Conference on System Sciences (HICSS)*, Kauai, HI, 1380–1988.

Storbacka, K., Brodie, R.J., Böhmann, T., Maglio, P.P. and Nenonen, S. (2015) "Actor engagement in service ecosystems: Directions for further research," *Working paper*, University of Auckland Business School.

Teece, D.J., Pisano, G. and Shuen, A. (1997), "Dynamic capabilities and strategic management," *Strategic Management Journal*, 18(7), 509–533.

Van Doorn, J., Lemon, K. E., Mittal, V., Naβ, S., Pick, D., Pirner, P. and Verhoef, P. C. (2010), "Customer engagement behavior: Theoretical foundations and research directions," *Journal of Service Research*, 13(3), 253–266.

Verhoef, P. C., Neslin, S. A. and Vroomen, B. (2007), "Multichannel customer management: Understanding the research-shopper phenomenon," *International Journal of Research in Marketing*, 24(2), 129–148.

Vargo, S. L. and Lusch R. F. (2004), "Evolving to a new dominant logic for marketing," *Journal of Marketing,* 68(1), 1–17.

Whitney, D. E. (2002), "Physical limits to modularity," *Working paper*, Massachusetts Institute of Technology Engineering Systems Division. ESD-WP-2003–01.03.

8 Customer engagement in technology-based and high-contact interfaces

Katrien Verleye and Arne De Keyser

Introduction

In today's dynamic marketplace characterised by demanding customers, increased competition and economic downturns, firms find themselves in a quandary about how to gain competitive advantage in a cost-effective manner. One popular strategy involves engaging customers in the creation and development of products and services (Lovelock and Wirtz, 2007). For instance, firms such as Starbucks, Lego, Unilever and H.J. Heinz have been found to stimulate customers to share new ideas in company-managed virtual environments (Sawhney et al., 2005; Breidbach et al., 2014; De Ruyck and De Wulf, 2013). In other cases, customers are encouraged to design their own solutions in collaboration with the firm (Franke and Piller, 2004; Thomke and Von Hippel, 2002). Nike, for instance, encourages its customers to design their own shoes by means of NikeID, an online design tool integrated in the Nike website.

In keeping with the aforementioned examples, customers are able to engage with the firm through shared inventiveness and co-design (Bolton and Saxena-Iyer, 2009; Mustak et al., 2013; Vargo and Lusch, 2008). In recent years, these discretionary behaviours with a brand or firm focus – after and beyond transactions – have also been labelled as customer engagement behaviours (Van Doorn et al., 2010; Jaakkola and Alexander, 2014). Customer engagement behaviours encompass not only customer behaviours seeking to benefit the firm (cf. customer voluntary performance or organisational citizenship behaviours), but also customer behaviours that are driven by customers' own motivational drivers, rather than those originating from the firm (Brodie et al., 2011; Van Doorn et al., 2010). Although customer engagement behaviour researchers often incorporate customers' communication about a brand or firm – such as customer referrals and word-of-mouth – as important behavioural manifestations of customer engagement, this chapter focuses solely on customer engagement behaviours in the creation, development and delivery of new products and services.

Previous research holds that customer engagement behaviours in new product and service delivery processes contribute to the firm's performance in three ways. First, these customer engagement behaviours help firms to define and create unique and/or personalised experiences for customers (Prahalad and Ramaswamy, 2003; Fang et al., 2008). Specifically, firms can more easily enter into a dialogue with customers engaged in the creation and development of new products and services, which allows for progressive learning from and about customers and improves their understanding of the customer's experience context (Payne et al., 2008; Sawhney et al., 2005). Second, customer engagement behaviours are associated with productivity and efficiency gains and consequently, decreased costs for new product and service development (Hoyer et al., 2010) based on customer contributions facilitating the generation of new ideas (Blazevic and Lievens, 2008), the speed of innovation (Fang, 2008), and the marketability and launch of new products and services (Melton and Hartline, 2010). Third, customer engagement allows the development of stronger customer relationships, as a result of which firms can better retain, sustain and nurture their customer base and consequently, generate long-term profitability and lifetime value, rather than short-term gains (Kumar et al., 2010; Van Doorn et al., 2010).

As a result of the aforementioned customer-related and firm-related benefits, firms increasingly recognise the value of customer engagement and, consequently, opt for a customer engagement strategy (i.e. a strategy deployed to boost customer engagement with the brand or firm). To achieve this end, company-customer contact interfaces – such as internet platforms – are adjusted to allow engagement behaviours to take place. Generally, firms use a combination of technology-based interfaces (i.e. technologies – such as websites, social media and mobile apps – that mediate interactions between customers and the firm) and high-contact interfaces (i.e. employees that mediate interactions between customers and the firm) to interact with their customers. In this chapter, we elaborate on the implications of a customer engagement strategy for the design and development of these company-customer contact interfaces, thereby explicitly taking into consideration that firms offer multiple company-customer contact interfaces and thus use multi-interface systems (Berry et al., 2010).

In both high-contact and technology-based interfaces, firms can introduce tools that foster customer engagement in new product and service development and innovation. To do so, firms need tools that anticipate customers' motivational drivers to engage with the brand or firm. In this chapter, we discuss three widely-used tools – experimentation, community-building and gamification – that can help management achieve better results in engaging customers in new product and service development (De Ruyck and De Wulf, 2013).

The chapter is organised as follows: First, we elaborate on the key characteristics and motivational drivers of customer engagement. Second, drawing from self-determination theory, we discuss how engaged customers expect unique combinations of extrinsic, internalised extrinsic and intrinsic benefits. We then show how firm investments in, respectively, experimentation, community-building and gamification can help generate these benefits. More particularly, the integration of these tools in technology-based and high-contact service interfaces helps firms to encourage and support customers in showing shared inventiveness, co-design and other discretionary behaviours. We conclude this chapter by discussing the hurdles to benefit from engaging customers in multi-interface systems.

Key characteristics of customer engagement

Customers who engage in the creation, production and delivery of products and services co-construct their own experiences and solutions (Pine and Gilmore, 1999). In other words, this type of customer engagement reflects customers' interactive, co-creative experiences with a focal object/agent, such as a brand or firm (Brodie et al., 2011). Although customer engagement takes place by virtue of interactions with a focal object/agent, behavioural manifestations of customer engagement can occur in interactions between the focal object/agent and/or other actors (Brodie et al., 2011; Jaakkola and Alexander, 2014; Verleye et al., 2014). Customers can, for instance, give input for new products and services to frontline employees, or they might report new product and service suggestions in a survey directed to the firm. In other cases, customers may launch ideas for product and service innovations in interactions with other customers, rather than in interactions with the firm and its employees.

Next, customer engagement behaviours in interactions with the firm and/or other actors can exist in both offline and online environments. On the one hand, firms can encourage their customers to participate in user meetings, face-to-face interviews and brainstorming or focus groups (Alam, 2002; Schirr, 2012). On the other hand, customers may post ideas in virtual customer environments (e.g. new product and service ideas posted on www.MyStarbucksIdea.com) or design their own products and services by means of user innovation toolkits and self-design tools (Franke and Schreier, 2010; Thomke and Von Hippel, 2002). The occurrence of customer engagement behaviours in offline and online environments implies that customer engagement can have not only a local scope (e.g. when customers verbally communicate a new product or service idea to employees), but also a global scope (e.g. when customers post new product and service ideas on the world wide web) (Van Doorn et al., 2010). As a result, firms need to take into consideration that their initiatives to boost customer engagement can have a broad geographic scope.

Furthermore, customer engagement occurs not only among customers who consume products and/or services of a brand or firm, but also among customers who do not directly consume these products and services. Family members of nursing home residents and parents of school children, for instance, do not consume nursing home or educational services themselves but they can give suggestions for service improvement to the nursing home or school personnel (Verleye et al., 2014). These examples illustrate that engagement behaviours can occur in the broader network of customers and/or other stakeholders. Jaakkola and Alexander (2014) argue that 'organisations can improve and differentiate their offering by incorporating the broad range of resources that customers and other stakeholders are willing to invest through co-developing or augmenting behaviours' (p. 257). As a consequence of this observation, firms might benefit from taking the broader network of customers and/or other stakeholders into consideration when opting for a customer engagement strategy.

As mentioned before, customer engagement is driven by customers' own and unique purposes and intentions, and not by the purposes and intentions of the firm (Jaakkola and Alexander, 2014). As a result, customer engagement behaviours are voluntary and the result of (multiple) motivational drivers (Van Doorn et al., 2010). In other words, customers decide whether or not to make voluntary resource contributions in terms of – among others – time, money and/or actions, by which the expected returns are – in line with social exchange theory – an important driver to engage in the creation, development and delivery of products and services by voluntary resource contributions (Verleye, 2015).

Finally, it is not inconceivable that customers' voluntary resource contributions do not accord to the purposes or intentions of the firm (Jaakkola and Alexander, 2014; Brodie et al., 2013; Van Doorn et al., 2010). In 2014, the initiator of www.IkeaHackers.net was asked to close this fan IKEA fan site, because IKEA argued that the fan site violated its brand rights by allowing their users to post ideas to turn IKEA furniture into classy and unique furniture (De Muynck, 2014). Although a worldwide storm of protest hampered IKEA to proceed, this example illustrates that customer engagement is not necessarily beneficial to the firm (Jaakkola and Alexander, 2014; Van Doorn et al., 2010). Moreover, customer engagement behaviours can even have detrimental effects for the firm and its stakeholders. Customers can, for instance, become competitors of the firm by developing competing versions of new products and services (Hoyer et al., 2010) or organise public actions against a firm (Van Doorn et al., 2010). In these situations, customers are disengaged instead of engaged with the firm (Kumar et al., 2010). In the next sections, we focus on motivational drivers of customer engagement.

Motivational drivers of customer engagement

Social exchange theory holds that people who put more resources and effort into an activity – such as customers engaged in specific creation, development and delivery of products and services – are motivated by the expected returns (Blau, 2004). The literature on customer motives to engage in the creation, production and delivery of new products and services confirms that customers expect different benefits in return for their engagement (see Table 8.1).

Several researchers group the six categories of motivational drivers of customer engagement into broader categories. Etgar (2008), for instance, identifies three broad categories. The first category refers to economic benefits, including reduction of risks associated with receiving inappropriate products or services (cf. pragmatic benefits) and a compensation in line with the effort made (cf. economic benefits). The second category refers to social benefits, including both opportunities for social contact (cf. social benefits) and better status and social esteem (cf. personal benefits). The third category refers to psychological

Table 8.1 Motivational drivers of customer engagement

		Hedonic benefits	Cognitive benefits	Social benefits	Personal benefits	Pragmatic benefits	Economic benefits
Motivational drivers in general	Etgar (2008)	Enjoyment, excitement and fun	Learning and mastering new skills and techniques	Opportunities for sharing activities with persons of similar interests and desires	Better status and social esteem	Reduction of risks associated with receiving inappropriate products or services and higher level of customisation	A compensation in line with the effort made (such as a cost reduction)
	Hoyer et al. (2010)	Enjoyment of contributing and intrinsic motivation	Gain technology, product or service knowledge	Strengthening of ties with relevant others	Increased status and social esteem		Monetary prizes or profit sharing from the firm that engages in co-creation with them, or intellectual property rights
Motivational drivers in technology-based interfaces	Nambisan and Baron (2009)	Pleasurable experiences	Knowledge about products, services and technologies	Strengthened relational ties among co-creation actors	Status and self-efficacy		
	Füller (2010)	Intrinsic playful tasks	Opportunities to keep up with new ideas and develop skills	Opportunities to connect with like-minded people	Self-efficacy and recognition	Solutions that better meet personal needs	Monetary rewards

benefits, which include enjoyment, fun and excitement (cf. hedonic benefits), as well as learning and mastering new skills and techniques (cf. cognitive benefits). Hoyer et al. (2010) propose a similar categorisation, except for the fact that cognitive benefits are considered as a separate category of expected co-creation benefits. All aforementioned categorisations are – as also acknowledged by Verleye (2015) – in line with self-determination theory focusing on motives behind people's choices, in that the these drivers can be plotted on a continuum going from more intrinsic benefits (hedonic and cognitive benefits) over internalised extrinsic (social and personal benefits) to more extrinsic benefits (pragmatic and economic benefits).

Recent research shows that intrinsically and extrinsically motivated customers have different preferences in relation to the design of service interfaces (i.e. employees and/or technologies that mediate the interactions and relationships between customers and firms (Verleye, 2015). To ensure that engaged customers get rewarding experiences, firms need to understand customers' drivers to engage in the creation, production and delivery of products and services. If customers are intrinsically interested, firms might benefit from integrating hedonic elements into their service interfaces. In return, service interfaces with pragmatic and economic benefits might encourage extrinsically interested customers to engage in the creation, production and delivery of products and services. In a lot of situations, however, firms want to attract a wide variety of customers. In these situations, firms might benefit from integrating multiple, different benefits into their high-contact and technology-based interfaces. Specifically, the multi-interface system thus needs to (1) signal the potential benefits of customer engagement, and (2) aid engaged customers to act in ways that help them to get the expected benefits (Verleye, 2014). By balancing the expected benefits of engaging in the creation, development and delivery of products and services with the benefits received throughout the new product and service development and delivery process, firms can generate rewarding experiences for engaged customers (Zeithaml et al., 1990; Verleye, 2015).

Engagement tools in multi-interface systems

In this section, we present three tools to incorporate customer encouragement and support into multi-interface systems. These tools include experimentation, community-building and gamification, because these tools anticipate extrinsic, internalised extrinsic and intrinsic motivational drivers of customer engagement and are often used in practice (De Ruyck and De Wulf, 2013).

Experimentation

To encourage and support customers to engage in new product and service development, firms can provide their customers with *experimentation tools*. These tools allow customers to create, develop, design and test products and services in a more effective and efficient way (Franke and Schreier, 2010;

Thomke and Von Hippel, 2002). As a result, experimentation contributes to developing products and services that better meet customers' needs (i.e. pragmatic value) in a more efficient way (i.e. economic benefits), although the benefits can extend beyond these extrinsic benefits in both technology-based and high-contact interfaces.

An example of the integration of experimentation toolkits in technology-based interfaces is the 'Do Us a Flavour' website of Lay's. This website provides tools to engage customers in the creation of new flavours for potato chips. Customers are able to use the 'Create My Flavour' tool to design and visualise their own chip styles (e.g. flavour name and main ingredients) and the 'Flavour Gallery' tool to learn more about favourite flavours per location and their friends' favourite flavours (more information: see www.dousaflavor.com). By offering these tools, the 'Do Us a Flavour' website of Lay's signals the opportunity to engage in the design of a personalised product in an efficient way (cf. economic benefits). Moreover, these tools also allow customers to learn their preferences iteratively (cf. cognitive benefits). Previous research confirms that customers learn their preferences iteratively until the optimal product or service is created if experimentation toolkits allow for visualisation and trial-and-error experimentation (Thomke and Von Hippel, 2002; Franke et al., 2008).

Furthermore, firms can also provide customers with experimentation toolkits in high-contact interfaces. One such example comes from German manufacturer of personal care products Beiersdorf. To preserve its status as a provider of popular body care brands, such as NIVEA and Eucerin, the company's research centre invested in on-site bathrooms designed solely for the purpose of gaining insight into how characteristics of creams, shaving foams, shampoos and soaps are experienced, judged and desired by their customers. To gather this information, Beiersdorf product developers observe how customers use a variety of products and actively discuss usage, habits and expectations stemming from these customers (for more information: see www.beiersdorf.com). By participating in this initiative, customers gain new knowledge about the company, its products and body care (cf. cognitive benefits). In the meanwhile, it is not inconceivable that highly engaged customers also get social and personal benefits from engaging in Beiersdorf's product development processes, because it allows them to connect with Beiersdorf product developers and signal these connections to their peers.

To ensure that experimentation toolkits in high-contact interfaces aid customers in getting the expected benefits, firms need to invest in customer-oriented employees. Customer orientation implies that employees do not only need to seek dialogue with customers, but also need to find ways to process what they learn from customers to keep the customers' interest and bring the dialogue forward (Prahalad and Ramaswamy, 2000). In technology-based interfaces, firms need to invest in developing user-friendly tools. User-friendliness involves information provision to use the innovation tools, since this helps customers to use these tools more efficiently (Zeithaml et al., 2002). Next, firms also need to avoid technology failures (e.g. temporarily unavailable online tools) and/or process failures (e.g. tool not remembering choices made in an earlier stage), because these failures decrease the customer experience (Meuter et al., 2000). Zeithaml et al. (2002) confirm the importance of reliability (i.e. technical functioning of the website and its functions) and fulfillment (i.e. accuracy of service promises) to generate a better customer experience.

Community-building

To ensure that customers also have opportunities to obtain social benefits in return for their engagement in the creation, development and delivery of new products and services (cf. internalised extrinsic benefits), firms can also invest in building customer communities. Although customers can also create their own communities (e.g. Ikea Hacking), this section specifically focuses on firm initiatives aimed at creating opportunities for customers to connect with one another and the firm. In technology-based interfaces, firms can build customer communities in various ways. On the one hand, firms can use several external social media platforms – such as Twitter and Facebook – to encourage customers to connect with the firm and one another. Social media can connect customers with firms and one another by providing access to online content and facilitating communication (Hollebeek et al., 2014). The 'Do Us A Flavour' contest of Lay's, for instance, started with a big media campaign, by which social media were used to create buzz around the contest and by which Lay's fans and followers could actively discuss the contest. Participants were also encouraged to promote their own potato style via these platforms. On the other hand, firms can integrate a virtual customer community within their own, internal interfaces. Starbucks, for instance, offers a direct link on its website to the company-owned webpage 'mystarbucksidea.com', which is an online community where customers can share and comment on ideas for new products and services. This community allows customers to connect with each other and company representatives who manage the community (cf. social benefits), and enables them to learn from one another (cf. cognitive benefits).

To improve the customer experience, virtual customer communities – such as mystarbucksidea.com – need to be continuously monitored in order to guarantee the working of the platform and to avoid situations in which customer ideas do not get posted or community members start offending each other's ideas (Meuter et al., 2000, Weijters et al., 2007). Hence, company monitoring and support are key to the success of these communities. Zeithaml et al. (2002), for instance, underline the importance of assisting customers when problems occur (cf. responsiveness) and allowing customers to communicate with the firm (cf. contact). At the MyStarbucksIdea website, a couple of Starbucks employees – labelled as 'Starbucks Idea Partners' – are appointed to listen to customers' ideas and answer and ask questions. Moreover, MyStarbucksIdea members can also support one another by commenting on each other's ideas (more information: see www.mystarbucksidea.com). In other words, both company-to-customer support and customer-to-customer support can aid customers to get the expected benefits and consequently, improve their customer experience.

In some situations, firms may benefit from bringing customers physically together by means of events. In 2013, for instance, the potato chip styles of the three finalists of the 'Do Us a Flavour' contest in Belgium ended up in all retail outlets of Lay's and Lay's also organised a closing event for all finalists, fans, press and other interested parties to announce the winner and hand over the financial award to the finalists. By doing so, the finalists get appreciation for their input, which can increase their status and self-esteem (cf. personal benefits). In the meantime, these events allow finalists, fans, press and other interested parties to connect with one another, because they experience the same event (cf. social benefits). Therefore, while the underlying mechanisms are the same in offline and online community-building, we consider events as an interesting community-building mechanism in high-contact interfaces, which can complement virtual customer communities.

Gamification

To anticipate customers' need for hedonic and cognitive returns on their engagement in new product and service development and innovation (cf. intrinsic benefits), firms may opt for gamification. Gamification involves inserting (video) game dynamics in customer-firm interfaces, and often involves specific competition (e.g. gathering more points than others) and co-operation (e.g. helping each other to reach target goals) mechanisms aimed at stimulating desired behaviours (Harman et al., 2014; Bailey et al., 2015). For example, mystarbucksidea.com explicitly incorporates multiple game elements into the online community to ensure that their members experience fun in interacting with the platform (cf. hedonic benefits). Moreover, all members can vote for other customer's ideas and become part of the Leaderboard if they get high scores from other customers (more information: see www.mystarbucksidea.com). As a consequence of gamified functionalities like voting and influence scores, customers can increase their self-esteem and status by visualising their achievements (cf. personal benefits). Another example involves FoldIt, which is a 3D online puzzle developed by the University of Washington in collaboration with the biochemistry industry. The aim of this application is to help advance one of biology's most prominent problems today: the folding of proteins. As this folding can be done in numerous ways and the current professional research community is limited, Foldit brings in the help of outside players who compete folding proteins in the best possible and most efficient way. In doing so, they advance science by discovering new solutions that complex mathematical models had not uncovered before (more information: see www.fold.it). The players involved can experience multiple benefits: the fun of solving a puzzle (cf. hedonic benefit), an increased self-esteem upon finding more efficient ways to solve a puzzle (cf. personal benefits), an increased knowledge of biology (cf. cognitive benefits) and a sense of community (cf. social benefits).

Although gamification is most often applied in a technology-based context, its benefits can also be introduced in high-contact interfaces. Looking back at

Lay's 'Do Us A Flavour' contest, multiple gamification elements were adopted in offline events. For instance, Lay's battles were organised in supermarkets where people got to taste and vote for the different new flavours that were developed. In doing so, customers cannot only derive pleasurable experiences from the battles (cf. hedonic benefits), the discussion amongst and competition between fans of different flavours also results in social experiences (cf. social benefits).

To ensure the success of gamifying the company-customer interfaces, firms need to ensure customers are intrigued and challenged by the gamified elements (e.g. obtaining a specific badge) in order to ensure continuous levels of customer engagement (Zichermann and Cunningham, 2011). Specifically, this implies developing games that do not exceed the skill-level of the customer base and allow them to reach specific target goals (Novak et al., 2000). However, firms should guarantee a minimum level of challenge in the long run as people might lose interest if they can achieve specific targets too easily and the gamified element loses its fun-factor. Hence, negative outcomes – such as not reaching a specific level of achievement or reaching it too easily – might cause customer to disengage in the long run. Ideally, gamification also enables immediate gratification through real-time feedback (e.g. whether or not one has obtained a badge; notification if other customers like your posts, etc.), while allowing the customer to share his/her achievements with his/her friends and family (Zichermann and Cunningham, 2011). Importantly, firms should be prudent with automatic sharing of customer achievements as they may harm the customer's self-esteem (e.g. when a customer performs worse than his/her friends). Therefore, it is advisable to let the customers choose whether or not they want to publicly share their current accomplishments on the gamified platform.

Combinations

Many companies combine experimentation, community-building and gamification in order to create compelling environments that foster engagement behaviours. OpenIDEO, for instance, explicitly integrates experimentation, community-building and gamification in its online interface. This open innovation platform, managed by design company IDEO, attempts to bring together people from all over the world to solve social problems by means of collaborative thinking (cf. community-building). Every social cause that is discussed is backed-up by one or more sponsoring firms with a specific interest in solving this issue. At all times, multiple challenges are posted in which members can contribute their ideas and solutions. Other members can comment, vote and 'applaud' potentially valuable research ideas that they feel would advance the project (cf. gamification). Furthermore, every member is assigned a specific 'Design Quotient' that is based on his/her number of research ideas, comments and votes on the platform, reflecting the status of that member (cf. gamification). OpenIDEO also provides all its subscribers with specific design tools that can help them think of and develop their research ideas (cf. experimentation tools; more information: see www.openideo.com).

As illustrated by the case of OpenIDEO, online interfaces lend themselves to simultaneous integration of experimentation, community-building and gamification. The integration of these tools, however, can also extend beyond the boundaries of a specific interface. The 'Do Us A Flavour' contest of Lay's, for instance, combines online experimentation, community-building and gamification (cf. www. dousaflavor.com) with community-building and gamification in high-contact interfaces (cf. events and battles in supermarkets). In other words, firms can also opt for integrating experimentation, community-building and gamification in the multi-interface system. By doing so, firms can further increase the likelihood of customers engaging in the creation and development of new products and services.

Benefit-inhibiting hurdles from engaging customers in multi-interface systems

To ensure that firms benefit from investing in tools to encourage and support customer engagement in multi-interface systems, it is not sufficient to signal the potential benefits and ensure that customers also get the expected benefits. Additionally, it is of the utmost importance that engaged customers use the interfaces in ways that do not harm the firm (cf. key characteristics of customer engagement). Firms, for instance, might be hurt by customers using their interfaces to spread negative word-of-mouth or acting as competitors by developing competing versions of the firm's products and services (Hoyer et al., 2010; Prahalad and Ramaswamy, 2000). To avoid this situation, firms might benefit from providing engaged customers with information about their role. Drawing from role theory, this process of giving guidelines to customers has been labelled as customer socialisation (Verleye, 2014). In the next paragraphs, we elaborate on the concretisation of customer socialisation in high-contact and technology-based interfaces.

Regarding technology-based interfaces, customers are often asked to create an account and accept the terms and conditions of use. The terms of use of MyStarbucksIdea, for instance, stipulate that users are – among others – prohibited from 'creating any frames at any other sites pertaining to any portion of this site', 'posting submissions or using the site in such a way that damages the image or rights of Starbucks, other users or third parties' or 'using the site to send or post harassing, abusive, or threatening messages' (Starbucks, 2015). By doing so, Starbucks attempts to avoid that customer engagement in the MyStarbucksIdea platform harms the firm and/or its stakeholders. Additionally, these terms of use also specify the firm's rights in relation to customer input (e.g. 'You give Starbucks a non-exclusive, free, worldwide license for the duration of the applicable author's rights, to publish your remarks, ideas, graphics, photographs or other information communicated to Starbucks through this site'; Starbucks, 2015). In sum, clarification of the role expectations can help firms to ensure that their investments in customer engagement in new product and service development in technology-based service interfaces benefit both customers (cf. motivational drivers) and firms (cf. new product and service development).

In high-contact interfaces, firms need to ensure that customer engagement does not consume too many resources. Moreover, customer engagement in high-contact interfaces can also harm the firm by placing an excessive burn on frontline employees. Previous research has merely shown that customers who engage in the firm's processes often claim less responsibility than the firm for failure and more responsibility than the firm for success in situations where they take over tasks from the frontline employees (Bendapudi and Leone, 2003). Since customers who engage in the creation, development and delivery of new products and services also take over tasks previously performed by frontline employees, it is not inconceivable that these employees experience job stress. To avoid job stress among frontline employees, firms might benefit from informing customers about their role in new product and service development initiatives. A case study in nursing homes, for instance, revealed that these organisations invest in role alignment discussion between customers and frontline employees in combination with written role information in folders and brochures (Verleye et al., 2014). By investing in communication about the role expectations, firms can avoid that customer engagement in new product and service development harms the firms and/or their frontline employees.

Conclusions

This chapter shows that customer engagement has the potential to generate both customer-related benefits (unique and personalised customer experiences) and firm-related benefits (productivity and efficiency gains and/or long-term profitability). To achieve these benefits, firms need to find ways to encourage their customers to engage in the creation, development and delivery of new products and services. Drawing from social exchange theory, this chapter holds that people who put more effort into an activity – such as engaged customers – are motivated by the expected returns. Specifically, customer engagement is – in line with self-determination theory – seen as a unique function of extrinsic, internalised extrinsic and intrinsic benefits. Therefore, firms need to anticipate these benefits into their multi-interface system through respectively experimentation, community-building and gamification, but the concretisation depends on the level of technologisation.

In technology-based interfaces, firms can encourage and support their customers to engage in the creation and development of products and services by providing experimentation toolkits, creating virtual customer communities or adding gamification elements to the company-customer interface. By doing so, firms signal the potential benefits of engaging in the creation, development and delivery of products and services. To support customers in also getting the expected benefits in technology-based interfaces, firms need to ensure that experimentation tools, communities and games are user-friendly. In high-contact interfaces, firms can similarly encourage their customers to engage in the creation and development of products and services by means of experimentation toolkits, community events and gamification. In all these initiatives, it is important that employees and/or other customers are open to customer engagement and support the input of engaged customers to ensure a rewarding customer experience.

User-friendly online tools, communities and games in technology-based interfaces and customer-oriented employees in high-contact interfaces help generate compelling experiences for customers engaged in new product and service development initiatives. However, these initiatives are a necessary but insufficient condition for firms to benefit from opting for a customer engagement strategy. Drawing from role theory, firms need to inform customers about their role – including rights and duties – when engaging in the creation, development and delivery of products and services. By doing so, firms can avoid customers feeling exploited and ensure that customers do not harm the firm.

In sum, we used social exchange theory, self-determination theory and role theory to advance our understanding of the implications of a customer engagement strategy for the design and development of multi-interface systems. It is not inconceivable that the design of compelling multi-interface systems requires initial investments. Kumar et al. (2010) hold that these investments have the potential to generate higher profits in the long run through the creation of customer engagement value. In the meanwhile, Hoyer et al. (2010) argue that the trade-offs between the costs and benefits of customer engagement in general – both in the short and the long run – deserve further investigation. Therefore, future research is warranted on the trade-offs between the creation of customer engagement value and the investments needed to design multi-interface systems that generate value for the customer and the firm.

References

Alam, I. 2002. An exploratory investigation of user involvement in new service development. *Journal of the Academy of Marketing Science*, 30, 250–261.

Bailey, P., Pritchard, G. and Kernohan, H. 2015. Gamification in market research: Increasing enjoyment, participant engagement and richness of data, but what of data validity? *International Journal of Market Research*, 57, 17–28.

Bendapudi, N. and Leone, R.P. 2003. Psychological implications of customer participation in co-production. *Journal of Marketing*, 67, 14–28.

Berry, L.L., Bolton, R.N., Bridges, C.H., Meyer, J., Parasuraman, A. and Seiders, K. 2010. Opportunities for innovation in the delivery of interactive retail services. *Journal of Interactive Marketing*, 24, 155–167.

Blau, P.M. 2004. *Exchange and power in social life*. New York: Wiley.

Blazevic, V. and Lievens. A. 2008. Managing innovation through customer coproduced knowledge in electronic services: An exploratory study. *Journal of the Academy of Marketing Science*, 36, 138–151.

Bogers, M., Afuah, A. and Bastian, B. 2010. Users as innovators: A review, critique, and future research directions. *Journal of Management*, 36, 857–875.

Bolton, R. and Saxena-Iyer, S. 2009. Interactive services: A framework, synthesis and research directions. *Journal of Interactive Marketing*, 23, 91–104.

Breidbach, C.F., Brodie, R. and Hollebeek, L. 2014. Beyond virtuality: From engagement platforms to engagement ecosystems. *Managing Service Quality*, 24, 592–611.

Brodie, R.J., Hollebeek, L.D., Juric, B. and Ilic, A. 2011. Customer engagement: Conceptual domain, fundamental propositions, and implications for research. *Journal of Service Research*, 14, 252–271.

Brodie, R. J., Ilic C, A., Juric, B. and Hollebeek, L. 2013. Consumer engagement in a virtual brand community: An exploratory analysis. *Journal of Business Research*, 66, 105–114.

De Muynck, E. 2014. IKEA legt grootste fansite restricties op. De Standaard, 19 June.

De Ruyck, T. and De Wulf, K. 2013. The Consumer Consulting Board, Ghent, Belgium. InSites Consulting.

Etgar, M. 2008. A descriptive model of the consumer co-production process. *Journal of the Academy of Marketing Science*, 36, 97–108.

Fang, E. 2008. Customer participation and the trade-off between new product innovativeness and speed to market. *Journal of Marketing*, 72, 90–104.

Fang, E., Palmatier, R. W. and Evans, K. R. 2008. Influence of customer participation on creating and sharing of new product value. *Journal of the Academy of Marketing Science*, 36, 322–336.

Franke, N., Keinz, P. and Schreier, M. 2008. Complementing mass customization toolkits with user communities: How peer input improves customer self-design. *Journal of Product Innovation Management*, 25, 546–559.

Franke, N. and Piller, F. 2004. Value creation by toolkits for user innovation and design: The case of the watch market. *Journal of Product Innovation Management*, 21, 401–415.

Franke, N. and Schreier, M. 2010. Why customers value self-designed products: The importance of process effort and enjoyment. *Journal of Product Innovation Management*, 27, 1020–1031.

Fuller, J. 2010. Refining virtual co-creation from a consumer perspective. *California Management Review*, 52, 98–122.

Harman, K., Koohang, A. an Paliszkiewicz, J. 2014. Scholarly interest in gamification: A citation network analysis. *Industrial Management & Data Systems*, 114, 1438–1452.

Hollebeek, L. D., Glynn, M. S. and Brodie, R. J. 2014. Consumer brand engagement in social media: Conceptualization, scale development and validation. *Journal of Interactive Marketing*, 28, 149–165.

Hoyer, W. D., Chandy, R., Dorotic, M., Krafft, M. and Singh, S. S. 2010. Consumer cocreation in new product development. *Journal of Service Research*, 13, 283–296.

Jaakkola, E. and Alexander, M. 2014. The role of customer engagement behavior in value co-creation: A service system perspective. *Journal of Service Research*, 17, 247–261.

Kumar, V., Aksoy, L., Donkers, B., Venkatesan, R., Wiesel, T. and Tillmanns, S. 2010. Undervalued or overvalued customers: capturing total customer engagement value. *Journal of Service Research*, 13, 297–310.

Lovelock, C. H. and Wirtz, J. 2007. *Services marketing: People, technology, strategy.* New Jersey: Prentice Hall.

Melton, H. L. and Hartline, M. D. 2010. Customer and frontline employee influence on new service development performance. *Journal of Service Research*, 13, 411–425.

Meuter, M. L., Ostrom, A. L., Roundtree, R. I. and Bitner, M. J. 2000. Self-service technologies: Understanding customer satisfaction with technology-based service encounters. *Journal of Marketing*, 64, 50–64.

Mustak, M., Jaakkola, E. and Halinen, A. 2013. Customer participation and value creation: A systematic review and research implications. *Managing Service Quality*, 23, 341–359.

Novak, T. P., Hoffman, D. L. and Yung, Y. F. 2000. Measuring the customer experience in online environments: A structural modeling approach. *Marketing Science*, 19, 22–42.

Payne, A. F., Storbacka, K. and Frow, P. 2008. Managing the co-creation of value. *Journal of the Academy of Marketing Science*, 36, 83–96.

Pine, J. B. and Gilmore, J. H. 1999. *The experience economy: Work is theatre and every business a stage*. Boston, Massachusetts: Harvard Business School Press.

Prahalad, C. K. and Ramaswamy, V. 2000. Co-opting customer competence. *Harvard Business Review*, 78, 79–87.

Prahalad, C. K. and Ramaswamy, V. 2003. The new frontier of experience innovation. *MIT Sloan Management Review*, 44, 12–18.

Sawhney, M., Verona, G. and Prandelli, E. 2005. Collaborating to create: the internet as platform for customer engagement in product innovation. *Journal of Interactive Marketing*, 19, 4–17.

Schirr, G. R. 2012. Flawed tools: The efficacy of group research methods to generate customer ideas. *Journal of Product Innovation Management*, 29, 473–488.

Starbucks. 2015. MyStarbucksIdea.com Terms of Use [Online]. Available: http:// mystarbucksidea.com/ [Accessed March, 20 2015].

Thomke, S. and Von Hippel, E. 2002. Customers as innovators: A new way to create value. *Harvard Business Review*, 80, 74–81.

Van Doorn, J., Lemon, K. N., Mittal, V., Nass, S., Pick, D., Pirner, P. and Verhoef, P. C. 2010. Customer engagement behavior: Theoretical foundations and research directions. *Journal of Service Research*, 13, 253–266.

Vargo, S. L. and Lusch, R. F. 2008. Service-dominant logic: Continuing the evolution. *Journal of the Academy of Marketing Science*, 36, 1–10.

Verleye, K. 2014. Designing service interfaces for customer engagement in the creation of value. In: Kandampully, J. (ed.) *Customer experience management: Enhancing experience and value through service management*. Dubuque, Iowa: Kendal Hunt Publishing Company.

Verleye, K. 2015. The co-creation experience from the customer perspective: Its measurement and determinants. *Journal of Service Management*, 26, 321–342.

Verleye, K., Gemmel, P. and Rangarajan, D. 2014. Managing engagement behaviors in a network of customers and stakeholders: Evidence from the nursing home sector. *Journal of Service Research*, 17, 68–84.

Weijters, B., Rangarajan, D., Falk, T. and Schillewaert, N. 2007. Determinants and outcomes of customers' use of self-service technology in a retail setting. *Journal of Service Research*, 10, 3–21.

Zeithaml, V. A., Parasuraman, A. and Berry, L. L. 1990. *Delivering quality service. Balancing customer perceptions and expectations*. New York: The Free Press.

Zeithaml, V. A., Parasuraman, A. and Malhotra, A. 2002. Service quality delivery through Web sites: A critical review of extant knowledge. *Journal of the Academy of Marketing Science*, 30, 362–375.

Zichermann, G. and Cunningham, C. 2011. *Gamification by design*. Sebastopol, Canada: O'Reilly Media.

9   Website engagement

Antonio Hyder and Enrique Bigné

Introduction

Beyond customer engagement with brands (Martí, Bigné and Hyder, 2014), engagement in Web settings is gaining focus as the digital consumer industry pays attention to the term *Web site engagement* (Forrester, 2015). Despite the growing use of this term, it is yet to be conceptualised from an academic perspective. Broadly speaking to engage is to 'involve (a person or his or her attention) intensely' (Collins Essential English Dictionary, 2006). Whereas industry focuses mainly on the use of clickstream metrics for its assessment, it has not yet been clarified how Web site engagement should be measured. The aims of this research are to clarify what is Web site engagement, to identify its dimensions and to suggest a Web site engagement measurement. Our proposal is based on the engagement with the technology scale developed by O'Brien (2008). The implications of this article are relevant for both academics and practitioners and opens paths for further research.

Online retention and Web site engagement

Within the context of digital marketing, there is a growing body of literature that relates to both the psychological and behavioural retention of consumers. Research can be found on concepts such as stickiness (Li, Browne and Wetherbe, 2006), cognitive lock-in (Zauberman, 2003) and cognitive absorption (Agarwal and Karahanna, 2000). Retention constructs are particularly valuable within online contexts as they are difficult to develop and are not as strong as commitment in other offline contexts (Li, Browne and Wetherbe, 2007). Understanding how online consumers engage with a digital medium such as a Web sites, and how this phenomenon can be measured, is relevant for both academia and industry.

Researchers have argued that given the increased emphasis on online user experience, it is no longer sufficient to ensure that an information system's results are merely usable (Blythe, Overbeeke and Monk, 2003). O'Brien (2008) affirms that successful technologies *engage* users. When justifying the need for an *engagement with technology* construct, O'Brien (2008) affirmed that 'failing to engage users equates with no sale on an electronic commerce site and no transmission of information from a Web site'. She defines *engagement with technology* as 'a holistic construct that fits within the context of experience and encapsulates users' perspectives of the human-computer interaction, as well as its system and user constituents'. According to the results from a global survey conducted by McKinsey & Company (2014), the top strategic priority is digital engagement of customers, with 69 per cent ranking engagement among their top-three priorities of the six identified.

At present there seems to be a contradiction regarding whether Web site engagement should be measured with clickstream data downloaded from Internet servers (e.g. Bucklin and Sismeiro, 2009) surveys (e.g. O'Brien, 2008) or a combination of both. Industry relies on the use of clickstreams. Consultancy firm McKinsey (2008) affirmed 'The Web is the most measurable medium in the history of marketing. Now all that's left is figuring out how to measure it.' In their report they suggest that the digital world has developed faster than the tools that are required to measure it. In this direction, software *Google analytics* offers Web site managers the possibility of measuring engagement with their sites. According to the Google analytics Web site, managers can measure their site engagement goals against threshold levels that they define (Google, 2015). However, these thresholds are primarily determined solely with clickstream variable, such as visit duration and page depth and do not take into account consumer experiences. In this chapter we argue that experience is a part of engagement and should be included in any measurement of Web site engagement.

Definitions of engagement

In plain English language, to *engage* is to '*involve (a person or his or her attention) intensely*' (Collins Essential English Dictionary, 2006). In academic research something that 'engages' us is something that draws us in, that attracts and holds our attention (Chapman, 1997; see Martí, Bigné and Hyder, 2014 for further detail on customer engagement). Within the context of multimedia, Jacques, Preece and Carey (1995) suggest an engaging experience is an active process, in which a system 'catches', 'captivates', 'holds' and 'retains' the 'interest' and 'attention' of the user. In the context of advertising, Lin, Gregor and Ewing (2008) consider that engagement is an activity that occurs when a person's attention is focused on the activity. For O'Brien (2008), *engagement with technology* is 'a holistic construct that fits within the context of experience and encapsulates user's perspectives of the human-computer interaction, as well as its system and user constituents'. Being engaged could also be consider as being 'biologically connected', as Nahl and Bilal (2007) consider being engaged as 'the opposite of being disconnected'.

Academic research on engagement in technology-related contexts

Since Laurel's (1993) first use of the term, engagement has also been applied in the context of technology, and for more than two decades, researchers have been undertaking research utilising the term. Jacques et al. (1995) consider engagement in their research in the field of learning with multimedia, describing how an understanding of engagement can aid in the process of designing multimedia technology (e.g. computers and mobile telephones) or different applications, such as TV series, web sites or social media. They give examples of interactions that are found to be engaging and provide methods for evaluating their impact on students. The researchers state that learners were engaged with education multimedia when these systems held their attention. They also affirm that well-designed multimedia systems would draw learners in, motivate interaction and help them to accomplish learning goals without distraction. Within the field of multimedia presentations, Webster and Ho (1997) suggest that developing presentations that provide greater *challenge, feedback, control* and *variety* could increase engagement. They also described that *attention focus, curiosity* and *intrinsic interest* have an influence on engagement.

Similarly, Garris, Ahlers and Driskell (2002) use the term *motivation* to refer to the desire to engage in a task. More specifically, these researchers used motivation to describe an individual's choice to engage in an activity, and the intensity of effort or persistence in that activity. Individuals who are highly motivated are more likely to engage, devote effort and persist longer in a particular activity. Also Mallon and Webb (2000) studied engagement in the computer games industry, as the entertainment industry particularly focuses on capturing and holding the attention of their audience. Building open notions of enjoyment and flow, Agarwal and Karahanna (2000) propose a multidimensional construct called *cognitive absorption*, which they define as a 'state of deep involvement with software'. Also McMillan and Hwang (2002) refer to the relationship between engagement and the time spent on a Web site, suggesting that an increased time controlling a site could also be a result of intense engagement, and that time-related factors, such as two-way communication are relevant to engagement on the Web. Studying participant engagement and retention with a physical activity Web site at a workplace, Leslie, Marshall, Owen and Bauman (2005) use repeat visits to the home page and subsequent page views on the physical activity Web site in order to measure engagement.

Within the contexts of media and advertising, Calder and Malthouse (2008) refer to reader engagement with the media, and define engagement as 'the collective experiences that a reader has with the editorial content'. The dimensions they utilise to measure media engagement are utility of the medium, transportation and the degree that the reader felt both smarter and sophisticated. In a subsequent research, Calder, Malthouse and Schaedel (2009) extended their work differentiating between personal engagement and social-interactive engagement. Mollen and Wilson (2010) propose a conceptual online-engagement framework taking into account the viewpoints of both practitioners and academics. They interpret online engagement as a cognitive and affective commitment to an active relationship with a brand as personified by a Web site. According to Mollen and Wilson (2010), engagement is a mental state that is accompanied by active, sustained and complex cognitive processing. They affirm that engagement involves emotional bonding or impact, emotional congruence and pleasure and satisfaction. Based on the Stimulus-Organism-Response model (S-O-R; Eroglu, Machleit and Davis, 2003) they propose an online engagement conceptual framework where a consumer's experiential response to a stimulus passes through three stages: perceived interactivity, telepresence and finally engagement. In their article, Mollen and Wilson (2010) also describe three differences between involvement and engagement. First, consumer involvement requires a consumption object. In their research, the consumption object was the 'brand personified by the Web site'. Second, they suggested that engagement goes beyond involvement as that it should also encompass an active relationship with a brand. Third, engagement requires more than performing cognition, as it requires satisfying both experiential and instrumental values.

Kumar, Aksoy, Donkers, Venkatesan, Wiesel and Tillmanns (2010) also refer to 'customer engagement' as a behavioural construct and define it as active interactions of a customer with a firm, with prospects and other customers, whether they are transactional or non-transactional in nature. Likewise in this direction, Brodie, Hollebeek, Jurić and Ilić (2011) have developed a successful research stream also focusing on the same 'customer engagement' concept (e.g. Hollebeek, 2011a; Hollebeek, Glynn and Brodie, 2014) which they consider a psychological state with emotional, cognitive and behavioural dimensions, and define consumer engagement as a motivational state that occurs by virtue of interactive, co-creative customer experiences with a focal agent/object (e.g. a brand) in focal brand relationships.

O'Brien (2008) conducted prominent research on technology-related engagement. Based on previous research (O'Brien and Toms, 2008) and *flow theory* (Csikszentmihalyi, 1996), this researcher deconstructed the term 'engagement' as it applies to people's experiences with technology. She conducted exploratory research using semi-structured interviews with users of four different technology applications – Web searching, online shopping, Webcasting and gaming applications – in order to explore their perception of being engaged with the technology. Based on the outcome of this analysis, she operationally and conceptually proposed a definition of the multidimensional concept of *engagement with technology*. In order to propose this construct, O'Brien (2008) undertook a series of three research efforts described in Table 9.1. We shall refer to these three research efforts as stage 1, 2 and 3 in the development of an engagement with technology construct.

In the first stage of the research O'Brien and Toms (2008) suggest that the engagement process is characterised by attributes that pertain to users, an information system and user-system interaction; suggest that engagement with technology comprises four different stages; and propose the dimensions of a Web site engagement construct illustrated in Table 9.1. The four different stages are: point of engagement, period of engagement, disengagement (i.e. withdrawal) and re-engagement. They also refer to a state of non-engagement. As a conclusion of their first stage of research, O'Brien and Toms (2008) suggest that engagement with technology can be measured with 11 variables, in particular, aesthetic and sensory appeal, affect, awareness, challenge, feedback, interactivity, interest, motivation, novelty, perceived control and perceived time.

In the second stage of research, O'Brien (2008) reduced the period engagement dimensions from 11 to 10. Interactivity was excluded from the first proposal of the engagement with technology construct, and focused attention was included. Items that originally composed interactivity overlapped with other items and this construct was therefore eliminated. Also, the combined 'aesthetics and sensory appeal' dimension was reduced to just 'aesthetics'. The 10 dimensions of the construct, in total, contained 31 items or *indicators*. Table 9.1 illustrates the proposed dimensions of engagement with technology of stage 2, alongside the dimensions of stage 1 and stage 3. In the third stage of the development of an engagement with technology construct, 31 indicators from

Table 9.1 Three-stage proposal of dimensions of *engagement with technology*

Stage 1 O'Brien and Toms (2008) 11 dimensions	Stage 2 O'Brien (2008) 10 dimensions	Stage 3 O'Brien (2008) 12 dimensions
Aesthetic and sensory appeal	Aesthetics	Aesthetics
Affect	Affect	Positive affect Negative affect
	Focused attention	Attention
Awareness	Awareness	
Challenge	Challenge	Challenge Engagement
Feedback	Feedback	Feedback
Interactivity		
Interest	Interest	
		Intention to return
Motivation	Motivation	Motivation
Novelty	Novelty	Novelty
Perceived control	Control	Control
Perceived time	Perceived time	Perceived time

Source: O'Brien and Toms (2008)

stage 2 were subjected to an exploratory analysis and rearranged into 12 sub-scales: aesthetics, attention, positive affect, negative affect, challenge, control, engagement, feedback, intention to return, motivation, novelty and perceived time. This is O'Brien's (2008) final proposal of a scale of *engagement with technology* and is illustrated in Table 9.1.

Towards a Web site engagement measurement

Overall, it seems that there are different types of engagement. Calder, Malthouse and Schaedel (2009) suggest that engagement pertains to a group of people and consider a *social engagement* perspective. Brandtzaeg, Følstad and Heim (2005) and Webster and Ho (1997) approach engagement from a *personal engagement* perspective. In this direction Brodie, Hollebeek and colleagues refer to 'customer engagement' and 'customer brand engagement' perspectives across their research stream (e.g. Brodie, Hollebeek, Jurić and Ilić, 2011; Hollebeek, 2011).

There are multiple approaches for approaching the engagement concept, and we postulate that engagement should be context-dependent. In this research, and within the context of consumer-digital technologies, we pursue the development of a personal Web site engagement measurement seen from the perspective of how an individual engages with an e-commerce Web site (Li et al., 2006). In fact, we argue that the dimensions of engagement across different digital interactive contexts might even change: the dimensions of engagement with a Web site might be different to the dimensions of engagement with a smart phone, although they are both consumer-digital devices, simply because the situations of use can be different per se, and therefore engagement could also be different. We argue that each communication activity may lead to different dimensions of engagement, where the activity is the key, overcoming characteristics inherent in the particular. In this vein, apart from laptops or tablet computers, a mobile device can also be used for searching on the Internet.

Accordingly, based on the definitions of Chapman et al. (1997), Jacques et al. (1995) and Brandtzaeg et al. (2005) and due to the fact that our proposal of engagement will be specific for the context of Web sites, we suggest the following definition of Web site engagement:

> *Web site engagement is a consumer experience that occurs when a user's attention is captivated and held by a Web site, and the user wants to remain interacting with the Web site in a concentrated fashion during a period of time.*

We base our proposal of a Web site scale adopting and adapting the engagement with technology construct suggested by O'Brien (2008). This researcher suggests that engagement can be measured with 12 subscales grouped in six factors, which are: aesthetics, focused attention, endurability, involvement, novelty and perceived usability. Focusing on factor perceived usability, O'Brien (2008) suggests that challenge and control are subscales of this factor. *Challenge* is a construct that refers to how difficult is it to use a Web site, relative to the skills of the user (Ghani, 1995) and therefore, researchers have related this construct to the usability of a Web site (Huang, 2003; Guo and Poole, 2008). In flow theory, challenge has been considered as a dimension of flow by some researchers (e.g. Csikszentmihalyi, 1996; Hoffman and Novak, 2000) and excluded by others (Chen, 2006; Lu, Zhou and Wang, 2009). Furthermore, Guo and Poole (2008) specifically highlight that it is difficult to assess how challenging a Web site can be during its design due to the different levels of skills of its different users. This implies that it is not clear whether challenge is a construct that should be assessed from the point of view of consumers, or from a combined consumer-technology viewpoint. Should challenge be a dimension of Web site engagement, this would mean that it is a variable that depends on the levels of skill held by a Web site user combined with the level of usability of a Web site. If it is not a dimension of Web site engagement, this would mean that engagement experiences only occur within the eyes of consumers and is subject to the architecture of a Web site.

With regards to *control*, this construct is closely related to interaction, as within the context of Web site-related research, control refers to the individual's perception that she or he exercises control of the interaction with a Web site (Guo and Poole, 2008; Huang, 2003) or with technology in general (Ghani and Deshpande, 1994; O'Brien, 2008). Teo, Oh, Liu and Wei (2003) operationalise a seven-level scale of control, based on the level of control that consumers had over different levels of interactivity. In this scale, different levels of control are required for different levels of interactivity. Likewise, in flow research, control has been recognised as one of the six dimensions of flow (Csikszentmihalyi, 1988) and has also been considered as a dimension of this construct in online-related research. Also Brandtzaeg et al. (2005) affirm that engagement makes users feel in control during an interaction. Accordingly, due to the interaction that can take place between a Web site and a user, and due to the close relationship between control and interactivity, it is not clear if control over interaction should be a dimension of Web site engagement.

As overall conclusion of this discussion is that it is not clear whether control and challenge are dimensions of Web site engagement. If they are, it could be argued that Web site engagement is a state that takes place between a system and a consumer. If they are not, it could be concluded that Web site engagement is a psychological state that takes place in the minds of people.

Potential dimensions of Web site engagement

The eight dimensions that we suggest would compose a Web site engagement scale are *positive affect, focused attention, challenge, control, curiosity, involvement, transformation of time* and *up-to-dateness of information*. In what follows each of these is described.

Positive affect Some researchers have used the term affect to equally refer to what psychology research calls *feelings* or *emotions* (Peterson, Hoyer and Wilson,

1986). Jennings defines affect as 'the emotional investment users make in order to be immersed in an environment, and sustain their involvement in the environment' (Jennings, 2000). When studying the role of affect in human computer interaction, Hudlicka (2003) affirms that an 'affective HCI' is an 'effective HCI'. Webster and Ahuja (2004) suggest that engagement in the context of online shopping could be not only purposeful but also pleasurable, and that affect could make people return to a specific product or company Web site.

Focused attention has been defined in online consumer research as 'the degree to which a user's attention is focused on Web site interaction' (Huang, 2003). Grounded on the fact that focused attention is also considered equal to concentration (e.g. Guo and Poole, 2008) and also that numerous researchers consider focused attention a dimension of flow applicable to online environments, we postulate that this construct will be a component of Web site engagement, and not *attention*, which refers to the allocation of cognitive resources.

Challenge The challenge of an activity is to apply one's knowledge of the functional capabilities of a tool, such as a Web site, thus the challenge derives from the difficulty of the task relative to one's skill (Ghani, 1995). O'Brien (2008) considers challenge as a component of engagement with technology, and defines this construct as 'the cognitive and physical effort users perceive they are expending when interacting with technology'. We propose challenge as a component of Web site engagement. This is further supported by the notion that the Web is able to provide immediate challenge to a user's level of skill and interest (Pace, 2004).

Control Siekpe (2005) uses this dimension in order to capture a user's individual's perception that she or he exercises control over the interaction with technology. Within online consumer behaviour research based on flow theory, this construct refers to 'the control a user exercises over interaction with a Web site' (Huang, 2003) and suggested that 'control is a facilitator of Web performance'. This suggests a possible relationship between control and interactivity, and also between control and usability. O'Brien (2008) defines control as 'how in charge' users feel over their experience with a technology. Following research based on flow theory, it seems that it is not interactivity that is important to a Web user, but the control the user exercises over interactivity (Teo et al., 2003).

Curiosity means tapping into the extent an experience arouses an individual's sensory and cognitive curiosity (Agarwal and Karahanna, 2000). Instead of curiosity, O'Brien (2008) considers novelty as a component of engagement with technology, referring to the extent a technology was perceived as novel. However, the Internet has surpassed the early adopter stage (Hoffman, Novak and Venkatesh, 2004).

Involvement is a needs-based cognitive/affective state of psychological identification with an object or activity. It depends on the needs of the individual and on his or her perception about the need-satisfying potential of the object or situation, and is sometimes considered a phenomenon synonymous to motivation (Kappelman, 1995). Elliot and Speck (2005) suggest that online vendors should emphasise Web features that best suit the involvement and experience profile of the primary users of the Web site. O'Brien (2008) considered involvement as part of engagement with technology.

Transformation of time is a perception that time appears to pass very slowly or very rapidly compared to ordinary experience (Guo and Poole, 2008). Considered by Csikszentmihalyi (1998) as one of the original components of flow, this construct is equally referred to as *time distortion, time dissociation* (Guo and Poole, 2008) and *distorted sense of time* (Pace, 2004). O'Brien (2008) suggests 'perceived time' as a component of engagement with technology. In this research we shall refer to this construct as 'transformation of time' as utilised by Guo and Poole (2008).

Up-to-dateness of information refers to the freshness of information presented on a Web site. Novelty can be created with the freshness of information contained within a Web site (Huang, 2003). According to Supphelen and Nysveen (2001), Web site revisits can be encouraged by changing information content frequently so that sites always have something new to offer. Bigné, Aldás and Andreu (2008) reveal that future shopping intentions are influenced by consumer dependency on online shopping information, as well as the innovativeness of the consumer; it seems to makes sense that Web sites should offer their visitors up-to-date information.

The proposed dimensions were tested in an experimental data acquisition Web site based on an improved version of *mouselab* (Johnson, Payne, Schkade and Bettman, 1989) that allowed to remotely trace eye movements. Respondents were asked to complete a travel package choice task where only 1 of the 12 cells, showing a travel package description, was visible at the time as the mouse pointer was rolled over each of the cells. We utilised a sample of 336 respondents gathered on a real e-commerce platform, *Citylogo.com* (Bigné and Hyder, 2012). Based on two self-reported questionnaires, conducted before and after the navigation process, clickstreams and elementary information process data (EIP) (Bettman, Johnson and Payne, 1990; Bucklin and Sismeiro, 2009), a model of web site engagement dimensions was tested using partial least squares path modelling (PLSPM).

The dimensions of Web site engagement were estimated with partial least squares path modelling (PLSPM) (Ringle, Wende and Will, 2005). The results revealed how this construct comprises five dimensions only. These are: positive affect (β = 0.120; p<0.01), focused attention (β = 0.120; p < 0.01), challenge (β =-0.109; p < 0.01), curiosity (β = 0.182; p < 0.01) and involvement (β = 0.351; p < 0.01). These findings are summarised in Table 9.2.

Table 9.2 Dimensions of Website engagement

PATH	Standarised path coefficients	t-value (bootstrap)	Web site engagement dimension?
Positive affect → Web site engagement	0.120**	2.31	Yes
Focused attention → Web site engagement	0.120**	3.3	Yes
Challenge → Web site engagement	–0.109**	2.06	Yes
Control → Web site engagement	0.058	1.52	No
Curiosity → Web site engagement	0.182**	2.7	Yes
Involvement → Web site engagement	0.351**	6.41	Yes
Transformation of time → Web site engagement	0.013	0.52	No
Up-to-dateness of information → Web site engagement	0.01	0.32	No

The other three variables not found to be dimensions of Web site engagement are control (β = 0.058), transformation of time (β = 0.013) and up-to-dateness of information (β = 0.01). The output of this analysis, therefore, reveals how to measure Web site engagement.

Conclusions and implications

The outcomes of this research extend the existing body of knowledge on engagement in consumer-technology contexts, by proposing a Web site engagement measurement. From the eight expected dimensions of the Web site engagement construct, we found that, in fact, it has five dimensions, which are positive affect, focused attention, challenge, curiosity and involvement. When a user becomes engaged with a Web site she or he experiences these five qualities simultaneously. Three dimensions – control, transformation of time and up-to-datedness of information – were not found to form part of this construct. The first two, control and transformation of time, are not emerging probably due to the fact that browsing is nowadays a common daily task controlled by users and developed as one of the common activities in a typical day. To illustrate, more than 50 per cent of people in emerging and developing nations posit that the Internet produces a good influence in education, personal relationships and the economy (Pew Research Centre, 2015). Regarding up-to-datedness of information, our research approach did not show participants in different, non-updated scenarios.

Our results are in line with the results of other researchers who have conceptually studied engagement in contexts other than Web sites (e.g. Chapman, 1997; Jacques et al., 1995; Brodie et al., 2011). The overall findings allow the development of a greater understanding of Web site engagement

Table 9.3 Dimensions of the Website engagement measurement

DIMENSIONS OF WEB SITE ENGAGEMENT	
Positive affect	The emotional investment users make in order to be immersed in an environment and sustain their involvement in the environment (Jennings, 2000)
Focused attention	The concentration of mental activity. Concentrating on one stimulus only and ignoring all others (Huang, 2003)
Challenge	The amount of effort users perceive they are expending when using a Web site (Chen, 2006)
Curiosity	Tendency to seek out elements that are new, interesting, or unusual in one's environment (Huang, 2003)
Involvement	The inherent interests, values, or needs that motivate users towards using a Web site (Based on Chen 2006; Zaichkowsky, 1994)

and how it can be measured. This leads to theoretical and practical implications that are detailed in the following sections. Table 9.3 provides a definition of the five dimensions of the Web site engagement measurement.

We conclude that Web site engagement takes place in the eyes of online consumers and it does not occur inside a Web site. It could also be argued that Web site engagement takes place in an intermediate position between a Web site and its users, as the negative loading sign of challenge indicates that if users perceive a Web site to be challenging they will not engage with the Web site. This perception is subject to personal issues of each user regarding his or her level of familiarity with a Web site and the degree of skill with Web sites and the Internet in general. If Web designers develop Web sites that are usable, this will benefit their users as discussed in previous literature. A similar argument occurred regarding where does *interactivity* takes place, as is it still not clear. Liu and Shrum (2009) affirm that interactivity is a multi-dimensional construct that can reside among different entities such a computer, within humans, and between humans and a computer. However, Song and Zinkhan (2008) affirm that interactivity is only related to the behaviour of consumers, as it fully resides in their eyes and not within an information system itself. Regarding where Web site engagement takes place, our results are consistent with the position of Song and Zinkhan (2008).

Comparing the Web site engagement construct resulting from our research with other similar online consumer cognitive and experiential constructs, it seems that Web site engagement is different to other previous constructs such as cognitive absorption (Agarwal and Karahanna, 2000), enduring involvement (Huang, 2006), online flow (Hausman and Siekpe, 2009), engagement with technology (O'Brien, 2008), customer engagement (Kumar et al., 2010; Brodie, et al., 2011) and customer brand engagement (Hollebeek, 2011; Hollebeek et al., 2014).

As an outcome to our findings, we suggest the following definition of Web site engagement:

> *'Web site engagement' is a consumer experience that occurs when a user's attention is captivated and held by a Web site, and the user wants to remain interacting with the Web site in a concentrated fashion during a period of time. The five dimensions of Web site engagement are positive affect, focused attention, curiosity, challenge and involvement.*

Our findings can help digital marketing companies to better understand their relationships with online consumers. We provide online marketers with a tool for understanding if the visitors to Web sites have become engaged with them. Table 9.4 provides a checklist of aspects that can be carefully considered before

Table 9.4 Survey checklist for measuring Website engagement

ITEM No.	FACTOR	ITEMS
		Whilst I navigated on the Website I felt . . .
1 – PA1	Positive affect	excited
2 – PA2		energetic
3 – PA3		happy
4 – PA4		satisfied
5 – PA5		bold
6 – FA1	Focused attention	When navigating this Website, I didn't think about other things (R)
7 – FA2		When navigating this Website, I wasn't aware of distractions (R)
8 – FA3		When navigating this Website, I was totally absorbed in what I was doing
9 – CH1	Challenge	This Website was easy to use
10 – CH2		Using this shopping Website was not mentally taxing
11 – CH3		This shopping experience was not demanding
12 – CH4		Shopping on this Website was not too much trouble
13 – CU1	Curiosity	I continued to shop on this Website out of curiosity
14 – CU2		This shopping experience satisfied my sense of curiosity
15 – CU3		The content of the shopping Website incited my curiosity
16 – IN1	Involvement	I felt involved in this shopping task
17 – IN2		It was easy to get wrapped up in this shopping experience
18 – IN3		I was really drawn into my shopping task

(R) Reverse coded

commencing the design of e-commerce sites and can be used to directly assess consumers' Web site engagement.

Regarding the limitations of this research, the main one is that both the Web site engagement construct and the research model have been contrasted with data proceeding from only one Web site simulating an online travel agency. This could limit the overall applicability of the findings to other industries, as the dimensions of Web site engagement could be different in different contexts, in different ranges of travel products, or in a different nature of products all together such as could occur with tangible products. The data acquisition Web design was designed based on mouselab and only one holiday package was presented at the time when the mouse pointer was rolled over each of the 12 cells. Whilst this was the only method that could remotely trace mouse movement and behaviour of the respondents, this limitation could be surpassed utilising an eye-tracking device. Another limitation of this research is that the online travel Web site developed for this research was not a real e-commerce site where visitors could make purchases but an experiment.

Regarding our recommendations for future research, first it is a priority to consolidate the Web site engagement construct, paying special attention to the three dimensions that were not found to form part of Web site engagement: control, transformation of time and up-to-dateness of information. Second, we suggest studying the effect of Web site engagement over time, as engaging experiences could differ as users pay repeated visits to a same Web site. Third, further research should concentrate on understanding drivers of engagement, therefore research on further antecedents of Web site engagement should be undertaken. Fourth, whilst data was obtained uniquely with the data acquisition Web site developed for this research, it would be useful to revalidate the Web site engagement construct utilising an eye-tracking device. Finally, we suggest consolidating the Web site engagement construct in using different devices, such as mobile phones or tablet computers.

References

Agarwal, R.; Karahanna, E. (2000): 'Time flies when you're having fun: Cognitive absorption and beliefs about information technology usage'. *MIS Quarterly*, pp. 665–694.

Bettman, J. R.; Johnson, E. J.; Payne, J. W. (1990): 'A componential analysis of cognitive effort in choice'. *Organizational Behavior and Human Decision Processes*, Vol. 45(1), pp. 111–139.

Bigné, J. E.; Aldás, J.; Andreu, L. (2008): 'B2B services: IT adoption in travel agency supply chains'. *Journal of Services Marketing*, Vol. 22(6), pp. 454–464.

Bigné, E.; Hyder, A. (2012): 'A combined consumer-technology methodology for the assessment of online consumer'. *Frontiers of Service Research Conference 2012*. University of Maryland.

Blythe, M. A.; Overbeeke, K.; Monk, A. F. (2003): *Funology: From usability to enjoyment*. Kluwer Academic Publishers.

Brandtzaeg, P.; Følstad, A.; Heim, J. (2005): 'Enjoyment: lessons from Karasek'. *Funology*, pp. 55–65.

Brodie, R. J.; Hollebeek, L. D.; Jurić, B. and Ilić, A. (2011): Customer engagement: conceptual domain, fundamental propositions and implications for research. *Journal of Service Research*, Vol. 14(3), pp. 252–271.

Bucklin, R. E.; Sismeiro, C. (2009): 'Click here for Internet insight: advances in clickstream data analysis in marketing'. *Journal of Interactive Marketing*, Vol. 23, pp. 35–48.

Calder, B. J.; Malthouse, E. C. (2008): 'Media engagement and advertising effectiveness'. In B. Calder (Ed.), *Kellogg on advertising and media* (pp. 1–36). New York, NY: John Wiley & Sons.

Calder, B. J.; Malthouse, E. C.; Schaedel, U. (2009): 'An experimental study of the relationship between online engagement and advertising effectiveness'. *Journal of Interactive Marketing*, Vol. 23(4), pp. 321–331.

Chapman, P. (1997): Models of engagement: Intrinsically motivated interaction with multimedia learning software. Unpublished masters of applied science, University of Waterloo, Waterloo, ON.

Chen, H. (2006): 'Flow on the net-detecting web users' positive affects and their flow states'. *Computers in Human Behavior*, Vol. 22(2), pp. 221–233.

Collins Essential English Dictionary (2006): HarperCollins Publishers, 2nd Edition, 2006.

Csikszentmihalyi, M. (1988): 'The flow experience and human psychology'. In M. Csikszentmihalyi and I. S. Csikszentmihalyi (Eds.), *Optimal experience: Psychological studies of flow in consciousness* (pp. 15–35). Cambridge: Cambridge University Press.

Csikszentmihalyi, M. (1996): *Creativity: Flow and the psychology of discovery and invention*. New York: HarperCollins.

Dennis, C.; Merrilees, B.; Jayawardhena, C.; Wright, L. T. (2010): 'E-consumer behaviour'. *European Journal of Marketing*, Vol. 43(9/10), pp. 1121–1139.

Elliott, M. T.; Speck, P. S. (2005): 'Factors that affect attitude toward a retail web site'. *Journal of Marketing Theory and Practice*, Vol. 13(1), pp. 40–51.

Eroglu, S. A.; Machleit, K. A.; Davis, L. M. (2003): 'Empirical testing of a model of online store atmospherics and shopper responses'. *Psychology & Marketing*, Vol. 20 (2), pp. 139–150.

Forrester (2015): https://www.forrester.com/Create+A+Customer+Engagement+Network+For+Your+BT+Agenda/fulltext/-/E-res122043. Last accessed 13 April 2015.

Garris, R.; Ahlers, R.; Driskell, J. E. (2002): 'Games, motivation, and learning: A research and practice model'. *Simulation & Gaming*, Vol. 33(4), pp. 441–467.

Ghani, J. A. (1995): 'Flow in human computer interactions: test of a model'. *Human Factors in Information Systems: Emerging theoretical bases*, pp. 291–311.

Ghani, J. A.; Deshpande, S. P. (1994): 'Task characteristics and the experience of optimal flow in human-computer interaction'. *Journal of Psychology*, Vol. 128, pp. 381–391.

Google (2015): Google analytics. www.google.com/intl/en_uk/analytics

Guo, Y. M; Poole, M. S. (2008): 'Antecedents of flow in online shopping: a test of alternative models'. *Information Systems Journal*, Vol. 19(4), pp. 369–390.

Hausman, A. V. and Siekpe, J. S. (2009): 'The effect of web interface features on consumer online purchase intentions'. *Journal of Business Research*, Vol. 62(1), pp. 5–13.

Hoffman, D. L; Novak, T. P. (2000): 'How to acquire customers on the web'. *Harvard Business Review*, Vol. 78(3), pp. 179–188.

Hoffman, D.L.; Novak, T.P.; Venkatesh, A. (2004): 'Has the Internet become indispensable?'. *Communications of the ACM,* Vol. 47(7), pp. 37–42.

Hollebeek, L.D. (2011): 'Demystifying customer brand engagement: exploring the loyalty nexus'. *Journal of Marketing Management,* 27(7-8), pp. 785–807.

Hollebeek, L.D.; Glynn, M.S.; Brodie, R.J. (2014): 'Consumer brand engagement in social media: conceptualization, scale development and validation'. *Journal of Interactive Marketing.* Vol. 28(2), pp. 149–165.

Huang, M.H. (2003): 'Designing website attributes to induce experiential encounters'. *Computers in Human Behavior,* Vol. 19(4), pp. 425–442.

Huang, M.H. (2006): 'Flow, enduring, and situational involvement in the web environment: a tripartite second-order examination'. *Psychology and Marketing,* Vol. 23(5), pp. 383–411.

Hudlicka, E. (2003): 'To feel or not to feel: the role of affect in human-computer interaction'. *International Journal of Human-Computer Studies,* Vol. 59(1–2), pp. 1–32.

Hyder, A.; Bigné, E.; (2012): 'A Web site engagement model. Analysis of the influence of intra Web site comparative behaviour'. *AEMARK, Spanish Marketing Association Conference 2012,* University of Mallorca, Spain.

Jacques, R.; Preece, J.; Carey, T. (1995): 'Engagement as a design concept for hypermedia'. *Canadian Journal of Educational Communications,* Special issue on multimedia development, pp. 49–59.

Jennings, M. (2000): 'Theory and models for creating engaging and immersive ecommerce websites'. In *Proceedings of the 2000 ACM SIGCPR Conference on Computer Personnel Research,* pp. 77–85. ACM New York, NY.

Johnson, E.J.; Payne, J.W.; Schkade, D.A.; Bettman, J.R. (1989): *Monitoring information processing and decision: the Mouse-Lab system.* Unpublished manuscript. Centre for Decision Studies, Fuqua School of Business, Duke University, Durham, NC.

Kappelman, L.A. (1995): 'Measuring user involvement: a diffusion of innovation perspective'. *Data Base Advances,* Vol. 26, (2/3). pp. 65–86.

Kumar, V.; Aksoy, L.; Donkers, B.; Venkatesan, R.; Wiesel, T.; Tillmanns, S. (2010): 'Undervalued or overvalued customers: capturing total customer engagement value'. *Journal of Service Research,* 13(3), pp. 297–310.

Laurel, B. (1993): *Computers as theatre.* Reading, MA: Addison-Wesley.

Leslie, E.; Marshall, A.L.; Owen, N., Bauman, A. (2005): 'Engagement and retention of participants in a physical activity website'. *Preventive Medicine,* Vol. 40(1), pp. 54–59.

Li, D.; Browne, G.J.; Wetherbe, J.C. (2006): 'Why do Internet users stick with a specific Web Site? A relationship perspective'. *International Journal of Electronic Commerce,* Vol. 10(4), pp. 105–141.

Li, D.; Browne, G.J.; Wetherbe, J.C. (2007): 'Online consumers switching behavior: A buyer-seller relationship perspective'. *Journal of Electronic Commerce in Organizations,* Vol. 5(1), pp. 30–42.

Lin, A.; Gregor, S.; Ewing, M. (2008): 'Developing a scale to measure the enjoyment of Web experiences'. *Journal of Interactive Marketing,* Vol. 22(4), pp. 40–57.

Liu, Y.; Shrum, L.J. (2009): 'A dual-process model of interactivity effects'. *Journal of Advertising,* Vol. 38(2), pp. 53–68.

Lohse, G.L.; Johnson, E.J. (1996): 'A comparison of two process tracing methods for choice tasks'. *Organizational Behavior and Human Decision Processes,* Vol. 68(1), pp. 28–43.

Lu, Y.; Zhou, T.; Wang B. (2009): 'Exploring Chinese users' acceptance of instant messaging using the theory of planned behavior, the technology acceptance model, and the flow theory'. *Computers in Human Behavior,* Vol. 25(1), pp. 29–39.

MacInnis, D. J.; Jaworski, B. J. (1989): 'Information processing from advertisements: Toward an integrative framework'. *The Journal of Marketing,* Vol. 53 (4), pp. 1–23.

Mallon, B; Webb, B. (2000): 'Structure, causality, visibility and interaction: propositions for evaluating engagement in narrative multimedia'. *International Journal of Human-Computer Studies,* Vol. 53(2), pp. 269–287.

Martí, J.; Bigné, E.; Hyder, A. (2014): 'Brand engagement'. In *The Routledge Companion to the Future of Marketing,* pp. 250–257.

McGinnis, T.; Bustard, D. W.; Black, M.; Charles, D. (2008): 'Enhancing e-learning engagement using design patterns from computer games'. In *Advances in Computer-Human Interaction, 2008,* pp. 124–130.

McKinsey & Company (2008): 'How poor metrics undermine digital marketing'. *McKinsey Quarterly,* Vol. 4, 38–61.

McKinsey & Company (2014): 'The digital tipping point: McKinsey Global Survey results'. June 2014. Available from http://www.mckinsey.com/insights/business_technology/The_digital_tipping_point_McKinsey_Global_Survey_results?cid=other-eml-nsl-mip-mck-oth-1407

McMillan, S. J; Hwang, J. S. (2002): 'Measures of perceived interactivity: an exploration of the role of direction of communication, user control, and time in shaping perceptions of interactivity'. *Journal of Advertising,* pp. 29–42.

Mollen, A.; Wilson, H. (2010): 'Engagement, telepresence and interactivity in online consumer experience: reconciling scholastic and managerial perspectives'. *Journal of Business Research,* Vol. 63(9–10), pp. 919–925.

Nahl, D.; Bilal, D. (2007): *Information and emotion.* Medford, NJ: Information Today, Inc.

O'Brien, H. L. (2008): *Defining and measuring engagement in user experiences with technology.* PhD Dissertation, Dalhousie University, Halifax, N.S.

O'Brien, H. L.; Toms, E. G. (2008): 'What is user engagement? A conceptual framework for defining user engagement with technology'. *Journal of the American Society for Information Science and Technology,* Vol. 59(6), pp. 938–955.

Pace, S. (2004): 'A grounded theory of the flow experiences of Web users'. *International Journal of Human-Computer Studies,* Vol. 60(3), pp. 327–363.

Peterson, R. A.; Hoyer, W. D.; Wilson, W. R. (1986): *The role of affect in consumer behavior: Emerging theories and applications.* Lexington, MA: Lexington Books.

Pew Research Center (2015): 'Internet seen as positive influence on education but negative influence on morality in emerging and developing nations'. Available from http://www.pewglobal.org/files/2015/03/Pew-Research-Center-Technology-Report-FINAL-March-19-20151.pdf. Last accessed 13 April 2015.

Ringle, C. M.; Wende, S.; Will, A. (2005): SmartPLS 2.0 (beta). Hamburg, Germany: University of Hamburg.

Siekpe, J. S. (2005): 'An examination of the multidimensionality of flow construct in a computer-mediated environment.' *Journal of Electronic Commerce Research,* Vol. 6(1), pp. 31–43.

Song, J. H.; Zinkhan, G. M. (2008): 'Determinants of perceived Web site interactivity'. *Journal of Marketing,* Vol. 72(2), pp. 99–113.

Supphellen, M.; Nysveen, H. (2001): 'Drivers of intention to revisit the websites of well-known companies'. *International Journal of Market Research,* Vol. 43(3), pp. 341–352.

Teo, H.H.; Oh, L.B.; Liu, C.; Wei, K.K. (2003): 'An empirical study of the effects of interactivity on web user attitude'. *International Journal of Human-Computer Studies,* Vol. 58(3), pp. 281–305.

Webster, J.; Ahuja, J.S. (2004): 'Enhancing the design of web navigation systems: the influence of user disorientation on engagement and performance'. Unpublished manuscript.

Webster, J.; Ho, H. (1997): 'Audience engagement in multimedia presentations'. *SIGMIS Database,* Vol. 28(2), pp. 63–77.

Zaichkowsky, J.L. (1994): 'The personal involvement inventory: Reduction, revision, and application to advertising'. *Journal of Advertising,* Vol. 23(4), pp. 59–70.

Zauberman, G. (2003): 'The intertemporal dynamics of consumer lock-in'. *Journal of Consumer Research,* Vol. 30(3), pp. 405–419.

Part III

Managerial applications of engagement

10 Strategic drivers of customer and employee engagement

Practical applications

Christopher Roberts, Frank Alpert and Carissa Roberts

Introduction

If an organisation takes steps beyond just encouraging customers to make once-off purchases, and instead, attempts to create engaged customers, they can dramatically increase business performance, including sales and growth. However, it is easier to acknowledge that engaged customers are valuable, than it is to earn them. This chapter draws on and expands the discussion around our earlier article, 'Total Customer Engagement: Designing and Aligning Key Strategic Elements to Achieve Growth' (Roberts and Alpert, 2010). With five more years' experience of working with companies using the Total Engagement Model® to create customer engagement since our earlier article, our confidence in the model has grown, and there are new insights to share.

A key factor we have identified when investigating customer engagement is understanding how engaged customers are more likely to deliver positive recommendations or word-of-mouth marketing for the brand. Customer engagement has many benefits, but this is a key one. It would be expected that 'Promoters' (those more likely to recommend as per the Net Promoter model, who would be positively engaged customers) would be more likely to provide positive comments than 'Detractors' (those less likely to recommend). The 2014/15 Engaged Marketing consumer benchmarking study found that Promoters (the most engaged customers) typically make almost *five times more* positive comments than Detractors across five categories.

Engaged Marketing conducted a survey of 4,815 respondents in the general population in our location, Australia, to investigate both the extent and importance of word of mouth (WOM). How important are WOM comments in influencing purchasing decisions? Respondents were asked which of the marketing channels detailed in Table 10.1 had the greatest influence on them when making a purchase decision. The results indicate that WOM by people we know and trust has by far the greatest influence on purchase decisions. Specifically, WOM was found to be the most influential channel for almost half the respondents (46.8 per cent). The next most popular choice was 'Product Reviews', which was selected by 22.5 per cent of respondents, which is effectively a peer assessment. Taken in combination this means that nearly

Table 10.1 Marketing channels which have the greatest influence on purchase decisions

Response	Percentage
Recommendation from a friend, family member or colleague	46.8%
Product review websites or publications	22.5%
TV advertising	10.0%
Internet advertising	2.7%
Direct mail	1.9%
Newspaper advertising	1.7%
Social media advertising (e.g. ads on Facebook, LinkedIn, MySpace, etc.)	1.3%
Magazine advertising	1.2%
Email marketing	1.1%
Press articles	1.0%
Blogs	0.9%
Radio advertising	0.6%
Sports sponsorships	0.2%
Celebrity endorsements	0.1%

70 per cent of participants are most influenced by what an organisation does (i.e. the customer experience and proposition that is actually delivered to customers and stimulates WOM), as opposed to what an organisation says (organisation-initiated marketing and advertising activities). Good WOM follows from customer engagement.

The chapter is organised as follows. First we describe the Total Engagement Model, as the model completely reflects our perspective on how to achieve customer engagement. Second, we provide some general observations based on five years of consumer benchmarking that outline the key distinguishing factors of loyalty leaders in relation to the Total Engagement Model. In particular, we focus in on the importance of employee engagement and present new survey evidence regarding the state of employee engagement today and how that affects customer engagement. Finally, we present five case studies that illustrate total customer engagement, and draw our conclusions.

Total engagement model

Our definition of an engaged customer is one that is loyal to a focal brand and actively recommends the brand and its products and services to others. Our suggestion for how to create engaged customers is via the Total Engagement Model, which is presented as Figure 10.1.

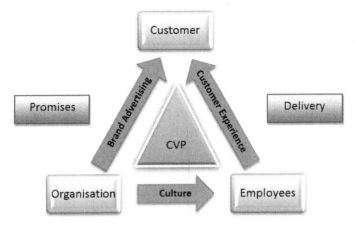

Figure 10.1 The Total Engagement Model (Roberts and Alpert, 2010)

The model starts with the proposition that key strategic elements of a business need to be **designed and aligned** to create engaged customers. These elements are present in most organisations and the individual benefits of these are well documented. They are:

- Your Customer Value Proposition (CVP) in simple terms is the value you offer your customers. In other words, this is the reason customers should purchase from you over your competitors.
- Brand is effectively the sum total of who you are and what you stand for, not just your logo or name. Your value proposition must form a key part of your brand and your brand advertising, which is how you communicate the brand to consumers.
- Culture refers to 'the way we do things around here', and represents the internal aspects of the organisation, such as its goals, values and internal behaviours. This should be designed to create an environment where staff have the capability to consistently deliver the brand's value proposition and planned customer experience.
- Customer Experience is a combination of physical and emotional elements, which customers experience when they interact with the brand and the organisation.

The design and, more importantly, alignment of these elements to specifically drive loyalty and engagement forms the basis of the Total Engagement Model. The model was developed by first author Christopher Roberts and is described more fully in Roberts and Alpert (2010). The model was developed when Christopher Roberts was Head of Marketing and Communications at a major utility. It was used to effectively recover a severely damaged brand from being the worst in its category, to being the best in its category.

Essentially, the model poses the following question: How often are an organisation's intent, or what they think (i.e. value proposition), who they are (i.e. culture), what they say (i.e. brand advertising) and what they do (i.e. value delivered and customer experience) *in perfect harmony, from a customer perspective?*

Considering the challenges that brands face today, every communication and customer interaction should be fully leveraged, optimised and treated as an opportunity to create engaged customers. These linkages are brought together in the Total Engagement Model, which focuses on *aligning the four key elements* of customer value proposition, brand advertising, culture and customer experience. To create engaged customers an organisation should implement the following steps:

1   Develop a unique *value proposition* based on strong customer insight and competitor positioning.
2   It should then communicate this value proposition to customers consistently in its *brand advertising.*
3   This promise is then ideally delivered by engaged staff that support and understand the strategy and, importantly, *understand* their individual role in making it a success.
4   This *cultural* foundation results in the delivery of a planned customer experience that delivers strongly against the promise made in the brand's advertising.

Benchmarking studies about drivers of customer engagement

The real world of business represents a very complex and dynamic environment. The key drivers of customer engagement can be examined by investigating how leading brands achieve their success within their respective sector. Engaged Marketing's consumer benchmarking studies span 9 industries in Australia and include 40,000+ category-specific responses. The studies measure NPS (Net Promoter Score), stated loyalty, recommendation, brand strength, performance of key touch points and attributes, and customer experience elements. Our key findings show that the two elements that drive advocacy and recommendation more than anything else are the *delivery of a strong and unique value proposition*, and *great customer experiences* that include key emotions.

We now elaborate further on some of the key findings from Engaged Marketing's benchmarking studies.

Customer value propositions

Examining Engaged Marketing's consumer benchmarking 'Loyalty Leaders' (i.e. organisations which have achieved the highest category-specific Net Promoter

Score across Engaged Marketing's consumer benchmarking studies) over the years, their commonality is a unique value proposition. For example:

- Apia Insurance – for the over-50's market
- Youi Insurance – pay for what you use
- ING Direct – branchless banking
- Bank of Queensland – personalised service because it is owner operated
- Virgin Mobile – challenging the status quo

This is a fundamental principle of marketing, makes intuitive sense and would be consistent with most people's experience. Think about the last time you recommended a product or service to someone, it would have been because of the delivery of a distinct value proposition, which may include product dimensions such as functionality, price, image, fashion or innovation. Alternatively, it would have been because the customer experience with the organisation was great.

Customer experiences and emotions

The other unique aspect of loyalty leaders is their ability to deliver great customer experiences. Great customer experiences typically consist of functional (e.g. reliable, timely, knowledgeable) and emotional elements (e.g. supported, happy, valued). The distinguishing factor of Loyalty Leaders is the transfer of key positive emotions, such as 'valued' or 'cared for'. There is increasing interest in the customer experience aspect of customer engagement. We next provide more detail on a key driver of, and key challenge for delivering, great experience for customers: employee engagement.

Importance of employee engagement

In order to deliver great customer experiences, in particular through the transfer of key *positive emotions from customer-facing employees to customers,* employee engagement is very important. In our experience it is one of the key differentiators between organisations that do and do not achieve superior experiences for their customers. Employee engagement is easy to pay lip service to but hard to truly deliver in hierarchical organisations. It is often the key hurdle, and thus worth focusing on. In order to better understand what is actually happening with employee engagement today from employees' perspective, which is how it must be measured, Engaged Marketing conducted a nationwide survey. A total of 3,361 employees across Australia were recruited from an independent market research panel for an online opt-in email survey. This provided a high quality sample of participants from small and large organisations and from all levels of the organisational hierarchy. The key measures were eNPS (employee likelihood to recommend their company as a great place to work) and NPS (employee likelihood to recommend their organisation's products and services). These were measured using an 11 point scale from 0–10, where 0 is 'not likely at all to recommend' and 10 is 'extremely likely to recommend', as per standard NPS measurement (Reichheld, 2006). Scores of 0–6 are labelled Detractors, 7 to 8 are labelled Passives, and scores of 9 or 10 are referred to as Promoters. Both eNPS and NPS are calculated by subtracting the percentage of Detractors from the percentage of Promoters. Other ratings are measured on satisfaction or agreement scales ranging from 1–10.

Frontline staff engagement

The results show staff are substantially less engaged than the leadership. Despite common admonitions in the management literature to empower employees, those lower in the organisational hierarchy appear to be less engaged. We would intuitively expect lower level staff engagement to be less, but this survey quantifies the degree of engagement by employee level. There are more organisation Promoters than Detractors at the very top of the organisation hierarchy in comparison to lower levels. The critical aspect of great customer experiences is the transfer of key positive emotions from staff to customers. This will be a challenge if staff do not feel positive emotions. Can they fake positive emotions in the customer interaction? Even if they tried to, there is a risk the faked emotion would be detected as inauthentic.

Understanding and commitment to strategy

Discretionary effort is a rating of employees' likelihood to do more than what is expected in their day-to-day job/function. Staff members that give their companies discretionary effort are, typically, the ones that deliver experiences worthy of recommendation. Simultaneously, these staff members are often motivated to find new ways to increase efficiencies and reduce costs. The Champion Analysis examines the composition of employees who understand the brand's strategy in conjunction with their levels of personal commitment to it. Kevin Thomson, who at the time worked for MCA Communications, developed the champion approach (Thomson, de Chernatony, Arganbright and Khan, 1999). It is based on two simple axes. One axis reflects the intellectual understanding of an organisation's strategy, while the other axis reflects the personal commitment employees have towards making the strategy successful.

Results from the survey (Figure 10.2), show that *Champions' stated discretionary effort is 61 per cent higher than that expressed by Weak Links* (7.1 vs. 4.4), thus indicating the importance of staff understanding and commitment towards organisational strategy. While it may be expected that Champions' discretionary effort would exceed that of Weak Links, these results quantify the difference. The Champion Analysis lends more insight than simply looking at the average discretionary effort, as it provides the link between discretionary effort, understanding of strategy and personal commitment to the strategy.

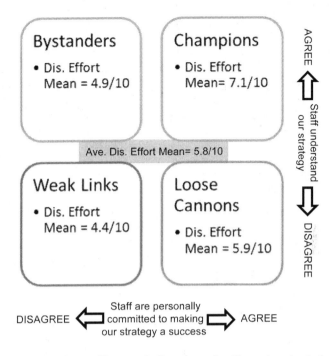

Figure 10.2 Discretionary effort results based on the Champion Analysis

To address this result leaders not only need to inform staff of the organisation's strategy and direction (i.e. 'tell' staff so that they truly understand), but also need to 'sell' it (i.e. earning staff commitment). Thus, senior management that do not invest in either activity (i.e. neither telling nor selling) risk creating Weak Links.

Employees' likelihood to recommend their organisation's own products and services

A key statistic rarely discussed or measured is employees' likelihood to recommend their own organisation's products or services. The results in the survey on the NPS question revealed that while 30 per cent of employees were Promoters for their company's products or services, 36 per cent of employees were Detractors. Note that this NPS measure differs from eNPS as it measures, where appropriate, an employee's likelihood to recommend their company's products and services to their friends and family, rather than as a place of work, which forms the basis of eNPS. The 30 per cent Promoters vs. 36 per cent Detractors results in a shocking NPS score of −6 per cent. More than one-third of employees reported a low likelihood to recommend their own organisation's products and services. *Less than a third of employees were actually strongly willing to recommend their very own organisation's products and services.*

These findings beg the question: If your own employees are not willing to recommend your products and services to other people, what chance do you have? A score like this is indicative of employees who lack understanding of key organisational strategic elements. If staff do not understand the organisation's strategy, direction or value propositions, it is no mystery as to why they do not feel comfortable recommending your products and services to their friends and family. Alternatively, a more worrying explanation may be that staff simply do not believe that their organisation delivers high-quality products or services.

Purpose beyond economics

Our experience with implementing the model suggests that the secret ingredient that can truly power your brand is an internal purpose beyond economics. Taking this perspective, 'leads to a strategy that is concerned with what an organisation wants to achieve and how that will happen, purpose deals with why the organisation exists in the first place and what ultimately matters in its work' (Ledwith and Springett, 2004).

A clear and strong organisational purpose beyond profit and shareholder return is essential to motivate employees beyond pure economics. Those financial purposes are considered central to capitalism and would be the dominant paradigm, but if financial returns are the only purpose for the organisation it can leave employees cold.

Critically if you can align the organisational purpose with a noble purpose that individual employees can get behind, then you have something very powerful. For example, when you look at the brands in the case studies to follow, the underlying purpose beyond economics is:

*   TUH – the health of its members
*   Jetts – passionate about inspiring others to enhance their health and fitness
*   PETstock – pets are loved so much that they are family

What if a brand does not have a natural, somewhat altruistic purpose like the above brands? Then it should focus on either (a) being extremely customer focused as customers and employees want to be associated with a customer-focused brand, (b) take on a strong competitor focus such as destroying the competition (e.g. Coke vs. Pepsi, Nike vs. Adidas, etc.), or (c) challenge the status quo of a whole category, which is a strategy that brands such as Virgin and Apple have utilised over the years. These are also purposes that can motivate employees.

Link between customer and staff emotions

In the previous section we suggested the importance of emotions within the customer experience. Our assertion is that there is an *inextricable link* between employee engagement and customer engagement. Our view is that, ultimately, emotions play a key role when it comes to employee and customer engagement. Pugh (2001) found that employees' displayed positive emotions were not only associated with customers' positive emotions post-interaction, but also their service evaluations. Many aspects of a service experience can be automated. We believe that staff must feel a particular emotion before they can transfer this across to customers. As an example, a staff member cannot make customers feel valued if they do not feel valued as employees. This observation is illustrated by the following analysis drawn from Engaged Marketing's nationwide benchmarking study of the financial institutions category and nationwide employee engagement insights.

The surveys also provide new evidence on the importance of emotion to customer engagement and employee engagement. NPS will be the measure of engagement used throughout the data we present here. Likelihood to recommend is a higher-order measure of engagement in comparison to satisfaction. The following from the financial institutions benchmarking study illustrates the variation in NPS based on whether the customer felt 'valued' or not:

- Average NPS across the financial institution category = –6 per cent
- NPS when customers felt 'valued' = +33 per cent
- NPS when customers did not feel 'valued' = –29 per cent

Thus, customers who felt valued are more likely to recommend the company than customers who did not feel valued. This data quantifies the difference, and it shows that shifting customers from not feeling valued to feeling valued has a huge effect (raising NPS from –29 per cent to +33 per cent).

We then looked at similar data in the employee survey, again in terms of eNPS. The following results indicate the key role that emotions play in eNPS.

- Average eNPS across Australia = –23 per cent
- eNPS when staff felt 'valued' = +11 per cent
- eNPS when staff did not feel 'valued' = –41 per cent

Thus, the same effect holds for employees. The size of the effect is in the same ball park, a 52 per cent shift in eNPS compared to a slightly larger 62 per cent shift for NPS. These are large changes. Shifting employees from not feeling valued to feeling valued would make a huge positive change in employees' likelihood to recommend their workplace to others.

Case studies

The Total Engagement Model requires a complete picture of what a company does; hence what would it look like if an organisation met the criteria of the Total Engagement Model? To illustrate what this would look like, we present examples across five industries. These case studies were developed from interviews with senior executives in these organisations, and address all aspects of the Total Engagement Model. The case studies show a wide-lens snapshot of current industry trends across several different types of companies and industry categories. After presenting the case studies we examine the key alignment factors that lead to engagement.

Case Study 1. TUH

Background	TUH is a health insurance brand based in Queensland, Australia. It is a not-for-profit brand that has traditionally served union members within the education sector. In addition to providing health insurance it also has a Health Care Centre incorporated into its Head Office. This centre acts as a 'one-stop shop' offering optical, dental, physiotherapy and a range of other medical services to members on-site. It has recently expanded its offerings so that it is also available to union members outside of the education domain.
Loyalty and Growth	TUH has a very high Net Promoter Score and approximately 45% of new sales are sourced via word of mouth. Their growth rate has doubled in recent times, a testament to the excellent service they offer members.
Brand Communications	The positioning line for TUH is 'It's my health fund' to highlight that it is a not-for-profit organisation that is owned by members, not shareholders. It communicates that TUH is driven to meet members' needs not the profit needs of shareholders. Therefore being member-focused is a part of its core DNA.
Customer Value Proposition	TUH competes with much larger health insurance brands. In this category adequate health insurance coverage is key, but what is unique about TUH is that it truly cares about its members. Hence their value proposition, 'Covered with Care', not only perfectly encapsulates TUH's positioning (which is about offering great coverage) but also emphasises a sense of unrivalled personal care that can only come from an organisation that is owned by its members and not driven by profit.
	According to the Chief Executive Officer of TUH, Rob Seljak, the health insurance market is becoming increasingly competitive: 'Some insurance funds offer low cost packages especially to younger segments to

make it attractive and affordable, but this means excluding some critical coverage. TUH never excludes serious medical conditions. So all our products always cover cancer and cardiac, because it does happen and so I guess it is just part of our value proposition that is in line with our member focus and values.'

Customer
Experience

The people at TUH are what make the experience unique with high NPS scores driven by high ratings around emotional elements such as feeling 'valued' and 'cared for'.

This is best highlighted by a story Seljak describes: 'A few weeks ago we had really bad rains in Brisbane and roads were being closed and we decided it was too dangerous for people to come in to the Health Care Centre so we decided to close it. We had around 100 people booked so we contacted every person and rescheduled all their appointments. There was one person who was an older dental patient who we could not contact. She did not have a mobile and was not at home so one of our dentists made the decision to keep the place open until she got here. She got here after everybody else had left, and the place was closed but he let her in, provided her with her treatment and then closed up.'

Seljak continues, 'Five to seven years ago we started looking at how we could increase member focus and it was not just what we could provide the member but it was what we could provide staff so that they could do more in the way they could benefit the member. So we looked at the "one-stop shop" approach – before if you phoned in to do a claim and then you wanted to change your address you had to be transferred to someone else as they did not have the system on their desk to be able to change it. Now the person you call can do most things without transferring you.'

Culture

The culture is driven by a sense of purpose which is all about caring for members and their health. Staff are recruited and rewarded based on whether they have empathetic skills. Cathy McGuane, Executive Manager Member Services, says 'I still remember one of the stories about a dental hygienist who was seeing a patient and this lady was a bit elderly and she says that the TUH carpark was full here so she parked down the road somewhere and this lady had no idea where her car was and this dental hygienist walked this lady to one or two of the local car parks until they found it. Interestingly, we would have never have found out but the member called us the next day to tell us. The great thing about this story is that the staff member did not expect to be recognised; it's just the way we do things at TUH.'

Disciplines and Accountability	TUH uses the NPS discipline. Overall member relationships are measured as well as the performance of key touch points via transactional surveys. Detractors are called back to understand member issues and determine ways to improve the overall experience.

Case Study 2. Apia

Background	Apia is an Australian based insurance company for the over-50's market.
Loyalty and Growth	Apia has headed up the leader board as the most recommended Australian insurer in recent years. Based on nationwide, independent benchmarking they have been the most recommended property insurance provider for five years running and the most recommended motor insurance brand four times in the last five years.
Brand Communications	As Apia focuses on the over-50's segment their communication is tailored for this segment. In addition to using imagery around over 50, they do not discourage customers from calling them and they do not push customers towards self-serve and online channels.
Customer Value Proposition	Apia's value proposition is quite clear. If you are over 50 then this is the insurance company for you, as they understand the needs of this segment better than any other brand.
Customer Experience	The customer experience is tailored to this segment very carefully.

As an example the call centre does not utilise IVR systems. When customers call they are greeted by a real person. The focus is on customer intimacy and not operational efficiency, so there are no 'Grade of Service' measures in place. Effectively, Apia representatives can speak to customers for as long as they want.

Geoff Keogh, Executive Manager for Apia, says 'We are about understanding, not just insurance, and this is reflected in every interaction we have with our customers.'

Staff are multi-skilled and therefore a customer is not transferred from one department to another. In addition, staff are delegated powers to resolve customer issues in one conversation. Apia deploy a personal advice model that is unique in the industry.

Culture

Apia has a strong internal culture driven by engaging staff around the fact that they offer understanding not just insurance.

Keogh elaborates, 'Sales and service staff are encouraged to visit customers with claims assessors and see first-hand what customers are going through, providing the mechanism for greater levels of empathy when dealing with clients on the phone.'

A positive culture has been achieved by empowering staff through multi-skilling, deploying a personal advice model unique to the industry and finally the right delegation levels. All this ensures a personalised experience that sincerely meets the needs of the over-50's market.

Disciplines and Accountability

Regular NPS surveys are conducted at an overall relationship level and by key touch points after an interaction.

Importantly the results (whether good or bad) are shared with frontline teams. Staff can actually listen to a recording where a customer has given them a rating of ten out of ten.

Finally, it does not stop at just sharing results in a top-down fashion. At a granular team level, staff develop initiatives to improve their customer rating scores.

Case Study 3. Nimble

Background

Nimble as a brand was launched in 2012, previously under the name Cash Doctors. It offers small short-term loans from $100 to $1,600. Key features are a fast application process without paperwork and quick decisions, which means approved customers get their money fast.

Loyalty and Growth

Since 2005 Nimble has provided close to 900,000 small loans and continues to grow rapidly. Nimble's NPS is higher than any other major financial institution in Australia, based on the industry benchmarking study conducted by Engaged Marketing.

Brand Communications

The tag line is 'Smart Little Loans' with a Jack Rabbit as the logo.

Customer Value Proposition

The core value proposition, which is also their mission, is 'To delight people by making borrowing simple, fast and stress-free'.

Customer Experience

The customer experience carefully implements the slogan of simple, fast and stress free. This is regardless of whether it is on the phone, on mobile app or on their website.

Andrew Kirkwood, Head of Operations at Nimble elaborates, 'Customer service is part of our very DNA at Nimble. It is ingrained in our hiring and development practices and is a core differentiator within the financial services industry in Australia. For this reason, NPS is a top-3 business objective for us, and will continue to be a focus as long as we are in business, and we don't plan on going anywhere soon.'

Culture

The internal culture is very customer focused, best illustrated by the fact that customers rate Nimble staff extremely highly. Great customer experiences are always a reflection of a positive culture. Nimble makes sure it maintains a strong culture by conducting regular employee engagement surveys.

Kirkwood details: 'At Nimble one of our core philosophies and values is "it's all about the people". This is true when speaking not only of our customers but also our employees, as we truly believe that happy employees lead to happy customers. We strongly believe that Engaged People drive Innovation and Customer focus, and as such make sure our frontline employees are given the opportunity and voice to help shape EPIC, our customer service strategy, at every turn. It is this strategy that has enabled us to increase our NPS score to a stable 57%, and it is this strategy that will allow us to push on past our ultimate goal of over 70% NPS each month.'

Disciplines and Accountability

NPS is a top-3 initiative at Nimble. NPS targets are a key KPI for all senior executive and staff. Customer feedback is reviewed and corrective action is taken regularly. As an example, due to sheer growth contact centre wait times dropped below satisfactory levels of 80% of all calls answered within 20 seconds. Nimble was quick to monitor the impact on NPS via its transactional surveys and rather than accept second-rate service for a period of time, quickly increased resources to this despite the significant cost and time involved.

Case Study 4. PETstock

Background

PETstock is pet retailer in Australia with over 100 retail stores. The Young family (David and Shane) took ownership of Ballarat Produce in 1991 but it was not until 2002 and 11 stores later that the PETstock franchise was born. PETstock was and still remains a family-owned and -operated organisation, with 100+ stores and 1000+ team members Australia wide.

Loyalty and Growth

PETstock has a high NPS score within the market it operates. Its growth is illustrated by going from 11 stores to more than 100 stores in the space of around 12 years.

Brand

In Australia pet supplies can be purchased from a range of retailers. Supermarkets offer a largely transactional service with minimal range, little expertise and limited personal service. You then have the specialist pet shops that are owned by individuals or families, which offer personalised service and specialised knowledge but perhaps limited range due to their size. In this market PETstock's unique positioning offers the consistency of a large chain, a large range of products and the personalised service and knowledge you previously would only receive from a family-owned specialised pet shop.

PETstock's brand elements are communicated internally via PETstock's 'Kennel'. The Kennel's purpose is to ensure all staff fully understand and live the PETstock brand and is a constant reference point for all staff.

Customer Value Proposition

PETstock's value proposition is 'Engaging specialists who truly care'. A demonstration of just how deeply this sentiment is embedded within staff can be found from the actions of over 250 PETstock staff members who salary sacrifice to PETstock Assist, which is PETstock's very own charity foundation dedicated to the rescue, rehabilitation and rehoming of pets and the support of organisations focused on improving the quality of life for disabled or disadvantaged people through animal-based companion projects.

Customer Experience

The backbone of PETstock are its people who truly care about animals. It is not unusual for a staff member to remember your pet's name and the ailment they were suffering from last week. It is normal practice to take large dog food bags out to the customers' car while still talking to them. David Young, Managing Director of PETstock, provides an example of how staff find clever ways to engage with customers even in uncommon situations: 'At the launch of a new vet hospital as part of the grand opening we had sessions where we would take the families through and the kids would come through the operating room. We would have a stuffed teddy so we would put the gown on the kids and give them the utensils and ask them what is wrong with the stuffed dog and the Vet would pull out a lolly out of the dog and say obviously he has eaten a lot of lollies and had a pain in the stomach and then we would give them a certificate to say that they have completed our Vet Training course at PETvet.'

Culture

The culture at PETstock revolves around a couple of key aspects: (1) truly living 'engaging specialists that truly care', a 'family-owned' culture, and (2) leadership that are happy to go to the front and get their hands dirty.

Young goes on to say: 'we live and breathe engaging specialists who truly care and we have done this without even realising that we were doing this way before we actually formally developed the value proposition with Engaged Marketing. Obviously we were able to build a business up through word of mouth rather than going out to advertise to the market to say 'we are here'. We had customers doing it for us without even realising that they were doing it. We wouldn't ask any of our staff to do anything that we wouldn't do ourselves. I went to an opening of a new store and while I am not great on the floor anymore in terms of product knowledge I was still out there and helping taking bird cages and kennels to the cars. The traditional way of going to a store and still being served in the way in which you want to be served. I believe this is still very much why customers still warm to us as we are not serving from behind the counter; we are going out and engaging with them. This is a behaviour exhibited by all leaders in the organisation.'

Staff have regular yoga classes at work and the flexibility to pick up the kids from school and have them at the head office at 3pm. There are regular staff activities such as a Run for Kids and Boot Camps, which again adds to the family-owned culture and atmosphere.

Selection of the right staff is key. Staff do not have to own a pet but they have to at least love animals and they have to have a sense of empathy and share the PETstock family values.

Disciplines and Accountability

Besides regular organisational KPI's, PETstock also uses NPS as a regular discipline. In addition to all stores and other key staff having near real-time access to customer feedback via sophisticated dashboards, there is a regular discipline around calling customers that are unhappy with the service and resolving their issues.

Case Study 5. Jetts

Background	Jetts is a family-owned gym fitness chain based on the Sunshine Coast, Australia. It was founded by husband-and-wife team Brendon and Cristy Levenson, with the opening of the very first Jetts Club on the Gold Coast in 2007.
Loyalty and Growth	From its humble beginnings in 2007 Jetts now has more than 220 gyms across three countries (Australia, New Zealand and the Netherlands), which is an impressive expansion rate. Jetts has a high NPS driven largely by consistent service and the passionate Jetts staff.
Brand	The Jetts brand established itself as the first 24/7 fitness chain in Australia. In addition they offer no lock-in contracts. Effectively the brand positioning is all about convenience encapsulated in their current positioning line: 'workout on your terms'. Essentially, Jetts eliminated two key customer complaints about gyms: limited hours and lock-in contracts. Jetts' goal is to be the 'most loved gym'.
Customer Value Proposition	The value proposition is convenience, 24/7 access and no lock-in contracts. In addition Jetts is aimed at regular people not serious body builders.
Customer Experience	Jetts has been voted the Number 1 gym in Australia in terms of customer satisfaction two years in a row, independently measured by Canstar. According to Elaine Jobson, Country General Manager of Jetts, 'we focus on the "brilliant basics" as we call it and then having the "wow" experience on top of that. I think Jetts is consistently better at delivering the basics that members want on a consistent basis: a clean environment, equipment that works. You can guarantee that when you get into the Club you will have a consistent, quality team member who is able to be knowledgeable because all of our people are qualified and we only recruit people that are fitness passionate.'
Culture	Jetts has an amazing internal culture. Its employee engagement score is much higher than the Australian average. A majority of staff would happily recommend

Jetts to others as a great place to work. Feeling 'love' for Jetts and other team members is a common theme in verbatim employee engagement staff comments. Jobson outlines how they have achieved this amazing culture: 'internal culture is definitely our strength. We do a number of things; it is not just one silver bullet. To make sure our culture is alive it has to be absolutely lived and breathed by the leadership, then with the office support teams. This allows us to hold our Business Owners to high account on being outstanding and being educated in that culture. So when we recruit Business Owners into Jetts we make sure that they go through that kind of 'brand filter' and they understand what the culture is and we resist the temptation to bring people in that are not of that type that they will never get our culture. So we recruit to this end and then we look at every possible way to communicate with them. We have newsletters go out, we put it in every single communication on our email, we make sure it is on our voicemail messages, it's on our Power Point slides. Whenever I speak to a Business Owner I make sure culture is part of the conversation in some capacity. So living our culture is a borderline obsession.'

Disciplines and Accountability

Jetts uses the NPS discipline for customers and conducts a comprehensive employee engagement study for its staff and measures and manages both down to a granular level of individual Clubs. Detractors are regularly called back and key staff have near real-time dashboards so they can monitor customer feedback. NPS is a key organisational metric. Jobson explains, 'I am actually less interested in our overall NPS score than I am in what conversations are happening on the ground. The reason for that is it is about the conversation happening with our Club staff and members. I ask Clubs what they are doing to fix issues highlighted in the research. If you do this and talk to members then the natural outcome will be our overall NPS score improves and members will stay longer.'

Table 10.2 Key alignment factors leading to engagement

Case 1 TUH	'Covered with Care' is the sentiment that best glues TUH's brand, customer experience and culture together as they are member owned
Case 2 Apia	Understanding the needs of the over-50's segment better than any other brand and not just providing insurance is the mechanism Apia uses to align their brand, culture and customer experience
Case 3 Nimble	Gearing up the entire organisation in terms of people, process and systems 'To delight people by making borrowing simple, fast and stress-free'
Case 4 PETstock	Family-owned 'can do' culture with a true sense of caring for animals
Case 5 Jetts	An internal culture driven by its mission, which is to 'inspire people to live a better life' with a no-strings, convenient product offering

A further examination of these case studies reveals a number of common threads, which are summarised in Table 10.2.

First, all of these organisations have invested a substantial amount of time in creating a clear strategic intent around their brand, customer experience, propositions and culture. While most organisations do this, for these brands it is more than just words on a poster or in an annual report; they have actually operationalised these strategic intents into regular disciplines and essentially this drives the entire ethos of these organisations.

Value propositions tend to be functional in nature but this can be enriched by an internal purpose that extends beyond economics. PETstock truly care about pets and this drives their charitable foundation, whom they employ and their decision to not sell puppies and kittens. Another example is Jetts since not only does everyone who works at Jetts truly value fitness but more importantly they values fitness to the point to where they are passionate about helping others achieve their fitness goals. The strong connection between an individual's purpose in life and the organisation's purpose can propel a business forward if it is widespread enough. In essence, an internal purpose beyond economics provides true gravitas to the delivery of the organisation's propositions and experiences. We spend a considerable amount of our lives at work so who wouldn't want to work for a company which has a purpose beyond economics?

Another common factor across the five case studies above is an engaged culture. A culture which is truly customer-focused, takes customer feedback very seriously, and where excellent customer service is a priority is a culture which attracts and retains a customer-focused employee.

While the elements discussed so far can be strategically designed, a critical aspect for organisations is to utilise effective disciplines. All of the case studies have embraced the Net Promoter Score discipline and have systems and processes in place allowing them to live and breathe it. A simplistic overview of this process begins with simply capturing regular and timely insight at a relationship and transactional level and taking action at both a top-down (involving strategic action planning around organisation-wide pain points and drivers) and bottom-up level (operational action planning where teams, at a granular level, develop initiatives based on customer feedback).

Finally, what all these brands have in common is strong executive support. Customer measures are a key performance indicator, executives visibly show their support of customer strategies and executives are not afraid to go out to the frontline. Without this key leadership element, these organisations would not have achieved the success they have attained.

Conclusion

In an increasingly competitive world, customer engagement is absolutely critical, yet difficult to achieve. Single-factor principles to achieve customer engagement are positive steps, yet insufficient without consideration of the total company interaction with customers. The Total Engagement Model addresses total company interaction with customers, and identifies the strategic drivers of customer engagement. This chapter expands discussion of the Total Engagement Model, and contributes new evidence. The key finding attained from nine industry benchmarking studies is that a great customer value proposition combined with delivering a great customer experience are the major drivers of industry-leading customer brand loyalty.

Employee engagement represents a key driver, given that employees deliver the relevant value propositions and experiences required to create engaged customers. New evidence suggests that employee engagement is far from being as high as we would like or expect, which translates into less discretionary effort than we would hope to see, and even far less employee recommendation of their company's own products and services than would be expected. Achieving total customer engagement is a complex picture involving all the company's operations. To demonstrate what it looks like in the real world for a company to achieve total customer engagement, five case studies of high customer engagement companies were presented, which reflected each of the dimensions of the Total Engagement Model. Specifically, the findings were based on insider descriptions attained from interviews with senior management and close author observation. Further, this chapter contributes to the literature on customer engagement by providing additional evidence on a model that was designed and tested over time within a series of real-world settings and sectors.

Notes

The section 'Total engagement model' is drawn from our article 'Total Customer Engagement: Designing and Aligning Key Strategic Elements to Achieve Growth' (Roberts and Alpert, 2010). More detail is available in that article.

Please note that Net Promoter®, NPS®, eNPS® and Net Promoter Score® are trademarks of Satmetrix Systems, Inc., Bain and Company and Fred Reichheld. The Total Engagement Model is a registered trademark of Engaged Marketing.

References

Ledwith, M. and Springett, J. 2010. *Participatory Practice: Community-based Action for Transformative Change.* University of Bristol, UK: Policy Press.

Pugh, S. D. 2001. Service with a smile: Emotional contagion in the service encounter. *Academy of Management Journal,* 44, 1018–1027.

Reichheld, F. F. 2006. *The Ultimate Question: Driving Good profits and True Growth.* Boston, MA: Harvard Business School Press.

Roberts, C. and Alpert, F. 2010. Total customer engagement: Designing and aligning key strategic elements to achieve growth. *Journal of Product and Brand Management,* 19, 198–209.

Thomson, K., de Chernatony, L., Arganbright, L. and Khan, S. 1999. The buy-in benchmark: How staff understanding and commitment impact brand and business performance. *Journal of Marketing Management,* 15, 819–835.

11 Customer engagement with a service offering

A framework for complex services

Sylvia Ng, Carolin Plewa and Jillian C. Sweeney

Introduction

Customer engagement (CE) represents a topic of rapidly increasing interest to academics and practitioners, largely due to its focus on the interactions between the consumer and the brand, which in the context of services represents a key 'building block' of service delivery. Indeed, the Marketing Science Institute (MSI), which develops research priorities to reflect the most pressing needs and interests of marketers in business, identifies the conceptualisation, definition and measurement of engagement as a Tier 1 priority (2014–2016). To date, CE research has centred on customer interactions with brands and organisations (Brodie, Hollebeek, Juric and Ilic, 2011), with other literature streams focusing more specifically on employee engagement (e.g. Kahn, 1990, 1992; Salanova, Agut and Peiro, 2005) and school engagement (e.g. Fredricks, Blumenfeld and Paris, 2004; Li and Lerner, 2013). However, while CE is often contextual and unique to an individual, existing literature rarely sheds light on actor engagement (Chandler and Lush, 2015) or, more specifically, the engagement with a complex service offering, which is likely to comprise engagement with the service provider, their advice and the service process.

We address this gap by broadly examining CE with a service offering (CESO) in a setting of complex services. For the purposes of the present study, we use the term 'complex' to represent services, which are relational, require a number of interactions between provider and customer, and are high in credence-based qualities, such that the quality and value of the service is never fully known, as is the case with credence services. In such services, CESO is likely to be more elaborate, compared to CE with a brand in other settings, given the possibility for the undertaking of complex interactions between two actors throughout an extended service process. CESO also embodies a particular level of relationship building that is process-intensive, and requires responsive, assuring and empathetic service over time (Parasuraman, Berry and Zeithaml, 1991). This research, therefore, responds to the call by Brodie et al. (2011) to explore customer engagement beyond brands and organisations, adding valuable insights into the conceptualisation of engagement from the perspective of complex ongoing services, consistent with key MSI objectives.

This chapter contributes to the engagement literature by addressing the following objectives: (1) to investigate how customers engage with a service offering (CESO), in the context of complex services, and clearly define the individual components of CE under such circumstances; (2) to identify different antecedents driving individual components of CESO in a complex setting; and finally, (3) to identify the outcomes of CESO in complex services. We examine these specifically by leveraging on the financial planning industry as the context for this research. The finance industry is an appropriate setting for studying CESO, as it is characterised by high levels of interaction (Yoo, Arnold and Frankwick, 2012), interdependence and transfer of rich information between the customer and the service provider (Auh, Bell, McLeod and Shih, 2007). Further, the setting is ongoing for many customers, such that repeated interactions with the same service provider are experienced over time (Gremler and Gwinner, 2000). These characteristics suggest a rich setting to explore in detail the many ways in which customers engage with focal firms' service offerings within this particular sector.

Background

Given the dynamic actor interactions in complex service contexts, CESO is likely to be elaborate. In particular, CESO differs from customer brand engagement, in that the service offering is a multi-faceted, interactive engagement object. Specifically, we argue that researchers examining CE in a complex service environment should employ a comprehensive approach that considers CE with regard to the service provider, their advice and the service process, in order to examine and understand the complexities of CESO (Li and Lerner, 2013). In the context of this study, the service offering is complex in that it comprises three aspects working in synergy with each other, namely, the financial planner as the service provider whom the client interacts with, the planner's advice, as well as the service process, during which the planner develops and delivers the advice. As such, our discussion of CESO includes activities reflecting engagement with the resources that comprise the offering, that is, the provider, the advice, as well as the service process.

Facilitated by interactions with the financial planner, customers are able to experience varying levels of behavioural, cognitive and emotional activities. This is consistent with discussions in recent literature, where customer engagement is viewed as a multi-faceted construct comprising behavioural, cognitive and emotional engagement (e.g. Brodie et al., 2011; Hollebeek, 2011; Li and Lerner, 2013). Drawing on existing knowledge from customer brand engagement research, we concur that a positive valence underlies customer engagement (e.g. Hollebeek, Glynn and Brodie, 2014; Brodie et al., 2011; Hollebeek, 2011), which is particularly relevant to CESO. Positive CE has positive financial and non-financial consequences for the firm, both in the short and long run (Van Doorn et al., 2010). Consequently, building on

Hollebeek et al.'s (2014) definition, we define CESO as the customer's positively valenced behavioural, cognitive and emotional activities related to the provider, the advice and/or the service process. This definition enables us to capture the dynamic interactive nature that exists between two focal actors (Lusch and Vargo, 2014; Kohli, 2006).

In line with this definition, we describe the behavioural component of CESO as 'any positive activities that the customer willing engages in, related to the provider, the advice and/or service process'. Cognitive CESO refers to 'any positive internal thought processes or projected thoughts that the customer experiences, related to the provider, the advice and/or service process'. Likewise, emotional CESO refers to 'any positive emotions that the customer has towards the provider, the advice and/or the service process'. These three dimensions of CE with the service provider are likely to change across situations, resulting in various levels of intensity and complexity over time (Brodie et al., 2011). Nonetheless, it is crucial to acknowledge that certain behavioural, cognitive and emotional experiences connecting the two actors could persist after the service interaction (Chandler and Lusch, 2015).

Our work rests on the following assumptions: (i) CESO can occur during the service interaction between a focal customer and provider; (ii) CESO can occur beyond the service interaction, as prompted by the provider; (iii) CESO can occur beyond the service interaction, as initiated by the customer. That is, any positive feelings, thoughts or actions as experienced by the customer with respect to the service offering signifies an ongoing form of engagement, independent of whether they occur during or outside of the service interaction. Indeed, CESO is not confined to 'an orderly, sequential progression of phases over time' (Brodie, Ilic, Juric and Hollebeek, 2013, p. 110). Nonetheless, each aspect of the service offering can be linked naturally to a component of CE – for instance, the planner, emotionally; the advice, cognitively; and the process, behaviourally.

Presently, there are limited empirical insights on CE in the area of services. However, we expect some differences in terms of the antecedents and outcomes of CESO, compared to CE in other contexts (e.g. digital or brand-based settings). This is because CE represents a context-dependent variable (Brodie et al., 2011; Chandler and Lusch, 2015). Conceptually, specific to the focal service setting, fostering post-failure customer satisfaction and relationship closeness, increasing repurchase intentions (or loyalty), and reducing negative word-of-mouth have been suggested as outcomes of CE (Patterson et al., 2006). Other outcomes of CE include trust, satisfaction, commitment, empowerment, customer value and loyalty (Brodie et al., 2013). On the other hand, possible antecedents of CE are involvement, interactivity and flow (Hollebeek, 2011; Hollebeek, 2009), with little information specific to antecedents of CE in services. Hence, we advance understanding of CE by investigating the various components of CESO, as well as their drivers and outcomes, in the context of complex services.

Method

To achieve our objectives, 26 semi-structured interviews were carried out across three Australian states. The semi-structured approach was employed to promote consistency, offering a wider scope for data collection (Corley and Gioia, 2004). As the study context was financial planning, the sample included 15 financial planners and 11 existing customers of financial planners (cf. Tables 11.1 and 11.2). Existing customers were characterised by a variety of ages, occupations and relationship experience with financial planners. Similarly, the financial planners represented a range of experience in the industry, firm sizes and locations (both regional and metropolitan). The interviewees were primarily contacted through convenience sampling, complemented by snowball sampling. The latter technique was useful in identifying suitable candidates to be included in the study, due to the nature of the targeted population that is small and unique (Lukas, Hair, Brush and Ortinau, 2005).

All three authors participated in the collection of the qualitative data; each was assigned to one of the three Australian states to conduct the relevant interviews. The interviews lasted between 40 to 120 minutes. In-depth interviews were appropriate for this study as the aim was to derive rich insights on the process and development of customer engagement through interactions. Customers were asked to talk about their engagement with their current and (if relevant) previous financial planners, from the first time they started seeking advice to the present. Likewise, financial planners reflected on their engagement with various customers and their role in facilitating it.

The interviews were later transcribed and analysed using the categorizing process by Lincoln and Guba (1985). The aim was to identify recurring patterns of thoughts, ideas and perceptions which interviewees had that were related to the concept of customer engagement (Gremler and Gwinner, 2000). Multiple

Table 11.1 Customer profiles

Code	Relationship Length	Occupation	Age	State
C1	1.5 months	Lecturer	30s–40s	WA
C2	3–4 months	Recruitment Consultant	30s–40s	NSW
C3	1 year	Nurse	30s–40s	SA
C4	1 year	Retired	60s–70s	SA
C5	2 years	Finance Manager	30s–40s	NSW
C6	3 years	Shift Supervisor	50s	SA
C7	4 years	General Manager	50s	SA
C8	4 years	Adjunct Lecturer	50s	SA
C9	6 years	Retired	60s–70s	SA
C10	13 years	Retired	60s–70s	SA
C11	27 years	Retired	60s–70s	SA

Table 11.2 Financial planners' profiles

Code	Experience in Financial Planning Industry	Firm Size (Number of Employees)	Location	State
FP1	4 months	30	M	NSW
FP2	1 year	6	M	NSW
FP3	1 year	40	M	NSW
FP4	1.5 years	200	M	SA
FP5	3 years	6	M	NSW
FP6	4 years	1	M	NSW
FP7	5 years	1	M	NSW
FP8	5 years	2	M	WA
FP9	6 years	100–200	M	NSW
FP10	7 years	6	M	WA
FP11	12 years	2	M	WA
FP12	12 years	200	M	NSW
FP13	20 years	3	R	SA
FP14	21 years	2	R	SA
FP15	37 years	2	M	WA

Notes: M = Metropolitan area, R = Rural area. NSW = New South Wales, WA = Western Australia, SA = South Australia.

investigator triangulation was carried out by the authors to minimise discrepancies in data, allowing a single reality to emerge (Grove and Fisk, 1992). After several rounds of negotiation and revision, we achieved theoretical saturation (Shah and Corley, 2006) and reached consensus on the components that defined each of the three dimensions of customer engagement, as well as its drivers and consequences. These steps contributed towards the credibility of the qualitative data collected (Lincoln and Guba, 1985).

Facets of customer engagement with a service offering (CESO)

Behavioural engagement with a service offering

Data analysis addressing behavioural engagement with the service offering showed several positive activities related to the planner, the advice or the service process that customers engage in. We argue that customers exhibit positive engagement behaviours if they willingly engage in activities out of their own accord, rather than obligated participation to complete a required task as set by the financial planner (such as filling out forms). Hence, behavioural engagement with a service offering encompasses contacting, informing and engaging in service-related activities.

Contacting: Customers may exhibit behavioural engagement by initiating contact with the financial planner. In particular, behaviours are evident when customers actively seek out their financial planner, as stated by this interviewee: *'The other contact has been from myself to the planner, and that's often in relation to what's happening with the market, whether we should change the profile and so on. So, the contact is probably more so from me to the planner now' (C9)*. While either party is able to initiate interaction in a relational service context, organisations often take the initiative to do so (Vivek, Beatty and Morgan, 2012). In instances where contact is initiated by the planner, the extent to which the customer responds willingly and positively is also a reflection of CESO. Hence, a customer's proactive initiation of contact and willingness to extend contact initiated by the planner are valuable signals of engagement with the financial planner and the planner's work.

Informing: CESO can be initiated by a customer who provides his/her financial planner with up-to-date information. In ongoing complex services, the personal interface (whether online or offline) between the customer and financial planner is crucial in enabling customers to contribute directly throughout the service process (Auh et al., 2007). Information provided by the customer that is both useful and timely is fundamental to higher-quality service output (Schneider and Bowen, 1995). Hence, timely notifications by the customer to inform the financial planner with relevant information can be regarded as an act of engagement with the planner: *'The biggest thing I do on an ongoing basis is just to tell him what's going on in our lives, so that he can decide from there to review or adjust the plan or do anything different' (C5)*. In doing so, the customer respects the need for his/her financial planner to gain access to relevant personal information so as to make better judgements, and makes the effort to do so: *'He can only do his job if he knows what's happening and so you know if we're deviating from the plan, the sooner he knows then the more easily he can adjust to the plan' (C5)*.

Engaging in service-related activities: The engagement in activities relating to the service process signals another component of behavioural engagement as reflected in our data. For example, customers may request for materials from their planners that are of interest to them or prepare their budgets diligently. However, the extent to which customers engage in such activities differs. Customers may choose to engage fully or partially in activities suggested by the financial planner, for instance, reading relevant information materials: *'If he gets a new something of information, he just asks am I interested or not . . . I probably do 20, 25 per cent' (C6)*. This is consistent with previous findings, which have shown that customers vary in terms of the degree to which they participate in the service process with the provider (McColl-Kennedy et al., 2012).

Likewise, the customer can be deemed engaged if he/she follows the advice of the financial planner by attending suggested functions. Such functions could include professional networking sessions, social events or educational seminars.

Companies often organise financial-related events as part of their strategic efforts to engage customers: *'They would organise pretty regular seminars and invite all their financial planning customers along'* (C8). The customer's behaviour therefore signifies behavioural engagement with the advice and service process, triggered by the financial planner: *'Like if (he) said, look there's an investment opportunity, I think you should be there . . . Go and have a listen. You know, it's only time'* (C6). Hence, the extent to which the customer actively engages in service-related activities that have been sought for or provided by the financial planner denotes CESO.

Cognitive engagement with a service offering

Cognitive engagement processes have been examined in the literature with regards to students/school, employees/work and consumers/brands. Specifically, these entail students' self-regulation or strategic approach towards learning (Fredricks et al., 2004), employees' absorption and attention to their work (Ho, Wong and Lee, 2011; Rothbard, 2011 and customers' immersion in brands (Hollebeek and Chen, 2014), respectively. That is, cognitive engagement with a focal object or task that is less relational or dynamic in nature, compared to a service offering. To account for this, we specifically examine positive cognitive activities related to the planner, the advice or service process. Here, cognitive processes refer to both internal thought processes and projected thoughts by customers. Results suggest that when engaging with a service offering, customers' cognitive activities consist of learning, evaluating, deciding and reflecting.

Learning: The understanding and absorption of information by customers from their financial planners through communication represents cognitive engagement with the advice. This may happen either online or offline through clarifications or discussions. Clarification occurs when the customer has specific concerns for the planner to address: *'He has been very helpful and understanding, and nothing seems to be too much effort for him to explain'*(C4). In particular, customers with lower levels of financial knowledge often request their planners to simplify information in order for them to absorb: *'And that then is where I look to (his) skills to make it simple: "Explain to me in English what are we talking about"'(C11)*.

On the other hand, financial planners may also engage customers in discussions that stimulate customer learning. Customers who are open to such discussions often improve their financial knowledge over time, as it helps them to understand and internalise new information: *'We've already had some mild discussions about it and I've already learnt a lot about different products that I didn't even know existed before'* (C5). Through these dialogs, customers are able to receive educational support from their financial planners, enabling them to absorb information more meaningfully by relating new information to existing knowledge (Walker, Greene and Mansell, 2006).

Evaluating: Customers engage with their financial planners on a cognitive level when they evaluate various options together before making a decision. This involves sharing or debating ideas related to the advice. While evaluating options, customers and financial planners often engage through the exchange of ideas: '*They give you ideas and you give them ideas*' (C1). In line with the finding by Grönroos and Voima (2013), cognitive engagement can run both ways where either party is able to actively influence each other's thinking, aligning themselves to a common vision that is of value to the customer, impacting the evaluation of options: '*I expect in return that they . . . [take] care to understand my ambitions and dreams and getting an assessment of what will work*' (C1). In this scenario, the higher the customer's financial knowledge, the more he/she will be able to debate ideas actively, leading to higher levels of cognitive engagement with their planners. Additionally, rigorous cognitive activity in customers may be further encouraged, when financial planners challenge customers to think more broadly when assessing options: '*[He] made us think about some things that we hadn't really considered*' (C3).

Deciding: The customer working with the financial planner to think through decisions together also represents cognitive engagement with the advice. This may take the form of joint decision-making: '*We went through all the accounts that we had, [and] we rationalised them and we ensured that using our language basically we wanted to have a bank account with a sign on it and certain money would go into certain accounts and other money would go in other accounts*' (C7). Conversely, certain customers may prefer more decisional authority over their finances. Under such circumstances, these customer exhibit cognitive engagement by requesting their financial planners to review their intended plans during the process of finalising a decision: '*In times when you need decisions made, contacting the financial advisor makes the decision easier, because you're getting a perspective of someone who works in the industry and knows what's happening*' (C9). The results suggest that the level of cognitive engagement during the decision-making process is likely to depend on whether the customer has sufficient knowledge and skills to make sound judgements independently, and the extent to which the customer prefers to have control over his/her finances.

Reflecting: Cognitive engagement also takes place when customers evaluate past service experiences, review financial strategies and performances of their financial planners during the service process, or formally at the end of a service cycle (i.e. annual review). Existing customers tend to have a more developed set of stable, evaluative criteria to assess consumption situations (Bowden, 2009) due to numerous service interactions. Thus, customers are able to reflect with their financial planners on their own processes and how they work with each other (Payne, Storbacka and Frow, 2008) to meet financial objectives: '*We reflect where [we] are and we get our original goals and we're just seeing what we're ticking off . . . But we're also starting to think, "Oh, what next"*' (C6). Proper evaluation demands a high level of cognitive processing in terms of knowledge and experience on the part of the customer. Hence, customers who are able to provide useful insights and feedback are likely to engage better with their financial planner.

Emotional engagement with a service offering

Interview data revealed several positive emotions that customers have towards the service offering. In contrast to affective states as discussed in the context of customer brand engagement (e.g. feeling happy, good or positive; cf. Hollebeek et al., 2014), we conceptualise emotions as a strong sense of connectedness or attachment (Luthans and Peterson, 2002; Chandler and Lusch, 2015), as such feelings ensure that meaningful effort is exerted (Li and Lerner, 2013). The management literature also specifies different forms of emotions during actor-to-actor interactions, such as experienced emotions, expressed emotions and emotional regulation (Bono, Foldes, Vinson and Muros, 2007). However, our study focuses on emotions as experienced by the customer towards the service offering. In this context, it is found that emotional engagement is often naturally linked to the planner. These include the customer's ability to relate and be inspired by their financial planners.

Relating: The customer's ability to identify with their planner is another sign of emotional engagement. The ability to relate denotes a sense of connection and an intimate relationship (Klassen, Perry and Frenzel, 2012) with the planner. This is because by being transparent and open about their inner thoughts and feelings, customers engage in a form of self-revelation (Gremler and Gwinner, 2000), requiring them to be vulnerable or fully present (Kahn, 1992) in the presence of their financial planner. Aptly described by a customer, *'You can already see so much of me so I might as well tell you all my dreams, my hopes and ambitions. I'm putting a lot of myself out there, right?' (C1).* This may embody a form of secure attachment (King, 2015; Furrer and Skinner, 2003) to the planner, whom the customer is able derive support from: *'We look at him like a father figure . . . just like a second coach' (C6).* As customers relate better to their planner, they become more aligned with each other, encouraging more cognitive activities.

Feeling inspired: Customers may also experience a sense of inspiration instilled when dealing with their planner (Patterson et al., 2006) during the service process, which connotes a high level of activation (Macey and Schneider, 2008). Customers described that they feel *invigorated* when their financial planners help them to understand what is going on, by equipping them with sufficient knowledge and engaging them further through their expertise: *'I want the person to invigorate me, educate me so I can take more responsibility or more ownership or interest in how my money is working for me' (C1).* Further, customers' interests may be *stimulated* or *excited* by new prospects that are proposed by their planners, thereby becoming emotionally engaged as a result (Li and Lerner, 2013):

'*And I said wow that's very stimulating for me. I like that personally because I think this person is now giving me all these options*' (C1). In this case, through a meeting and evaluation of options, the customer experiences a feeling of inspiration as an outcome of behavioural and cognitive activities. This indicates that the emotional, behavioural and cognitive dimensions may not occur at the same time, but as an outcome of one another, as the latter defines the situation.

Antecedents of customer engagement with a service offering

CESO as detailed in the previous section is enhanced by a number of factors, such as self-asserted responsibility, personal commitment, perceived complexity, initial rapport and the desire to learn. In this context, attitudinal components such as self-asserted responsibility, personal commitment and the desire to learn are found to be drivers of CESO. Some factors impact on all three dimensions of CESO, namely self-asserted responsibility, personal commitment and perceived complexity, while antecedents such as initial rapport and the desire to learn have a stronger effect on one dimension in particular.

Self-asserted responsibility: The positive attitude that customers have towards their own participation during the service process is a pivotal force in driving CESO. Customers with a strong sense of responsibility tend to play a more active role, with a higher propensity to engage with the service offering: '*It's definitely a partnership. I think we would be irresponsible . . . just to wash our responsibility away. I don't want to be a passenger in this situation*' (C3). This is due to a strong sense of self-ownership: '*I'm not making him responsible for, I don't make him responsible for my success*'(C6); or, as pointed out by another customer: '*You can't have it both ways. You can't say "I went and got advice but I don't want to do that"*' (C8). Such customers are inclined to invest more thoughts, actions and feelings into the relationship. Customers are likely to be more proactive in interacting with their planners and learning to increase their financial skills and knowledge.

Personal commitment: Customers may engage with the service offering due to their personal commitment towards their planner, their advice and the service process, as indicated by the following quote: '*You don't want him to think that you're not serious about it, right? So I think it's healthy if he has expectations that he sees a budget the next time we meet because that's what we're committed to*' (C1). In another words, their positive outlook towards self-participation drives CESO. The results also suggest that financial planners may stimulate the customer to act on his/her commitment, for example by offering relevant reminders: '*He reminds me that it's on me to participate in this, and that you know he's making a recommendation for a reason, so I need to do some homework from time to time and work with him*' (C5). Behaviourally, this relates more to the completion service-related activities and attending functions that are initiated by the planner.

Due to large investment that customers make in terms of the time and effort in behavioural and cognitive activities, they are likely to develop an attachment towards their current planner.

Perceived complexity: The results indicate that the perception of financial planning as complex, whether in terms of products or process, acts as another driver of CESO. Customers commonly engage with the service offering due to their lack of financial expertise or interest in gaining a high level of financial knowledge, as exemplified in the following quote: *'A lot of the products and services are really complex, and I don't have the time or the knowledge or the patience to understand them all' (C5)*. As complexity increases, so does engagement on all three levels – behavioural, cognitive and emotional. Customers may also engage with the service offering to acquire sufficient knowledge for decision-making purposes, or to solve an issue. Furthermore, customers with complex and diverse portfolios may require more assistance from their planners, leading to more interactions: *'Not only was it the investment advice but it was fitting in with what else you were trying to do. So it was linking in with our business, and our superannuation fund and our tax. It was bringing it all together' (C8)*. As customers learn to depend on their planner's expert guidance, they may develop more trust in their planner over time, becoming emotionally engaged in the process.

Initial rapport: Depending on the context, rapport has been seen as either an antecedent or outcome of CE (Hollebeek, 2011). However, in the setting of complex services, we propose initial rapport as an antecedent of CESO in this context, enabling deeper levels of emotional engagement to develop over time. Rapport can be characterised by enjoyable interactions and a personal connection between the customer and the service offering (Gremler and Gwinner, 2000). As stated by a customer: *'You make that assessment initially about whether you can work with this person, whether that person, you know, whether you connect and have some early rapport and trust with that person' (C9)*. An initial assessment is often made by the customer to gauge to what extent he/she is able to connect with the financial planner, the advice and how he/she delivers the service: *'I mean, if I go to a doctor and I don't like the doctor, I'm going to go somewhere else' (C8)*. That is, a planner who is able to align with the customer's values, and is understanding and caring towards them (Gremler and Gwinner, 2000). Further, it is found that a simple connection needs to be established first, prior to forming a deeper relationship, relating emotionally with the planner. That is, before hiring a planner, customers need to feel comfortable with the person first, in order to relate with him/her on an ongoing basis: *'In order to feel comfortable to talk about your circumstances about your finances you need to be comfortable with the person you're talking to' (C2)*.

Desire to learn: The desire to extend financial knowledge emerged in the data as a facilitator of cognitive engagement. This means that cognitive engagement is stronger for customers seeking financial education while engaging with the service offering: *'I don't know enough about it to have a decent opinion. However, I'm happy to be guided and to learn about it'* (C3). In particular, some customers may expect general discussions about processes involved in financial planning: *'I wish we had of had a more detailed discussion about the processes by which underwriting organisations actually assess these forms'* (C2); others may want to deepen their existing knowledge about financial products with more in-depth information: *'I personally expect more than that because I am quite a savvy investor myself. I like understanding financial instruments'* (C1). While the desire to learn facilitates positive cognitive engagement with the advice, it does not naturally translate to positive engagement with the planner (emotionally) or service process (behaviourally). For instance, it may be confronting for a customer who receives advice that drastic behavioural lifestyle changes are necessary to achieve set goals: *'We had to change things and face up to things . . . So there is a bit of an emotional cost there because you have to confront a few things'* (C5). Thus, positive engagement with the service offering – the planner, the advice and the service process – need to be in sync for stronger positive outcomes of CESO to occur.

Outcomes of customer engagement with a service offering

Trust, loyalty, customer empowerment, customer capability, service quality and customer's co created value emerged as outcomes of CESO. While the first three are engagement outcomes in the customer brand engagement setting (e.g. Brodie et al., 2013; Hollebeek, 2011; 2009), we contribute to the existing service literature by identifying increased customer capability, service quality and customer's co created value as outcomes of CESO. Capability development is important due to increasing emphasis placed on customer learning in the service literature (Hibbert, Winklhofer and Temerak, 2012).

Trust: Feelings of trust can occur as a result of experiencing behavioural, cognitive and emotional activities in relation to the planner, the advice or the service process. Customers are able to gauge the planner's level of *'sincerety, honesty and authenticity'* (C2), in terms of the way he/she communicates. As elaborated by another customer, *'I trust [the planner] because he explains things in a way that I understand and I feel comfortable that I'm making the right decision'* (C5), that is, the customer has trust in the planner's advice. In this context, feelings of trust is active and ongoing throughout the service process, and established over time, which leads to customer loyalty: *'He's already built up that trust that when we're ready to get a mortgage or talk about a mortgage, we should talk to him'* (C5). Trust is often a prerequisite to other forms of engagement with the planner, as summed up by another customer, *'You need to be able to trust, you need to be able to trust the person that you're dealing with as a financial planner'* (C2).

Loyalty: Ongoing engagement, particularly due to an emotional connection between the customer and planner, results in the formation of strong relationships and the development of loyalty: *'I think we trust [him] a lot actually and we're in for the long haul' (C3)*. The idea that their financial planner was part of their 'team' was also highlighted several times: *'I see he is part of our team, and that's my wife and my daughter and myself' (C6)*. Another customer explained: *'It's like, a strange sort of analogy, but it's like we're getting to this time where we have a GP, so that, we know, we've got the same person, we've got a relationship, we've got a planner. We've got a bank, we've got a dentist; got a vet. . . . And he's part of that team, if you know what I mean' (C3)*. In this regard, CESO strengthens relationships, facilitating customer retention through customer loyalty. While customer satisfaction was not explicitly mentioned, loyalty can be seen as an indicator of satisfaction, given the intention to continue with the service.

Customer empowerment: Engagement with the service offering also empowers the customer to take responsibility for his/ her own financial matters: *'I knew what the rules were, which is really important because . . . I could actually do some things that were beneficial and quite within the rules in terms of how I manage my affairs' (C8)*. This is mostly due to behavioural and cognitive activities relating to the advice and service process. For instance, customers could contact their planners at any point, to clarify doubts or ask questions, as necessary, as mentioned by a customer, *'I can tap in whenever I've had any queries' (C4)*. Customer empowerment also enables the customer to take more ownership of his/her financial matters, which can help to alleviate blame on the financial planner if things go wrong: *'I don't make him responsible for my success . . . and the consequence of what I choose to do' (C6)*. As a result, customers may experience a strong sense of accomplishment from being accountable for their own finances: *'I guess we make it a bit of a joke that we're finally being grown-ups. I feel like we're actually being grown up' (C3)*.

Increased customer capability: Cognitive engagement with the advice through the planner can contribute towards the customer's existing financial knowledge: *'We've certainly learned a bit through the process. Learnt a bit about what we can do now . . . what he's done really well for us, is to teach us about thinking about our long term future' (C3)*. For some customers, their capabilities were further developed with the additional knowledge, assisting them with future decision-making: *'My major thing was that I knew what the rules were, which is really important because . . . I could actually do some things that were beneficial and quite within the rules in terms of how I manage my affairs' (C8)*. Consequently, the increase in financial literacy may give them additional confidence to deal with more complex processes and products in future.

Service quality: The quality of a service depends on inputs from both parties (Auh et al., 2007), especially so in ongoing complex services. As such, high levels of behavioural engagement are expected during the service process, as customers interact frequently with planners to customise the service. Cognitive activities also help to align expectations between the customer and the planner: *'I'm putting a* *lot of myself out there . . . I expect in return that they . . . [take] care to understand my ambitions and dreams and getting an assessment of what will work'* (C1). Conversely, planners who did not take the effort to align with customers' expectations were seen as providing bad service: *'I felt like I was just a number and there wasn't much education going on'* (C1). Moreover, customer's trust in the planner helped to promote confidence in the planner in providing optimal service: *'I have confidence as far as the planner goes, I have confidence that he understands our profile enough to invest in the right things'* (C5).

Customer co created value: Depending on the extent to which customers choose to engage with the service offering, they are likely to experience different types of value. For instance, customers may benefit from increased drive and interest to meet financial goals they have set (Ng, Plewa and Sweeney, 2015), requiring high levels of behavioural, cognitive and emotional engagement with the service offering. As elaborated by a planner; *'It's like I'm your personal trainer. When you actually go to gym trainer, they don't do the exercise for you, but what they do is stand next to you and tell you the right plan for your diet, the right plan for your exercise. You have to do what they [tell you to] do, they will keep checking on [you]'* (FP3). On the other hand, for customers who value the ability to outsource the responsibility for managing their financial affairs to an expert (Ng, Plewa and Sweeney, 2015), they are able to do so with low levels of CESO. As explained by another planner; *'You know at a very simplistic level it's like when somebody outsources, [like] when they get a cleaner to clean a house'* (FP6).

Managerial implications

This chapter provides a basis on which managers can understand and facilitate customer engagement during complex services. First, the research clearly distinguishes between, and defines, three different dimensions of CESO. This enables managers to gauge the extent to which their customers are engaged with their service offering behaviourally, cognitively and emotionally. Yet, a behaviourally compliant customer does not necessarily equate to a fully engaged customer. Simply put, a customer who is engaged is one who *wants* to do something, rather than *has to* do something (Li and Lerner, 2013). For stronger positive CESO outcomes, positive engagement with the service offering needs to be in sync across all aspects, that is, the planner, their advice and the service process. Nonetheless, higher CESO does not necessarily translate into value for customers; managers have to take into consideration the extent to which customers are willing to invest in engagement activities. Companies should then put their resources towards developing relevant activities that will trigger customers' interest to engage wholeheartedly.

In cases where customers are looking to develop their financial knowledge further, service providers should initiate learning opportunities through cognitive activities. Customers can benefit from increased knowledge, empowering them and increasing their capabilities to better engage with the service offering, deriving more value as a result. Moreover, customers engage in cognitive-related activities mostly because they require expert knowledge in solving problems or making decisions, to meet set objectives. Therefore, it is crucial for service providers to offer insights, thoughts or recommendations that will help to solve issues that are of concern to their customers.

Providers should also put effort into understanding their customers on a deep level, to relate and form emotional bonds with their customers. Customers tend to engage best with empathetic planners whom they can relate to as a friend – that is, going beyond the highly task-oriented focus on achieving set objectives. Engaged customers often look to build an authentic relationship with their service provider, someone they can share their aspirations with and trust. They tend to associate their provider as being part of the team, someone whom they are likely to share a long-term relationship with, establishing loyalty with the financial planner. Hence, it is worthwhile to invest time and effort to connect with customers individually.

Service providers can facilitate CESO by creating enjoyable interactions (Gremler and Gwinner, 2000) and aligning themselves to the customers' values to create rapport. It is essential to ensure that customers feel comfortable in their presence, a prerequisite for engagement in the context of ongoing services. Thus, providers should look to develop their relational skills on top of industry-related qualifications. Importantly, certain customers may be more averse to relationship building (Gremler and Gwinner, 2000) or find it intrusive (Adelman, Ahuvia, and Goodwin, 1994). In such cases, providers can focus on engaging them in quality behavioural and cognitive activities to achieve set objectives.

Limitations and future research

This study provides rich valuable insights in customer engagement with the service offering. Although the focus here is on a single industry, financial planning, we expect that the results are highly relevant to other complex services, that is, those that are relational, require a number of interactions between provider and customer, and are credence-based. Examples include health services and other professional services, such as accountants, physicians (including specialists), lawyers and education.

Moreover, it is also critical for service providers to consider customer preferences for engagement on an individual basis, in the context of CESO. This is because preference for the level of CESO is likely to vary amongst individual customers, as it requires a fair amount of time, effort, feeling and thinking on the part of the customer. However, the difficulty lies in the provider's ability to locate a suitable level of activities for each customer in order to stimulate customer engagement. Thus, future research may develop a scale to measure the level of CESO in the context of complex services, based on extant scales of customer engagement with the brand or organisation (e.g. Hollebeek et al., 2014).

Such a scale will enable generalisation beyond the sample of this study, and can be used to test the antecedents and outcomes of CESO empirically in the financial planning and other complex service contexts. Future research can then explore the extent to which service providers should interact with customers, and how they can support customers in terms of the resources that they can provide (i.e. what service providers can do). This information will be invaluable to firms, enabling them to utilise resources more effectively when strategising.

Conclusion

This chapter has offered an examination of customer engagement with a service offering (CESO) in a complex service setting, and provided insights to the antecedents and outcomes of such engagement. Advancing our understanding of customer engagement by going beyond engagement with brands or organisations, we also captured the multi-faceted nature of CESO founded in the complex interactions of actors. Service providers may facilitate CESO by stimulating cognitive thinking and establishing emotional connections with customers through behavioural activities. The resultant engagement with the service provider not only develops customer capabilities and enables customer empowerment, but could also lead to customer co created value, enhanced quality perceptions, trust and loyalty.

Acknowledgements

The authors express their sincere gratitude for the support of this research by the Commonwealth Government as part of the ARC Linkage Grant Scheme and of our industry partner, the Financial Services Council.

References

Adelman, M.B., Ahuvia, A. and Goodwin, C. (1994) "Beyond Smiling: Social Support and Service Quality," in R.T. Rust and R.L. Oliver (eds.), *Service Quality: New Directions in Theory and Practice*. Thousand Oaks, CA: Sage.

Auh, S., Bell, S.J., McLeod, C.S. and Shih, E. (2007) "Co-production and Customer Loyalty in Financial Services," *Journal of Retailing*, 83(3): 359–370.

Bono, J.E., Foldes, H.J., Vinson, G. and Muros, J.P. (2007) "Workplace Emotions: The Role of Supervision and Leadership," *Journal of Applied Psychology*, 92(5): 1357–1367.

Bowden, J.L. (2009) "The Process of Customer Engagement: A Conceptual Framework," *Journal of Marketing Theory and Practice*, 17(1): 63–74.

Brodie, R.J., Hollebeek, L.D., Juric, B. and Ilic, A. (2011) "Customer Engagement: Conceptual Domain, Fundamental Propositions, and Implications for Research," *Journal of Service Research*, 14(3): 252–271.

Brodie, R.J., Ilic, A., Juric, B., and Hollebeek, L. (2013) "Consumer Engagement in a Virtual Brand Community: An Exploratory Analysis," *Journal of Business Research*, 66: 105–114.

Chandler, J. D. and Lusch, R. F. (2015) "Service Systems: A Broadened Framework and Research Agenda on Value Propositions, Engagement, and Service Experience," *Journal of Service Research*, 18(1): 6–22.

Corley, K. G. and Gioia, D. A. (2004) "Identity Ambiguity and Change in the Wake of a Corporate Spin-off," *Administrative Science Quarterly*, 49: 173–208.

Fredricks, J. A., Blumenfeld, P. C. and Paris, A. H. (2004) "School Engagement: Potential of the Concept, State of the Evidence," *Review of Educational Research*, 74(1): 59–109.

Furrer, C. and Skinner, E. (2003) "Sense of Relatedness as a Factor in Children's Academic Engagement and Performance," *Journal of Educational Psychology*, 95(1); 148–162.

Gremler, D. D. and Gwinner, K. P. (2000) "Customer-Employee Rapport in Service Relationships," *Journal of Service Research*, 3(1): 82–104.

Grönroos, C. and Voima, P. (2013) "Critical Service Logic: Making Sense of Value Creation and Co-creation," *Journal of the Academy of Marketing Science*, 41: 133–150.

Grove, S. J. and Fisk, R. P. (1992) "Observational Data Collection Methods for Services Marketing: An Overview," *Journal of the Academy of Marketing Science*, 20(3): 217–224.

Hibbert, S., Winklhofer, H. and Temerak, M. S. (2012) "Customer as Resource Integrators: Toward a Model of Customer Learning," *Journal of Service Research*, 15(3): 247–261.

Ho, V. T., Wong, S. and Lee, C. H. (2011) "A Tale of Passion: Linking Job Passion and Cognitive Engagement to Employee Work Performance," *Journal of Management Studies*, 48(1): 26–47.

Hollebeek, L. D. (2009) "Demystifying Customer Engagement: Toward the Development of a Conceptual Model," in *Proceedings of ANZMAC Conference*, Melbourne, VIC, 30 November – 2 December.

Hollebeek, L. D. (2011) "Demystifying Customer Brand Engagement: Exploring the Loyalty Nexus," *Journal of Marketing Management*, 27(7–8): 785–807.

Hollebeek, L. D., Glynn, M. S. and Brodie, R. J. (2014) "Consumer Brand Engagement in Social Media: Conceptualization, Scale Development and Validation," *Journal of Interactive Marketing*, 28: 149–165.

Hollebeek, L. D. and Chen, T. (2014) "Exploring Positively- Versus Negatively-valenced Brand Engagement: A Conceptual Model," *Journal of Product & Brand Management*, 23(1): 62–74.

Kahn, W. A. (1990) "Psychological Conditions of Personal Engagement and Disengagement at Work," *Academy of Management Journal*, 33(4): 692–724.

Kahn, W. A. (1992) "To Be Fully There: Psychological Presence at Work," *Human Relations*, 45(4): 321–349.

King, R. B. (2015) "Sense of Relatedness Boosts Engagement, Achievement, and Well-Being: A Latent Growth Model Study," *Contemporary Educational Psychology*, 42: 26–38.

Klassen, R. M., Perry, N. E. and Frenzel, A. C. (2012) "Teacher's Relatedness with Students: An Underemphasized Component of Teachers' Basic Psychological Needs," *Journal of Educational Psychology*, 104(1): 150–165.

Kohli, A. K. (2006) "Dynamic Integration: Extending the Concept of Resource Integration," *Marketing Theory*, 6(3): 290–291.

Li, Y. and Lerner, R. M. (2013) "Interrelations of Behavioral, Emotional, and Cognitive School Engagement in High School Students," *Journal of Youth and Adolescence,* 42: 20–32.

Lincoln, Y. S. and Guba E. G. (1985) *Naturalistic Inquiry.* Thousand Oaks, CA: Sage Publications.

Lukas, B. A., Hair, J. F., Bush, R. P. and Ortinau, D. J. (2005) *Marketing Research.* New South Wales: McGraw-Hill Australia Pty. Ltd.

Lusch, R. F. and Vargo, S. L. (2014) *Service-Dominant Logic.* New York: Cambridge University Press.

Luthans, F. and Peterson, S. J. (2002) "Employee engagement and manager self-efficacy," *Journal of Management Development,* 21(5): 376–387.

Macey, W. H. and Schneider, B. (2008) "The Meaning of Employee Engagement," *Industrial and Organizational Psychology,* 1: 3–30.

McColl-Kennedy, J. R., Vargo, S. L., Dagger, T. S., Sweeney, J. C. and van Kasteren, Y. (2012) "Health Care Customer Value Cocreation Practice Styles," *Journal of Service Research,* 15 (November): 370–389.

Ng, S., Plewa, C. and Sweeney, J. C. (2015) "Service Provider Value Cocreation Styles: Supporting Customers' Value Creation in Complex Services," *Working paper,* University of Adelaide and University of Western Australia.

Parasuraman, A., Berry, L. L. and Zeithaml, V. A (1991) "Understanding Customer Expectations of Service," *Sloan Management Review,* 32(3): 39–48.

Patterson, P., Yu, T. and De Ruyter, K. (2006) "Understanding Customer Engagement in Services," in *Proceedings of ANZMAC Conference,* Brisbane, QLD, 4–6 December.

Payne, A., Storbacka, K. and Frow, P. (2008) "Managing the Co-Creation of Value," *Journal of the Academy of Marketing Science,* 36: 83–96.

Rothbard, N. R. (2011) "Enriching or Depleting? The Dynamics of Engagement in Work and Family Roles," *Administrative Science Quarterly,* 46: 655–684.

Salanova, M., Agut, S., and Peiro, J. M. (2005) "Linking Organizational Resources and Work Engagement to Employee Performance and Customer Loyalty: The Mediation of Service Climate," *Journal of Applied Psychology,* 90(6): 1217–1227.

Schneider, B. and Bowen, D. E. (1995) *Winning the Service Game.* Boston, MA: Harvard Business School Press.

Shah, S. K. and Corley, K. G. (2006) "Building Better Theory by Bridging the Quantitative-Qualitative Divide," *Journal of Management Studies,* 43(8): 1821–1835.

Van Doorn, J., Lemon, K. N., Mittal, V., Nass, S., Pick, D., Pirner, P., and Verhoef, P. C. (2010), "Customer Engagement Behavior: Theoretical Foundations and Research Directions," *Journal of Service Research,* 13(3): 253–266.

Vivek, S. D., Beatty, S. E. and Morgan, R. M. (2012) "Customer Engagement: Exploring Customer Relationships Beyond Purchase," *Journal of Marketing Theory and Practice,* 20(2): 127–145.

Walker, C. O., Greene, B. A. and Mansell, R. A. (2006) "Identification with Academics, Intrinsic/Extrinsic Motivation, and Self-Efficacy as Predictors of Cognitive Engagement," *Learning and Individual Differences,* 16(1): 1–12.

Yoo, J. J., Arnold, T. J. and Frankwick, G. L. (2012) "Effects of Positive Customer-to-Customer Service Interaction," *Journal of Business Research,* 65(9): 1313–1320.

12 Brand co-creation through social actor engagement

Kamer Yuksel, David Ballantyne and Sergio Biggemann

Introduction

Since the Internet has become prominent, the world has become a more connected place. Online brands with innovative business models were born; conventional methods of production, consumption and communication have changed too. The Internet, however, has become much more sophisticated with social media platforms, yielding even more novel ways of interaction, participation, and collaboration for brands and consumers alike (Lassila and Hendler, 2007). Brand development is today more dynamic and involves several parties that indulge in interaction, potentially affecting even the most traditional organisations.

Traditional brand management literature presents serious limitations in reflecting this dynamic and interactive nature of brand development, fostered by the changing social environment (Merz, He, and Vargo, 2009; Payne, Storbacka, and Frow, 2008; Payne, Storbacka, Frow, and Knox, 2009). Traditionally, marketers' dominant view has been that brand management is a one-way, top-down and inside-out communication process and the main responsibility of brand management is to find effective ways to favourably influence consumer perceptions. Therefore, brand managers' task has been to position brand associations into consumers' minds, with a focus on 'awareness and reach' (Tripathi, 2009, p. 138). This view, according to Ballantyne and Aitken (2007), is underlined by an implicit assumption that consumers are passive receivers of what is on offer as value, while the company is the sole creator of value.

More recently, however, there have been calls for a new understanding of brand management in which brand development is characterised as an *interactive process*, with recognition of the role of consumers and other stakeholders as co-creators of the brand (Ballantyne and Aitken, 2007; Brodie, Glynn, and Little, 2006; Merz et al., 2009; Prahalad and Ramaswamy, 2004). This new dimension runs parallel with the value co-creation perspective proposed by Vargo and Lusch (2004) and Prahalad and Ramaswamy (2004), and challenges the conventional supplier and consumer roles respectively as the owners/creators and users/destroyers of the brand and brand value. We argue that brands can no longer simply be seen as an entity or a process to be managed per se, when they are the consequence of firm-consumer and consumer-consumer interactions in a broader network eco-system context.

In this emerging brand development context, we put forward the concept of *social actor engagement* as important for understanding brand development from a network point of view. Hanna, Rohm, and Crittenden (2011) argue 'marketing can no longer solely be about capturing attention via reach; instead, marketers must focus on both capturing and continuing attention via engagement'. Ramaswamy (2011) advises companies to engage their consumers through the use of engagement platforms with the aim of creating valuable experiences together. Fournier and Avery (2011) and Brodie, Ilic, Juric, and Hollebeek (2011) urge scholars to update their understanding of the brand and brand management in the presence of engagement. Exploring what this might mean and the managerial consequences is the subject of this chapter.

Drawing on a single case study of the brand development experience of Beautylish, this chapter investigates brand development from emerging interactive perspectives, and introduces the concept of *social actor engagement* as a means to understand how brand management is changing in a network configuration of brand co-creation. The case study exemplifies an organisation, which since inception adopted an interactive approach to brand development, by strategically engaging a broad range of social actors. More specifically, the issues we wish to explore focus on these questions:

- What does social actor engagement mean in an interactive/co-creative brand development context?
- What are the roles of the organisation and social actors when brand is strategically co-created?
- Why do the organisation and social actors engage and how do they benefit from their engagements?

Traditional perspectives on brands and brand management

An overview of various conceptualisations of the brand and its associated managerial approaches, based on Brodie (2009), is provided in Figure 12.1. What

Traditional brand managerial perspectives

Brand as a company-concept	Brand as a consumer-concept	Brand as a relational-concept
CORPORATE BRAND MANAGEMENT • *corporate identity* • *corporate reputation*	EQUITY-BASED BRAND MANAGEMENT • *Brand image* • *Brand positioning* • *Brand personality*	RELATIONAL BRAND MANAGEMENT • *Brand relationship* • *Brand promise*

Figure 12.1 Traditional brand management perspectives

is common in all of the three perspectives is a holistic view of the brand, focusing on the intangibles which enhance the value of the product beyond its functional purpose (Farquhar, 1989). However, what is not as easily revealing among the three concerns is with whom to attribute the brand and brand value, and who controls the branding process.

The dominant view in the literature has evolved to see the brand as a consumer-concept (Kapferer, 2008), but still subject to the authority of the firm in making these determinations. According to Leone et al. (2006), perception of the brand as a consumer-concept no longer grounds brand meaning in the perceptions of the company; instead, consumer thoughts and feelings give meaning to brands. At this point, a dilemma presents itself as to the real nature of the brand. Brand as a company-concept locates the sources of brand internally (e.g. corporate identity), whereas brand as a consumer-concept locates them outside the firm, within the minds of consumers. However, this does not imply that the latter defines the brand as a consumer-concept, in the literal sense. Ultimately, both view the brand as a 'company-asset', yet each articulates 'different tactics to serve the same concealed intent, that is to exercise the firms' authority over the branding process' (El-Amir and Burt, 2010, p. 74).

Furthermore, traditional brand management perspectives views brand communications as a carefully crafted and disseminated, 'one-way message making system' (Ballantyne and Varey, 2006, p. 224), in which brand managers control all the essential facets – channel, content and impact (Godes et al., 2005) – of brand development. Thus, customers are treated as passive agents – even in their own brand meaning formation (Boyle, 2007; Coupland, 2005; Gensler, Völckner, Liu-Thompkins, and Wiertz, 2013).

To a certain extent, relational brand management challenges this dominant view by offering an alternative conceptualisation of brand meaning formation, and service production and consumption. Instead of a cognitive psychology–based view typically defining equity-based models (e.g. Keller, 2003), scholars like Fournier (1998) introduce a phenomenological view of consumer brand meaning formation. This reinforces the idea that consumers are their own animals who cannot be controlled as commonly assumed, but does not ignite a major shift in the managerial view of brand development as an interactive and/or network-based process. Stakeholder-based equity models (e.g. Brodie, 2009; Brodie, Glynn, and Van Durme, 2002; Jones, 2005) try to close this gap by introducing a network dimension to brand development. Yet, they rely upon brand equity framework as their theoretical foundation – a concept that is inherently company-biased and managerial in its intentions. More specifically, the framework of 'brand as a promise' (Brodie et al., 2006) aims to offer a more balanced and interpretive dimension to brand development. However, the promises that a customer can make reciprocally/interactively are not articulated in a way to suggest a fundamental shift in the role of the customer in the brand development process. It is also important to note that, even though services and relationship marketing scholars acknowledge a relational mode of exchange between customers and organisations (Merz et al., 2009), this perception is mainly a contextual necessity.

The customer is perceived as an organisational resource, whose main role is to serve organisational needs, within the *organisationally defined and imposed bound-aries* (Czepiel, 1990; Jaakkola and Alexander, 2014).

Overall, for the reasons discussed here, even brand management models that aspire to be relational and break free from the restrictive understanding of tra-ditional brand management are vulnerable by basing their foundations on the concept of brand equity, which sees brands as *hard-won corporate assets* (Fournier and Avery, 2011). This concept positions customers as *organisational resources* that are 'available to the firm that enable it to produce efficiently' (Hunt and Morgan, 1995), attempts to maintain authority over the brand (El-Amir and Burt, 2010) and does not acknowledge consumers *who are not part of the buying process* also as influential in brand development (Van Doorn et al., 2010).

Transformative agendas of brand development

In time, what has started as a relationship focus in brand management literature has further evolved with the introduction of ideas, such as co-creation of brands and brand value (Iglesias, Ind, and Alfaro, 2013), and network/eco-system views of brand development (Breidbach, Brodie, and Hollebeek, 2014; Gensler et al., 2013; Gyrd-Jones and Kornum, 2013). Today, these ideas represent emerging phenomena in marketing and potentially a fundamental shift in how we think about brands, consumers and the overall process of brand formation. Thus far, co-creation has been approached from various theoretical perspectives (e.g. service dominant logic) and in various contexts (e.g. product innovation). However, its application to brands and brand development has been limited, particularly in online contexts, which enables interactions to take place in unex-pected places, at unexpected times, among a variety of actors who may or may not have a direct brand focus. Most conceptualisations of brand co-creation hint towards an iterative, social and process-based view of brand and brand value that is co-created via interactions between brands, customers and other stakeholders (Brodie and De Chernatony, 2009; Golant, 2012; Iglesias et al., 2013; Merz et al., 2009; Payne et al., 2009), and materialised through value-in-use (Merz et al., 2009) and customer experiences (Payne et al., 2009; Ramaswamy, 2011). Implicit in this view is the expectation of a direct customer brand contact/interface via product or service provision; whereas, another emerging view makes more explicit the ability of other actors who may not be at the organisational radar (from a strategic point of view), and potentially exist 'at the periphery of the eco-system' (Gyrd-Jones and Kornum, 2013) to con-tribute to brand development in valuable ways.

The latter supports a broader network-based view of brand development, in which brands are viewed as part of wider eco-systems, exact boundaries of which may never be realistically assessed and controlled in the traditional sense. Accord-ingly, brands are more spontaneously defined and redefined (co-created through interaction), beyond a practical organisational control, thus representing a stark contrast to the strategic formation of brand for a pre-defined purpose by the brand manager (Varey, 2008), as well as to the stakeholder perspectives which still in part subscribe to organisational control through management of key stakeholders based on their expected value contributions to the brand (e.g. Jones, 2005). One common theme that is making these concepts more relevant and their theoretical maturity more urgent is the advances in online digital platforms (e.g. Facebook, Twitter; Fournier and Avery, 2011; Gensler et al., 2013). This broad array of platforms is seen as game changers, markedly influencing how online users interact, communicate and relate to one another. They connect users at a global scale and offer unique multiverse experiences that are not possible offline. More importantly, they make information and consumer stories abundant and accessible, enabling many voices to be heard – not just the voices of the few, better-funded or the well-orchestrated.

Online brand communities support this extended view of brand development (e.g. Wirtz et al., 2013). However, the eco-system view goes beyond brand communities, by extending to consumer collectives on online digital platforms (Hanna et al., 2011; Muñiz and Schau, 2011). In this context, co-creation of brand and brand value is 'grounded in patterns of communicative interaction' and is 'emergent in kind' (Ballantyne, Frow, Varey, and Payne, 2011). This view was echoed early on the in the practitioner world by the authors of the Cluetrain Manifesto who redefined markets as conversations – and not as mere marketing messages (Levine, Locke, Searls, and Weinberger, 2000).

Simultaneously, this technology-infused trend is forcing traditional organisations to adapt from a closed, company-controlled and one-way view of brand management to an open, interactive/co-creative and network view of brand development, which cautiously welcomes brand managers into an environment 'where anyone and everyone had a say in matters of the brand' (Fournier and Avery, 2011, p. 194). Most traditional organisations are trying to claim their place by merely extending their offline brand management practices to online, as they are called upon to 'develop consumer engagement as part of the marketing mix' (Woodcock, Green, and Starkey, 2011, p. 59) or treat social media as an alternative channel of brand communications (e.g. Mosadegh and Behboudi, 2011, p. 66). As a result, the status of consumers who engage resemble somewhat *unwelcomed guests*, with whom organisations have to find effective ways to deal with or accommodate within the bigger (organisational) scheme of things. What is noticeably missing in the literature are organisations that exemplify – in the true spirit of the word – co-creative/interactive brand development, in which brand managers not only envision, but also develop their brands by embracing engagement in a network context, making it a core organisational philosophy and part of the brand experience for every social actor involved. The case study presented in this chapter is one such organisation and offers unique insights into brand co-creation through social actor engagement.

Engagement: the concept and boundaries

The term engagement has been used by consultants and management authors for some time. Marketing scholars have more recently started to examine its use and range of meanings (e.g. Bowden, 2009; Brodie, Hollebeek, Jurić, and

Ilić, 2011; Hollebeek, 2011a, 2011b; Van Doorn et al., 2010). The concept is therefore still in its formal stages and yet to achieve theoretical maturity (Gambetti and Graffigna, 2010; Hollebeek, 2011a). Some of the conceptualisations identified from the marketing literature are summarised in Table 12.1. As to be expected in the development of a new concept, there are a number of differing and contradictory themes.

Table 12.1 Various conceptualisations of engagement in the marketing literature

Author	Concept	Concept Definition	Dimensions	Research Method
Engagement as a psychological concept				
McEwans (2004)	Customer engagement	CE is a measure of the overall strength of a company's customer relationships; it reflects the degree to which customers have formed emotional as well as rational bonds to the brands they buy and own.	Cognitive Affective	Conceptual
Bowden (2009)	Customer engagement	CE is a psychological process that models the underlying mechanisms by which customer loyalty forms for new customers of a service brand as well as the mechanisms by which loyalty may be maintained for repeat purchase customers of a service brand.	Cognitive Affective	Conceptual
Calder and Malthouse (2008)	Media engagement	Engagement is the sum of the motivational experiences consumers have with the media product.	Cognitive Affective	Conceptual
Higgins and Scholer (2009)	Engagement	Engagement is a state of being involved, occupied, fully absorbed or engrossed in something – sustained attention.	Cognitive Affective	Conceptual
Calder et al. (2013)	Consumer engagement	Engagement is a highly personal and motivational state arising out of consumer experiences with a product or service.	Cognitive Affective	Empirical – based on two large scale surveys

Engagement as a behavioural concept

Kumar et al. (2010)	Customer engagement	Active interactions of a customer with a firm, with prospects and with other customers, whether they are transactional or non-transactional in nature, can be defined as customer engagement.	Behavioural	Conceptual
Van Doom et al. (2010)	Customer engagement behaviours	Engagement is the customers' behavioural manifestation toward a brand or firm, beyond purchase, resulting from motivational drivers.	Behavioural	Conceptual

Engagement as both a psychological and behavioural concept

Hollebeek (2010)	Customer brand engagement	The level of an individual customer's motivational, brand-related and context-dependent state of mind characterised by specific levels of cognitive, emotional and behavioural activity in direct brand interactions	Cognitive Affective Behavioural	Conceptual
Hollebeek (2011b)	Customer brand engagement	The level of a customer's cognitive, emotional and behavioural investment in specific brand interactions	Cognitive Affective Behavioural	Empirical – based on a qualitative study

Online engagement conceptualisations

Mollen and Wilson (2010)	Online engagement	Online engagement is a cognitive and affective commitment to an active relationship with the brand as personified by the website or other computer-mediated entities designed to communicate brand value. It is characterised by the dimensions of dynamic and sustained cognitive processing and the satisfying of instrumental value (utility and relevance) and experiential value (emotional congruence with the narrative schema encountered in computer-mediated entities).	Cognitive Affective	Conceptual

(*Continued*)

Table 12.1 (Continued)

Author	Concept	Concept Definition	Dimensions	Research Method
Brodie et al. (2011)	Online consumer engagement	Consumer engagement is a context-dependent, psychological state characterised by fluctuating intensity levels that occur within dynamic, iterative engagement processes. Consumer engagement is a multidimensional concept comprising cognitive, emotional, and/or behavioural dimensions.	Cognitive Affective Behavioural	Empirical-based: netnography

Early conceptualisations (e.g. Bowden, 2009; McEwen, 2004) view customer engagement as certain psychological states of customers leading to brand loyalty and/or other conspicuous consumption behaviours. Taking a more process-based view, some scholars define engagement as an emergent state of mind, more grounded in personal experiences with media and service/product (e.g. Calder, Isaac, and Malthouse, 2013; Calder and Malthouse, 2008), or with the pursuit of a bigger consumer goal (Higgins and Scholer, 2009). Some scholars take a tripartite (i.e. cognitive, affective and/or behavioural) view. As such, Hollebeek (2011b) defines '"customer brand" engagement as customers' cognitive, emotional, and behavioural investments in a brand', and more specifically, as 'the level of an individual customer's motivational, brand-related and context-dependent state of mind characterised by specific levels of cognitive, emotional and behavioural activity in direct brand interactions' (Hollebeek, 2011a, p. 790).

Aiming to consolidate prior conceptualisations, Brodie, Hollebeek, et al. (2011) emphasise the multidimensional, context-dependent, and process-based nature of the concept, resulting from interactive experiences, within a network of service relationships, revealing different levels of engagement intensities. According to the scholars, customer engagement occurs in a way that 'requires first-hand experiences' with the focal agent/object, and can be directed towards brands, products/services, a piece of communication, a communication channel, user message or content interactions, human/computer-mediated interactions and/or interpersonal interactions. Online-based definitions do not necessarily bring any further clarification to the confusion surrounding the engagement concept. For example, Mollen and Wilson (2010) define online engagement as 'cognitive and affective commitment to an active relationship with the brand as personified by the website'. Brodie, Ilic, Juric, and Hollebeek (2013) define online customer engagement as 'a context-dependent, multidimensional psychological state characterised by fluctuating intensity levels that occur within dynamic, iterative engagement processes'.

All in all, despite offering a broader conceptualisation of engagement by perceiving it as a multidimensional concept, some scholars suggest that such conceptualisations risk being too broad, making it difficult to offer enough practical guidance and distinguish it from other rival concepts (e.g. consumer involvement, consumer brand relationships) (Mitchell, 2012; Van Doorn, 2011). Thus, solely focusing on the behavioural dimension, Kumar et al. (2010) define customer engagement as 'customers' transactional and non-transactional interactions with the firm and with other customers, in ways that generate value for the firm'. Accordingly, not every interaction with the firm is considered, but the ones that actually contribute value (e.g. positive valenced) to the firm are recognised. Taking a similar stance, Van Doorn et al. (2010, p. 254) define such behaviours as 'customers' behavioural manifestations that have a brand or firm focus, beyond purchase, resulting from motivational drivers'. They deviate from Kumar et al. (2010) by excluding repurchase behaviours. Instead, they call attention to all non-transactional behaviours (e.g. word of mouth), while also pointing out that an exhaustive understanding of such behaviours as currently missing.

In this chapter we propose an alternative view of engagement and offer the following definition:

> Social actor engagement is a form of communicative interaction with the focal firm (e.g. employees) and/or other social actors, beyond routine commercial interactions, in ways that support or hinder brand development.

There are three aspects of this definition that need to be emphasised. First, *communicative interaction* is posited as a new analytical framework to view the engagement concept. It implies that online interactions are communicative by nature, and have an enhanced potential to generate a response from other social actors. Thus, it delimits engagement to communicative phenomena only, and cannot include interactions with product/service (as in product usage or participation in service production/consumption) or product (re)purchase as part of the concept. The emphasis on *beyond routine commercial interactions* excludes interactions that do not support (co-creative) brand development, despite being potentially communicative by nature (e.g. emailing customer service about an order status). Finally, the emphasis on *brand development* and not associating the concept with a particular constituency (e.g. customer) aims to liberate the brand from the managerial catch-and-conquer mentality. It also stresses that brand development is not confined within the organisational boundaries; that is, it is a network process. The case study presented next will substantiate this suggested analytical framework, while also revealing a deeper understanding for brand co-creation through social actor engagement.

Case study

Research approach

This research was qualitative in nature and adopted a single holistic case study approach (Yin, 2003), utilising in-depth interviews with key brand managers and naturalistic observation of the brand and community-created content on the brand website (beautylish.com) and on social media sites (e.g. Facebook and Twitter). The primary researcher has registered as a community member as part of this research, and observed the community engagements for over two years. Naturalistic observation was used to generate new insights, which were not revealed with the interviews, as well as for overall triangulation purposes of the literature, in-depth interviews and observational data.

About the brand

Beautylish was established in 2010 as a beauty- and make-up-focused online social community site. In two years, it has reached over one million members on the brand site and a substantial community on various social media sites (e.g. Pinterest: 3 million). The site provides specialised content such as product reviews, how-to-tips, photos and video tutorials contributed by *community members* and *the organisation* itself. In 2012, after two years of intense focus on growing the community, Beautylish has added an e-commerce option to its social brand experience. Thus, the brand experience now also involves, but does not necessitate, buying some of the products as seen on the website.

Brand vision

The initial vision of the organisation was to create a unique community that can support people's ability to learn and apply make-up, by combining and enhancing some of the elements of offline and online experiences readily available. The offline beauty experience typically involves a make-up counter at a retail store, in which a beauty consultant personally attends to the customer by assessing her skin type/tone, and makes product recommendations and demonstrations – generally incentivised by certain brands; or it involves a beauty magazine that tailors the brand experience towards a specific customer segment, promoting certain looks (e.g. blonde, slender figure) and brands. In the online context, the typical beauty (shopping) experience, through a retailer like Amazon, involves product photos, descriptions and some aggregate product ratings/reviews, based on which the customer makes a purchase decision – without any personal feedback or consultation.

Beautylish's vision was to provide an alternative experience in a way that replicates the social and consultative nature of the offline make-up counter, and takes it further with online social and community capabilities (e.g. community members asking questions and getting unbiased feedback). Also, in contrast to beauty magazines targeting certain customer groups, Beautylish is a gathering place for people from all backgrounds, races and gender, including people with unconventional looks.

Brand development of Beautylish

Figure 12.2 depicts the brand development process of Beautylish. The brand has evolved gradually and dynamically. This has been through social media, followed by the brand community, and then e-commerce as the latest brand initiative. Initially, there was heavy reliance on social media platforms for community building purposes. However, in time, as the community aspect became stronger and richer, with the growing number of community members and community-created content, the initially rather sequential process between social media and the brand community has become more of a fluid, parallel-functioning and cross-fertilising process.

Figure 12.2 Brand co-creation through social actor engagement: the case of Beautylish

I think one of the things that helped us grow early on was actually being really active with people on social networks, especially on Twitter. We were really active in terms of responding to people's questions, people would ask for beauty tips. And we would tweet out our own beauty tips. If they have questions we would answer them. . . . So, we did the same sort of thing on other platforms, like Facebook, and on our own site . . .

(Sameer Iyengar, Co-founder)

I would say it [social media] is almost 50 per cent of the endeavour. So what you see on the web site is only a portion of our activity, and the full story is something that is told across all of the mediums. It is told on the web site but also on the Pinterest, also on the emails that we send to people, on Twitter, on Facebook, on Tumblr.

(Bec Stupak, Creative Director)

The *engagement eco-system* which encapsulates all social media platforms and the online brand community – leaving out e-commerce (transactional aspects) – represents all the communicative interactions that are taking place among social actors interacting across time and space, supporting brand co-creation. All social actors that are part of the eco-system constitute of the focal firm, company employees, online brand community members (members of Beautylish.com) – who could be either customers or non-customers – and all other social actors interacting on social media platforms with direct or indirect brand focus. Company employees are also part of the brand community, and interact with the community members and other social actors on a regular basis.

Meaning of engagement in a brand co-creation context

In a brand co-creation context, a common theme concerning engagement emerges as 'being active' both on the brand community site and on social media platforms. We interpret this activity as a form of communicative interaction between the organisation and other social actors taking place on various platforms, which leaves a trace, and are visible to the organisation and/or other social actors, thus has a potential to generate further engagements.

I mean a lot of [engagement] is just by being active. So if they have products that they review, if they upload photos or videos, they comment on things, if they follow other people, you know comments on their photos. You know, these are kind of all the ways that they do. And then also, if they see something that they like and they share it on their own Facebook, or they share it on their own Twitter, or Tumblr, or Pinterest.

(Bec Stupak, Creative Director)

At a broad level, our analysis reveals that engagement processes, concerning all social actors taking place within the engagement eco-system, involve the following communicative interactions:

- creating and sharing own content (e.g. make-up photos, hair tutorials, beauty articles)
- curating and sharing other social actors' content (e.g. photos, tutorials)
- endorsing (e.g. liking, following)
- asking questions/commenting (e.g. writing product reviews)
- responding to questions/comments

An important observation is that the organisation's engagement processes are not significantly different than that of the community members and other social actors. The organisation and its employees engage very much the same way via all of the aforementioned means.

> *I would be very active on the articles so when people are commenting on the questions, I respond, or I leave my own comments just responding to the articles, the photographs that people upload I share them on Pinterest, and we make sure that if there is something that we really like that it gets shared on Facebook, or, I leave comments on people's photos . . . We also follow people, that sort of behaviour that people are familiar with on Facebook.*
>
> (Bec Stupak, Creative Director)

There are, however, exceptions, and it involves engagement content of incentivising (e.g. offering free-gifts who registered with the community site) and call-to-action (e.g. 'like' this post, if you like this quote) as being somewhat more exclusive to organisations. Naturally, social actors who engage without any professional agenda do not commonly rely on this form of communicative interaction. However, we have also observed that some actors (e.g. people with more professional aspirations or community members who are also professional make-up artists) can exhibit these processes as well. They do it, for example, by sharing their personal website and/or blog address, and ask others to 'visit my page'.

As social actors become more sophisticated with their online (marketability) skills, they can also be expected to excel in these engagement forms. Despite, however, counting these types of engagements as communicative interaction, our focus in this chapter is on more organically emerging engagements that can potentially generate valuable co-creative outcomes such as conversation and dialogue.

The role of the organisation in brand co-creation

It is important to note that traditional roles concerning 4Ps, customer service and technical support are naturally still within the role definitions of the organisation. However, in each of these elements, social actor engagement is considered and integrated at varying degrees. For example, the organisation supports the community by providing technology solutions, such as interactive capabilities and integration to other social media platforms. The organisation specifically focuses on *access and sharing capabilities*, so that social actors can access the brand community site from many different platforms and devices, and share as conveniently as possible. This chapter, however, focuses on newly emerging organisational roles that make brand co-creation possible, including the roles of moderating, facilitating, interpreting and inspiring. Figure 12.3 provides a brief overview of these roles, in the context of brand co-creation, followed by a detailed discussion on each role.

Moderating: This role involves moderating the community by setting the ground rules, and restricting faulty and unconstructive engagements. This is not about censuring negative engagements which might potentially hurt the focal firm (e.g. customer complaints); instead the main aim is to provide a safe space for everyone to engage in a productive and meaningful way. Therefore, the types of engagements that are moderated out include direct attack to community content using unconstructive language and member questions that may

Figure 12.3 Newly emerging roles of the organisation in a brand co-creation context

potentially attract unconstructive engagements. Engagement netiquette posted on the site encourages kindness, thoughtful contribution and respecting others' creative content by crediting the original source when shared. Even though the organisation allows all social actors to endorse and/or share community content without becoming a community member, it does require membership – detailed identity revealed – for certain engagement processes (i.e. creating content and commenting). This simultaneously supports the goal of creating a safe space for engagement.

> *What we don't want [is] people leaving anonymous comments; we want people [to] stand by the thing that they are saying. So, it is a conversation between two individuals and that they know who they are.*
>
> (Bec Stupak, Creative Director)

The moderator role is shared with the community, thus carried out in collaboration with several community members who are not company employees. Therefore, it assigns a broader responsibility to community oversight, promoting self-control mechanisms instead of brand-only oversight.

Facilitating: This role involves facilitating community members' construction of (online) identities and self-concept by encouraging them to create more of their own content and share more of the community-created content. At a more holistic level, the organisation recognises the important role a brand can play in furthering or hindering a community member's sense of self, and considers this aspect in designing its own engagement processes.

> *. . . so it is not just about these products, but it is also about kind of what it [brand] does for peoples' sort of sense of self-confidence, their self-expression and so forth . . .*
>
> (Bec Stupak, Creative Director)

The organisation acknowledges community members' high-quality content, and encourages them to create more by, for instance, regularly featuring community-created content on its main page, as well as on other social media platforms. The organisation facilitates self-expression through the customisation of online profiles (e.g. photos, hair/eye colour) and by embracing individuals with different races, genders and unconventional looks as community members and also as focal subjects of the company-created content.

Interpreting: One of the most important roles that emerges in a brand co-creation context for the organisation is to make sense of social actor engagements (e.g. comments, product reviews) and make them actionable in a way that will benefit the whole community – not only the company. This is done primarily by having a conversation and a dialogue with as many social actors as possible within the engagement eco-system. Many conventional organisations prefer not to get involved directly with the conversation, and try to gauge the brand sentiments from a distance. When/if they engage, they focus on solving product- and/or service-related issues. What we observe in this case study is a continuous and intentional effort to engage at multiple levels, including employees, so that a better sense of the engagement eco-system could be grasped in ways that can guide the organisation.

> *It is not so much about they are having a conversation that we are watching; it is kind of like we are all having a conversation. So we all try to be very active on the site in terms of engaging with the users when they upload photos and videos, when they comment on articles, we'll comment as well. We also talk with people on Twitter . . . having a whole conversation with people there.*
>
> (Bec Stupak, Creative Director)

Making engagements actionable is a crucial and a challenging aspect of this role. One way this is done which is potentially unique to this case is that, before even introducing e-commerce, the company encouraged community members to contribute to a product database, which at the time of the fieldwork already had ratings and reviews for over 30,000 products. Having gathered this information voluntarily from many social actors guides the organisation on deciding what might be an appropriate product/merchandising strategy for the community overall.

> *. . . we use cues from what's popular, what people are recommending to each other, what people like within the community to help drive those partnerships as well . . . If you were setting up a traditional sort of e-commerce retail, you would probably just find a list of the biggest most popular brands and kind of just go after them one by one.*
>
> (Samer Iyengar, Co-founder)

Inspiring: One of the most critical roles that emerge for successful brand co- creation is organisational ability to inspire the community and other social actors. The organisation does this by providing artistic-driven content that gets shared a lot, and raises the bar for everyone else wishing to engage. Compared to other social actors, the organisation, with its access to resources and ties to a network of influential social actors (e.g. professional make-up artists), still has a unique advantage which can be put to the benefit of the community and the wider eco- system. By trying to be inspirational, the organisation also sets, by example, higher standards for engagement, consequently enhancing the social experience for every social actor involved. This effort raises the standard for every social actor who wants to engage, and motivates them to excel in their own engagements.

> *So we have our own design and editorial team, we shoot our own photos or videos and write our own articles, and those tend to be in the spectrum of things pretty high quality. . . . And one of the things we saw after releasing those things to the community is the level of the quality of the community photos.*

Because, I think in the community people look around for cues to see like OK what kind of community is this. And if you look around, and all you see are really high quality photos, then you know this isn't probably the place to take your flip phone camera and take a simple picture, and put it up.

(Sameer Iyengar, Co-founder)

The role of community members in brand co-creation

On the surface, community members contribute to brand development by 'simply being active'. As argued previously, their communicative interactions, like the brand, involve the following: creating content, curating and sharing content, endorsing, asking questions/writing comments and responding to questions/comments. Their engagements within the community, however, are explicitly and implicitly governed by some structural and moral boundaries, and underlined by certain rituals and responsibility (Muñiz and O'Guinn, 2001). Explicit norms are easier to see as they are immediately presented to the social actor once she or he becomes a member (e.g. via engagement netiquette). Implicit norms are more likely to take time to understand and adapt. At this stage, the organisation has a more critical role in terms of driving engagements and energising all social actors. However, as the community progresses, it forms its own culture and norms of acceptable behaviour, influenced not solely by the organisation but all members; thus the organisation's initial role as being the main driver of social actor engagements lessens, as other social actors engage in multitude of ways.

One way members act responsibly within community boundaries is engaging in a way that would not jeopardise the integrity of the community and other member engagements. Also, they are motivated, by the organisation and their peers, to put a certain level of effort and thought into their engagements (e.g. product reviews and content). Even though, this is not mandatory, and subpar engagements are not filtered out, it does not fit well within the norms of the community. The most important cue with respect to gauging a community member's quality of engagement is through its ability to generate further engagements quantitatively (e.g. number of shares, likes etc.) and/or qualitatively (e.g. nature of comments) from other members of the community and the wider eco-system. This seems to act like a self-check and a reward mechanism, signalling community members that their engagement is appropriate and contributes to the community in positive ways.

Community members who excel in their engagements, particularly in their own content creations (e.g. make-up tutorials), *inspire* other community members, and may also encourage others to do better.

. . . some of those people have fantastic work. I think it is really interesting where it is like: oh this person at home in her bedroom in Ohio is doing amazing stuff. So there is a whole level of people who have risen up, sort of from anonymity to be very prominent in this field.

(Bec Stupak, Creative Director)

What is further observed is that many community members support each other's content with constructive comments, praising each other's efforts of personal expression. In these respects, they also share the brand's *facilitating role,* which aims to enhance community members' self-concept and self-expression. It is important to note that, since unconstructive engagements are generally moderated out, we cannot observe such engagements.

Finally, some community members directly help the organisation with the moderator role as they oversee the community member engagements and make sure that they are constructive and support the community in positive ways.

The role of other social actors – who do not have a direct brand focus – in brand co-creation

The communicative interactions of these social actors with the brand occur rather indirectly through more complicated network routes. These social actors may endorse (e.g. like) or comment on another social actor's (e.g. a Facebook friend) 'shared' community content without even realising the brand connection of the content. This communicative interaction simultaneously becomes visible to the actors' whole social network, which may then trigger other social actors within the network to follow suit. Alternatively, by following the source of one of the 'shared' brand-related content (e.g. link origin), they may stumble upon the community site, and take a piece of the community content, and share it with their own networks on various social media sites.

> . . . one of the behaviours we see, for example, is people come to our photo section and use that, they browse the photos on Beautylish and look for things to pin to their pin-board. So then it creates this interesting eco-system where people see these photos and come to our web site, they kind of take piece of it, and curate it in their pin-board, and when other people see that they will come to our site . . .

(Sameer Iyengar, Co-founder)

Interestingly enough, in none of these situations do these social actors need to become a member of the brand community or a customer to the company in order to support brand development. This supports the eco-system view of brand development, involving many social actor engagements. Thus, it offers support to our argument that brand is co-created within the engagement eco-system, as a result of numerous communicative interactions – with direct or no direct brand focus – involving many social actors.

Drivers of organisation and community member engagements

Particularly, at the initial phases of brand development, prior to the introduction of e-commerce, the main drivers of company engagement was to develop the brand in a way that supports the brand's vision, which involved creating a space for everyone who is interested in beauty and make-up to engage with the organisation and with other like-minded social actors. The organisation has primarily achieved that by being *active and responsive* to all social actors within the engagement eco-system, which was influential in reinforcing further engagements and the development of the brand community.

> . . . *if you ask a brand a question and they don't respond, well that's not so great, right. Just being able to be there and just connect with the users has just been valuable, and that's what people really like about what we are doing. I think it gives them a reason to keep coming back.*
>
> (Sameer Iyengar, Co-founder)

The organisation intended to build a community, which is safe and inspires people, thus motivating other social actors to join the effort; so the organisation is not the sole actor making most of the brand development effort. This is reflected in the organisation's engagement processes, particularly with respect to content creation, as well as sharing of other social actors' content. By using professional photos and writing editorial articles in collaboration with professional artists they enhance the quality of their own engagements. And by sharing other social actors' content, they acknowledge and encourage similar efforts – which, in turn, contributes to the whole community by increasing the number of people visiting the site, asking questions, commenting, endorsing and/or sharing the community content out.

With the exception of small monetary incentives (e.g. gifts, store credit), the organisation does not employ a regular incentive program to encourage engagement. Therefore, besides some social actor engagements that are a direct response to incentivising and/or call-to-actions, the non-monetary drivers of community member engagement emerge as to learn/discover new skills, get feedback from an impartial crowd, share their knowledge with others (altruistic), get recognised (non-monetarily) for their talent/effort and socialise with others. Some community members are professional make-up artists or people who aspire to become professionals; what drives them to engage appear to have different motivations. These members, however, might still share the aforementioned motivations; at the same time, they also try to support their professional endeavours.

> . . . *it is a very generous community, and I think that what people are finding is that any social engagement they have just helps them in their career, and it just helps elevate their status.*
>
> (Bec Stupak, Creative Director)

It is important to highlight that this research did not directly investigate with the community members; therefore, these findings draw from the interviews with brand managers and the main researcher's observation of the brand's

230 Kamer Yuksel et al.

community site as a passive community member for over two years. Additionally, this research cannot reveal insights as to what drives other social actors who do not have a direct brand focus to engage, as theorised previously.

Discussion

This chapter has drawn upon the brand co-creation effort of an organisation, which successfully engaged a broad range of social actors, through the use of social media platforms and its brand community. We presented an alternative view of engagement, in the form of social actor engagement, and defined it as a form of communicative interaction taking place within the engagement eco-system, amongst a broad array of social actors, affecting brand development in both positive and negative ways.

Given the ongoing debate concerning what engagement is or what it might be, we align more closely with the behavioural perspective of Van Doorn et al. (2010). Concomitantly, however, we differ from them in some respects. Our view is grounded in communications theory, rather than consumer behaviour, and is process-focused, rather than outcome focused. Thus, our approach foregrounds different brand co-creation processes, such as conversation and dialogue, rather than traditional brand outcomes, such as brand loyalty and brand equity. We also acknowledge that interactions of other social actors – who are not community members and/or customers – with no direct brand focus are also important for brand development. Finally, our conceptualisation focuses on online interactions only, offering a unifying framework to view specific processes of online engagement.

The specific engagement processes that we have identified include creating and sharing own content, curating and sharing other social actors' content, endorsing, asking questions/commenting and responding to questions/comments. Our findings parallel Brodie et al. (2013)'s online engagement sub-processes (i.e. sharing, co-developing, learning, advocating and socialising). However, we think that some of their processes (i.e. learning, co-developing and socialising) are better treated as potential consequences and/or antecedents of social actor engagements. Also, among all engagement forms, we highlight *sharing* as particularly powerful in the context of brand co-creation. We argue that sharing capability effectively extends the boundaries of the engagement eco-system, by enabling numerous social actors, who may or may not have a direct brand focus, to participate in brand co-creation.

Our research also reveals that community members engage with the focal firm and other social actors for various reasons including learning/discovery, getting unbiased feedback, sharing knowledge/skills with others (i.e. altruistic), being recognised (non-monetarily) for talent/effort and socialising. In an extensive survey of consumers using web-based consumer opinion platforms, Hennig-Thurau, Gwinner, Walsh, and Gremler (2004) also find that social benefits, concern for others, advice seeking and extraversion/self-enhancement as the main (non-monetary) reasons why consumers articulate their brand experiences. Our findings broadly fall into these categories, but the individual nature of each factor does not necessarily overlap, due to different study contexts. Also, our study indirectly infers the potential drivers of community member engagements, thus is limited in its scope, requiring further empirical investigation.

In a brand co-creation context, even the traditional brand management practices are revisited (e.g. Frow, Payne, and Storbacka, 2011); however, most critically, new roles emerge for the organisation, involving the roles of moderating, facilitating, interpreting and inspiring. These roles are not traditionally managerial in nature and intentions; instead they focus on enabling and bringing to light the potential of the community and other social actors as brand co-creators. So far, DART, by Prahalad and Ramaswamy (2004), has been the guiding model for the co-creative enterprise. However, our findings suggest that, in the context of brand co-creation, other organisational roles need to be more prominent. Our study, thus, uncovers these roles.

From inception, the organisation strategically recognises the value that the community and the engagement eco-system can generate, and builds many mechanisms to support their ability to engage (Muñiz and Schau, 2011). The organisation acknowledges other social actors, who are not community members or customers, but still contribute to brand development, and engages with them mainly through social media platforms. By not restricting engagement (e.g. not requiring community membership) and allowing any social actor to share and endorse content, the brand relaxes the control and ownership of its own and the community-created content.

In a brand co-creation context, the organisation does not try to cling to the brand development process; instead there is confidence in the brand and its value proposition that it will be accepted favourably by enough number of social actors within the network. Here, the main assumption is that, as long as the organisation and other social actors operate in a way that is supportive and helpful to the whole network, everyone wins. IMP researchers (e.g. Håkansson and Snehota, 1989; Olkkonen, Tikkanen, and Alajoutsijarvi, 2000) long challenged the fundamental assumption of traditional view of competition as a win-or-lose process; instead, they suggested, if companies strive to improve their networks through win-win strategies, that would also strengthen their network position.

A lot of people say, well look people are putting your photos from your community and posting them under Pinterest; isn't Pinterest now competitive with you because they can now just go to Pinterest, and get all of the beauty photos. And I think that's kind of a concern that a lot of businesses have, that they are really keeping a tight stronghold over their content . . . So we kind of take the approach that if we really have good stuff, which we feel like we do, in terms of whether it is the community content or our own, then if that stuff gets shared out, people will sort of find their way back to our site; because they will be looking for more like it.

(Sameer Iyengar, Co-founder)

Finally, none of these newly emerging organisational roles is typically fulfilled with an exchange-driven and product-focused mentality, but requires a more holistic vision, a will to collaborate with others and successfully integrating that vision to company's engagement processes. A holistic vision further entails that the organisation learns and grows with the community. It does subdue immediate opportunistic tendencies, and mainly derives its energy from what is exciting for the community. This does not mean that the organisation does not have any financial concerns, but it is not the starting point or the core of the brand co-creation effort. This vision is particularly evident in the company's intentionally refraining from an exchange-based model, and solely focusing on building a community in the initial years of its life. This choice enabled the organisation to build trust in ways that may not have been possible otherwise, if the starting point of brand development was in reverse order: as an exchange-based mentality leading to a community-building effort later on, which represents the community-building initiatives of most organisations.

References

Ballantyne, D., and Aitken, R. (2007). Branding in B2B markets: Insights from the service-dominant logic of marketing. *Journal of Business & Industrial Marketing,* 22(6), 363–371.

Ballantyne, D., Frow, P., Varey, R. J., and Payne, A. (2011). Value propositions as communication practice: Taking a wider view. *Industrial Marketing Management,* 40(2), 202–210.

Ballantyne, D., and Varey, R. J. (2006). Introducing a dialogical orientation to the service-dominant logic of marketing. In R. F. Lusch and S. L. Vargo (Eds.), *The Service-Dominant Logic of Marketing: Dialogue, Debate, and Directions.* New Delhi: Prentice-Hall of India.

Bowden, J. (2009). The process of customer engagement: A conceptual framework. *Journal of Marketing Theory & Practice,* 17(1), 63–74.

Boyle, E. (2007). A process model of brand cocreation: Brand management and research implications. *Journal of Product & Brand Management,* 16(2), 122–131.

Breidbach, C. F., Brodie, R. J., and Hollebeek, L. D. (2014). Beyond virtuality: From engagement platforms to engagement ecosystems. *Managing Service Quality: An International Journal,* 24(6), 592–611.

Brodie, R. J. (2009). From goods to service branding. *Marketing Theory,* 9(1), 107–111.

Brodie, R. J., and De Chernatony, L. (2009). Towards new conceptualizations of branding: Theories of the middle range. *Marketing Theory,* 9(1), 95–100.

Brodie, R. J., Glynn, M. S., and Little, V. (2006). The service brand and the service-dominant logic: Missing fundamental premise or the need for stronger theory? *Marketing Theory,* 6(3), 363–379.

Brodie, R. J., Glynn, M. S., and Van Durme, J. (2002). Towards a theory of marketplace equity. *Marketing Theory,* 2(1), 5–28.

Brodie, R. J., Hollebeek, L. D., Jurić, B., and Ilić, A. (2011). Customer engagement. *Journal of Service Research,* 14(3), 252–271.

Brodie, R. J., Ilic, A., Juric, B., and Hollebeek, L. D. (2011). Consumer engagement in a virtual brand community: An exploratory analysis. *Journal of Business Research.*

Brodie, R. J., Ilic, A., Juric, B., and Hollebeek, L. D. (2013). Consumer engagement in a virtual brand community: An exploratory analysis. *Journal of Business Research, 66*(1), 105–114.

Calder, B. J., Isaac, M. S., and Malthouse, E. C. (2013). *Taking the Customer's Point of View: Engagement or Satisfaction?* Marketing Science Institute.

Calder, B. J., and Malthouse, E. C. (2008). Media engagement and advertising effectiveness. In B. J. Calder (Ed.), *Kellogg on Advertising and Media* (1–36). Hoboken, NJ: Wiley.

Coupland, J. C. (2005). Invisible brands: An ethnography of households and the brands in their kitchen pantries. *Journal of Consumer Research, 32*(1), 106–118.

Czepiel, J. A. (1990). Service encounters and service relationships: Implications for research. *Journal of Business Research, 20*(1), 13–21.

El-Amir, A., and Burt, S. (2010). A critical account of the process of branding: Towards a synthesis. *Marketing Review, 10*(1), 68–86.

Farquhar, P. H. (1989). Managing brand equity. *Marketing Research, 1*(3), 24–33.

Fournier, S. (1998). Consumers and their brands: Developing relationship theory in consumer research. *Journal of Consumer Research, 24*(4), 343–353.

Fournier, S., and Avery, J. (2011). The uninvited brand. *Business Horizons, 54*(3), 193–207.

Frow, P., Payne, A., and Storbacka, K. (2011). *Co-creation: A typology and conceptual framework.* Paper presented at the ANZMAC, Perth, Australia.

Gambetti, R. C., and Graffigna, G. (2010). The concept of engagement. *International Journal of Market Research, 52*(6), 801–826.

Gensler, S., Völckner, F., Liu-Thompkins, Y., and Wiertz, C. (2013). Managing brands in the social media environment. *Journal of Interactive Marketing, 27*(4), 242–256.

Godes, D., Mayzlin, D., Chen, Y., Das, S., Dellarocas, C., Pfeiffer, B., . . . Verlegh, P. (2005). The firm's management of social interactions. *Marketing Letters, 16*(3/4), 415–428.

Golant, B. D. (2012). Bringing the corporate brand to life: The brand manager as practical author. *Journal of Brand Management, 20*(2), 115–127.

Gyrd-Jones, R. I., and Kornum, N. (2013). Managing the co-created brand: Value and cultural complementarity in online and offline multi-stakeholder ecosystems. *Journal of Business Research, 66*(9), 1484–1493.

Håkansson, H., and Snehota, I. (1989). No business is an island: The network concept of business strategy. *Scandinavian Journal of Management, 5*(3), 187–200.

Hanna, R., Rohm, A., and Crittenden, V. L. (2011). We're all connected: The power of the social media ecosystem. *Business Horizons, 54*(3), 265–273.

Hennig-Thurau, T., Gwinner, K. P., Walsh, G., and Gremler, D. D. (2004). Electronic word-of-mouth via consumer-opinion platforms: What motivates consumers to articulate themselves on the Internet? *Journal of Interactive Marketing, 18*(1), 38–52.

Higgins, E. T., and Scholer, A. A. (2009). Engaging the consumer: The science and art of the value creation process. *Journal of Consumer Psychology, 19*(2), 100–114.

Hollebeek, L. D. (2011a). Demystifying customer brand engagement: Exploring the loyalty nexus. *Journal of Marketing Management, 27*(7–8), 785–807.

Hollebeek, L. D. (2011b). Exploring customer brand engagement: Definition and themes. *Journal of Strategic Marketing, 19*(7), 555–573.

Hunt, S.D., and Morgan, R.M. (1995). The comparative advantage theory of competition. *The Journal of Marketing, 59*(2), 1–15.

Iglesias, O., Ind, N., and Alfaro, M. (2013). The organic view of the brand: A brand value co-creation model. *Journal of Brand Management, 20*(8), 670–688.

Jaakkola, E., and Alexander, M. (2014). The role of customer engagement behavior in value co-creation: A service system perspective. *Journal of Service Research, 17*(3), 247–261.

Jones, R. (2005). Finding sources of brand value: Developing a stakeholder model of brand equity. *Journal of Brand Management, 13*(1), 10–32.

Kapferer, J.N. (2008). *The New Strategic Brand Management: Creating and Sustaining Brand Equity Long Term* (4th ed.). London, UK: Kogan Page.

Keller, K.L. (2003). Brand synthesis: The multidimensionality of brand knowledge. *Journal of Consumer Research, 29*(4), 595–600.

Kumar, V., Aksoy, L., Donkers, B., Venkatesan, R., Wiesel, T., and Tillmanns, S. (2010). Undervalued or overvalued customers: Capturing total customer engagement value. *Journal of Service Research, 13*(3), 297–310.

Lassila, O., and Hendler, J. (2007). Embracing "Web 3.0". *IEEE Internet Computing, 11*, 90–93. Retrieved from http://www.computer.org/portal/web/csdl/doi/10.1109/mic.2007.52.

Leone, R.P., Rao, V.R., Keller, K.L., Luo, A. M., McAlister, L., and Srivastava, R. (2006). Linking brand equity to customer equity. *Journal of Service Research, 9*(2), 125–138.

Levine, R., Locke, C., Searls, D., and Weinberger, D. (2000). *The Cluetrain Manifesto: The End of Business as Usual.* Cambridge, MA: Perseus Books.

McEwen, W.J. (2004). Why satisfaction isn't satisfying. *Gallup Management Journal Online.*

Merz, M., He, Y., and Vargo, S.L. (2009). The evolving brand logic: A service-dominant logic perspective. *Journal of the Academy of Marketing Science, 37*(3), 328–344.

Mitchell, A.A. (2012). The brand engagement myth. *Marketing,* 32–34. Retrieved from http://search.ebscohost.com/login.aspx?direct=true&db=bth&AN=71170443&site=ehost-live&scope=site.

Mollen, A., and Wilson, H. (2010). Engagement, telepresence and interactivity in online consumer experience: Reconciling scholastic and managerial perspectives. *Journal of Business Research, 63*(9–10), 919–925.

Mosadegh, M.J., and Behboudi, M. (2011). Using social network paradigm for developing a conceptual framework in CRM. *Australian Journal of Business and Management Research, 1*(4), 63.

Muñiz, A. M., and O'Guinn, T.C. (2001). Brand community. *Journal of Consumer Research, 27*(4), 412–432.

Muñiz, A. M., and Schau, H.J. (2011). How to inspire value-laden collaborative consumer-generated content. *Business Horizons, 54*(3), 209–217.

Olkkonen, R., Tikkanen, H., and Alajoutsijarvi, K. (2000). The role of communication in business relationships and networks. *Management Decision, 38*(6), 403–409.

Payne, A., Storbacka, K., and Frow, P. (2008). Managing the co-creation of value. *Journal of the Academy of Marketing Science, 36*(1), 83–96.

Payne, A., Storbacka, K., Frow, P., and Knox, S. (2009). Co-creating brands: Diagnosing and designing the relationship experience. *Journal of Business Research, 62*(3), 379–389.

Prahalad, C. K., and Ramaswamy, V. (2004). Co-creation experiences: The next practice in value creation. *Journal of Interactive Marketing, 18*(3), 5–14.

Ramaswamy, V. (2011). It's about human experiences . . . and beyond, to co-creation. *Industrial Marketing Management, 40*, 195–196.

Tripathi, M. N. (2009). Customer engagement – Key to successful brand building. *Vilakshan: The XIMB Journal of Management, 6*(1), 131–140.

Van Doorn, J. L. (2011). Comment: Customer engagement. *Journal of Service Research, 14*(3), 280–282.

Van Doorn, J. L., Lemon, K. N., Mittal, V., Nass, S., Pick, D., Pirner, P., and Verhoef, P. C. (2010). Customer engagement behavior: Theoretical foundations and research directions. *Journal of Service Research, 13*(3), 253–266.

Varey, R. J. (2008). Marketing as an interaction system. *Australasian Marketing Journal 16*(1), 79–94.

Vargo, S. L., and Lusch, R. F. (2004). Evolving to a new dominant logic for marketing. *Journal of Marketing, 68*(1), 1–17.

Wirtz, J., den Ambtman, A., Bloemer, J., Horváth, C., Ramaseshan, B., van de Klundert, J., . . . Kandampully, J. (2013). Managing brands and customer engagement in online brand communities. *Journal of Service Management, 24*(3), 223–244.

Woodcock, N., Green, A., and Starkey, M. (2011). Social CRM as a business strategy. *Database Marketing & Customer Strategy Management, 18*(1), 50–64.

Yin, R. K. (2003). *Case Study Research: Design and Methods* (3rd ed.). USA: Sage Publications Inc.

13 Extending the tourism experience

The role of customer engagement

Kevin Kam Fung So, Ceridwyn King and Beverley Sparks

Introduction

Tourism products and services are experiential in nature. The fundamental offering provided by the tourism industry is a travel experience, which results from a combination of a wide variety of services that a tourist consumes while travelling. These services range from hotel accommodation to airline services, from a tour at Yellowstone National Park to a delightful theme park experience at the Magic Kingdom in Disney World. The essence of tourism is the development and delivery of travel experiences to individuals or groups who wish to see, understand, and experience the nature of different destinations and the way people live, work, and enjoy life in those destinations (Ritchie et al., 2011). Tourism products generally consist of multiple service touch points which customers evaluate prior, during, and after their tourism experience (Stickdorn and Zehrer, 2009).

Given this ongoing evaluative process, tourism organisations, such as a hotel or airline, even destinations such as Australia, New Zealand, and New York, have extensively implemented customer engagement (CE) strategies, in one form or another, to engage with their customers at various stages of consumption: pre, during, and post. During each stage, certain CE strategies become more prevalent than others. For example, at the pre-consumption stage, CE may be primarily driven by a need to obtain or seek consumption-related information. Asking questions or commenting in an online forum help the individual form a consumption vision necessary to determine product choice. In contrast, during the consumption stage, CE may be motivated by the desire to share the experience with others, by checking in or liking a post on Facebook, etc. At the post-consumption stage customers may still be motivated to share their experiences personally with their friends and relatives, but also may desire maintaining a relationship with the tourism organisation, through following the brand via various social media outlets to receive updates and newsletters. In addition some, but not a large percentage of customers, may also write comments and reviews publicly on third-party websites.

The prevalence of CE activities in the tourism industry is suggested to be the result of tourism products' heavy emphasis on the experience. While tourism can be considered a part of the service sector, and therefore subject to the well-established inherent service characteristics, the experiential nature of a tourism product suggests that tourism consumers may be more likely to participate in CE activities in contrast to other service products. In the context of tourism, or other experiential purchases, customers often rely on CE activities to make or reinforce purchase decisions, as evident in the previous discussion. As such, from a tourism perspective, CE is an extremely relevant and integral element of a customer's experience, thus emphasising its significance for management of tourism organisations. For tourism organisations, CE extends the customer experience beyond the actual service encounter, providing multiple opportunities, if managed well, for organisations to have a positive and meaningful influence with respect to consumer attitudes and behaviour. It is from this perspective that the insight of this chapter is illuminated. While CE can be considered a volitional act on behalf of individuals, the experiential nature of tourism motivates consumers to participate in such activities, at a minimum to make an informed decision thereby reducing perceived risk, but ideally, from an organisational perspective, to participate in conspicuous consumption. As such, the concept of CE has the potential to extend the tourism experience beyond the service encounter through interacting and engaging with the customers beyond purchase, particularly in the pre- and post-consumption period. Tourism brands and organisations, therefore, have a unique opportunity, and to some extent obligation, to effectively manage these interactions to enhance positive customer experiences. It is from this perspective that we propose CE as being a necessary requirement for experiential brands to manage, and rather than being seen as an additional benefit of a satisfied customer, being seen as integral for a satisfied customer to be realised.

The remainder of this chapter is arranged as follows. The ensuing section presents an introduction to the emergence of the CE concept, followed by a review of the conceptual roots and definitions of CE. The subsequent section briefly reviews the characteristics of tourism services. Next, the chapter provides discussion of three dominant CE activities in tourism including online reviews, blogging and social networking. While CE is a phenomenon that could occur both in an online as well as offline environment, this chapter focuses predominantly on engagement behaviour through an online or social media platform. From a practitioner perspective, these customer engagement behaviours (CEBs) are the ones that tourism organisations are most focused on and active in. Interestingly, however, these CEBs emphasise engagement between customers or prospective customers rather than engagement directly with the organisations. As such, the brand/organisation is more of a bystander that has limited control over the content and messages of these communications. Nonetheless, these CEBs are a key determinant in a tourism organisation's success given the dominant role they play in shaping new and existing customers' perceptions of the brand and, by default, extending the tourism experience beyond the service encounter. The chapter concludes with a summary, highlighting the importance of understanding CE not only from a behavioural perspective, but for a tourism organisation, the importance of influencing the psychological perspective which subsequently informs CEBs.

The rise of customer engagement

Entering a new technology era that is characterised by a tremendous increase in the popularity of social media and the Internet, the emerging concept of CE has dominated many recent discussions among marketing academics (Brodie et al., 2011, Verhoef et al., 2010, van Doorn et al., 2010) and practitioners (Econsultancy, 2011). A significant level of interest in the CE concept was stimulated by the 3rd Thought Leadership Conference on Customer Management held in Montabaur, Germany in 2009. More than 40 leading scholars in the field of marketing intensively discussed key issues in customer engagement. This conference resulted in a special issue of articles that constitute seminal discussions of this relatively new, yet highly relevant, marketing concept published in the *Journal of Service Research*. The articles provided critical new insights for managers wrestling with these issues (Verhoef et al., 2010) as well as sparked a significant line of continued academic investigations in the marketing literature. A Google Scholar search with the term 'customer engagement' generated approximately 1,300 results prior to 2008. Following the illumination of the concept, academic attention started to increase with 448 results identified in 2009, 619 results in 2010, 949 results in 2011, 1,170 results in 2012, 1,550 results in 2013 and, most recently, 1,780 articles were published in 2014 that related to CE. This exponential growth pattern suggests that academic interest in CE is likely to further intensify in the years to come.

The importance of CE is increasingly recognised from a practitioner perspective as well. For example, Econsultancy (2011) surveyed more than 1,000 companies and agencies across various industries worldwide and found that 50 per cent of the companies regard CE as 'essential' for their organisations, with 33 per cent considering CE as 'important'. The Gallup Group (2010) suggests,

> *World class organizations unleash their potential for growth by optimizing their customer relationship. Organizations that have optimized engagement have outperformed their competitors by 26% in gross margin and 85% in sales growth. Their customers buy more, spend more, return more often, and stay longer.*

(p. 1)

While not using the exact same term of CE, marketing scholars have long promoted the relevance of engagement, suggesting that the strongest affirmation of brand loyalty occurs when customers are willing to invest time or other resources in the brand beyond those expended during purchase or consumption of the brand (Keller, 2003). Typical examples of such consumer activities include joining a club centred on the brand, visiting brand-related websites and participating in chat rooms, which are forms of CE behaviours (Verhoef et al., 2010,

Marketing Science Institute, 2010). More recently, the Marketing Science Institute (2014) has identified CE as one of the key priority areas for 2014–2016. Academic research has highlighted the benefits of deliberately enhancing CE activities. For example, Sashi (2012) argues that CE expands the role of consumers by including them in the value-adding process as co-creators of value, which enhances need satisfaction of both customers as well as the firm. Wirtz et al. (2013) suggest that when delighted or loyal customers share their brand enthusiasm or delight in interactions with others via social networks they become brand advocates, laying a strong foundation for an enduring relationship with the brand. Empirical research indicates that CE in social media enhances self-brand connection and brand usage intent (Hollebeek et al., 2014). CE has also been found to enhance consumers' evaluation of a service brand and trust level attributed to the brand, as well as their subsequent brand loyalty (So et al., 2014b). Furthermore, according to the Marketing Science Institute (2010), non-transactional activities are increasingly seen as a route for creating, building and enhancing customer-firm relationships, described as the 'expanded domain of relationship marketing' (Vivek, Beatty and Morgan, 2012, p. 129).

Definition of customer engagment

The term engagement, in a business-related context, originally referred to employee engagement (EE), which is described as 'the simultaneous employment and expression of a person's preferred self in task behaviors that promote connections to work and to others, personal presence, and active, full role performances' (Kahn, 1990). EE has been conceptualised as a motivational construct comprising attention and absorption (Rothbard, 2001), and may include an identification dimension (Bakker et al., 2008, Demerouti and Bakker, 2008). EE is 'a positive, fulfilling, work-related state of mind that is characterized by vigor, dedication and absorption' (Schaufeli et al., 2002), suggesting that EE is a persistent and pervasive affective-cognitive state (Schaufeli and Bakker, 2004). Consistent in these definitions is the focus on psychological aspects.

In contrast, marketing scholars have conceptualised CE to include a strong behavioural focus. For example, the Marketing Science Institute (2010) identifies CE as a priority topic and describes the concept as 'customers' behavioral manifestation toward a brand or firm *beyond purchase*, which results from motivational drivers including: word-of-mouth activity, recommendations, customer-to-customer interactions, blogging, writing reviews, and other similar activities'. The academic (e.g., van Doorn et al., 2010, Bijmolt et al., 2010, Verhoef et al., 2010) and practitioner (e.g., Shevlin, 2007) literature also demonstrate a behavioural orientation.

However, several scholars argued that the conceptualisation of CE needs to go beyond a pure action focus to incorporate both psychological and behavioural dimensions (e.g., Patterson et al., 2006, Hollebeek, 2011a, Hollebeek, 2009, Brodie et al., 2011). In particular, support for broadening the conceptual domain of CE was grounded in the thinking that pure behavioural participation in CE activities does not necessarily mean true CE with a brand. A customer may engage in a brand discussion forum to acquire product information or reduce perceived risks (Brodie et al., 2013), rather than to be connected to the brand. As the truly engaged customer must have an enduring psychological connection with the brand in addition to behavioural participation (So et al., 2014a, Hollebeek, 2011b), a multidimensional approach captures the full conceptual domain of the CE concept.

Consistent with this approach, several multidimensional conceptualisations of CE have been proposed (e.g., Brodie et al., 2013, Hollebeek, 2011b, van Doorn et al., 2010, So et al., 2014a), which provide a significant conceptual foundation for CE. Based on an extensive review of the use of the term 'engagement' in the social science, management, and marketing literature, Brodie et al. (2011) define CE as a *psychological state* that occurs by virtue of *interactive, cocreative* customer experiences with *a focal object* such as a brand in focal service relationships. They further describe that CE happens under a specific set of context dependent conditions generating differing CE levels, and suggest that CE is a *multidimensional concept* subject to a context- and/or stakeholder-specific expression of relevant cognitive, emotional and/or behavioural dimensions.

This definition provided an important contribution to the advancement of the CE concept, particularly by describing the nature of CE as well as its boundaries from a definitional point of view. In advocating that CE may require consideration be given to the psychological aspects of engagement, as well as behavioural participation, this conceptual definition also underlines that CE is context specific, suggesting understanding of CE requires consideration being given to the context of the research settings. This is because CE will vary in its levels of intensity and complexity, as well as potentially at different points in time, based on the interactive experiences between a focal CE subject (customer) and object (brand) under a specific set of situational conditions (e.g. CE in online versus offline environment) (see Brodie et al., 2011 for a detailed discussion). This consideration of context is also highlighted by Hollebeek (2011a) who suggests that CE is a context-dependent state of mind characterised by specific levels of cognitive, emotional, and behavioural activity in brand interactions.

While highlighting the propensity of CE to vary dependent upon the individual and the object, the original multidimensional conceptualisations of CE stopped short of articulating the attributes upon which this variability would be evident. Therefore, in seeking to build on the work of Brodie et al. (2011) and others, So et al. (2014a) advanced a more prescriptive definition of the concept, thereby affording a more nuanced, and therefore applied construct that could be easily operationalised. Defining CE as a customers' personal connection to a brand as manifested in cognitive, affective and behavioural responses outside of the purchase, So et al. (2014a) conceptualised CE as a higher-order construct comprising five first-order factors, including *enthusiasm* (or *vigor*), *attention*, *absorption*, *interaction*, and *identification*.

Enthusiasm represents an individual's strong level of excitement and interest regarding the focus of engagement, such as a brand. In a work context, engagement encompasses the employee's sense of significance, enthusiasm, inspiration, and pride (e.g., Schaufeli and Bakker, 2004, Salanova et al., 2005). An engaged employee feels enthusiastic and passionate about his/her work and role in the organisation, consistent with the CE dimensions of vigor (Patterson et al., 2006) and activation (Hollebeek, 2009). *Attention* describes a consumer's attentiveness to the brand. Within the EE literature, attention is the duration of focus on, and mental preoccupation with, work (Rothbard, 2001). Regulatory engagement theory also defines engagement as sustained attention, where behaviourally turning attention away from something lowers the level of engagement (Scholer and Higgins, 2009). *Absorption* is a pleasant state in which the customer is fully concentrated, happy, and deeply engrossed while playing the role as a consumer of the brand. In a work context, absorption partially defines engagement (Hakanen et al., 2008), which is characterised by being so fully concentrated and engrossed that time passes quickly and one has difficulty detaching from his/her role. In the marketing domain, scholars have also argued that strong engagement extends beyond concentrating on something to being absorbed or engrossed with it (Scholer and Higgins, 2009). *Interaction* refers to a customer's online and offline participation with the brand, or other customers, outside of the purchase transaction. Marketing researchers promote CE as manifesting in behaviours such as customer interactions (Bijmolt et al., 2010, Marketing Science Institute, 2010, van Doorn et al., 2010). The relevance of customer interaction at the brand level is supported by the well-established notion of brand community, which represents a structured set of social relationships among admirers of a brand (Muniz and O'Guinn, 2001). *Identification* is an individual's perceived oneness with, or belongingness to, the brand. Work engagement is characterised by a strong identification with one's work (Bakker et al., 2008). Similarly, strong consumer-company relationships are based on consumers' identification with the companies that help them satisfy one or more important self-definitional needs (Bhattacharya and Sen, 2003).

The five underlying dimensions collectively reflect the psychological and behavioural aspects of CE. In describing the different dimensions of CE from both a psychological and behavioural standpoint, So et al.'s (2014a) conceptualisation affords insight with respect to not only how CE is realised, but also provides a diagnostic tool for determining areas of variability as well as drivers of CE within different contexts. While informative to all contexts that seek to examine CE, So et al.'s (2014a) work is particularly insightful for experiential brands given that it was originally developed within the tourism industry, where consumer attitudes and behaviour are influenced pre-, during, and post-encounter due to the experiential nature of the tourism product. For example, while the actual service encounter may have the most significant impact on a customer's evaluation of that particular transaction, experiences pre-encounter determine consumer choice and those post-encounter not only have the potential to solidify customer preference, but also have a ripple effect by impacting new consumer's pre-encounter experience via word of mouth (WOM) communications. It is for this reason that the conceptualisation of CE is considered to have extended our understanding of experiential organisations' relationships with their customers, beyond that of the core service encounter.

In a tourism context, where today's CE activities, particularly those that are generated via online mediums such as Tripadvisor and Yelp, are prevalent in management decision-making processes, the ability to appreciate the psychological mechanisms that drive CE behaviour is considered to be essential for being able to measure the effects of various initiatives that are instigated for the sole purpose of generating CE. To appreciate how CE is an integral element of experiential services, consideration, therefore, is given to its application in a tourism setting.

Tourism services: a case of experiential services

A tourism experience involves the provision and consumption of a collection of individual service components. Within the service marketing literature, in differentiating between goods and services, scholars have identified several unique features of services that distinguish them from goods, namely *intangibility, inseparability, heterogeneity,* and *perishability* (e.g., Zeithaml et al., 1985, Zeithaml et al., 2006). While the difference between services and goods has been increasingly challenged (e.g., Vargo and Lusch, 2004), these characteristics still present a number of difficulties to tourism marketers and potential tourists. For example, on the one hand, from a marketing perspective, the intangible nature of services creates difficulty for marketers to display, demonstrate or effectively communicate a service offering to customers (Grönroos, 1998), thus making the articulation of service attributes or benefits a challenge for service marketers (Mattila, 2000).

On the other hand, from a consumer perspective, the intangibility and heterogeneity features of services make pre-purchase evaluation of a service more difficult than that of a manufactured good, because manufactured goods are usually associated with a greater level of search qualities (Mittal and Baker, 2002). For example, tangible products, such as mobile phones and clothing, can be easily seen, touched, and tried on prior to the actual purchase (Zeithaml et al., 2006). In contrast, intangible services, such as hotel accommodations or holidays, have few physical elements of the service performance for consumers to easily inspect prior to the actual experience (Mittal and Baker, 2002). In addition, services are characterised by experience qualities (e.g., Zeithaml et al., 2006), and the quality of the purchase can only be evaluated after the service experience. For example, for a hotel stay the consumer can assess many aspects of service only after checking in, such as the quality of the facilities provided, the cleanliness of the rooms, and the friendliness of the staff. Therefore, despite the substantial changes in the marketing literature that occurred in the last two decades, the aforementioned challenges are still critically relevant, particularly for experiential products such as a tourism experience.

In addition to its service characteristics, tourism has long been described as an information-intense industry (Sheldon, 1997), making it critical to understand changes in technologies and consumer behaviour that impact the distribution and accessibility of travel-related information (Xiang and Gretzel, 2010). Technology has dramatically changed the landscape of many industries including tourism. In particular, the web, and what is known as Social Media or Web 2.0, have given consumers much more control, information, and power over the market process, posing tourism operators with important challenges (Constantinides et al., 2009). Conversely, Web 2.0 features such as interactivity and user-generated content advance the potential for brand-to-customer and customer-to-customer interactions, providing increased opportunities for tourism firms to engage with their customers outside of the service encounter through non-transactional customer activities such as writing reviews, joining a Facebook community, blogging, or similar activities collectively termed CE behaviour (CEB) (van Doorn et al., 2010, Verhoef et al., 2010).

The significance of these beyond-purchase interactions is highlighted by Verhoef et al. (2009) who posit that customer experience encompasses the *total* experience, including the search, purchase, consumption, and after-sale phases of the experience, thus extending customer experience beyond the service encounter. The significance of these 'outside of transaction' experiences is evident in the attention they get in both academia and industry. There has been a significant increase in the number of tourism and hospitality articles dedicated to research related to online consumer-oriented platforms in recent years and the overwhelming majority of tourism providers, large and small, have a presence in a variety of social media platforms. With this in mind, discussion turns to the emphasis of both tourism academic and practitioner interest with respect to CE, namely CEB. Specifically, three of the more dominant forms of CE activities in the tourism industry are reviewed, highlighting their integral role in shaping a consumer's tourism experiences.

Online reviews

One of the most common forms of CEB that are ubiquitous in tourism is customer participation in online travel reviews. An AC Nielsen (2012) study attests that the primary reason for the growth of this form of CEB is indicated by the fact that of the many forms of media, online reviews are the second most trusted form of communication after personal recommendations, with 70 per cent of global consumers surveyed indicating they trust this platform. Online consumer reviews, as a type of CEB highlighted by the Marketing Science Institute (2010), as well as a form of electronic WOM, are having an unprecedented impact on how consumers view tourism and hospitality products and services (Xiang and Gretzel, 2010). They are considered to be a powerful source of information affecting tourists' pre-purchase evaluation of a holiday experience (Browning et al., 2013, Hudson and Thal, 2013). The advent of the Internet has made it even easier for consumers to interact with other customers or even the business firms, by posting or accessing online reviews anonymously evaluating hotels and restaurants in any tourist destination (Buhalis and Law, 2008). These interactions allow potential customers to leverage the highly experiential aspects of people's knowledge and information, making aggregated individual experiences available to many others (Flanagin and Metzger, 2013). Information exchanged or obtained as a result of the interactions are often perceived by consumers as having a higher level of credibility and trustworthiness than traditional marketing communications (Akehurst, 2009), thus providing a quick way for potential customers to evaluate a holiday destination or a particular hotel before their actual visitation, and subsequently, a more influential way to shape consumer expectations of the experience than any form of communication channel that an organisation may have control over.

While common platforms for travellers to share their travel experiences include many online review websites such as Yahoo! Travel, Igougo, and Lonely Planet (Lee et al., 2011), one particular platform that is worthy of mentioning is TripAdvisor, an American travel website that provides reviews of travel-related content as well as interactive travel forums for travelers at difference stages of their consumption journey: pre- (reading), during (reading and/or writing) and post-consumption (writing). TripAdvisor is the world's largest travel site (comScore, 2014), enabling travelers to plan and book the perfect trip (Trip-Advisor, 2015). As one of the largest platforms for customer interactions, it offers trusted advice from travelers and a wide variety of travel choices and planning features with seamless links to booking tools that check hundreds of websites to find the best hotel prices. TripAdvisor branded sites make up the largest travel community in the world, reaching 315 million unique monthly visitors (Google Analytics, 2014), with more than 200 million reviews and opinions covering more than 4.5 million accommodations, restaurants, and attractions. The proliferation of third-party review sites, such as TripAdvisor, provides consumers with significantly expanded opportunities to generate publicly available commentaries on a hotel or destination. In addition to facilitating asynchronous customer connections, these third-party sites also facilitate customer-brand connections by allowing the organisations that customers provided feedback about to openly comment and respond to customer feedback.

As such, from an organisational perspective, the increasing usage of such a platform for customers to engage in WOM related to a particular tourism organisation or destination has allowed tourism operators to actively engage with their customers outside of the encounter. Responding to consumer comments or questions, whether positive or negative, result in a dialogue that is characteristic of CE benefits for both the consumer and the organisation. Therefore, while online reviews are based on user-generated content, which gives them a heightened level of credibility with respect to influencing consumers, the ability for interaction affords the tourism organisation an opportunity to indirectly shape consumer attitudes and behaviour (Sparks, So & Bradley, 2016), thereby expanding the customer's experience with a tourism brand.

The overwhelming significance of online reviews can be attributed to this one platform facilitating engagement in several ways. For example, consumers can create content, while others may seek information. As such, in the tourism domain, the impact of online reviews has attracted a number of studies examining the effects of online review as a form of CEB from both the consumer's and the firm's perspective. Specifically, previous studies have mainly focused on the increased use of review sites and the influence that online reviews have on firm performance indicators such as hotel room bookings (e.g., Ye et al., 2009) and restaurant popularity (e.g., Zhang et al., 2010), as well as consumer outcomes such as consideration of hotel (e.g., Vermeulen and Seegers, 2009), trust in the hotel and intention to book the hotel (e.g., Sparks and Browning, 2011), as well as their potential consumers' attributions of service quality and firms' ability to control service delivery (Browning et al., 2013). This line of research clearly demonstrates that CEBs in the form of online reviews is a significant and influential factor shaping consumer attitudes and behaviour, and has the potential to alter the consumer's evaluation of the service encounter, thereby highlighting the significance of CE for experiential brands.

Travel blogs

Another prominent platform that facilitates CEBs for experiential brands such as those in the tourism industry is blogging. The popularity of blogs has grown substantially over the past few years as advancements in communication technology have become more accessible, allowing consumers to engage more easily in social commentaries. Blogging is one of the most increasingly popular forms of social media, where people are engaged through being part of a conversation. The conversation begins with one person publishing an article, in which readers give their comments (Stickdorn and Zehrer, 2009). Blogs in the context of tourism, often described as travel blogs, are defined by Pühringer and Taylor (2008) as individual entries which relate to planned, current or past travel. Travel blogs have increased in use and popularity over the last few years (Pan et al., 2007). Travel blog sites such as TravelBlog.org and TravelPost.com continue to grow in popularity, resulting in a growing recognition that they facilitate powerful discussions that could affect consumer decisions and evaluations of destinations and even reshape the communication networks previously dominated by traditional information suppliers (Xiang and Gretzel, 2010, Bosangit et al., 2012).

The most obvious form of blogs in tourism is those written by travelers who publish their travel stories and recommendations online. The interaction occurs when blog contributors share detailed narratives of their recent experience with specific tourism products leading to recommendations, while users acquire information from them to base future purchase decisions on (Zehrer et al., 2011). Unlike online reviews, which allow consumers to provide both qualitative and quantitative reviews of tourism products such as hotels, attractions, and other travel experiences, travel blogs are online diaries and stories meant to provide information and engage the reader in the travel experience (Banyai and Glover, 2012). They are made up of one or more individual entries strung together by a common theme (for example, a trip itinerary or the purchase of a round-the-world ticket). They are often written by tourists to report back to friends, families or other potential tourists about their activities and experiences during trips. BlogPulse and Technocrati reported that the number of monitored blogs had increased significantly from 3 million in 2004 to 164 million in 2011 (Trenor, 2011), and the 2009 'State of Blogosphere' reported that 20 per cent of the blogs surveyed were tagged as travel blogs (Banyai and Glover, 2012). This global phenomenon underlies the critical role of travel blogs as a CE activity for travelers. TravelBlog.org, one such travel blog website, hosts more than 700,000 blog entries with more than 200,000 members, increasing by about 100 new members that join daily (TravelBlog, 2015). It provides an important platform for customer interactions by offering worldwide access to people looking to share information with others about their travel experiences (Banyai and Glover, 2012).

One of the major reasons for customers engaging in this form of CEB, particularly at the pre-purchase stage, is the perceived higher credibility of consumer opinions compared to traditional tourist information sources (Zehrer et al., 2011, Schmallegger and Carson, 2008). This is because they view blogs as authoritative WOM communication. From a tourist's perspective, blogs, therefore, are a form of digitized WOM communication enabling consumers to gain insight from other consumers regarding tourism products (Zehrer et al., 2011). In contrast, at the post-purchase consumption stage, millions of individuals have joined travel blog web sites to share their travel experiences online thereby reinforcing their consumption memories. Through sharing their travel stories online, tourists communicate with an audience and construct their identities that often include a brand and/or destination identity, thus strengthening the psychological bond between the customer and the organisation/destination. Scholars have suggested that blogging has become an aspect of the tourist production and consumption process (Bosangit et al., 2009a), forming part of the tourist experience (Bosangit et al., 2012). As such, blogging as a dominant platform that facilitates CEBs, consistent with online reviews, is thought to extend the tourism experience beyond the service transaction. Bosangit et al. (2012) suggest that an examination of travel blogs and considering how tourists reconstruct their travel experiences and the actions behind the blogging can provide a deeper understanding of the post-consumption behaviour of tourists.

From an organisational point of view, tourism firms or destinations can also leverage CE in blogging. As travel blogs express the tourists' experience at a specific destination, marketers need to view blogs as a new technological phenomenon with implications for marketing and promotion of a destination (Pan et al., 2007). The constraint-free feedback offered by tourists on their travel blogs provide destination marketing organisations (DMOs) with information about tourists' perceptions and impressions of the destination, thus shedding light on how tourists interpret the destination (Banyai and Glover, 2012). As such, destination marketers need to pay particular attention to this type of CEB given the wealth of insight about particularities of a destination including attractions, facilities, infrastructure, and, at a more abstract value, the overall atmosphere of the destination that is provided (Tussyadiah and Fesenmaier, 2008). Furthermore, travel blog content can be used for improving and monitoring destination images and products by responding to tourists' demands and expectations, and also adjusting competitive strategies (Litvin et al., 2008, Pan et al., 2007, Carson, 2008). This is in addition to the deeper understanding of bloggers' consumption and evaluation of tourism products that is also revealed (Tussyadiah and Fesenmaier, 2008, Bosangit et al., 2009b). The experience of travel blogging, whether that be as an author or reader/responder, is significant CEB that affords access to vital marketing information that is both relevant to consumers and the organisation, thereby extending the tourism experience.

Social networks

Since their introduction, social network sites (SNSs) such as MySpace, Facebook, Cyworld, and Bebo have attracted millions of users, many of whom have fully integrated these sites into their daily lives. Social network sites (SNSs) are increasingly attracting the attention of academic and industry researchers intrigued by their affordances and reach (Boyd and Ellison, 2007). Of particular significance is Facebook, which emerged as a leading social networking site with 350 million active users in July 2009 (Treadaway and Smith, 2010) and grew to 500 million active users in 2010, which soon doubled to 1 billion in 2012 (Facebook, 2015). Through enhancing personal connections through the site's news feed, chat and messaging features, Facebook has become the website Internet users spend the most time on.

While the emergence of social network sites such as Facebook has fundamentally changed the marketing landscape in recent years, the CEBs exhibited in these platforms is of special relevance to tourism. According to the 2013 Portrait of American TravelersSM study, Facebook users are passionate about sharing their travel experiences. In 2012, Facebook reviewed the top stories people shared to their Facebook timelines and discovered that the top story being shared by users was travel experiences with 42 per cent of stories shared to users Facebook timelines related to travel experiences, more than double that of the next category. In the evolving digital marketing landscape, it is clear that consumers want to share their travels with others (MMGY Global, 2014).

As the tourism experience is the dominant type of experience shared on Facebook, this platform for CEBs offers many benefits to tourism brands. Facebook is a gathering place of a large pool of consumers and this social networking site is also a mine of consumer information and a means of spreading information to build market presence (Hsu, 2012). For example, in 2011, VisitBritain invited consumers to register for a Unite the Invite app. Individuals were invited to upload a picture of themselves and they were then sent the photo of another random registrant, which they were asked to upload to their Facebook wall, encouraging Facebook friends to share so that they could locate their match on the social network. The fastest pair to 'unite their invite' each won a trip for two to the United Kingdom. The campaign's goal was to attract people to visit the Love UK Facebook page. Twelve thousand people entered Unite the Invite, and the Love UK Facebook page shortly gained 25,000 fans during the campaign (Hudson and Thal, 2013, Birkner, 2011).

The platform has also evolved to facilitate business connections with consumers. Social network sites such as Facebook serve as an important tool that supports both eMarketing and viral marketing, enabling the process of building connections to a network or social circle (Zarella, 2010). Through Facebook Pages, Facebook Advertising, and Facebook Applications, brands are able to build long-term online dialogs and relationships with consumers while telling their unique story to the world. Facebook offers travel brands, such as Hilton, Cathay Pacific, Shangri-La, and even destinations including London, New York, and Australia, the ability to identify prospective travelers, communicate directly with users, engage with advocates and create branded customer experiences through advertisements and custom-developed Facebook applications, making it the most powerful social media channel for travel marketers (MMGY Global, 2014). For example, Tourism Australia's official Facebook page has attracted more than 6 million followers. Every day the organisation posts images of beautiful parts of Australia, which attract thousands of likes and shares among its followers, creating tremendous marketing exposure. Furthermore, Facebook allows people to gather and form relationships within a virtual space and build personal pages and then connect with friends to communicate and share content (Treadaway and Smith, 2010).

The effects of CE via a social network site on customer's perceptions or evaluation of a tourism service are supported in the literature. For example, Maurer and Wiegmann (2011) suggest that Facebook provides the ideal platform for direct communication between organisations and customers. In the context of special events, Paris et al. (2010) found that users' trust and expected relationship through Facebook had a significant effect on users' acceptance of Facebook and their intended offline behaviour to attend the event. The results of their study suggest that businesses should actively seek to build trust with their consumers using their Facebook pages, and that their efforts should be made to focus on making their Facebook Events straightforward and entertaining to be most effective. The findings also suggest that users' acceptance of Facebook Events can influence their actual intentions to attend an event. Similarly, Leung et al. (2013) found that hotel customers' social media experiences in Facebook and Twitter influence their attitudes-toward-social-media-site, which in turn influences their attitudes-toward-hotel-brand, and that hotel customers' attitudes-toward-hotel-brand affects their hotel booking intentions and, in turn, intentions to spread electronic WOM.

Conclusion

This chapter has argued that CE plays a significant role in expanding the tourism experience of customers. The chapter discussed three dominant forms of CEB in the tourism industry including online reviews, travel blogs, and social networks. This is important, as there has been a sustained growth in these forms of communication with customers and as such, an increase in the need for business and research attention into ways to further engage customers using these channels is vital. While the extant literature overwhelmingly supports the effects of these CEBs on how consumers think and feel about a brand, it is worth noting that they are behavioural manifestations of CE. Although these CEBs can occur pre-, during, and post-consumption, and therefore be considered prolific, it is important to note that they only represent the outcome of CE. While practitioners' interests in fostering these CEBs are heightened, it should be noted that customers that engage in these actions may not necessarily be truly connected or engaged with the brand.

Furthermore, as evident in the previous discussion, CEBs in a tourism context are predominantly focused on customer-to-customer interactions, given its experiential nature, in contrast to customer-to-brand. So what, therefore, is the role of the tourism organisation in facilitating CE? For CEBs to be evident, the psychological aspects of CE, such as identification, Enthusiasm, and attention, need to be considered. Through the provision of a service experience that enables consumers to create a psychological connection to the organisation, management can be assured that the exhibition of CEBs pre-, during, and post-consumption are not just driven by transactional motives (e.g., searching for information), but rather a deeper and more enduring desire to want to maintain a relationship with the brand.

While the emphasis of this chapter was on illuminating how CE has extended the tourism experience beyond the core service encounter, it is important to note that to only focus on the outcome (i.e. CEBs), which is not within the control of the organisation, in contrast to focusing on developing the psychological connection, of which the organisations has more direct influence, will be to the long-term detriment of any tourism organisation wanting to engage in a meaningful way with customers. CE is more than behavioural participation. As identified in previous literature, there are many facets of CE that lead to behavioural engagement (So et al., 2014a, Vivek et al., 2012). Advancing the concept of CE necessitates not only an understanding of mere participation by customers, but also what drives that behaviour, aspects of which organisations must be aware of when developing a meaningful CE strategy.

References

Ac Nielsen. 2012. *Nielsen: Global consumers' trust in 'earned' advertising grows in importance* [Online]. Available: http://www.nielsen.com/us/en/press-room/ 2012/nielsen-global-consumers-trust-in-earned-advertising-grows.html [Accessed 23 Oct 2013].

Akehurst, G. 2009. User generated content: The use of blogs for tourism organisations and tourism consumers. *Service Business,* 3, 51–61.

Bakker, A. B., Schaufeli, W. B., Leiter, M. P. and Taris, T. W. 2008. Work engagement: An emerging concept in occupational health psychology. *Work & Stress,* 22, 187–200.

250   *Kevin Kam Fung So et al.*

Banyai, M. and Glover, T. D. 2012. Evaluating research methods on travel blogs. *Journal of Travel Research*, 51, 267–277.

Bhattacharya, C. B. and Sen, S. 2003. Consumer-company identification: A framework for understanding consumers' relationships with companies. *Journal of Marketing*, 67, 76–88.

Bijmolt, T.H.A., Leeflang, P.S.H., Block, F., Eisenbeiss, M., Hardie, B. G. S., Lemmens, A. and Saffert, P. 2010. Analytics for customer engagement. *Journal of Service Research*, 13, 341–356.

Birkner, C. 2011. Marketing a country: The British are coming. *Marketing News*, May 24.

Bosangit, C., Dulnuan, J. and Mena, M. 2012. Using travel blogs to examine the postconsumption behavior of tourists. *Journal of Vacation Marketing*, 18, 207–219.

Bosangit, C., Mccabe, S. and Hibbert, S. 2009a. Understanding consumption experiences: A discourse analysis of travel blogs. *ENTER 2009*. Amsterdam, Netherlands.

Bosangit, C., Mccabe, S. and Hibbert, S. 2009b. What is told in travel blogs? Exploring travel blogs for consumer narrative analysis. *In:* Hoepken, W., Gretzel, U. and Law, R. (eds.) *Information and communication technologies in tourism.* Springer: Vienna.

Boyd, D.M. and Ellison, N.B. 2007. Social network sites: Definition, history, and scholarship. *Journal of Computer-Mediated Communication*, 13, 210–230.

Brodie, R. J., Hollebeek, L. D., Juric, B. and Ilic, A. 2011. Customer engagement: Conceptual domain, fundamental propositions, and implications for research. *Journal of Service Research*, 14, 252–271.

Brodie, R. J., Ilic, A., Juric, B. and Hollebeek, L. 2013. Consumer engagement in a virtual brand community: An exploratory analysis. *Journal of Business Research*, 66, 105–114.

Browning, V., So, K.K.F. and Sparks, B. A. 2013. The influence of online reviews on consumers' attributions of service quality and control for service standards in hotels. *Journal of Travel & Tourism Marketing*, 30, 23–40.

Buhalis, D. and Law, R. 2008. Progress in information technology and tourism management: 20 years on and 10 years after the Internet – The state of eTourism research. *Tourism Management*, 29, 609–623.

Carson, D. 2008. Theblogosphere'as a market research tool for tourism destinations: A case study of Australia's Northern Territory. *Journal of Vacation Marketing*, 14, 111–119.

Comscore. 2014. *Media metrix for TripAdvisor sites, worldwide* [Online]. [Accessed March 1 2015].

Constantinides, E., Romero, C. and Boria, M. G. 2009. Social media: A new frontier for retailers? *In:* Swoboda, B., Morschett, D., Rudolph, T., Schnedlitz, P. and Schramm-Klein, H. (eds.) *European Retail Research.* Gabler Verlag.

Demerouti, E. and Bakker, A. B. 2008. The Oldenburg Burnout Inventory: A good alternative to measure burnout and engagement. *In:* Halbesleben, J.R.B. (ed.) *Handbook of stress and burnout in health care.* Hauppauge, NY: Nova Science.

Econsultancy. 2011. *Customer engagement report* [Online]. Available: http://econsultancy.com/us/reports/customer-engagement-report [Accessed 15 October 2014].

Facebook. 2015. *About Facebook: Milestones* [Online]. Available: https://www.facebook.com/facebook/info?tab=milestone [Accessed 25 March 2015].

Flanagin, A. J. and Metzger, M. J. 2013. Trusting expert-versus user-generated ratings online: The role of information volume, valence, and consumer characteristics.
Computers in Human Behavior, 29, 1626–1634.

Google Analytics 2014. Average monthly unique users, Q3 2014.

Grönroos, C. 1998. Marketing services: The case of a missing product. *Jornal of
Business and Industrial Marketing,* 16, 322–338.

Hakanen, J. J., Schaufeli, W. B. and Ahola, K. 2008. The Job Demands-Resources
model: A three-year cross-lagged study of burnout, depression, commitment, and
work engagement. *Work & Stress,* 22, 224–241.

Hollebeek, L. D. Demystifying customer engagement: Toward the development of
a conceptual model. ANZMAC 2009 conference, 2009 Monash University, Melbourne, VIC 30 November – 2 December.

Hollebeek, L. D. 2011a. Demystifying customer brand engagement: Exploring the
loyalty nexus. *Journal of Marketing Management,* 27, 785–807.

Hollebeek, L. D. 2011b. Exploring customer brand engagement: Definition and
themes. *Journal of Strategic Marketing,* 19, 555–573.

Hollebeek, L. D., Glynn, M. S. and Brodie, R. J. 2014. Consumer brand engagement
in social media: Conceptualization, scale development and validation. *Journal of
Interactive Marketing,* 28, 149–165.

Hsu, Y.-L. 2012. Facebook as international eMarketing strategy of Taiwan hotels.
International Journal of Hospitality Management, 31, 972–980.

Hudson, S. and Thal, K. 2013. The impact of social media on the consumer decision process: Implications for tourism marketing. *Journal of Travel & Tourism
Marketing,* 30, 156–160.

Kahn, W. A. 1990. Psychological conditions of personal engagement and disengagement at work. *Academy of Management Journal,* 33, 692–724.

Keller, K. L. 2003. *Strategic banding management: Building, measuring, and managing brand equity.* Upper Sanddle River, NJ: Prentice Hall.

Lee, H. A., Law, R. and Murphy, J. 2011. Helpful reviewers in TripAdvisor, an
online travel community. *Journal of Travel & Tourism Marketing,* 28, 675–688.

Leung, X. Y., Bai, B. and Stahura, K. A. 2013. The marketing effectiveness of social
media in the hotel industry: A comparison of Facebook and Twitter. *Journal of
Hospitality & Tourism Research,* 1096348012471381.

Litvin, S. W., Goldsmith, R. E. and Pan, B. 2008. Electronic word-of-mouth in
hospitality and tourism management. *Tourism Management,* 29, 458–468.

Marketing Science Institute 2010. *2010–2014 Research priorities.* Boston, MA: Marketing Science Institute.

Marketing Science Institute 2014. *2014–2016 Research priorities.* Cambridge, MA:
Marketing Science Institute.

Mattila, A. 2000. The role of narratives in the advertising of services. *Journal of
Services Research,* 3, 35–45.

Maurer, C. and Wiegmann, R. 2011. *Effectiveness of advertising on social network
sites: A case study on Facebook.* Springer.

Mittal, B. and Baker, J. 2002. Advertising strategies for hospitality services. *Cornell
Hotel and Restaurant Administration Quarterly,* 43, 51–63.

MMGY Global. 2014. *Facebook marketing for tourism organizations* [Online]. Available: www.mmgyglobal.com.

Muniz, A. M. and O'Guinn, T. C. 2001. Brand community. *Journal of Consumer
Research,* 27, 412–432.

Pan, B., Maclaurin, T. and Crotts, J.C. 2007. Travel blogs and the implications for destination marketing. *Journal of Travel Research*, 46, 35–45.

Paris, C.M., Lee, W. and Seery, P. 2010. The role of social media in promoting special events: Acceptance of Facebook 'events'. *Information and Communication Technologies in Tourism 2010*, 531–541.

Patterson, P., Yu, T. and De Ruyter, K. Understanding customer engagement in services. ANZMAC 2006: Advancing Theory, Maintaining Relevance, 2006 Brisbane, QLD 4–6 December.

Pühringer, S. and Taylor, A. 2008. A practitioner's report on blogs as a potential source of destination marketing intelligence. *Journal of Vacation Marketing*, 14, 177–187.

Ritchie, B., Tung, V.W.S. and Ritchie, R.J. 2011. Tourism experience management research: Emergence, evolution and future directions. *International Journal of Contemporary Hospitality Management*, 23, 419–438.

Rothbard, N.P. 2001. Enriching or depleting? The dynamics of engagement in work and family roles. *Administrative Science Quarterly*, 46, 655–684.

Salanova, M., Agut, S. and Peiro, J.M. 2005. Linking organizational resources and work engagement to employee performance and customer loyalty: The mediation of service climate. *Journal of Applied Psychology*, 90, 1217–1227.

Sashi, C.M. 2012. Customer engagement, buyer-seller relationships, and social media. *Management Decision*, 50, 253–272.

Schaufeli, W.B. and Bakker, A.B. 2004. Job demands, job resources, and their relationship with burnout and engagement: A multi-sample study. *Journal of Organizational Behavior*, 25, 293–315.

Schaufeli, W.B., Salanova, M., González-Romá, V. and Bakker, A.B. 2002. The measurement of engagement and burnout: A two sample confirmatory factor analytic approach. *Journal of Happiness Studies*, 3, 71–92.

Schmallegger, D. and Carson, D. 2008. Blogs in tourism: Changing approaches to information exchange. *Journal of vacation marketing*, 14, 99–110.

Scholer, A.A. and Higgins, E.T. 2009. Exploring the complexities of value creation: The role of engagement strength. *Journal of Consumer Psychology*, 19, 137–143.

Sheldon, P.J. 1997. *Tourism information technology*. Wallingford, Oxon: CAB International.

Shevlin, R. 2007. *Customer engagement is measurable* [Online]. Available: http://marketingroi.wordpress.com/2007/10/02/customer-engagement-is-measurable/ [Accessed 18 August 2010].

So, K.K.F., King, C. and Sparks, B.A. 2014a. Customer engagement with tourism brands: Scale development and validation. *Journal of Hospitality & Tourism Research*, 38, 304–329.

So, K.K.F., King, C., Sparks, B.A. and Wang, Y. 2014b. The role of customer engagement in building consumer loyalty to tourism brands. *Journal of Travel Research*, doi: 10.1177/0047287514541008.

Sparks, B.A. and Browning, V. 2011. The impact of online reviews on hotel booking intentions and perception of trust. *Tourism Management*, 32, 1310–1323.

Sparks, B.A., So, K.K.F. and Bradley, G.L. 2016. Responding to negative online reviews: The effects of hotel responses on customer inferences of trust and concern. *Tourism Management*, 53, 74–85.

Stickdorn, M. and Zehrer, A. Service design in tourism: Customer experience driven destination management. First Nordic Conference on Service Design and Service Innovation. DeThinkingService-ReThinking-Design, Oslo, Norway, 2009.

The Gallup Group. 2010. *Customer engagement – Unleashing the potential for growth* [Online]. Available: http://www.gallup.com/consulting/49/Customer-Engagement. aspx [Accessed 5 December 2010].

Travelblog. 2015. *About TravelBlog* [Online]. Available: https://www.travelblog. org/about.html [Accessed 18 March 2015].

Treadaway, C. and Smith, M. 2010. *Facebook marketing: An hour a day*. Indianapolis, IN: Wiley Publishing Inc.

Trenor, T. 2011. *2011 Blogging statistics (infographic)* [Online]. Available: http://www. rightmixmarketing.com/right-mix-blog/blogging-statistics/ [Accessed 18 March 2015].

Tripadvisor. 2015. *About TripAdvisor* [Online]. Available: http://www.tripadvisor. com/PressCenter-c6-About_Us.html [Accessed 1 March 2015].

Tussyadiah, I. P. and Fesenmaier, D. R. 2008. Marketing places through first-person stories – an analysis of pennsylvania roadtripper blog. *Journal of Travel & Tourism Marketing*, 25, 299–311.

Van Doorn, J., Lemom, K. N., Mittal, V., Nass, S., D., P., Pirner, P. and Verhoef, P. C. 2010. Customer engagement behaviour: Theoretical foundations and reserach directions. *Journal of Service Research*, 13, 253–266.

Vargo, S. L. and Lusch, R. F. 2004. Evolving to a new dominant logic for marketing. *Journal of Marketing*, 68, 1–17.

Verhoef, P. C., Lemon, K. N., Parasuraman, A., Roggeveen, A., Tsiros, M. and Schlesinger, L. A. 2009. Customer experience creation: Determinants, dynamics and management strategies. *Journal of Retailing*, 85, 31–41.

Verhoef, P. C., Reinartz, W. and Krafft, M. 2010. Customer engagement as a new perspective in customer management. *Journal of Service Research*, 13, 247–252.

Vermeulen, I. E. and Seegers, D. 2009. Tried and tested: The impact of online hotel reviews on consumer consideration. *Tourism Management*, 30, 123–127.

Vivek, S. D., Beatty, S. E. and Morgan, R. M. 2012. Customer engagement: Exploring customer relationships beyond purchase. *Journal of Marketing Theory & Practice*, 20, 122–146.

Wirtz, J., Den Ambtman, A., Bloemer, J., Horváth, C., Ramaseshan, B., Van De Klundert, J., Gurhan Canli, Z. and Kandampully, J. 2013. Managing brands and customer engagement in online brand communities. *Journal of Service Management*, 24, 223–244.

Xiang, Z. and Gretzel, U. 2010. Role of social media in online travel information search. *Tourism Management*, 31, 179–188.

Ye, Q., Law, R. and Gu, B. 2009. The impact of online user reviews on hotel room sales. *International Journal of Hospitality Management*, 28, 180–182.

Zarella, D. 2010. *The social media marketing book*. Sebastapol, CA: O'Reilly Media, Inc.

Zehrer, A., Crotts, J. C. and Magnini, V. P. 2011. The perceived usefulness of blog postings: An extension of the expectancy-disconfirmation paradigm. *Tourism Management*, 32, 106–113.

Zeithaml, V. A., Bitner, M. J. and Gremler, D. D. 2006. *Services marketing: Integrating customer focus across the firm*. New York: McGraw-Hill/Irwin.

Zeithaml, V. A., Parasuraman, A. and Berry, L. L. 1985. Problems and strategies in services marketing. *Journal of Marketing*, 49, 33–46.

Zhang, Z., Ye, Q., Law, R. and Li, Y. 2010. The impact of e-word-of-mouth on the online popularity of restaurants: A comparison of consumer reviews and editor reviews. *International Journal of Hospitality Management*, 29, 694–700.

Part IV

Emerging customer engagement contexts

14 Developing a spectrum of positive to negative citizen engagement

Jana Lay-Hwa Bowden,
Vilma Luoma-Aho
and Kay Naumann

Introduction

In democratic societies the fundamental aim of public sector services is to serve citizens, rendering citizen engagement essential. Despite this, citizen disengagement is widespread in public administration, and as such, remains a key challenge within contemporary governance. A cursory glance of satisfaction statistics illustrates the extent of discontent with public sector performance. A recent study in the UK reported that only 20 per cent of citizens were satisfied with their Local Government's service provision (Mitchem, 2014), and a mere 25 per cent felt that their Local Government understood their needs. Over 30 per cent of citizens in America and Canada are also dissatisfied with their Local Government (Dorazio, 2014). This level of citizen disaffection is also mirrored in Australia where satisfaction with the performance of Local Government within specific service categories hovers around 20 per cent (e.g. road and transport infrastructure and town planning; Evans and Reid, 2013). Importantly, these citizens report feeling disgruntled, frustrated and in some cases alienated from their Local Government.

Whilst research has been conducted on the importance of citizen-centric governance, much of what we understand about citizen-centred governance is simply 'window dressing' (Evans and Reid, 2013). Such research is often bureaucratically motivated and results in rhetoric rather than an understanding of what drives citizen engagement. Attempting to understand citizen engagement is not merely an exercise in increasing citizen satisfaction, nor is it merely a new label for managing citizen relationships. Engagement has emerged as a mechanism for public sector organisations to interact with its citizens to better understand their citizens' wants, needs and expectations, and therefore, connect with them in a more collaborative manner (Holmes, 2011; Grant et al., 2011; Stewart, 2009; McCabe et al., 2006). Adopting a more holistic approach to understanding citizen engagement from both a theoretical and practical perspective, and drawing upon conceptualisations of engagement from services marketing may allow management to more effectively develop and employ engagement practices, and enhance citizen well-being (Herriman, 2011; Holmes, 2011).

Local Government context

Traditionally, Local Governments, or councils, have been responsible for providing communities with a range of day-to-day services, such as transport and waste collection. However, the focus of Local Government has gradually been expanding and councils are now responsible for providing services that enhance the cultural, social and environmental well-being of their residents (Dollery et al., 2005; Local Government Acts Taskforce, 2013). As explained by Dollery et al. (2006, p.555), 'Australian councils are moving away from their traditional narrow emphasis on "services to property" towards a broader "services to people" approach.' This broadened approach has been driven by a number of factors, including the devolution of service responsibilities from State and Federal Governments to local councils, and the increased pressure for councils to deliver a more holistic range of services tailored to the needs of their individual communities (Dollery et al., 2006; Thompson and Maginn, 2012; State of Australian Cities, 2012). Therefore, there is a need for councils to establish better relationships with their communities (Herriman, 2011) in order to deliver services that are more reflective of their needs (Dollery et al., 2006; Thompson and Maginn, 2012).

Despite these changes, many Local Governments continue to prioritise their bureaucratic obligations and legislative requirements at the expense of their relationship with their community (Artist et al., 2013). Local Government continues to be criticised on a range of issues including: low citizen involvement in service design and delivery; a focus on internal bureaucratic process as opposed to end user value and benefit; limited responsiveness to public opinion; poor benchmarking of service standards; and significantly, a lack of strategic understanding and focus on citizens needs and expectations (Evans and Reid, 2013). Reported levels of citizen disengagement with their Council services are therefore high. Yet, despite the determinants of citizen engagement remain under researched. This is somewhat surprising since the success of public sector reform is fundamentally based on the development of citizen-centred governance, which must inherently be underpinned by high levels of engagement (Holmes, 2011).

In the next section we develop a conceptual model of citizen engagement, disengagement and negative engagement. We do so by comparing current conceptualisations of engagement within the civic literature to conceptualisations of engagement in the service marketing literature. We then proceed to discuss the hallmarks, nature and triggers for each of the engagement valences, and the ways in which the propensity for positive and negative manifestations of engagement are shaped. Following this we present and discuss a case study of the Local Government context within Australia.

Developing a theoretical framework for citizen engagement

The relationships that citizens form towards their public sector organisations are complex, multidimensional unions that are subject to a range of contextual and temporal influences (Dwyer et al., 1987; Ng, Russell-Bennett and Dagger, 2007). Not all citizens value their relationships in the same way (Anderson and Narus, 1991; Cannon and Perreault, 1999) and motivations to form and maintain these relationships can differ across contexts (Bendapudi and Berry, 1997; Prahalad and Ramaswamy, 2003; Palmer, 2010).

The roots of citizen engagement in the public sector context lie in civic and political engagement. These concepts are related to, but distinct from our conceptualisations of citizen engagement. Civic engagement has been defined as 'people participating together for deliberation and collective action within an array of interests, institutions and networks, developing civic identity, and involving people in governance processes' (Cooper, 2005, p. 534). The concept of 'civic' implies that engagement occurs in the public sphere, instead of the private lives of citizens (Dahlgren, 2005, p. 58), and consists of voluntary activity aimed toward solving problems in the community and helping others. In addition, civic engagement is argued to occur through an engagement 'spectrum' that ranges from informing to consulting, involving, collaborating and, ultimately, empowering (Grant et al., 2011; Herriman, 2011). Equally, discussions on engagement within industry tend to revolve around achieving three major objectives: increasing citizens' access to government information, enhancing consultation between residents and their government, and increasing public participation (Holmes, 2011). Conversely, political engagement refers to activity oriented toward influencing governmental action (Dahlgren, 2005).

Civic engagement is considered to be a precondition for political engagement to occur as it infers improved governance capacity in a community and higher levels of social capital. However, these conceptualisations of civic and political engagement are at odds with marketing-based definitions of engagement. Whilst the rhetoric of policy makers emphasises the importance of citizen 'participation' and interactivity, in practice the reality of this 'participation' is often basic and one-way 'consultation'. Evans and Reid (2013, p.13) argue that this gap between the rhetoric of governance and the reality is culturally engrained in the sector as 'the idea of sharing the process of decision making itself is unpalatable to most policy makers'. Battalino, Beutler and Shani (1996 cited in Sanger 2008, p.78.), therefore, urge that a paradigmatic shift is required with regard to public sector conceptualisations of engagement – 'the shift is from public interest to results that [citizens] value; from efficiency to quality and value; from a justify-costs mentality to delivery-value mentality, from functions, authority and structure, to identifying a mission, services, customers and outcomes'.

Conceptualising positive engagement within the public sector

Marketing conceptualisations of engagement are considered much broader, dynamic and networked than conceptualisations of civic and political engagement (Bowden, 2009; Bowden-Everson and Naumann, 2013; Brodie et al.,

2011, 2011a; Van Doorn et al., 2010; Hollebeek, 2011a, 2011b; Hollebeek, 2012; Sashi, 2012; Kumar et al., 2010). Brodie et al. (2011, p. 260) define engagement as 'the psychological state that occurs by virtue of interactive, co-creative customer experiences with a focal agent/object (e.g. a brand) in focal service relationships. It occurs under a specific set of context dependent conditions generating differing customer engagement levels; and exists as a dynamic, iterative process within service relationships that co-create value'. Within this definition, the outcomes of engagement include cognitive, behavioural (Van Doorn et al., 2010), affective (Brodie et al., 2011a) and social expressions of engagement (Vivek et al., 2012). The major benefit of understanding engagement is in its contribution to understanding how value is co-created within the service relationship (Jaakkola and Alexander, 2014).

This contrasts to civic and political engagement, as customer engagement views interactivity, collaboration and co-creation of the service both between customers and between customers and their service providers as central to the creation of service value (Anderson et al., 2013; Rosenbaum et al., 2011), as well as customer well-being. Importantly, the process of engagement is not a one-way, linear or terminal one. Marketing conceptualisations of engagement suggest that relational connections evolve in response to stakeholder/actor inputs and exchanges and provide a feedback loop into the future development of the relationship, as well as the future propensity for engagement (Chandler and Lusch, 2014). We, therefore, view civic engagement and citizen engagement as interrelated, yet conceptually distinct constructs.

In order to advance our understanding of citizen engagement we adopt the definitional perspective on engagement put forward by Brodie et al. (2011a), and we argue that citizen engagement can be defined as a form of interactive participation, which aims to involve and/or re-involve citizens in the processes of governance. In our view, citizen engagement is context-specific and involves two focal service relationships. The first focal relationship is that of the horizontal engagement that occurs between members of the citizenry. Engagement within this horizontal actor-to-actor platform refers to the interactions that take place between the community members of a Local Government. These interactions are based on a sense of equality, mutuality, rapport and altruism, and as such, promote the co-creation of value at an informal, relatively unstructured and grassroots-type level. The second of these focal relationships is the vertical brand engagement that occurs between citizens and their governing authority. This relationship is governed more so by exchange and norms of dependency and an asymmetry of power (Fennema, 2004; Putnam, 1995) since citizens rely on their Local Government to provide them with valued community services in exchange for revenue (Warner, 2001). As such, this brand-level engagement promotes a more formally structured potential for the co-creation of value.

Importantly, positive and negative forms of engagement may occur within horizontal actor-to-actor networks, as well as vertical brand engagement networks. However, the valence, intensity and subsequent dominance (positive or negative engagement) in each network may be subject to temporal influences and the political climate of the jurisdiction. Understanding how these two networks operate, as well as how they interdependently shape engagement, is important since they form a broader part of the overall service ecosystem within the Local Government context. Within a public sector context, consequently, just as civic engagement is seen as a necessary precondition for political engagement to occur, we view civic engagement as a necessary, but not sufficient condition for citizen engagement to occur. This is an important contribution since engagement research is in its infancy (Jaakkola and Alexander, 2013) and very limited attention to date has been given to its exploration in the context of public sector services.

Thus the nature of engagement in the sector is multilayered and complex, and each unique type of engagement, which occurs in each of the vertical and horizontal networks, affects and is affected by the other. This complexity is reflective of the work of Chandler and Lusch (2014) who argue for a more encompassing view of service within service systems. In other words, we suggest that citizen engagement occurs within a constellation of service actors that, in turn, engage in service interactions at varying levels, including at the individual, group, organisational, and collective or societal level (Chandler and Lusch, 2014). This service ecosystem perspective posits that a single actor (individual or collective) or exchange event does not define positive engagement or otherwise; rather, engagement, 'depends on many actors, times, contexts or meanings' (Chandler and Lusch, 2014, p. 10). These can subsequently be symbiotic and mutually beneficial, or conversely, harmful and potentially collectively destructive to other actors (Chandler and Lusch, 2014). Citizen engagement is thus a highly organic and networked phenomenon in which actors continually influence and are influenced by one another. Whilst a citizen may at any one point predominantly display the characteristics of positive engagement within one network, this engagement is subject to variance and may potentially vacillate towards more neutral or even negative expressions of engagement within these networks depending on the prevailing relationships within the service context.

Conceptualising disengagement within the public sector

Disengagement refers to 'a process by which a customer-brand relationship experiences a trauma or disturbance, which may lead to relationship termination' (Bowden, Gabbott and Naumann, 2014, p. 6). We view citizen disengagement as distinct from citizen dissatisfaction and negative engagement, as in our view, disengagement represents a passive, yet still slightly negative, psychological orientation towards a service relationship that manifests when customers physically or emotionally distance themselves from involvement within the service process (Goode, 2012; Dolan, Conduit and Fahy, 2016). Conversely, dissatisfaction represents a failure of a service firm to meet customers' basic service expectations, a somewhat more linear and simple evaluative process. This is important since in commercial services, disengaged customers account for up to two-thirds of disaffected customers and are frequently described as those customers who take no action against a service provider; become apathetic from lack of success with past experiences (Anderson et al., 2013; Putnam, 2001); ignore or deny the severity of the problem; or worse still, engage in destructive engagement behaviours, such as negative recommendation and boycotting (Chebat, Davidow and Codjovi, 2005). Subsequently, disengaged customers often remain invisible to service providers (Bowden, Gabbott and Naumann, 2014; Dolan, Conduit and Fahy, 2016). They may remain with the service provider in their disengaged, or detached, state (Dolan, Conduit and Fahy, 2016), or if possible, they may leave the service provider and become negatively engaged.

Understanding citizens' disengagement with Local Government services, along with the propensity for this to develop into more deep-seated negative forms of engagement, is important since social services directly affect more holistic outcomes such as consumer well-being (Anderson et al., 2013; Donovon, 2011; Gainer and Padanyi , 2005; Becker-Olsen and Hill, 2006). Service delivery in the sector has the ability to influence not only transactional citizen satisfaction, but more importantly, citizen well-being across a range of life domains, including for example economic, emotional, social and health domains (Sirgy et al., 2008). Disengagement may, therefore, affect focal brand engagement and consumer well-being (Fournier and Alvarez, 2012, p. 254). Importantly, these disturbances within the citizen relationship may prevent citizens from developing positive affective bonds with their public sector organisation, and it may also decrease the quality of communication and interaction between the parties (Baxter 1984; Perrin-Martinenq 2004). Given the tendency towards inertia within the Local Government category as a result of the substantial switching barriers, understanding the hallmarks and processes of disengagement is essential. To summarise, in our view citizen dissatisfaction is a necessary but not sufficient condition for citizen disengagement to occur.

Conceptualising negative engagement within the public sector

Negative engagement is a new concept within the marketing literature (Juric, Smith and Wilks, 2016; Dolan, Conduit and Fahy, 2016). It is defined as '"unfavourable" brand-related thoughts, feelings and behaviours' within a service relationship (Hollebeek and Chen, 2014, p.62). Hollebeek and Chen (2013, p.2) suggest it is a process that results in 'focal brand-related denial, rejection, avoidance and negative word-of-mouth'. It is argued to manifest through a customer's negatively valenced immersion (cognition), passion (affect) and activation (behaviour), resulting in negative brand attitude and electronic word-of-mouth (eWOM; Hollebeek and Chen, 2014). Importantly, research has found that in some service contexts the presence of negative relationships may be more common than positive relationships. Fournier and Alavarez (2012), for example, note that the average split across categories of negative and positive relationships is 55 and 45 per cent, respectively. It is important, therefore, to understand both the positive and more negative manifestations of engagement as both influence the future propensity for engagement.

Within the context of Local Government services, we define negative engagement as a goal-directed process that involves citizens' active and persistent expressions of negativity towards some aspects of their Local Government, which has a detrimental effect on the service relationship and the value derived from the relationship. We suggest that negative engagement manifests through the active and spirited spread of negative word-of-mouth recommendation, co-opting others to adopt a particular attitudinal and/or behavioural position about a provider, the development of deeply negative attitudes, as well as potential retaliation and revenge behaviours (Juric, Smith and Wilks, 2016). Whereas disengagement adopts a passive orientation towards a service provider, negative customer engagement involves premeditated, activated and dedicated expressions of negativity throughout various aspects of the service process. Thus customers who are negatively engaged with their Local Government are indeed committed and involved within their service relationships, but they are committed in a deeply negative and engrained way. Thus the cognitive, affective and behavioural outcomes of their negative engagement have a detrimental effect on service value (Juric, Smith and Wilks, 2016; Hollebeek and Chen, 2013, 2014; Van Doorn et al., 2010). Displays of negative engagement have been found within the Local Government context and tend to revolve around boycotting, negative word-of-mouth and revenge-seeking behaviour (Luoma-aho, 2015). The concept of negative engagement needs to be more clearly understood so that Local Government authorities may develop strategies to reduce negative relationships with their citizens.

The next section presents a case study, which concentrates on describing the complex nature of the engagement that occurs, first, within citizens' horizontal actor-to-actor engagement with one another, and, second, within the context of a vertical brand engagement relationship that citizens have with the Local Government Authority itself (Fennema, 2004). We suggest that these two sets of relationships provide conditions, which are respectively conducive to the development of positive engagement, disengagement and negative engagement and that they, ultimately, affect and are affected by one another. In other words, the subsequent interaction between these two networks impacts positively or negatively on overall citizen well-being, as well as the broader outcomes of governance, social progress and democracy. We put forward a new framework for understanding citizen engagement within the Local Government sector. This framework acknowledges that citizen relationships can vacillate from positively engaged, to disengaged and negatively engaged within their horizontal and vertical networks and that citizens may move between these states depending on changes that occur within both their brand engagement (citizen-to-Local Government) and actor level engagement (citizen-to-citizen) networks. We note that positive and negative forms of engagement may occur within both horizontal actor-to-actor networks, and vertical brand engagement networks. However, the dominance of positive or more negative expressions of engagement within each network is subject to the prevailing political climate within any one jurisdiction.

Discussion

Developing a spectrum of citizen engagement: an Australian case study

In order to explore these three valences of citizen engagement, this study adopted a qualitative methodology. Focus groups were selected as they enabled an analysis of the meanings, processes and normative perceptions of the respondents, and allowed the researchers to gain a deep and applied understanding of the service context being explored (Creswell, 2012). The informants selected were rate-paying residents of a large, urban municipality within a major Australian capital city. The respondent profile was aged 25–55, of various ethnicities and split equally male/female. A total of ten focus groups containing eight to ten residents in each were conducted. Respondents were asked to discuss a range of positive and negative community experiences across their various Local Government relationships. Participants were encouraged to openly discuss important experiences, which allowed them to share their common thoughts, feelings and perceptions among the other respondents. The groups were further facilitated with word and image association tasks in order to explore the residents' underlying motivations, attitudes, values and perceptions. The data was analysed using the qualitative analytic program NVivo 10, which allowed for coding and thematic development.

Whilst we acknowledge that positive and more negatively valenced forms of engagement may occur within both horizontal, as well as vertical, actor-to-actor networks, brand engagement networks are a key finding of this specific case study and the focal jurisdiction was that positive engagement predominantly occurred within the citizen-to-citizen relationship, whilst disengagement and negative engagement predominantly occurred within vertical networks. Thus, this study highlights the unique complexity of exploring engagement within the current political context of this single, but large metropolitan jurisdiction in Australia. That is, engagement tended to operate positively at the actor-to-actor level between the citizenry, and disengagement and negative engagement operated at the brand engagement level with the Local Government itself. Whilst these two forms of engagement were found to occur within these two contextual sets of horizontal and vertical relationships, they were also inherently interrelated in that they affected each other. These equivalent engagement patterns may or may not manifest in other jurisdictions, which display different political climates. The next section reports the broad findings of this study.

Positive citizen engagement

Engagement in the marketing literature describes the process by which consumers form positive, emotionally laden and enduring relationships with the providers they patronise (Bowden, 2009; Verhoef et al., 2010; Hollebeek, 2011a/b, 2012). Achieving high levels of engagement within the context of the public sector is important since it facilitates community connection and belonging and assists in the development of social capital. Ongoing engagement with the citizen base and a deep commitment to the value of citizen participation in public policy is also an important precondition in the establishment of legitimacy and ownership of policy interventions (Evans and Reid, 2013). In a dynamic, networked, and unpredictable social environment, positively engaged citizens and their 'apostle-like' perceptions of their community may hold the key to enhancing community connection and citizen well-being (Hong and Yang, 2011). Engagement not only creates non-transactional social and emotional value amongst the community, but it may also transfer across to citizen's perceptions of the Local Government authority, and thus make the implementation of government policy more effective (Luoma-aho, 2010).

Within the current context, positive engagement was found to occur mostly between citizens within citizens' community networks, rather than with respect to the relationship between citizens and their Local Government authority. Positive engagement manifested through an intense interest in specific relationship(s) (cognitive dimension); positive feelings, satisfaction, happiness and pride towards the specific relationship(s) (affective dimension); and an above average amount of time spent engaging in behaviours associated with the specific relationship(s), including positive discussion and recommendation (behavioural and action-based dimension; Luoma-aho, 2007; 2015). These actor-to-actor level interactions were characterised by highly reciprocal, trusting and engaged exchanges, which prompted a shared sense of altruism, shared responsibility and mutual obligation throughout the community. The sociological literature labels these networks as horizontal networks (Onxy and Bullen, 2000). They are typically characterised by a number of factors including: reciprocity (Putnam, 1995; Foley and Edqards, 1996), mutuality (Theiss-Morse and Hibbing, 2005; Middleton et al., 2005), participation (Ferlander, 2007), trust (Putnam, 1993; Brown and Keast, 2003; Stolle, 2001) and a sense of belonging (Chiu and Wang, 2006; Gouveia and Clemente, 2003). Positive engagement enhances social capital (Stewart, 2009). This sense of equality is considered a 'crucial driver of engagement' (Putnam and Leonardi, 1993, pp. 173) as it motivates the formation of trusting and interactive relationships within a community.

Positive engagement amongst the citizenry was found to occur within this network since the relationships between citizens were focused on a sense of mutual goals and shared values. The engagement displayed was highly reflective of the interactive and co-creative value that is associated with customer engagement within the marketing literature (Brodie et al., 2011). These relationships appeared to be based on a sense of reciprocity, trust and interaction. They were affective and long-term in their orientation, which provided citizens with an intrinsic source of community value and a sense of belonging. These horizontal networks provided citizens with an intrinsic sense of community value and an invisible bond, which acted to connect the community and create a commonality of purpose and shared identity, and which ultimately created long-term, highly emotional attachments to the community. The positive bonds formed between residents were readily apparent when listening to the voice of citizens. Snapshot samples of this citizen interaction, affective bonding, reciprocity, trust and belonging are illustrated in the following citizen verbatim.

> . . . the people make the community, so I feel connected.
>
> Everybody in the street knows everybody, everybody helps out, so there's a big community spirit.
>
> For me it remind me of all the different suburbs coming together as being one big neighbourhood.
>
> I like the community and I've obviously lived here for a lot of years, it needs to be protected.
>
> We don't just have school friends, we have neighbours that are friends, the local people in the local shops, everyone . . .
>
> When I think of my neighbours – it conjures up a warm, fuzzy sort of feeling – village sort of . . .
>
> . . . they're all participating. There's a sense of you fit in and you belong.
>
> My grandparents loved it, and my parents love it, and now my husband and I have moved back.

Citizen disengagement

However, as Morgan and Hunt, (1994, p. 33) note, 'just as medical science should understand both sickness and health, marketing science should understand both functional and dysfunctional relationships'. Not all patrons within service relationships display positive forms of engagement. Disengagement within the marketing literature refers to those customers who may not display overtly negative brand thoughts, feelings and behaviour, but who nonetheless display a weakly, but negatively valenced form of engagement (Bowden, Gabbott and Naumann, 2014). This disengagement reduces the frequency and quality of interactivity between the parties and leads to a loss of affective bonding (Baxter, 1984; Perrin-Martinenq, 2004; Dolan, Conduit and Fahy, 2016). Whilst disengagement is seen as a relatively passive position, it is essentially a process driven by slightly negatively valenced perceptions about an exchange partner and their intentions (Coulter and Ligas, 2000; Price, Arnould and Deibler, 1995). These customers may or may not be sitting on the precipice of becoming negatively engaged within a service relationship (Bowden, Gabbott and Naumann, 2014).

This study found that within this jurisdiction with its associated unique political context, the propensity for disengagement was high within the vertical brand engagement relationship between citizens and their local governing body. The sociological literature describes these relationships as vertical networks. These networks are comprised of exchanges that feature an imbalance of power, status and resources between partners (Putnam and Leonardi, 1993; Stolle, 2001). Disengagement within this network relationship was driven strongly by a sense of inability to influence government decision making, which led to passivity, inaction and disenfranchisement. Citizens reported feeling that they were not benefitting from their interactions with government, perceived little value from engaging in the relationship and chose to either become passive and simply not engage in the relationship, or alternatively, actively decide to neglect their relationship with their Local Government. This contrasted markedly to the overwhelming positive forms of engagement experienced between the citizenry in their horizontal community networks. Importantly, disengagement negatively impacted upon citizens' overall perceptions, attitudes and opinions of their Local Government, and reduced the propensity for positive engagement to occur.

Citizens who potentially disengage from, or neglect, their relationship present a real problem for public managers. They begin to reduce their interaction within the focal relationship and subsequently treat their relationship with their government as a purely discrete and transactional exchange. In addition, their passivity towards the relationship distances citizens from their government, and delimits the ability of government to engage in soft governance (the power to persuade; Brandsen, Boogers and Tops, 2006). It also compromises opportunities to co-create and produce new policies and services designed to enhance citizens' social and economic outcomes. Withdrawal from the relationship may also have a negative spillover effect on other aspects of the civil experience such as their sense of community belonging and their contribution and connection to other citizens. This may ultimately affect a citizen's overall sense of wellbeing. A snapshot sample of this disengagement is illustrated in the following citizen verbatim.

> I used to be involved. I turned up to the Town Hall meetings. I had my say. But I realised they don't take in debate, they pay lip service to community consultation and community involvement and I just don't think they give two hoots. I thought 'what's the point' and just stopped going.
>
> It doesn't matter what rallies you have . . . they're still going to do what they want to do. So what's the use?
>
> I don't care anymore. I've learned that nothing I do or say changes anything. They will do what they want to. It's my choice – I've chosen to not care.
>
> Nowadays I just toss out their community newsletters, and ignore their meetings. My view as a member of the community obviously doesn't matter.
>
> I really don't need them much, and I don't want them in my life.

You know how there are some things you want to be involved with? This isn't one of them – I sit on the sidelines now.

You try to put them to the back of your mind – I don't want to think about what they do anymore.

Negative citizen engagement

A third condition, namely negative engagement, represents a more extreme negative condition than disengagement. It manifests as a goal-directed process, which involves dedicated and targeted expression of negative emotions, attempts to co-opt others to adopt a particular attitudinal and/or behavioural position, as well as, in some cases, direct and indirect attempts to retaliate and seek revenge (Juric, Smith and Wilks, 2016). Unlike the more passive conceptualisation of disengagement, negative engagement is considered to be a premeditated, activated and dedicated behaviour.

It is important to understand negative engagement within the current context as negatively engaged citizens may engage in value co-destruction. In this sense, negative engagement goes beyond mere disengagement, as it involves a clear target and stimulus, arises from anger, and results in deliberate, motivated and targeted negative action (Kuppens et al., 2003). The expression of anger has been shown to lead to a range of organisation-focused outcomes including exit, boycotting, negative word-of-mouth and revenge-seeking behaviour, all of which have profoundly negative effects on the Local Government's reputation as well as its ability to effectively govern its citizens (McColl-Kennedy et al., 2009). In other words, in a political context, negative brand engagement manifests through deeply negative thought processes, emotions and behaviours, which are targeted at the focal organisation. In addition, when anger is paired with perceptions of citizen efficacy within the context of public services, it may then produce what is termed anger activism, which may also lead to the establishment of oppositional lobby groups (Turner, 2007).

This study found that negative citizen engagement led to the creation of positive reward for the citizen engaging in it, therefore creating personal satisfaction and value. However, negative engagement also at the same time led to the co-destruction of value in that it damaged the focal brand and its reputation. In an environment where information is ubiquitous and brand meaning is frequently socially constructed, narratives generated by negatively engaged citizens have the potential to become a part of collective memory and contribute to citizens' negative perceptions of brand meaning (Luoma-aho, 2015). Thus the danger of negative engagement lies in the propensity for those who become negatively engaged to 'get even' and retaliate. In addition, since citizens often award their negative emotions with greater credibility compared to the positive information that may contradict these emotions (i.e. negative confirmatory bias), citizens involved in negative recommendation may quickly and powerfully shape the attitudes and brand meaning of other citizens (Schoenewolf, 1990). This emotional contagion can greatly damage brand equity and brand meaning and it may have the potential to convert otherwise disengaged and/or positively engaged citizens towards more negatively engaged states. A snapshot sample of this negative position is illustrated in the following citizen verbatim.

> You feel like you're being held hostage. I hate my Council. I want them out of my life but I'm trapped. I can't get rid of them unless I sell my house.
>
> I do everything I can to go to every Town Hall meeting. I stand up for what I believe in and I vocally oppose anything I object to at every opportunity. I want everyone to hear my views – the Council, the community, everyone. They might rule with an iron fist, but I'll damn well do my best to let them know I won't put up with being steamrolled.
>
> . . . we feel that the council bully and bulldoze – it's not appropriate but they always manage to go ahead without us.
>
> The amount of money it will cost the council to implement a city of well-being would be more than what their corporate greed would allow them to do.
>
> They think they're invincible. I might be the minority but I've joined all my local political lobby groups. Someone has to try to stop them. They don't listen to anything or anyone, except the media – we get our local rag to write opinion pieces on them – it's the only way.
>
> I feel like it's us against them. I feel very much like they're feathering their own nests.
>
> I love seeing stuff published about the latest scandal. I mean, I'm embarrassed to live in this council – but they deserve all they get.
>
> We were just walking down the street with placards and making the council very aware we were on to it and we were not going to settle for anything less than the best for the community – so residents stood up for one another and spoke.
>
> I walk into council and it's secretive and not transparent. When I think about them I feel anger bubbling up and frustration.
>
> My council – don't get me started. I write them scathing letters every year about how bad they are. I always tell me neighbours too and get them to write in. There's something satisfying about constantly complaining.

Concluding remarks

Seroka (1998) argues that the Local Government sector has undergone a number of changes with regard to how the sector performs their functions, how citizens relate to them, what citizens expect from them, as well as how the citizens relate to their community. Broadly speaking, these changes have led to enhanced citizen control, increased citizen responsibility and a heightened citizen awareness of the importance of community (Seroka, 1998). In this chapter we offered a new framework with which to view these changes. We have attempted to extend customer engagement theory by adapting it and placing it within a public sector context. We have developed a spectrum of types of citizen engagement including the strongly positively valenced engagement, the passive and weakly negative disengagement, and the highly activated, dedicated and destructive negative engagement.

We also explored the moderating role of vertical brand engagement networks and horizontal citizen-to-citizen actor networks on the propensity for each of these types of engagement to transpire. We note that positive and negative forms of engagement may occur within horizontal actor-to-actor networks, as well as vertical brand engagement networks. However, the expression of these forms of engagement, and their manifestation within vertical or horizontal networks, is significantly influenced by the political climate within the Local Government jurisdiction. Thus, whilst we find that citizens simultaneously feel positive and engaged with their community, whilst at the same time feeling disengaged or negatively engaged within this specific case study, this pattern of engagement may not be as pronounced within other Local Government jurisdictions. Management should therefore interpret their ability to engage their citizenry in light of their jurisdictions unique and nuanced political climate and conditions. Nonetheless, within the present context, this juxtaposition of directly opposing engagement forces creates an overall atmosphere of tension and unrest which impacts upon overall citizen well-being. These tensions between representative localism and community localism need to be resolved if public organisations are to learn from their citizenry, generate social capital, and foster democracy and social progress.

From a theoretical perspective, this study finds that the process of engagement in its various forms is not a linear or terminal one. The engagement that evolves between citizen 'actors' and also between citizens and their Local Government authority at the brand level are dynamic and provide a feedback loop into the future development of these focal relationships, as well as the future propensity for engagement, disengagement and negative engagement (e.g. Chandler and Lusch, 2014). Thus, 'ends and means develop co-terminously within connections that are themselves ever changing and thus always subject to re-evaluation and reconstruction' (Emirbayer and Mische 1998, p. 967). In other words, delivering upon a Local Government authority's value proposition at the brand level, and effectively and fully engaging citizens in positive ways at the community level, involves a network of continuous interactions, which, at the most fundamental level, occur between the Local Government itself and its citizens, but also the interactions between citizens (Gummesson, 2008). These two forms of engagement that occur at both the actor and brand level, affect and are affected by one another. Together they impact upon citizen well-being. Therefore, understanding citizen engagement requires Local Government to be cognisant of the fact that it is itself not restricted to simply developing and pitching a value proposition about its services and role to its community, but rather, it must actively and continually partake in value fulfilment with and among its citizen base in order to facilitate the outcomes of positive engagement and citizen well-being (Grönroos 2008). Interactive and mutual engagement between all stakeholders, irrespective of network level, is thus considered a critical element within the process of service system value creation (Brodie et al., 2011; Hollebeek, Glynn, Brodie, 2014).

From a managerial perspective, Local Government effectively need to adapt their policies and programs to the changing needs, expectations and relationship types of their citizens. They need to identify and harness the positive characteristics and resources that pre-exist in their highly engaged citizen-to-citizen networks, and nurture and transfer those capabilities to their citizen-to-government, brand engagement networks. As such, political ideologies that do not allow for the highly co-creative conditions of engagement to occur may delimit the extent to which citizen engagement can be achieved. This is because 'relationships both affect, and are affected by, the contexts in which they are embedded' (Fournier 1998, p. 346). Whilst negative forms of engagement were found to relate to vertical brand level engagement in this study, and positive engagement was found to relate to horizontal actor-to-actor citizen networks in this Australian context, there is evidence from other counties to suggest that positive engagement may also be associated with vertical networks and vice versa. Thus, historical political climate, as well as the philosophy of governance within any one country, may have an important influence on the propensity for positive and negative engagement within civil networks. The extent to which network type moderates the propensity for positive and negative engagement should be further explored within an international context.

In the current context, the findings of this study suggest that Local Government can, in effect, become the conduit and facilitator for positive engagement. To do so Local Government must adopt a bottom-up style of management, which places the citizen at the centre of public design, and which also devolves resources and, in part, power to the public. Whilst challenging to achieve, collective forms of interaction based on strongly interconnected community networks, and supported by Local Government, can in themselves be a strong motivator for participation, positive engagement and progressive social change. In addition engagement can facilitate and enhance co-creation of public service design; activate and energise citizens who seek to influence local governance; and foster and develop political literacy, confidence, innovation and ambition amongst the populous (Evans and Reid, 2013).

Perhaps one of the key opportunities in dealing with the disengaged, as well as the negatively engaged, citizens lies with the positively engaged citizens: only credible, good experiences of fellow citizens enable trust to spread and individuals to reconsider their stance. In political science this is referred to as the circle of trust; you trust others in society to do what is right, you do right yourself and you trust your authorities to do right. On the other hand, if the negatively engaged and disengaged citizens are left unattended, their distrust may quickly begin to dominate in society. Under these circumstances citizens do not trust others because they themselves are not trustworthy. Consequently, they do not trust their authorities and public sector organisations either. Governance in such an environment becomes increasingly challenging.

The crucial point here is that management need to pay more attention to the building blocks and foundation of democracy if our intentions are to not only ensure a positive reputation for our Local Governments, but to also build strong, sustainable and resilient local and national communities. Local Governments are the most fundamental element of governance and the lynchpin for positive social and economic progress. Whilst perhaps expressed rather extremely, (Seroka, 1998, p. 220) believes that 'to the extent that democracy is denied at the level of the local community, it has no chance for success at other levels of government. To the extent that citizens abandon their local institutions, their national institutions will wither and collapse from within.' Fundamentally then, citizen engagement, disengagement and negative engagement do not exist in isolation, but rather, exist within the context of other relationships. We need to understand not only how local and national institutions fit together, but also the intricately networked and complex structure of relationships that operate within the Local Government sector.

References

Anderson, J. and Narus, J. 1991. "Partnering as a focused market strategy." *California Management Review*, 33(3), 95–113.

Anderson, L., Ostrom, A. L., Corus, C., Fisk, R. P., Gallan, A. S., Giraldo, M., Mende, M., Mulder, M., Rayburn, S. W. and Rosenbaum, M. S. 2013. "Transformative service research: an agenda for the future." *Journal of Business Research*, 66(8), 1203–1210.

Artist, S., Grafton, D., Merkus, J., Nash, K., Sansom, G. and Wills, J. 2012. "Community engagement in Australian Local Government." *A Practice Review*, Centre for Local Government University of Technology, Sydney, NSW.

Baxter, Leslie A. 1984. "Trajectories of relationship disengagement." *Journal of Social and Personal Relationships*, 1(1), 29–48.

Becker-Olsen, K. L. and Hill, R. P. 2006. "The impact of sponsor fit on brand equity: The case of nonprofit service providers." *Journal of Service Research*, 9(1), 73–83.

Bendapudi, N. and Berry, L. L. 1997. "Customers' motivations for maintaining relationships with service providers." *Journal of Retailing*, 73(1), 15–37.

Bowden, J. L-H. 2009. "The process of customer engagement: a conceptual framework." *The Journal of Marketing Theory and Practice*, 17(1), 63–74.

Bowden, J. L-H., Gabbott, M., and Naumann, K. 2014. "Service relationships and the customer disengagement–engagement conundrum." *Journal of Marketing Management*, 31 (7–8), 774–806.

Bowden-Everson, J., and Naumann, K. 2013. "Us versus Them: The operation of customer engagement and customer disengagement within a local government service setting." Proceedings of ANZMAC, December 2013, The University of Auckland Business School, University of Auckland, Auckland, New Zealand.

Brandsen, T., Boogers, M. and Tops, P. 2006. "Soft governance, hard consequences: The ambiguous status of unofficial guidelines." *Public Administration Review*, 66(4), 546–553.

Brodie, R, J. and Hollebeek, L, D. 2011. "Advancing and consolidating knowledge about customer engagement." *Journal of Service Research*, 14(3), 283–284.

Brodie, R. J., Hollebeek, L.D., Jurić, B. and Ilić, A. 2011a. "Customer engagement conceptual domain, fundamental propositions, and implications for research." *Journal of Service Research*, 14(3), 252–271.

Brodie, R. J., Ilic, A., Juric, B. and Hollebeek, L. 2011. "Consumer engagement in a virtual brand community: An exploratory analysis". *Journal of Business Research*. 66, 105–114.

Brown, K.A. and Keast, R.L. 2003. "Citizen-government engagement: community connection through networked arrangements." *Asian Journal of Public Administration*, 25(1), 107–132.

Cannon, Joseph P. and Perreault Jr, William D. 1999. "Buyer-seller relationships in business markets." *Journal of Marketing Research*, 439–460.

Chandler, J.D. and Lusch, R.F. 2014. "Service systems: A broadened framework and research agenda on value propositions, engagement, and service experience." *Journal of Service Research*, 1–17.

Chebat, J-C., Davidow, M. and Codjovi, I. 2005. "Silent voices: Why some dissatisfied consumers fail to complain." *Journal of Service Research*, 7(4), 328–342.

Chitturi, R., Raghunathan, R. and Mahajan, V. 2008. "Delight by design: The role of hedonic versus utilitarian benefits." *Journal of Marketing*, 72(3), 48–63.

Chiu, C-M., Hsu, M-H. and Wang, E.T.G. 2006. "Understanding knowledge sharing in virtual communities: An integration of social capital and social cognitive theories." *Decision support systems*, 42(3), 1872–1888.

Cooper, T. 2005. "Civic engagement in the twenty-first century: Toward a scholarly and practical agenda." *Public Administration Review*, 65(5), 534–535.

Coulter, R.A., and Ligas, M. 2000. "The long good-bye: The dissolution of customer-service provider relationships." *Psychology & Marketing*, 17(8), 669–695.

Creswell, J.W. 2012. *Qualitative Inquiry and Research Design: Choosing among Five Approaches*. SAGE Publications.

Dahlgren, P. 2005. "The Internet, public spheres, and political communication: Dispersion and deliberation." *Political Communication*, 22(2), 147–162.

Delli Carpini, M.X., Cook, F.L., and Jacobs, L.R. 2004. "Public deliberations, discursive participation and citizen engagement: A review of the empirical literature." *Annual Review of Political Science*, 7(1), 315–344.

Dolan, R. Conduit, J. and Fahy, J. 2016. "Social media engagement: A construct of positively and negatively valenced engagement behaviours." In R. Brodie, L. Hollebeek, J. Conduit (Eds.) *Customer Engagement: Contemporary Issues and Challenges*. Routledge.

Dollery, B. and Johnson, A. 2005. "Enhancing efficiency in Australian Local Government: An evaluation of alternative models of municipal governance." *Urban Policy and Research*, 23(1), 73–85.

Dollery, B., Wallis, J. and Allan, P. 2006. "The debate that had to happen but never did: The changing role of Australian local government." *Australian Journal of Political Science*, 41(4), 553–567.

Donovan, R. 2011. "Social marketing's mythunderstandings." *Journal of Social Marketing*, 1(1), 8–16.

Dorazio, J. 2014. "Citizen engagement: 4 key insights from data on citizen satisfaction." http://www.visioncritical.com/citizen-engagement-4-key-insights-data-citizen-satisfaction/

Dwyer, F. R., Schurr, P. H. and Oh, S. 1987. "Developing buyer-seller relationships." *Journal of Marketing*, 51(2), 11–27.

Emirbayer, M. and Mische, A. 1998. "What is agency?." *American journal of sociology*, 103(4), 962–1023.

Evans, M. and Reid, R. 2013. "Public participation in an era of governance: Lessons from Europe for Australian Local Government." Australian Centre of Excellence for Local Government, University of Technology, Sydney.

Fennema, M. 2004. "The concept and measurement of ethnic community." *Journal of Ethnic and Migration Studies*, 30(3), 429–447.

Ferlander, S. 2007. "The importance of different forms of social capital for health." *Acta Sociologica*, 50(2), 115–128.

Foley, M.W. and Edwards, B. 1996. "The paradox of civil society." *Journal of Democracy*, 7(3), 38–52.

Fournier, S. 1998. "Consumers and their brands: Developing relationship theory in consumer research." *Journal of Consumer Research*, 24(4), 343–353.

Fournier, S. and Alvarez, C. 2012. "Brands as relationship partners: Warmth, competence, and in-between." *Journal of Consumer Psychology*, 22(2), 177–185.

Gainer, B. and Padanyi, P. 2005. "The relationship between market-oriented activities and market-oriented culture: Implications for the development of market orientation in nonprofit service organizations." *Journal of Business Research*, 58(6), 854–862.

Gao, C-Y. and Chen, M-L. 2013. "Customer engagement behavior: A new perspective in CRM." Paper presented at the 19th International Conference on Industrial Engineering and Engineering Management, Chinese Industrial Engineering Institution, CMES, China.

Goode, S. 2012. "Engagement and disengagement in online service failure: Contrasting problem and emotional coping effects." *Journal of Internet Commerce*, 11(3), 226–253.

Gouveia, V. V., Clemente, M. and Espinosa, P. 2003. "The horizontal and vertical attributes of individualism and collectivism in a Spanish population." *Journal of Social Psychology*, 143(1), 43–63.

Grant, B., Dollery, B. and Kortt, M. 2011. "Australian local government and community engagement: Are all our community engagement plans the same? Does it matter?" *Working Paper Series*, Centre for Local Government, School of Business, Economics and Public Policy, University of New England, Armidale NSW.

Grönroos, C. 2008. "Adopting a service business logic in relational business-to-business marketing: Value creation, interaction and joint value co-creation." in *Otago forum*, University of Otago, New Zealand, 2(1), 269–287.

Gummesson, E. 2008. "Extending the service-dominant logic: from customer centricity to balanced centricity." *Journal of the Academy of Marketing Science*, 36(1), 15–17.

Herriman, J. 2011. "Local government and community engagement in Australia." *Working Paper No. 5.* Australian Centre of Excellence for Local Government, University of Technology Sydney. http://www.acelg.org.au/file/1567/download?token=0JHw2u-JV7yHNZUBtIkvvQhmPtHG1wKNfI7tf41Bhg0.

Hollebeek, L. 2011a. "Exploring customer brand engagement: definition and themes." *Journal of Strategic Marketing*, 19(7), 555–573.

Hollebeek, L. D. 2011b. "Demystifying customer brand engagement: Exploring the loyalty nexus." *Journal of Marketing Management*, 27(7–8), 785–807.

Hollebeek, L. D. 2012. "The customer engagement/value interface: An exploratory investigation." *Australasian Marketing Journal*, 21(1), 17–24.

Hollebeek, L. D. and Chen, T. 2013. "Positively-vs. negatively-valenced engagement: Implications for SD logic." In Naples Forum on Service, Naples, Italy, 18–21 June.

Hollebeek, L. D. and Chen, T. 2014. "Exploring positively-versus negatively-valenced brand engagement: a conceptual model." *Journal of Product & Brand Management*, 23(1), 62–74.

Hollebeek, L. D., Glynn, M. S. and Brodie, R. J. 2014). "Consumer brand engagement in social media: Conceptualization, scale development and validation." *Journal of Interactive Marketing*, 28(2), 149–165.

Holmes, B. 2011. "Citizens' engagement in policymaking and the design of public services." *RESEARCH PAPER NO. 1, 2011–12,* Parliament of Australia Department of Parliamentary Services. http://www.aph.gov.au/About_Parliament/ Parliamentary_Departments/Parliamentary_Library/pubs/rp/rp1112/12rp01

Hong, S. Y. and Yang, S-U. 2011. "Public engagement in supportive communication behaviors toward an organization: Effects of relational satisfaction and organizational reputation in public relations management." *Journal of Public Relations Research*, 23(2), 191–217.

Jaakkola, E. and Alexander, M. (2014). "The role of customer engagement behavior in value co-creation." *Journal of Service Research*, 17(3), 247–261.

Juric, B., Smith, S., and Wilks, G. 2016. "Negative customer brand engagement: An overview of conceptual and blog-based findings." In R. Brodie, L. Hollebeek, J. Conduit (Eds.) *Customer Engagement: Contemporary Issues and Challenges.* Routledge.

Kumar, V., Aksoy, L., Donkers, B., Venkatesan, R., Wiesel, T. and Tillmanns, S. 2010. "Undervalued or overvalued customers: Capturing total customer engagement value." *Journal of Service Research*, 13 (3), 297–310.

Kuppens, P., Van Mechelen, I., Smits, D. J. M. and De Boeck, P. 2003. "The appraisal basis of anger: Specificity, necessity and sufficiency of components." *Emotion*, 3(3), 254.

Local Government Acts Taskforce. 2013. *A New Local Government Act for NSW-Discussion Paper.* NSW Government.

Luoma-aho, V. 2007. "Neutral reputation and public sector organizations." *Corporate Reputation Review*, 10(2), 124–143.

Luoma-aho, V. 2010. "Emotional Stakeholders: A threat to organizational legitimacy?" Paper presented at the ICA Conference 2010, on panel: "Nothing more than feelings", http://jyu.academia.edu/VilmaLuomaaho/Papers/185612/ Emotional-stakeholders – A-Threat-to-Organizational-Legitimacy-

Luoma-aho, V. 2015. "Understanding stakeholder engagement: Faith-holders, Hate-holders & Fakeholders." *Research Journal of the Institute for Public Relations,* 2(1). Retrieved from http://www.instituteforpr.org/understanding-stakeholder-engagement-faith-holders-hateholders-fakeholders/.

Mattila, A. S. and Enz, C. A. 2002. "The role of emotions in service encounters." *Journal of Service Research*, 4(4), 268–277.

McCabe, A. C., Keast, R. L. and Brown, K. A. 2006. "Community engagement: Towards community as governance." In *Governments and Communities in Partnership Conference*, 25–27 September 2006, Melbourne, VIC. http://eprints.qut. edu.au/7497/

McColl-Kennedy, J., Patterson, P., Smith, A. and Brady, M. 2009. "Customer rage episodes: Emotions, expressions and behaviors." *Journal of Retailing*, 85(2), 222–237.

Middleton, A., Murie, A. and Groves, R. 2005. "Social capital and neighbourhoods that work." *Urban Studies*, 42(10), 1711–1738.

Mitchem, Vi. 2014. "UK residents not satisfied with their local council." http://www.govtoday.co.uk/local-government-news/20-communities/18389-uk-residents-not-satisfied-with-their-local-council

Morgan, R.M. and Hunt, S.D. (1994), "The commitment-trust theory of relationship marketing." *Journal of Marketing*, 58(3), 20–38.

Ng, S., Russell-Bennett, R. and Dagger, T. 2007. "A typology of mass services: The role of service delivery and consumption purpose in classifying service experiences." *Journal of Services Marketing*, 21(7), 471–480.

Onyx, J. and Bullen, P. 2000. "Measuring social capital in five communities." *Journal of Applied Behavioral Science*, 36(1), 23–42.

Palmer, A. 2010. "Customer experience management: A critical review of an emerging idea." *Journal of Services Marketing*, 24(3), 196–208.

Perrin-Martinenq, D. 2004. "The role of brand detachment on the dissolution of the relationship between the consumer and the brand." *Journal of Marketing Management*, 20(9–10), 1001–1023.

Prahalad, C.K. and Ramaswamy, V. 2003. "The new frontier of experience innovation." *MIT Sloan Management Review*, 44(4), 12–18.

Price, L.L., Arnould, F.J. and Deibler, S.L. 1995. "Consumers' emotional responses to service encounters: The influence of the service provider." *International Journal of Service Industry Management*, 6(3), 34–63.

Putnam, R.D. 1995. "Tuning in, tuning out: The strange disappearance of social capital in America." *Political Science and Politics*, 28(4), 664–683.

Putnam, R. 2001. "Social capital: Measurement and consequences." *Canadian Journal of Policy Research*, 2(1), 41–51.

Putnam, R.D. and Leonardi, R. 1993. *Making Democracy Work: Civic Traditions in Modern Italy*. Princeton University Press.

Rosenbaum, M.S., Corus, C., Ostrom, A.L., Anderson, L., Fisk, R.P., Gallan, A.S., Giraldo, M., Mende, M., Mulder, M. and Rayburn, S.W. 2011. "Conceptualization and aspirations of transformative service research." *Journal of Research for Consumers*, 19, 1–6.

Sanger, M.B. 2008. "From measurement to management: Breaking through the barriers to state and local performance." *Public Administration Review*, 68 (s1), S70-S85.

Sashi, C. 2012. "Customer engagement, buyer-seller relationships, and social media." *Management Decision*, 50(2), 253–272.

Schoenewolf, G. 1990. "Emotional contagion: Behavioral induction in individuals and groups." *Modern Psychoanalysis*, 15(1), 49–61.

Seroka, J. 1998. "Trends in municipal administration and impact on democratization in the United States", *Law and Politics*, 1(2), 219–231

Sirgy, M.J., Lee, D-J., Grzeskowiak, S., Chebat, J-C., Johar, J.S., Hermann, A. and Webb, D. 2008. "An extension and further validation of a community-based consumer well-being measure." *Journal of Macromarketing*, 28(3), 243–257.

State of Australian Cities. 2012. Major Cities Unit, *Department of Infrastructure and Transport*, Australian Government.

Stewart, J. 2009. *Dilemmas of Engagement: The Role of Consultation in Governance*. ANU E Press. http://press.anu.edu.au/titles/australia-and-new-zealand-school-of-government-anzsog-2/dilemmas_citation/

Stolle, D. 2001. "Getting to trust: An analysis of the importance of institutions, families, personal experiences and group membership." In Dekker, P. and Uslaner, E. M. (Eds.) *Social Capital and Participation in Everyday Life*, 118–133. London: Routledge.

Theiss-Morse, E. and Hibbing, J. R. 2005. "Citizenship and civic engagement." *Annual Review of Political Science*, 8, 227–249.

Thompson, S. and Maginn, P. (2012), *Planning Australia: An Overview of Urban and Regional Planning.* Cambridge University Press.

Turner, M. M. 2007. "Using emotion in risk communication: The anger activism model." *Public Relations Review*, 33(2), 114–119.

Van Doorn, J., Lemon, K. N., Mittal, V., Nass, S., Pick, D., Pirner, P. and Verhoef, P. C. 2010. "Customer engagement behavior: Theoretical foundations and research directions." *Journal of Service Research*, 13(3), 253–266.

Verhoef, P. C., Reinartz, W. J. and Krafft, M. 2010. "Customer engagement as a new perspective in customer management." *Journal of Service Research*, 13(3), 247–252.

Vivek, S. D., Beatty, S. E. and Morgan, R. M. 2012. "Customer engagement: Exploring customer relationships beyond purchase." *The Journal of Marketing Theory and Practice*, 20(2), 122–146.

Warner, M. 2001. "Building social capital: The role of local government." *Journal of Socio-economics*, 30(2), 187–192.

15 Negative customer brand engagement

An overview of conceptual and blog-based findings

Biljana Juric, Sandra D. Smith and George Wilks

Introduction

> *Ryanair, I swore to exact my vengeance upon you. The fury of my pen shall never rest for as long as I'm an advocate against your inhumane and shameful conducts. May I urge you, dear readers, to join me for the boycott.*

(Ryanair, Blog 9)

In recent years, customer brand engagement has become a topic of immense interest, not only within the marketing and management disciplines, but also among business practitioners. Typically, customer brand engagement (CBE) is portrayed as a mechanism that serves to strengthen customers' relationships with brands, organisations and other individuals (Algesheimer, Borle, Dholakia and Singh, 2010). Furthermore, engagement is often recognised as a predictor of customer loyalty, (co-)created value, success and the financial performance of organisations (Brodie, Hollebeek, Juric and Ilic, 2011; Brodie, Ilic, Juric and Hollebeek, 2013; Luo, 2009). There is no doubt that brand engagement, engagement platforms and engagement outcomes are topics that should be and are of interest to practitioners and academics alike. However, not all CBE manifestations are positive. The Ryan Airline example above was posted by a resolute advocate against Ryanair, who intended to punish the company by not only warning existing or potential customers of the airline's poor performance, but also by rallying them to boycott the brand and tarnish its reputation. This example shows that there is a dark side to CBE.

A large body of marketing research that deals with word of mouth (WOM), and more recently electronic WOM, addresses negative WOM manifestations of customers dissatisfied with a particular brand (Luo, 2009; Park and Lee, 2009). Perceptions of a brand's poor customer service or unethical behaviour can lead to customers complaining, voicing or even taking part in revenge and sabotage behaviours (McColl-Kennedy, Sparks and Nguyen, 2011; Sparks and Browning, 2010; Zeelenberg and Pieters, 2004). Customers are increasingly expressing their negative views about particular brands through online social networks, forums and blogs. Whether customers use these communication channels because of the greater anonymity or greater communicative reach compared to offline channels, the reality is that companies have less control over communication pathways and messages than in the past. Customer online behaviours are increasingly gaining social acceptance as a valid way to communicate (Hsu and Lin, 2008) and such online behaviour is having an effect on brand equity, organisational reputation, market share and stock prices (Greun, Osmonbekov and Czaplewski, 2006; Tirunillai and Tellis, 2012). In addition, customers are using multiple behaviours and channels to express negative views about brands. For example, another angry Ryanair blogger told his readers that he had also written 'to many other organisations, including the BBC's Watchdog, the Air Travel Users Committee and the Anna Tims consumer page in *The Guardian* newspaper' (Ryanair, Blog 4).

The central theme of this chapter is a conceptualisation of negative customer brand engagement (NCBE), that is, negative customer engagement, which pertains to a brand or brands. Given the minimal attention marketing scholars have given to the concept of NCBE, the aim of this chapter is to provide, through conceptual and blog analysis, an overview of NCBE from a customer perspective. As Van Doorn, Lemon, Mittal, Nass, Pick, Pirner and Verhoef (2010) state, a piecemeal approach to examining customer engagement is no longer sufficient. NCBE is viewed as a holistic representation of negative customer behaviours (and associated mental states), such as negative WOM, protesting and revenge-based actions, which are triggered by perceptions that customer value has been co-destructed in a customer's exchange or exchanges with a brand or brands, and are undertaken with an intention to damage the brand's value. Due to the nature of triggers of NCBE, customer intentions towards the brand, related consequences and the overall nature of the engagement process, it is argued here that NCBE is not simply a negatively valenced form of customer brand engagement (Hollebeek and Chen, 2014; Van Doorn et al., 2010), but is a distinct phenomenon (Smith, Juric and Nie, 2013).

Emerging themes about negative engagement and negative customer brand engagement from the non-marketing and marketing literature are highlighted and an attempt is made to integrate central elements of these diverse literature streams. In order to extend Smith et al.'s (2013) original study, blogs from a range of brand and product contexts were analysed; thus, this chapter is also based upon the findings of a netnographic analysis of 75 anti-brand blogs, namely, Call of Duty (20), Facebook (25), iPhone (15) and Ryanair (15). Though online behaviour is only part of the negative engagement story, it is an important part, nonetheless. The analysis has given us further insights about the nature of NCBE versus engagement with a negative valence and has enriched the discussion about the selected themes. The theoretical foundations combine emergent S-D logic concepts of value co-destruction (Plé and Chumpitas-Caceres, 2010), value co-creation (Vargo and Lusch, 2004) and customer resource integration, specifically Conservation of Resource Theory (COR) (Hobfoll, 1989), which accommodates a customer perspective. Within the main tenet of COR's theory, which posits that individuals strive to protect the resources they value (Hobfoll, 1989; Smith et al., 2013), we use constructs of self-threat and dissonance to explain what triggers NCBE (Smith et al., 2013).

By conceptualising NCBE, this chapter makes a useful contribution to the current dialogue about CBE and, more generally, advances the theory of engagement within the marketing discipline. The chapter begins with a discussion about NCBE as it relates to customer engagement (CE); followed by a discussion regarding the process of NCBE. Future research directions are also discussed.

Conceptualising NCBE in relation to customer engagement

Negative engagement has been discussed within various disciplines, including abnormal childhood psychology (Dishion, Nelson, Winter, Bullock, 2004), educational psychology (Skinner and Belmont, 1993; Juvonen, Espinoza and Knifsend, 2012), information technology (Hedman and Sharafi, 2004), early childhood research (Vitiello, Booren, Downer and Williford, 2012), family and abnormal child psychology (Dishion, Nelson, Winter, and Bullock, 2004; Katz and Gottman, 1996) and information system science (Schmidt, 2010). Negative engagement is conceptualised as a sense of anxious, stressful and negative involvement (George, 1998) or non- involvement (Harrison, 2008), as criticism and blame (Dishin et al., 2004), and is used in conjunction with resistance, avoidance or fear of doing something (Davis, 2012). Contemporary thought on customer engagement posits that engagement is beyond involvement, resistance or avoidance due to its interactional nature and associated customer experiences. Moreover, negative employee engagement has been defined as including all negative behaviours irrespective of affect and all neutral behaviours with negative affect (Nordahl, Janson, Manger and Zachrisson 2014).

Marketing researchers have dealt with different aspects of specific negatively valenced consumer behaviours, emotional and cognitive states and goals (e.g. Kowalski, 2002), including in an online environment (Ward and Ostrome, 2006). To date, customer engagement scholars have tended to consider customer engagement to be beneficial to customers and firms, and only a few studies have recognised that customer engagement behaviours can be either advantageous or disadvantageous for the firm (e.g. Brodie et al., 2013; Hollebeek and Chen, 2014; Van Doorn et al., 2010). However, most customer engagement conceptualisations do not accommodate for manifestations of negative engagement. For example, Brodie et al.'s (2011) fundamental premises of engagement, which have increasingly been adopted by academics, depict engagement as a psychological state that is the result of core of interactive, co-creative customer experiences with an object (e.g. a brand). This definition assumes, however, that engagement behaviours are positively valenced, that is, generating co-creative, rather than co-destructive effects.

Only a few studies within marketing have focused on manifestations of customer negative engagement. For example, Van Doorn et al. (2010) suggest that customers' engagement behaviours can be either positive (e.g. posting a positive brand message on a blog) or negative (e.g. organising public actions against a firm). Most recently, drawing on Van Doorn et al. (2010), Hollebeek and

Chen (2014) developed a conceptual model providing key hallmarks, triggers and consequences of positively and negatively valenced brand engagement. For example, perceived brand value (an antecedent) is represented as having a direct relationship with 'immersion' (the level of a consumer's brand-related thoughts, concentration and reflection), which in turn may affect brand attitude. However, both these studies assume that positive and negative engagement are opposite forms of the same construct.

An alternative view is that negative engagement can be theorised as a distinct concept due to different underpinning nomological elements and processes (Smith et al., 2013). While manifestations of NCBE also occur through diverse states and behaviours embedded within the dynamic, iterative processes of relational exchange, the value is co-destructed for the brand and possibly other actors. Additionally, a nomological network, where customer engagement plays a central role, has different components; that is, it has conflict and dissonance, but not trust; flow, but not rapport with the brand; emotional brand dis-attachment and behavioural, but not attitudinal loyalty.

Why customers negatively engage: antecedents and triggers

Customers' negative engagement behavioural manifestations are preceded by events, such as negative direct and indirect experiences with a provider, concerns with service quality and/or perceived value, and dissatisfaction (De Matos and Rossi, 2008; Wangenheim, 2005). Overall, customer experiences and expectations of the brand, as well as competitive brands, are significant precursors of NCBE. The likelihood that customers will react negatively is associated with the level of perceived harm or risk related with or to the event, if the event happens unexpectedly or if customers believe that a firm could have prevented the incident (Choi and Mattila, 2006; Tsai, Yang and Chen, 2014). Furthermore, in the case of multiple events, the customer's negative perception of the brand is likely to increase and intensify (Johnston and Fern, 1999) and where switching costs are used to entrap customers, the negative response will be greatest (Ranaweera and Menon, 2013).

Antecedents predispose customers towards becoming negatively engaged once a critical event occurs. How antecedents are described within various disciplines is contingent upon how a particular behaviour is being observed, described or conceptualised. Van Doorn et al. (2010) categorise the antecedents of customer engagement behaviours as customer, firm and context-based. For example, consumption goals are customer-based, brand characteristics are firm-based and competitive factors are context-based. Within the context of WOM research, De Matos and Rossi's (2008) meta-analysis of various antecedents reveals that valence is a significant moderator. Some authors distinguish antecedents as distal and proximal, whereby the former are defined as background factors hypothesised to predispose an individual to a certain behaviour, and the latter are conceptualised as triggers (Waller, 2002). We posit that antecedents are conditions or predispositions to act while triggers are perceived and experienced by customers as critical events. In turn, these critical events spark a negative engagement process, which drives the customer to undertake one or a range of negative engagement behaviours. Mazzarol, Sweeney and Souter (2007) define triggers in relation to WOM as motivational factors unique to a particular situation.

Triggering events can be simple or complex; they may be a one-off event or cumulative. For example, a Ryanair customer created an entire website (Ryanair, Blog 1) due to a solo incident (threshold effect) and a Call of Duty blogger decided to blog about his or her dislike of a new game installment (Call of Duty, Blog 4). Others recalled multiple events that happened over a period of time (accumulation effect) as the following excerpt illustrates: 'However, after 3 agonizing and infuriating "incidents" with Europe's leading discount airline, I finally learned my lesson and firmly put my foot down and refused to fly Ryanair again' (Ryanair, Blog 5). Previous studies have also found that there is a progressive development in the frequency and severity of negative behaviours resulting from repeated incongruence between consumers' goals or values and a firm's actions (Chylinski and Chu, 2010).

Motivated by anxiety reduction, vengeance, concern for others and/or product involvement (e.g. Hennig-Thurau, Gwinner, Walsh, and Gremler, 2004; Mazzarol et al., 2007; Sundaram, Mitra, and Webster, 1998), customers undertake diverse actions. Some customers use negative WOM to reduce the anxiety and frustration caused by unpleasant consumption experiences. Others need to go beyond WOM, and therefore actively retaliate and punish an organisation, brand or employee. These customers may vindictively complain and spread malicious, negative WOM (Grégoire and Fisher 2008; Yagil, 2008). According to Berger (2014), WOM is predominantly the result of self- (rather than other) serving motivations.

The customer–brand relationship is also an important factor that might influence the nature and intensity of interactive experiences that customers initiate. Relational customers may forgive companies for an initial undesirable service or unethical conduct in situations when the level of harm is low, but as the harm increases, customers become progressively dissatisfied (Mattila, 2004; Tsai et al., 2014). Customers who are strongly attached to a brand feel betrayed and react more strongly than transactional customers, who are not so attached especially, in the case of unsuccessful service recovery (or double deviation) (Grégoire and Fischer, 2008; Grégoire, Tripp and Legoux, 2009).

The findings from our blog analysis indicate that low brand attachment, such as in the case of the Ryanair bloggers, seemed to amplify negative engagement with the brand. Bloggers were reporting that they predominantly used the brand because of perceived value from having a low-cost travel option. While the bloggers used a number of different metaphors to outline the various brands, in the case of Ryanair, descriptions such as 'a flying toilet', 'loophole predators' and 'spam-tinning factory' were amongst the most notable. Bloggers used such brand labels and expressed their expectation that the brand does not care about or respect its customers as the following example illustrates: 'For Ryanair is a notorious rip-off-savvy company. The more money in their pockets, the happier they are, and who cares about the customers anyway?' (Ryanair, Blog 14)

Bloggers across all the studied contexts displayed characteristics, such as individualism, assertiveness, opinion leadership, the need for self-enhancement and computer skills. Personality traits, such as altruism, individualism, assertiveness and especially customers' perceptions of injustice or an inclination to attribute blame (Richins, 1983; Folkes, Koletsky and Graham, 1987; Davidow and Dacin, 1997; Tax, Brown and Chandrashekaran, 1998) have also been shown as significant antecedents of different forms of negative engagement behavioural manifestations. Customers who pose a higher level of confidence, perceived control or self-efficacy, or who are risk takers are more inclined to voice their objections and suggestions to companies, or complain to friends and express their views online (Bearden and Teel, 1980; Bodey and Grace, 2006). Politeness, shame proneness and self-monitoring (Bodey and Grace, 2006; Mattila and Wirtz, 2004) negatively influence the propensity to voice or express negative WOM. Customer resources, such as their knowledge, or their communication and computer-related skills, are seen as enablers in the interactive process with a provider and other actors in the service context (Tronvoll, 2007).

Negative customer brand engagement or engagement with a negative valence

While antecedents might be necessary conditions for customer engagement, they do not explain why customers respond to these conditions with varying degrees of engagement, or why they engage negatively. Emergent S-D logic concepts of value co-destruction (Plé and Chumpitas-Caceres, 2010), value co-creation (Tronvoll, 2012) and Hobfoll's (1989) Conservation of Resource Theory might offer theoretical lenses that can explain the underlying causes of customers' negative reactions to a brand's and/or firm's actions.

A customer's negative cognitive, affective and behavioural responses, that is, negative engagement, occurs as a consequence of failed customer–firm resource integration or value co-destruction (Smith, 2013; Smith et al. 2013), a term Plé and Chumpitas-Caceres (2010, p. 431) employ to refer to 'an interactional process between service systems that results in a decline in at least one of the system's well-being'. Drawing again on S-D logic, service systems refer to individuals or firms who integrate resources to co-create value (Vargo and Lusch, 2004). An accidental or intentional 'misuse' of customers' resources by a brand and/or firm is seen as a decline of customers' well-being.

The blog analyses indicated that what triggered bloggers engagement, their intent towards a brand and intensity of dimensions differed. For example, NCBE was preceded by perceived co-destruction of customer value, such as resource loss or threat to self (Smith, 2013; Smith et al., 2013). The blogging was premeditated and it was conducted with awareness or intention to damage the brand. Often these bloggers expressed extreme negative emotions towards the brand and apart from emotional resources invested thoughts, time and other resources to damage the brand value. For example, in the following blog its clear intent is to describe not only the iPhone, but also iPhone users in a very negative light:

> *I am 100% serious when I say the iPhone . . . has actually made everyone's lives worse. I was at a birthday party last week and everyone's iPhone was illuminating their ugly faces as they were looking down ignoring each other.*
> (iPhone, Blog 6)

The notion of NCBE being multi-dimensional was confirmed in the blogs. The cognitive element emerged in the form of bloggers offering opinions, judgments and/or criticism, making comparisons and evaluations, integrating material from other sources and solving specific problems. Having greater informative value, negative stimuli elicit more cognitive work (e.g. information processing) and lead to more complex cognitive representations and stronger evaluations (Ito, Larsen, Smith and Cacioppo, 1998; Peeters and Czapinski, 1990; Price 1996) than do positive stimuli. For example, a study of members' engagement with an Air Miles loyalty program found that negatively valenced posts were up to three times longer than the typical post (I hate your brand, 2013).

Affective responses, adjacent to cognitive manifestations, were presented as a series of customers' emotions provoked by an event or events. Emotions carry specific information about a person's position (Zeelenberg and Pieters, 2004). As a response to a specific situation, negative emotions produce customer behaviour aimed at restoring the disturbed relationship with the situation. In addition to cognitive and affective elements, the blogs also provided behavioural components. The behavioural dimension is often expressed as the activities that bloggers undertook online (such as writing the blog) and reported offline activities or planned future behaviour. Blogs in their recounting of past events and future plans provide the reader with a range of cognitive, emotion-based and behavioural (past, future, hypothetical) statements. For example, in this excerpt from a blog about Call of Duty, the text provides a mix of cognitive (evaluation), emotion (frustration) and hypothetical behaviour:

> *I feel like that person in a bad horror flick where you want to yell at the screen "WATCH OUT YOU MORON!" just in time to get taken out by a sniper who's been sitting there for most of the match just to out camp me.*
> (Call of Duty, Blog 2)

We propose that the intensity of customer engagement is expressed in the complexity of cognitive 'processes', quality of emotional states and initiating and carrying out behaviours. Furthermore, blogging is a behavioural expression in itself.

In comparison to NCBE, customer engagement with a negative valence is characterised by a lack of intent to cause harm. Instead, the engagement behaviour is still focused on the co-creation of value for the brand. For example, the following Call of Duty user states 'Well the only way WE can help fix it is to report EVERY player and hammer them with data. I know this doesn't fix it. It will just show the scope of the problem' (Call of Duty, Blog 2). Such interactions might be seen as a part of the co-creation processes. Another example is a blogger posting a product review which critiques a particular brand and who may be trying to gain personal credence with his or her peers, rather than blogging from a sense of anger or injustice. These processes may still unwittingly cause harm to the brand, but the original harmful intent is not there.

Negative customer brand engagement as a state and a process

While increasingly customer engagement is viewed by academics as a dynamic and circular process-based concept that tends to occur in a series of iterations, there is no consensus on what that process signifies and encompasses. Higgins and Scholer (2009, p. 102) refer to customer engagement as 'the state of being involved, occupied, fully absorbed or engrossed in something'. Brodie et al. (2011) integrate the notion of state (Vivek, 2009) and process (Bowden, 2009) and posit that costumer engagement is a context-dependent, psychological state characterised by fluctuating intensity levels that occur within a dynamic, iterative engagement process during which co-creation of value occurs.

It could be said that NCBE is also a state and a process; furthermore, we propose that the phenomenon is an iterative process, which is made up of a series of states. Additionally, NCBE is enduring, but has a time frame and is episodic, rather than continuous. NCBE may be triggered by an event and also later when the event is remembered. The event, or a recounted version thereof, may again trigger negative emotions and the customer to act. The following working definition of NCBE reflects the findings and complexities outlined earlier:

> *Negative customer brand engagement is a series of mental states and an itera-tive psychological process, which is catalysed by perceived threats (or a perceived or reconstructed threat) to self. To reduce dissonance, associated with perceived self-threats, customers take part in premeditated, interactive experiences with or about the brand and associated actors through coping strategies, which result in positive value for the self and intended negative value for the brand. Nega-tive customer brand engagement is a complex, contingent, multi-dimensional construct.*

The role of self-threat and dissonance in NCBE

This section provides an analysis of how an event or critical incident triggers NCBE cognition, emotion and behaviour. A subjective evaluation of the critical event, and linking to and experiencing of the self-threat, is conducted by the customer. This kind of evaluation, that is, whether an individual has anything 'at stake' in an interaction, is called a cognitive appraisal (Folkman and Lazarus, 1984). Several empirical studies (e.g., Baumeister and Leary, 1995; Shapiro et al., 1996) in the psychology literature support the view that an individual's cognitive appraisal process (perceived threat to or violation of fundamental human needs) can act as a trigger of negative (aggressive, destructive) behaviours. Authors such as Schneider and Bowen (1999) and Patterson, Yu and De Ruyter (2006) argue that depriving customers of their fundamental human needs such as security, justice and self-esteem are much more potent drivers of customer behaviours than dissatisfaction with the service or product performance.

Smith et al.'s (2013) study revealed a connection between the objects of engagement of anti-Facebook bloggers (namely, privacy and ethics, lack of control, undesirable user behaviour and negative impacts on well-being) to the self-threats (outlined by Kliewer, Fearnow and Walton, 1998) as the damage to self-esteem, material loss or loss of relationship; and by Folkman and Lazarus (1984) as loss of control, injustice, insecurity, not attaining goals, harm to one's physical well-being or rejection by others). This finding was further explored and confirmed in this more extensive blog analysis. For example, in the case of a new iPhone owner not being able to attain consumption goals is the focus of the following comment:

> *Like many other iPhone 3GS owners, I am very disappointed in the actual battery life . . . I figured that I'd need to give it a few full charges and run downs to optimize the battery. I was wrong as it didn't change anything.*
>
> (iPhone, Blog 19)

A sense of injustice, and a loss of control are the foci of this blogger's comment about Facebook:

> *Bait-and-switch means that Facebook gets you to share information that you might not otherwise share, and then they make it publicly available. Since they are in the business of monetizing information about you for advertising purposes, this amounts to tricking their users into giving advertisers information about themselves.*
>
> (Facebook, Blog 3)

Furthermore, the non-marketing literature on negative engagement (e.g. Van Gaalen and Dykstra, 2006; Pater and Lewis, 2012) and Smith et al.'s (2013) findings indicate that the appraisal of the events by subjects led to an emotional response and conflict. The notion of internal conflict is associated in the psychology literature with (cognitive) dissonance. Some scholars (e.g. Dickerson, Thibodeau, Aronson and Miller, 1992) suggest that dissonance is directly caused by perceived threats to self. Dissonance refers to the pressure of an aversive motivational state when two opinions, beliefs or areas of knowledge, or cognitions about the self and about actual behaviour are inconsistent with each other

(Aronson, 1968; Festinger, 1957). Similarly, Stone and Cooper (2001) suggest that dissonance is aroused when people perceive a discrepancy between their behaviour, including advocating counter-attitudinal beliefs and making questionable decisions, and their personal standards for the self, including attributes of competence and morality.

Additionally, cognitive appraisal theory would suggest that a subjective individual's evaluation or cognitive appraisal that something is 'at stake', such as being threatened and/or losing self-esteem leads towards strong coping, negative emotional and behavioural responses (Folkman and Lazarus, 1988). If an event is perceived as a threat, harm to, or loss of personal significance, such as values or needs, then it is also likely to result in negative emotional responses. This type of appraisal can cause a psychological state of disequilibrium by which the person is driven to return to his or her normal state through coping responses. Coping refers to 'cognitive and behavioural efforts to manage specific external and/or internal demands that are appraised as taxing or exceeding the resources of the person' (Folkman and Lazarus 1988, p. 310). Generalised negativity theory developed by Aronson and Carlsmith (1963) suggests that any discrepancy of performance from expectations will disrupt the individual, producing 'negative energy'.

Grounded in the theoretical foundations of value co-destruction and conservation of resources, people are motivated to create and protect resources (Hobfoll, 1989) and their well-being (Moschis, 2007). Under the threat of stress they become increasingly motivated, dedicating more of their time, energy and attention to preserving their overall resource position (Hobfoll, 1989). Kowalski (2002) asserts that this self-focus initiates an evaluative process in which the current events are compared with individuals' standards for those events. It is argued by Kowalski (2002) that people who feel threatened must ascertain what the probability is that a behaviour, such as complaining, will serve to reduce the discrepancy. Individual bloggers evaluated the perceived utility of complaining in terms of promoting desired intra-psychic or interpersonal goals, such as reducing the discrepancy by altering others' perceptions and attitudes towards the brand and organisation, and seeking social support through the action of blogging, as the following example demonstrates: 'Anyway here are 10 reasons Facebook sucks. I think most of you guys will agree with me' (Facebook, Blog 1).

Outcomes

Negative customer brand engagement results in a number of different outcomes for diverse actors, including customers (individuals and groups) and targeted firms/brands. Although, to date, there is little examination of the outcomes of negative engagement within the marketing (engagement) literature, it was observed that customers might experience both positive and negative outcomes following manifestations of their negative engagement. Customers experience the reclamation of lost self-esteem, self-efficacy and a sense of control resulting in perceived increases of their subjective well-being (Smith, 2013). Dissatisfied customers, who are encouraged to complain directly to firms, experience reduced levels of dissatisfaction over time Gopinath and Nyer, 2009. However, it is also possible that customers experience further losses, or downward loss cycles (Hobfoll, 1989) of physical, psychological and social resources, resulting in a perceived overall loss of wellbeing. In both scenarios, positive or negative outcomes influence the reduction or increase of (or additional) dissonance creating a circular (iterative) loop between the outcomes and the evaluation and response to the critical event (or events).

Negative brand engagement behaviours such as negative WOM have wide-ranging negative brand equity impacts (Djelassi and Decoopman, 2013; Bambauer-Sachse and Mangold, 2011). Impacts may involve customers seeking financial compensation, withdrawing, and attempting to negatively influence other potential or existing customers through WOM; ultimately, firms may lose reputational, relational and financial resources as a result of NCBE behaviours undertaken by customers (Smith, 2013). Longer-term relational consequences may include increased distrust in the brand, which may manifest as behavioural, but not attitudinal loyalty, switching behaviour or a loss of customer–brand connection. Some forms of negative engagement behaviours such as negative WOM might have even long-term impacts on cash flows and stock prices (Luo, 2009).

NCBE is always preceded by customer value destruction and their negative reactions, which then have adverse consequences for firms. However, NCBE does not have to bring benefits only to customers; companies could profit as well if they listen to negatively engaged customers.

Conclusion

This chapter provides insight into the nature and process of NCBE within an online context and in relation to various brand-related blogs. It is clear that NCBE does not just occur online and in blogging forms, but this context was chosen because the internet and online engagement platforms are becoming increasingly prevalent in today's marketplace. In addition, by studying blogs specifically, reconstructions of events, cognitive appraisals, emotional states, proposed solutions, and reports of past and future actions were enabled. These texts enable researchers to analyse aspects of NCBE in a way that helps us to uncover a relatively nuanced view of NCBE.

In this chapter we have proposed that NCBE is more than just engagement with a negative valence. We posit that this phenomenon has a different process than negatively valenced engagement manifestations. NCBE tends to be premeditated and emerges as somewhat dedicated behaviour towards (or against) the brand, which is different from one-off or accidental negative actions towards the brand. Negative engagement is characterised by cognitive dissonance, which arises from cognitive appraisal of perceived threats. Furthermore, the critical event and subsequent triggering of customer negative brand engagement is in a form of interactional processes between a customer and a brand

and/or firm, in which customer value is co-destructed in the form of abuse of customer resources, such as self-esteem or time. A main difference is that negative customer engagement behaviours are undertaken with the intention to co-destruct, rather than co-create, brand equity and value.

Customers possess a set of fundamental human goals and needs (e.g. self-esteem and sense of control). When these are under threat or violated NCBE could be triggered. It is important for frontline staff, for example, to avoid any potential damage to these basic human needs of customers during service delivery (or recovery) and/or understand them and develop strategies that would prevent or recover. A similar suggestion could be made for engagement with negative valence, where the engagement behaviour is focused on the co-creation of value for the brand as in the case of changing customer expectations due to competitors' movements or desire to improve the brand. Understanding different intentions, motivations or triggers of negatively engaged customers would also help firms respond to, and possibly prevent, such behaviours, which have a negative impact on brand meaning and value. Distinguishing between a customer who wants to damage the brand and a customer who wants to help the brand would be central to a firm's management strategy given that NCBE and negatively valenced engagement are likely to require different recovery strategies.

Future research

The work discussed in this chapter opens up numerous research avenues. For example, what would be learned from exploring NCBE (or NCE more generally) in different contexts? Further work on the conceptual development of engagement constructs (i.e. engagement, engagement with a negative valence, negative customer engagement, disengagement, non-engagement) is needed. In addition, we need to understand the conditions under which some customers actively and negatively engage with a brand, while others disengage.

This research has shown that concepts of critical events (external stimulus) and triggers (internal response) of NCBE or NCE need further conceptual 'debate'. In fact, the interplay between different types of critical events, perceived self-threats and influence of antecedents (or moderators) is a fruitful area for research. Further, the question arises what is the role of dissatisfaction in the NCBE process? There is a need for longitudinal studies of brand engagement; for example, customer intent towards the brand and motivation of negative engagement could change through time, from first wanting to punish to altruism and wanting to help, even through to repentance.

More research is required to characterise the forms and channels of negative customer brand engagement and understanding how each channel potentially impacts customers' and firms' outcomes. As suggested by Van Doorn et al. (2010), further research is required to understand the related impacts of negative customer engagement behaviours on the firm and other actors. Lastly, the complexities and paradoxes of NCBE and NCE research provide fertile ground in this area, given that 'valence is in the eye of the beholder'.

References

Algesheimer, R., Borle, S., Dholakia, U. M., and Singh, S. S. (2010). The impact of customer community participation on customer behaviors: An empirical investigation. *Marketing Science*, 29(4), 756–769.

Aronson, E. (1968). Dissonance theory: Progress and problems. In R. P. Abelson, E. Aronson, W. J. Mcguire, T. M. Newcomb, M. J. Rosenberg, P. H. Tannenbaum (Eds.), *Theories of cognitive consistency: A sourcebook*, 5–27.

Aronson, E., and Carlsmith, J. M. (1963). Effect of the severity of threat on the devaluation of forbidden behavior. *Journal of Abnormal and Social Psychology*, 66, 584–588.

Bambauer-Sachse, S., and Mangold, S. (2011). Brand equity dilution through negative online word-of-mouth communication. *Journal of Retailing and Consumer Services*, 18(1), 38–45.

Baumeister, R. F., and Leary, M. R. (1995). The need to belong: Desire for interpersonal attachments as a fundamental human motivation. *Psychological Bulletin*, 117(3), 497.

Bearden, William and Teel, Jesse E. (1980). An investigation of personal influences on consumer complaining, *Journal of Retailing*, 56, 3–200.

Berger, J. (2014). Word of mouth and interpersonal communication: A review and directions for future research. *Journal of Consumer Psychology*, 24(4), 586–607.

Bodey, K. and Grace, D. 2006. Segmenting service "complainers" and "non-complainers" on the basis of consumer characteristics. *Journal of Service Marketing*, 20, 178–187.

Bowden, J.L.H. (2009). The process of customer engagement: A conceptual framework. *Journal of Marketing Theory and Practice*, 17(1), 63–74.

Brodie, R. J., Hollebeek, L. D., Juric, B., and Ilic, A. (2011). Customer engagement: Conceptual domain, fundamental propositions, and implications for research. *Journal of Service Research*, 1094670511411703.

Brodie, R. J., Ilic, A., Juric, B., and Hollebeek, L. Consumer engagement in a virtual brand community: An exploratory analysis. *Journal of Business Research*. 2013, 66(1), 105–114.

Choi, S., and Mattila, A. S. (2006). The role of disclosure in variable hotel pricing a cross-cultural comparison of customers' fairness perceptions. *Cornell Hotel and Restaurant Administration Quarterly*, 47(1), 27–35.

Chylinski, M., and Chu, A. (2010). Consumer cynicism: Antecedents and consequences. *European Journal of Marketing*, 44(6), 796–837.

Davidow, M., and Dacin, P. A. (1997). Understanding and influencing consumer complaint behavior: Improving organizational complaint management. *Advances in Consumer Research*, 24(1), 450–456.

Davis, M. (2012). A cognitive experiential avoidance model (C-EAM): Understanding non-suicidal self-injury as a form of avoidance (Doctoral dissertation).

De Matos, C. A., and Rossi, C. A. V. (2008). Word-of-mouth communications in marketing: A meta-analytic review of the antecedents and moderators. *Journal of the Academy of Marketing Science*, 36(4), 578–596.

Dickerson, C. A., Thibodeau, R., Aronson, E., and Miller, D. (1992). Using cognitive dissonance to encourage water conservation1. *Journal of Applied Social Psychology*, 22(11), 841–854.

Dishion, T. J., Nelson, S. E., Winter, C. E., and Bullock, B. M. (2004). Adolescent friendship as a dynamic system: Entropy and deviance in the etiology and course of male antisocial behavior. *Journal of Abnormal Child Psychology*, 32(6), 651–663.

Djelassi, S., and Decoopman, I. (2013). Customers' participation in product development through crowdsourcing: Issues and implications. *Industrial Marketing Management*, 42(5), 683–692.

Festinger, L. (1957). *A theory of cognitive dissonance*. Stanford, CA: Stanford University Press.

Folkes, V.S., Koletsky, S., and Graham, J.L. (1987). A field study of causal inferences and consumer reaction: The view from the airport. *Journal of Consumer Research*, 534–539.

Folkman, S. and Lazarus, R. S. (1988). The relationship between coping and emotion: Implications for theory and research. *Social Science Medicine*, 26(3), 309–317.

George, J.M. (1998). Salesperson mood at work: Implications for helping customers. *Journal of Personal Selling & Sales Management*, 18(3), 23–30.

Gopinath, M., and Nyer, P. U. (2009). The effect of public commitment on resistance to persuasion: The influence of attitude certainty, issue importance, susceptibility to normative influence, preference for consistency and source proximity. *International Journal of Research in Marketing*, 26(1), 60–68.

Grégoire, Y., and Fisher, R.J. (2008). Customer betrayal and retaliation: When your best customers become your worst enemies. *Journal of the Academy of Marketing Science*, 36(2), 247–261.

Grégoire, Y., Tripp, T.M., and Legoux, R. (2009). When customer love turns into lasting hate: The effects of relationship strength and time on customer revenge and avoidance. *Journal of Marketing*, 73(6), 18–32.

Gruen, T.W., Osmonbekov, T., and Czaplewski, A.J. (2006). eWOM: The impact of customer-to-customer online know-how exchange on customer value and loyalty. *Journal of Business Research*, 59(4), 449–456.

Harrison, S. (2008). *Masculinities and music: Engaging men and boys in making music*. Newcastle upon Tyne: Cambridge Scholars.

Hedman, L., and Sharafi, P. (2004). Early use of internet-based educational resources: Effects on students' engagement modes and flow experience. *Behaviour & Information Technology*, 23(2), 137–146.

Hennig-Thurau, T., Gwinner, K.P., Walsh, G., and Gremler, D.D. (2004). Electronic word-of-mouth via consumer-opinion platforms: What motivates consumers to articulate themselves on the internet? *Journal of Interactive Marketing*, 18(1), 38–52.

Higgins, E. T. and Scholer, A. A. (2009). Engaging the consumer: The science and art of the value creation process. *Journal of Consumer Psychology*, 19, 2100–2114.

Hobfoll, S.E. (1989). Conservation of resources: A new attempt at conceptualizing stress. *American Psychologist*, 44(3), 513–524.

Hollebeek, L., and Chen, T. (2014). Exploring positively-versus negatively-valenced brand engagement: A conceptual model. *Journal of Product & Brand Management*, 23(1), 62–74.

Hsu, C.L., and Lin, J.C.C. (2008). Acceptance of blog usage: The roles of technology acceptance, social influence and knowledge sharing motivation. *Information & Management*, 45(1), 65–74.

I hate your brand: How negative work-of-mouth can actually increase positive engagement (Aug. 24, 2013). Retrieved from http://www.tnooz.com/article/i-hate-your-brand-how-negative-word-of-mouth-can-actually-increase-positive-engagement.

Ito, T.A., Larsen, J.T., Smith, N.K., and Cacioppo, J.T. (1998). Negative information weighs more heavily on the brain: The negativity bias in evaluative categorizations. *Journal of Personality and Social Psychology*, *75*(4), 887.

Johnston, R., and Fern, A. (1999). Service recovery strategies for single and double deviation scenarios. *Service Industries Journal*, *19*(2), 69–82.

Juvonen, J., Espinoza, G., and Knifsend, C. (2012). The role of peer relationships in student academic and extracurricular engagement. In *Handbook of research on student engagement* (387–401). Springer US.

Katz, L.F., and Gottman, J.M. (1996). Spillover effects of marital conflict: In search of parenting and coparenting mechanisms. *New Directions for Child and Adolescent Development*, *1996*(74), 57–76.

Kliewer, W., Fearnow, M.D., and Walton, M.N. (1998). Dispositional, environmental, and context-specific predictors of children's threat perceptions in everyday stressful situations. *Journal of Youth and Adolescence*, *27*(1), 83–100.

Kowalski, R.M. (2002). Whining, griping, and complaining: Positivity in the negativity. *Journal of Clinical Psychology*, *58*(9), 1023–1035.

Lazarus, R.S., and Folkman, S. (1984). *Stress, appraisal, and coping*. Springer US.

Luo, X. (2009) Quantifying the long-term impact of negative word of mouth on cash flows and stock prices. *Marketing Science*, *28*(1), 148–165.

Mattila, A.S. (2004). The impact of service failures on customer loyalty: The moderating role of affective commitment. *International Journal of Service Industry Management*, *15*(2), 134–149.

Mattila, A.S. and Wirtz, J (2004). Consumer complaining to firms: The determinants of channel choice. *Journal of Services Marketing*, *18*(2), 147–155.

Mazzarol, T., Sweeney, J.C., and Soutar, G.N. (2007). Conceptualizing word-of-mouth activity, triggers and conditions: An exploratory study. *European Journal of Marketing*, *41*(11/12), 1475–1494.

McColl-Kennedy, J.R., Sparks, B.A., and Nguyen, D.T. (2011). Customer's angry voice: Targeting employees or the organization? *Journal of Business Research*, *64*(7), 707–713.

Moschis, G.P. (2007). Stress and consumer behaviour. *Journal of the Academy of Marketing Science*, *35*(3), 430–444.

Nordahl, K.B., Janson, H., Manger, T., and Zachrisson, H.D. (2014). Family concordance and gender differences in parent-child structed interaction at 12 months. *Journal of Family Psychology*, *28*(2), 253–259.

Park, C., and Lee, T.M. (2009). Information direction, website reputation and eWOM effect: A moderating role of product type. *Journal of Business Research*, *62*(1), 61–67.

Pater, R., and Lewis, C. (2012). Strategies for Leading Engagement Part 2. *Professional Safety*, *57*(6), 34.

Patterson, P., Yu, T., and De Ruyter, K. (2006, December). Understanding customer engagement in services. In *Advancing Theory, Maintaining Relevance, Proceedings of ANZMAC 2006 Conference, Brisbane* (4–6).

Peeters, G., and Czapinski, J. (1990). Positive-negative asymmetry in evaluations: The distinction between affective and informational negativity effects. *European Review of Social Psychology*, *1*(1), 33–60.

Plé, L., and Chumpitaz-Cáceres, R. (2010). Not always co-creation: Introducing interactional co-destruction of value in service-dominant logic. *Journal of Services Marketing*, *24*(6), 430–437.

Price, L. J. (1996). Understanding the negativity effect: The role of processing focus. *Marketing Letters*, 7(1), 53–62.

Ranaweera, C., and Menon, K. (2013). For better or for worse? Adverse effects of relationship age and continuance commitment on positive and negative word of mouth. *European Journal of Marketing*, 47(10), 1598–1621.

Richins, M. L. (1983). Negative word-of-mouth by dissatisfied consumers: A pilot study. *The Journal of Marketing*, 68–78.

Schmidt, P. J. (2010, January). The role of challenge in information systems use. In *System Sciences (HICSS), 2010 43rd Hawaii International Conference on* (1–10). IEEE.

Schneider, B., and Bowen, D. E. (1999). Understanding customer delight and outrage. *Sloan Management Review*, 41(1), 35–45.

Skinner, E. A., and Belmont, M. J. (1993). Motivation in the classroom: Reciprocal effects of teacher behavior and student engagement across the school year. *Journal of Educational Psychology*, 85(4), 571.

Smith, A. (2013). The value co-destruction process: A customer resource perspective. *European Journal of Marketing*, 47(11/12), 1889–1909.

Smith, S. D., Juric, B. and Niu, J. (2013). Negative consumer brand engagement: An exploratory study of "I Hate Facebook" blogs. Paper presented at the ANZMAC 2013 Conference.

Sparks, B. A., and Browning, V. (2010). Complaining in cyberspace: The motives and forms of hotel guests' complaints online. *Journal of Hospitality Marketing & Management*, 19(7), 797–818.

Stone, J., and Cooper, J. (2001). A self-standards model of cognitive dissonance. *Journal of Experimental Social Psychology*, 37(3), 228–243.

Sun, T., Youn, S., Wu, G., and Kuntaraporn, M. (2006). Online word-of-mouth (or mouse): An exploration of its antecedents and consequences. *Journal of Computer-Mediated Communication*, 11(4), 1104–1127.

Sundaram, D. S., Mitra, K., and Webster, C. (1998). Word-of-mouth communications: A motivational analysis. *Advances in Consumer Research*, 25(1), 527–531.

Tax, S. S., Brown, S. W., and Chandrashekaran, M. (1998). Customer evaluations of service complaint experiences: Implications for relationship marketing. *The Journal of Marketing*, 60–76.

Tirunillai, S. and Tellis, G. J. (2012). Does chatter really matter? Dynamics of user-generated content and stock performance. *Marketing Science*, 31(2), 198.

Tronvoll, B. (2007). Customer complaint behaviour from the perspective of the service-dominant logic of marketing. *Managing Service Quality: An International Journal*, 17(6), 601–620.

Tronvoll, B. (2012), A dynamic model of customer complaining behaviour from the perspective of service-dominant logic. *European Journal of Marketing*, 46(1/2), 284–305.

Tsai, C. C., Yang, Y. K., and Cheng, Y. C. (2014). Does relationship matter?: Customers' response to service failure. *Managing Service Quality*, 24(2), 139–159.

Van Doorn, J., Lemon, K. N., Mittal, V., Nass, S., Pick, D., Pirner, P., and Verhoef, P. C. (2010). Customer engagement behavior: Theoretical foundations and research directions. *Journal of Service Research*, 13(3), 253–266.

Van Gaalen, R. I., and Dykstra, P. A. (2006). Solidarity and conflict between adult children and parents: A latent class analysis. *Journal of Marriage and Family*, 68(4), 947–960.

Vargo, S. L., and Lusch, R. F. (2004). Evolving to a new dominant logic for marketing. *Journal of Marketing*, *68*(1), 1–17.

Vitiello, V. E., Booren, L. M., Downer, J. T., and Williford, A. P. (2012). Variation in children's classroom engagement throughout a day in preschool: Relations to classroom and child factors. *Early Childhood Research Quarterly*, *27*(2), 210–220.

Vivek, S. D. (2009). *A scale of consumer engagement.* Doctoral dissertation, The University of Alabama, Tuscaloosa.

Waller, G. (2002). The psychology of binge eating. In C. G. Fairburn and K. D. Brownell (Eds.), *Eating disorders and obesity: A comprehensive handbook*, 98–102. New York: Guilford Press.

Wangenheim, F. V. (2005). Postswitching negative word of mouth. *Journal of Service Research*, *8*(1), 67–78.

Ward, J. C., and Ostrom, A. L. (2006). Complaining to the masses: The role of protest framing in customer-created complaint web sites. *Journal of Consumer Research*, *33*(2), 220–230.

Yagil, D. (2008). When the customer is wrong: A review of research on aggression and sexual harassment in service encounters. *Aggression and Violent Behavior*, *13*(2), 141–152.

Zeelenberg, M., and Pieters, R. (2004). Beyond valence in customer dissatisfaction: A review and new findings on behavioral responses to regret and disappointment in failed services. *Journal of Business Research*, *57*(4), 445–455.

Index